In Lieu of Memory

Judaic Traditions in Literature, Music, and Art
Ken Frieden *and* Harold Bloom, *Series Editors*

Other titles in Judaic Traditions in Literature, Music, and Art

Badenheim 1939. Aharon Appelfeld; Betsy Rosenberg, trans.; Ken Frieden, ed.

Classic Yiddish Stories of S. Y. Abramovitsh, Sholem Aleichem, and I. L. Peretz. Ken Frieden, Ted Gorelick, and Michael Wex, trans.; Ken Frieden, ed.

Contemporary Jewish American Writers and the Multicultural Dilemma: The Return of the Exiled. Andrew Furman

The Dybbuk and the Yiddish Imagination: A Haunted Reader. Joachim Neugroschel, trans. & ed.

God, Man, and Devil: Yiddish Plays in Translation. Nahma Sandrow, trans. & ed.

The Image of the Shtetl and Other Studies of Modern Jewish Literary Imagination. Dan Miron

The Jewish Book of Fables: Selected Works. Eliezer Shtaynbarg; Curt Leviant, trans. & ed.

Jewish Instrumental Folk Music: The Collections and Writings of Moshe Beregovski. Mark Slobin, Robert A. Rothstein, and Michael Alpert, trans. & ed.

Nathan and His Wives. Miron C. Izakson; Betsy Rosenberg, trans.; Ken Frieden, ed.

Nineteen to the Dozen: Monologues and Bits and Bobs of Other Things. Sholem Aleichem; Ted Gorelick, trans.; Ken Frieden, ed.

Polish-Jewish Literature in the Interwar Years. Eugenia Prokop-Janiec; Abe Shenitzer, trans.

The Stories of David Bergelson: Yiddish Short Fiction from Russia. Golda Werman, trans.

A Traveler Disguised: The Rise of Modern Yiddish Fiction in the Nineteenth Century. Dan Miron

The Wishing Ring. S. Y. Abramovitsh; Michael Wex, trans.

In Lieu of Memory

Contemporary Jewish Writing in France

THOMAS NOLDEN

Syracuse University Press

Syracuse, New York 13244-5160

First Edition 2006
06 07 08 09 10 11   6 5 4 3 2 1

Permission to quote from the following sources is gratefully acknowledged:
Ami Bouganim, *Récits du Mellah* (Paris: Lattès, 1988);
Pierre Goldman, *Souvenirs obscurs d'un Juif polonais né en France*. © Editions du Seuil, 1975;
"Translation," copyright © 1977 by Viking Penguin Inc., from *Dim Memories of a Polish Jew Born in France* by Pierre Goldman, translated by Joan Pinkham. Used by permission of Viking Penguin, a division of Penguin Group (USA) Inc.;
Emmanuel Moses, "Deutéronome, 25, 17," in *Métiers* (Paris: Obsidiane, 1989);
Copyright © 1995 *Ellis Island* by Georges Perec. Reprinted by permission of The New Press. (800) 233-4830;
Henri Raczymow, *Un cri sans voix* (Paris: Gallimard, 1985). © Editions Gallimard;
Antoine Spire, *Le silence en héritage*. © Editions Robert Laffont, 1988.

The paper used in this publication meets the minimum requirements of American National Standard for Information Sciences—Permanence of Paper for Printed Library Materials, ANSIZ39.48–1984.∞™

Library of Congress Cataloging-in-Publication Data
Nolden, Thomas.
In lieu of memory : contemporary Jewish writing in France / Thomas Nolden.— 1st ed.
p. cm.— (Judaic traditions in literature, music, and art)
Includes bibliographical references and index.
ISBN 0-8156-3089-1 (alk. paper)
1. French literature—Jewish authors—History and criticism. 2. French literature—20th century—History and criticism. 3. Judaism and literature—France. 4. Jewish authors—France. 5. Holocaust, Jewish (1939–1945)—France—Influence. I. Title. II. Series.

PQ150.J4N65 2005
840.9'8924'09045—dc22   2005023940

Manufactured in the United States of America

To Sandy and our beautiful daughters

Thomas Nolden directs the comparative literature program at Wellesley College and has written widely on Jewish writing in contemporary Europe.

Contents

Acknowledgments *ix*

Introduction *xi*

1. Openings *1*

2. Departures *29*

3. Assertions *78*

4. Filiations *114*

5. Displacements *164*

6. Postscripts *214*

Works Cited *227*

Further Readings *241*

Index *247*

Acknowledgments

I acknowledge with gratitude the support of the many friends and colleagues who have read drafts of the manuscript. I can here mention only some of them. Odile Cazenave, Sam Engelstad, Helen Epstein, Barbara Honigmann, Christoph Miething, and Larry Rosenwald provided most helpful comments. Peter Patrikis, David Ward, Will Rollman, and Nathalie Rogers responded to individual queries and requests, David Price and Ted Kendris patiently went over the manuscript most perceptively.

I am also grateful to my research assistants Sarah Wall, Sarah Cussen, and Emily Coit who assisted me in all stages of the editing of this book—Emily also provided drafts of the translations from the French. Valerie Hotchkiss helped me find a title and a press, the staff of the Centre de Documentation Juive Contemporaine and Louise Magnichever from the Librairie du Temple in Paris secured for me hard-to-come-by copies of books, and, last but not least, Alan Astro, an exemplary colleague and scholar, shared with me most generously and graciously his vast knowledge of the subject matter at hand.

Wellesley College's supportive leave program allowed me to concentrate on the research for this book during several leave semesters. My wife Sandy and our daughters Lucie and Anna kept reminding me about the things that really matter.

Introduction

In Lieu of Memory: Contemporary Jewish Writing in France is a comprehensive study of works by French Jewish authors born after the Shoah. Although many of the authors have received prestigious prizes, the literary production of this group of writers, which comprises more than two dozen authors of both Sephardic and Ashkenazi background, has never before been the object of sustained critical attention in the English language. This study offers for the first time an introduction to these writers and a thorough review and analysis of the major themes, concerns, and stylistic features of their works.

The new generations of Jewish writers differ from their predecessors in several significant respects. First and foremost, while the latter were preoccupied with the Shoah and the problem of its representation, the former are engaged in elaborating strategies for the narration of Jewish life in the aftermath of both the Vichy experience and the Jewish exodus from the Maghreb. Regardless of whether the present generations of writers come from families leading an assimilated life, from homes shattered by the Nazi genocide, or from Orthodox families driven out of North Africa's Jewish quarters, they all face the task of working out their own attitudes toward history, toward the past of their families, and toward the future of the Jewish people. This means a negotiation with the missions and responsibilities imposed on them by the legacy of the victims of the Shoah, by the resistance to the Nazi occupiers and French collaborators, and by the emigration of their parents from the Maghreb during decolonization. Thus, these writers have not created a literature of the Shoah, nor have they presented the epic panoramas offered by older writers such as Marek Halter or André Schwarz-Bart, which scan the continuities and ruptures within Jewish history from its biblical beginnings to the present. Rather, they map in often autobiographically informed narratives the paths that led many of them from the political orthodoxies of the student rebellion to an appreciation of their cultural and ethnic heritage, from the study of Maoism to the study of Yiddish or Judeo-Espagnol, from the exegesis of Marx's *Capital* to the reading of Kafka's *Der Prozess* (The Trial).

Given the unique nature of their cultural, demographic, and political environment, the literature of the post-Shoah generations requires a new set of analytic tools to identify its place within literary and cultural history and to appreciate the striking diversity of voices it embodies. Although much good scholarly work presented in recent years has attempted to develop interpretative categories for the survivors' narratives (Elaine Marks's *Marrano as Metaphor* or Clara Lévy's *Écritures de l'identité* [Writings of Identity], none of these works acknowledges the specific character of the literary phenomenon presented by the *générations d'après*, by the writers born after the Shoah.

Contemporary Jewish writing responded historically, culturally, politically, and aesthetically to developments in the French society out of which it emerged: historically, to the dismantling of the Vichy syndrome and to the aftermath of decolonization; culturally, to French society's turn away from Jacobin uniformism; politically, to the demise of the ideological imperatives of the student movement; and aesthetically, to the exhaustion of the poetological paradigms of *littérature engagée* [political literature] or the *nouveau roman* [new novel]. The rich agenda of *jeune littérature juive* [young Jewish literature], whose beginnings date back to the late 1970s and which gained immense momentum in the 1980s and 1990s, also takes the form of a reassessment of changes and movements within modern Jewish life. It participates critically in the discourses both of France's Jewish communities as they have been shaped by complex demographic, religious, and cultural shifts and of the French nation at large. Scrutinizing the assimilationist course that French Jewry took after the French Revolution until it reached the dead end of Vichy, these writers narrate the biographies of Jews in France and in its colonies and protectorates while at the same time supplementing the collective memory of gentile France and pointing the way toward the future of Jewish culture in the New Europe.

Engaged in a dialogue with Alain Finkielkraut's influential critique *Le Juif imaginaire* [The Imaginary Jew]—a work that in 1980 challenged the post-Shoah generations to redefine Jewish identity in postwar France—these authors come face to face with the major events and forces in recent Jewish and French history (Shoah, decolonization, revisionism) as well as with the dynamics of contemporary Judaism (re-Judaization as well as de-Judaization, diasporic existence, and new militancy). What emerges, whether from the very absence of a Jewish past and tradition (as in Henri Raczymow, Gérard Wajcman, et al.), from a legacy of Jewish resistance (Pierre Goldman), or from the context of cultural and national displacement (Jean-Luc Allouche, Gil Ben Aych, Paule Darmon, Marco Koskas, Katia Rubinstein, et al.), is a form of writing that relates Jewish places of the past (the shtetl of Eastern Europe, the *mellah* and the *hara* of the Maghreb, the sites of combat of the Maquis) to present-day France and that gauges the historical, cultural, and generational distances between them. The traditions of Jewish literature prove only partially helpful in the project of creating a discourse that reflects, on the one hand, the desire for an autonomous beginning and, on the other, the attachment to the realm of the family and to the past of the Jewish people. Alain Gluckstein's postmodern adaptation of the genre of the *yizker-bukh* (the memorial book of Polish Jews), Gilles Rozier's narrative integration of Yiddish storytelling, and Ami Bouganim's literary adaptations of the oral traditions of the Moroccan ghetto all document a paradox that characterizes much of these writings: their authors' readiness to accept a canon while at the same time acknowledging the impossibility of conforming to it. These writers pick up the pen as *imaginative* rather than as *imaginary* Jews to engage in a reinvention of tradition—an act necessary, according to Albert Memmi, "si l'on veut survivre" (1997, 105) [if one wants to survive].

The American critic Alan Astro, who has pioneered the research on present-day Jewish writing in France, wondered in 1994 whether a French Jewish literature indeed exists (Astro 1994). Looking back at the literary production of the last twenty-five years and at the debates among the writers themselves, the answer to this question can only be an affirmative one: contemporary Jewish literature has come to represent one of the most exciting developments in France's recent cultural scene. Harold Bloom once eloquently stated that it is a shared canon of texts that informs the very community of the Jewish people (Bloom 1985). Instead of rereading the canonical texts and authors of the past, this book wants to direct attention to the contemporary texts as guarantors of the continuity of Jewish culture in the diaspora. It offers the readers a map to the dynamic landscape of this exciting part of contemporary French—and European—letters hitherto largely uncharted and still unknown territory to many.

In addition to the work of Alan Astro, this book is indebted to the literary criticism of Guy Dugas (France), Judith Klein (Germany), and (the French-Jewish writer) Henry Raczymow, among others, as well as to the ideas of several cultural critics and historians whose thoughts echo throughout the book. Accentuating certain dynamics of contemporary Jewish writing in France, this book does not claim to cover the corpus of this literature in its entirety; conceived as an introduction, it strives to balance the needs of the broad survey with the desire for close analysis. And rather than confining itself strictly to a discussion of the writers born after the Shoah, the study at times refers to authors who belong to an older age group (like Marcel Bénabou, Hélène Cixous or Georges Perec). I hope that these editorial decisions will allow the book to succeed as a liaison between American readers and this important segment of writing in present-day Europe. Unless noted otherwise, I am responsible for the translations of materials not yet published in English.

Illustrating the dynamics of contemporary Jewish writing with close readings of representative narratives by contemporary French Jewish authors, this book also aims to make a contribution to the theoretical debates on Jewish literature specifically and to minority discourse in general. It wants to point the current debate on the Jew and the process of writing in a new direction, avoiding the amalgamation of the two as well as the reduction of the Jew to a "generic social or moral critic, a reader of culture" (Ezrahi 2000, 14). The readings offered here will not provide the reader with a singular answer to the question of what the term "Jewish" means in the context of contemporary Jewish writing in France, as this answer necessarily has to be delineated in a manner wide enough to take into account that some of the contributors to the "nouvelle littérature juive française" [new French Jewish literature] grew up "sans histoire" [without history], while others spent their formative years in observant homes (Ascot 1987, 50; Ertel 1982, 90). The French literary critic Rachel Ertel presented as early as in 1981 an approach to this question that I would like to borrow for its inclusiveness. Aside from the historically, religiously, and nationally defined notions of Jewishness, Ertel wisely addressed "residual forms" of being Jewish consisting of real or imaginary memories, memories of memories, or fragments and splinters of it (1982, 90).

Once one has moved beyond what the Jewish-Quebecois critic and writer Régine Robin called the "le fallacieux problème de 'Qui est Juif' " (1986, 14) [the fallacious problem 'Who or what is Jewish?'], one can appreciate that Jewishness often appears as a form of self-understanding that is not necessarily derived from a simple identification with ethnic givens, religious rites, and cultural or historical traditions, but rather from the questioning and exploration of these. And it is exactly this kind of exploration that has turned out to be a strong type of engagement that has generated a highly intricate body of literary texts. It is an interest in this literary performance of *positioning* rather than in the static category of an *essence* of identity that guides this study (Hall 1990, 236). The readings of this literature will confirm that the notion of a brittle, mediated, and complex relationship toward Judaism on the one side and to secular France on the other side appropriately reflects the ambiguities displayed in contemporary Jewish writing whose vectors, however, are directed toward rather than away from the "lieux de mémoire juive" [sites of Jewish memory].

Following the imperative of *zakhor,* of remembering, this literature strives to unearth the strata of forgetting—the tightly woven chain of "L'oubli de l'oubli de l'oubli" (Boukhobza 1987, 235) [The forgetting of the forgetting of the forgetting], as one of the protagonists of Chochana Boukhobza's novels puts it, needs to be broken to allow the Jewish generations born after the Shoah to examine what has been lost as well as what can be and what should be preserved.

The first chapter of the study provides an introduction to the historical and societal changes in postwar France that led to a new appreciation of ethnic, religious, and cultural differences. Against this backdrop, the chapter looks at how the children of survivors and of Maghrebi immigrants created self-assertive forms of Jewish identity by focusing on attitudes different from those that previously prevailed within France's Jewish community. Chapter 2 reconstructs the beginnings of the careers of the new generations of authors, their initial stances in the discussions of Jewish writing, and their first works, which heralded Jewish literature in the aftermath of politicization (Patrick Modiano, Pierre Goldman, Henri Raczymow, Myriam Anissimov, Annie Goldmann). Chapter 3 discusses modes of autobiographical discourses and identifies the positions writers take in relationship to the difficult task of remembering in fiction events of a past that they often have not experienced themselves. Narrating and thereby interrupting the silence that surrounded the *années noires*, the period of Collaboration, is perhaps the major motive of contemporary Jewish writing that emerges as heir to Jewish resistance. Chapter 4 describes the tension between the principles of self-determination (Luc

Rosenzweig), filiation, and affiliation (Elisabeth de Fontenay) as one of the driving forces of the autojudeographic project. This tension informs emotive family tableaus in which young protagonists grapple with the legacy of problematic forms of Jewish life (the Israelite, the collaborationist Jew, the Maghrebi patriarch, the mute immigrant) as well as with the challenge of retaining or creating meaningful bonds between the generations despite a historical and cultural gap. Chapter 5 turns to both geographical and cultural forms of displacement and to the notion of diasporic experience. The chapter examines how the politics and poetics of *métissage* (Lionnet 1995) inform the postcolonial narratives dealing with immigration from the Maghreb: rejecting the literary convention of linguistic homogeneity, these stylistically complex texts commemorate former life in North Africa or portray the present of immigrant communities in France in a language that is not at all "acculturated." Capturing the nostalgia of the immigrant generations and articulating their *mutisme* [silence], Marlène Amar, Gil Ben Aych, Chochana Boukhobza, Marco Koskas, and Gilles Zenou appropriate the languages and the narrative traditions of their new and old homes to give voice no longer to the lot of the archetypical *Juif errant* [wandering Jew] but rather to their own now hybrid identities.

In Lieu of Memory

1 Openings

"Revival juif"

The revitalization of Jewish culture, or, to use Daniel Lindenberg's hybrid term, the "*revival* juif" [Jewish revival] undoubtedly is one of the most remarkable cultural developments in Europe's recent history (1990, 83). In the first decades after the end of World War II, no one could have foreseen that European Jewry would recover from the trauma and the losses caused by the Shoah. After all, only a fraction of the European Jewish population had survived persecution, and many of the survivors left their European homelands to settle in the New World or to make their aliyah to Israel. They left behind small enclaves of Jewish communities, which after the war suffered acutely from psychological and economic difficulties. European Jews were preoccupied with the need to provide social services for their communities and with the task of fighting for financial compensation and public recognition within societies prone to repress the past and to ignore the problems of the present. The Jews who had decided to stay in Europe initially had very little time and only limited means to reestablish a cultural life that could bear witness to the rich traditions of Jewish art, philosophy, and literature.

And yet, just a quarter century after the end of World War II, Jewish culture in countries such as France, Germany, Austria, Italy, England, Hungary, and even Poland began to prosper again. Since 1980, an ever-growing number of Jewish artists, writers, politicians, and intellectuals has been entering the public sphere, documenting how lively, productive, and diverse Jewish culture is. They have been responding to general societal developments and fundamental ideological changes brought about by the student rebellions in 1968, by the events in the Near East, by the new situation created by the end of the cold war, and by global migration. And they have been affected by changes in the demographic composition of Jewish communities both at the local level, where more and more members of the survivor generation have passed away, and at the global level, where the center of Jewish life has moved from Eastern Europe to Israel and the United States. Within Europe, France now has the largest Jewish community (around 650,000, or about 1.2 percent of the entire population), followed by Great Britain (approximately 315,000), Germany (approximately 60,000), and Hungary (circa 55,000). The situation of Europe's Jewish diaspora thus is a paradoxical one: while it may be demographically "vanishing" (Wasserstein 1996) due to intermarriage, politically and culturally it is flourishing and prospering.

In Austria and Germany, more than two dozen writers have emerged since Barbara Honigmann published in 1986 her first collection of stories, belying Germany's most prominent literary critic Marcel Reich-Ranicki's declaration in the late 1980s that the history of Jewish-German literature was "over, irrevocably finished" (1989, 57).[1] In England, the prolific literary production of second- and third-generation Jewish authors has been characterized as a kind of writing that—unlike the approach taken by the preceding generation of writers—addresses the issue of Jewishness "without universalizing it out of existence" (Cheyette 1993, n.p.).[2] In the Netherlands, Italy, Hungary, and Poland, Jewish writers have emerged to become important and influential voices in their countries' literary and cultural scenes, aspiring to go beyond the *letteratura memorialista* of their predecessors. In France, the number of publications from Jewish writers born after the Shoah began to surge in the late seventies and has continued to grow in both quantity and variety ever since. Approximately 350 books and innumerable journal and magazine articles covering various aspects of the past and the present of Judaism appear every year in France. More than three dozen Jewish writers born after the Shoah have found access to France's major publishing houses, joining the ranks of the prominent writers of the older generations.

Hand in hand with this reemergence of Jewish writing has come an increasing interest about Jewish matters in the French public—an interest in the situation of Jews in France that predates the emergence of virulent expressions of anti-Semitism by Islamic fundamentalists in the wake of September 11,

1. See also Gilman 1994 and Nolden 1995.
2. See also Cheyette's introduction in Cheyette 1998.

2001. After all, France is home to both the largest Jewish and the largest Muslim population (circa six million people) on the European continent.

Starting in 1978, the Centre Georges Pompidou has been hosting Journées on Yiddish and Sephardic Culture and, starting in 1982, an annual Jewish film festival. A Paris exhibition at the Porte de Versailles organized in 1989 by Chief Rabbi Joseph Sitruk and showcasing the religious aspects of Judaism drew the interest of more than 35,000 people. Public television channels devote programs to Jewish life in contemporary France, such as in the program "Être juif" [To Be Jewish], which aired in June 1991. The Musée d'Art et d'Histoire du Judaïsme in the Marais, opened in 1998 in the impressive Baroque Hôtel de Saint-Aignan, has met with huge success. Annual events like the Journée de la Thora [Torah Day] or the public reading of the names of the deportees at the Place des Martyrs-Juifs-du-Vélodrome d'Hiver, organized by the Mouvement juif libéral de France [Liberal Jewish Movement of France] continue to attract large audiences.

The process of re-Judaization has reversed the trend Judaism had been experiencing since the French Revolution when the French Jews were granted emancipation and when a transformation began that turned the *Juifs* [Jews] to *Israélites* [Israelites], to highly emancipated citizens. According to the historian Annette Wieviorka, the renewed interest in Judaism and Jewish life and culture has taken hold with incredible speed during the last fifteen years, bidding farewell to the notion of Jewish invisibility embodied by the "Israelite" that prompted Wieviorka to state in 2000: "Qu'on le veuille ou non, le modèle républicain traditionnel est derrière nous. Il n'y a plus, dans notre pays, de Français de confession mosaïque" (2000, 26) [Whether one likes it or not, the traditional republican model is behind us. There are no longer, in our country, any French of the faith of Moses].

This transformation has been carried out to a large degree by the children and grandchildren of the generation directly affected by the Shoah and by the children of the immigrants from France's former colonies and territories in North Africa. They have begun to search, often in different directions, for paths that would bring them back in touch with a Jewish past about which many of them have known very little. Cut off by the persecution of their ancestors and by the temptations of acculturation, they are trying to acquaint themselves with strains of traditions lost to acculturation, persecution, and emigration. The resulting "pluralization of ways to be Jewish" (David 1993, 27) has been taking place within a larger cultural context in the New Europe, one in which a public awareness welcomes religious, ethnic, cultural, and regional diversity in a manner unknown in previous times, and that no longer casts Jews as Europe's Other. There is even a discussion underway that looks at the Jewish people as a potential model for the European community as such. Alexandre J.-L. Delamarre's statement, which in 1979 sounded futuristic at best, has since met with much interest among European thinkers: "La judéité est donc comme le modèle implicite de l'identité européenne" (1979, 96) [Jewishness is like the implicit model of European identity].

A "Cacophony" of Voices

The years 1979 and 1980 mark the beginning of this remarkable process. When the French sociologist Dominique Schnapper, the daughter of the renowned thinker Raymond Aron, published her study *Juifs et Israélites* [Jews and Israelites] in 1980, she was astonished to find that she was not the only author trying to map the situation of contemporary French Jewry. The "nouvelle question juive" [new Jewish question], to borrow the title of the book by Shmuel Trigano that had appeared the previous year, reemerged on the surface of national consciousness. Claudine Vegh published her conversations with children of the deportees *Je ne lui ai pas dit au revoir* [I Never Told Him Goodbye], and Luc Rosenzweig (born in 1943) compiled his "Catalogue pour des Juifs de maintenant" [Catalogue for the Jews of Today], for which he had commissioned contributions through an announcement in the journal *Libération*. Admitting his surprise in view of the new "cacophony" of Jewish voices, he stated, "Ceux qui, aujourd'hui se mettent à l'écoute des voix juives sont peut-être surpris par la cacophonie des discours contradictoires qui émergent de ce monde tourbillonnant" (1997, 7) [Those who listen to Jewish voices today are perhaps surprised by the cacophony of contradictory discourses which are emerging from this turbulent world].

In 1979, Fernande Schulmann presented a collection of interviews with Jews born at the turn of the century. Her *L'enfance ailleurs: Mémoires juives* [Childhood Elsewhere: Jewish Memories] was driven by an "urgent" interest in preserving the memory of those capable of providing testimony of the period from 1915 on. Journals like *Esprit* and *Histoire* presented special issues such as "Les Juifs dans la modernité" [Jews in Modernity] and "Les Juifs en France" [Jews in France]. The editorial of the newly founded journal *Combat pour la diaspora* [Fight for the Diaspora] proclaimed, "La Diaspora doit trouver sa propre voix" (1979, 6) [The Diaspora must find its own voice]. Alain

Finkielkraut, who was born in 1949, in his seminal essay *The Imaginary Jew* explored self-critically the fallacies of the identity discourse prominent among his peers. This book would turn out to be one of the most influential documents of contemporary Jewish discourse, celebrated by the journal *L'arche* as a "a strong book, most especially a true book" (Malka 1980, 52).[3]

The same year, Luc Rosenzweig provocatively gave his collection of interviews with young Jews a title reminiscent of Edouard Drumont's notorious anti-Semitic pamphlet from 1886: *La jeune France juive* [Young Jewish France]. In his preface, he pointed quite paradigmatically to the fate of Pierre Goldman, his colleague at *Libération* who was assassinated in 1979, and to that of the student leader Daniel Cohn-Bendit. Born to Jewish-German parents but raised in France, Cohn-Bendit was expelled from France in 1968 as the "rouquin, l'apatride" [the stateless redhead]. The event elicited the famous slogan "Nous sommes tous des Juifs allemands" [We are all German Jews]. Rosenzweig celebrated the "*houtzpeh*, cette impertinence ravageuse qui permet de devenir fort lorsqu'on est faible et gai quand on est triste" [*chutzpah*, the raging impertinence that allows one to grow strong when weak and lighthearted when sad] with which Cohn-Bendit had led the very movement that would develop into a general strike and eventually lead to de Gaulle's fall a year later (1980, 10). The Algerian-born writer and journalist Jean-Luc Allouche remembers how he, the Sephardic Jew, felt vexed by the slogan celebrating the solidarity with Cohn-Bendit: "dans le secret de mon cœur, j'eusse préféré que fût célébré un Juif algérien et non pas un 'Pollak' " (Allouche 1984, 51–52) [at the bottom of my heart, I would have preferred that an Algerian Jew be celebrated, not a "Pollak"].

Arnold Mandel commented in an article with the programmatic title "Le néo-diasporisme culturel" [cultural neo-diasporism] in the same year on the younger generations' reappropriation of their Jewishness:

> Les mesures de la conscience juive ne signifient pas seulement dans des conduites existentielles, comme le port de la *Kipa* ou les thèmes et la tonalité de la jeune littérature, mais aussi et encore dans ce que l'on qualifie un peu hâtivement de "nouvelles tendances," comme si l'on se trouvait effectivement confronté avec une mutation idéologique, ce qui n'est pas tout à fait le cas. *Grosso modo* on peut désigner cette mouvance comme un néo-diasporisme. (Mandel 1980, 95)

3. See also Raczymow 1980.

> [The measures of Jewish consciousness signify not only in existential contexts, like the wearing of the *Kipa* or the themes and tonality of the new literature, but also and more so in that which is termed rather hastily the "new tendencies," as if a we actually found ourselves confronted with an ideological mutation, which is not at all the case. *Grosso modo* one can call these spheres of influence neo-diasporism.]

In 1980, the journal *L'arche* published the special issue "Les Juifs de France: Ce qui change" [The Jews of France: What Is Changing], and Dominique Schnapper presented with her study *Jews and Israelites* a thorough sociological analysis of the Jewish population, its demography, and its attitudes. After all, the new interest in the developments and movements within Jewish communities would be indicative not only of this segment of the French population, but also of the situation of France in general and its relationship to minorities and cultural diversification in general. Based on a large number of interviews, Schnapper drew a remarkable picture of the essential phenotypes prevalent in contemporary Jewish life in France. Her study differentiated between (1) the "pratiquants" [practicing] or observant Jews, whose lives are characterized by their strong adherence to the cultural and religious traditions of Judaism; (2) the "militants" [militants Jews], whose politics are consciously informed by their Jewish identity with a strong emphasis on their ties to the state of Israel; and (3) the "Israelites" [assimilated Jews], the ones who have severed their links to the culture and religion of Judaism altogether.

However, the insight that merits the most attention is Schnapper's description of the emergence of a fourth group that she called the "nouveaux-pratiquants" [new observant] or newly practicing Jews. More than a decade after the publication of her study, Schnapper elaborated on the rapid advance of this segment of the Jewish population, which in 1980 still was a statistically negligible minority:

> The return to Judaism in a religious sense takes many different forms, ranging from religious practices within the family to attendance at *yeshivot* or at study circles. The *yeshivot* offer Talmud study under the authority of a rabbi. . . . Above all, the *yeshivot* are concerned with reaffirming a form of return to traditional education. The study circles, in contrast, are a more innovative way of raising Jewish consciousness. Scattered in places where neither the Jewish religion nor Jewish communities have traditionally been well established, they attract Jews without much knowledge of Jewish tradition or culture to re-educate themselves together with their relatives or friends, primarily in

> response to the demands of a personal quest for identity. In this latter case, the concern is rather to situate oneself in a supportive milieu, to rediscover family memories, to reconstruct an identity on the basis of emotion rather than intellect, and to find ways of adapting the strictures of Jewish law to the modern world. At the same time, fundamentalist groups such as the Lubavitch Hasidim have engaged in substantial outreach activity and built up large communities of followers, impressive for their sheer size; the Liberal Jews, who tend to comprise members of the upper classes and intellectuals, have likewise revived their activity. The Consistoire, formally the official body of French Jewry, has no more than a minor regulatory impact on any of these groups. (Schnapper 1994, 174)

The vigor of the orthodox groups has resulted in more and more prominence within important representative bodies of France's Jewish community. In 1990, the success of the orthodox list *ACIP 2000* at the board elections for the Association Consitoriale Israélite de Paris [Israelite Council Association of Paris], an umbrella organization of Jewish groups in the Paris area, confirmed Schnapper's evaluation (even though the orthodox Benny Cohen then lost the presidency of the ACIP to a more moderate candidate in 1993). Leading the way for traditionalist politics, Benny Cohen's motto "La Torah, ce n'est pas le Coca-Cola" [The Torah is not Coca-Cola] urged his followers to continue on the old "chemin tracé par Maïmonide" (Lindenberg 1990, 83) [path followed by Maimonides].

The tensions between the radically orthodox minority and the largely unobservant majority have in the last few years elicited the call for a "dialogue *judéo-juif*" (Krygier 2000, 151) [Judeo-Jewish dialogue]. To prevent specific religious tendencies from becoming irreversible, as of 1981 France's chief rabbi is no longer nominated for life, but elected for a seven-year term. The campaign between the "philosopher" Gilles Bernheim (with Alsatian roots) and the conservative—and victorious—Joseph Sitruk (of Tunisian descent) preceding the election in 1994 showed the polarization within the Jewish community. For Sitruk, there is no question that Judaism has no future if left in the hands of those who—like Rivon Krygier, the 1957-born founder of Adath Shalom (the first conservative community of France) in Paris's XV district, or the liberal Pauline Bebe, France's first female rabbi—are reaching out to secular Jews flirting with religion: "Le judaïsme authentiquement religieux progresse, alors que sa version libérale régresse" (2000, 36) [Authentically religious Judaism progresses, while its liberal version regresses]. Rabbi Bernheim in his book *Un rabbin dans la cité* (1997) [A Rabbi in the City] appreciates the heterogeneous concert ranging from Orthodox (and Lubavitch, which nowadays attracts even Sephardic Jews from the Maghreb) to Reform within French Jewry but warns that the notion of a coherent Jewish community in France will disappear unless Jews return to a common denominator.

A look at the attendance of Jewish schools confirms this new interest in the old roots of Judaism: in 2000, there were no fewer than 220 Jewish schools in France with an enrollment of some 25,000 pupils (David 2000). Almost a fourth of the somewhat more than 100,000 Jewish children attend Jewish schools; similarly, the number of institutions of higher learning that offer programs in Hebrew has been growing steadily since 1975 as has the number of students taking courses on the religious aspects of Judaism (Birnbaum 1995, 206–7).

Retour identitaire and Re-Judaization

The most prominent example of the return to Judaism among the younger generations is the career of the intellectual Benny Lévy (born in Cairo in 1946). A student of Louis Althusser, Lévy founded in 1968 in Paris the Gauche prolétarienne [Proletarian Left] and later worked as the secretary of Jean-Paul Sartre until the philosopher's death. In 1983, Lévy left Paris for the yeshiva of *rav* Abitbol in Strasbourg to study the Scriptures. He later moved to Israel where he is currently directing an institute devoted to the works of the Jewish philosopher Emmanuel Lévinas.

The process of re-Judaization and the renewed interest in Jewish religion (of which Lévy figures as the most prominent example) have stimulated responses from nonreligious intellectuals and secular groups trying to counterbalance what many of them see as the "danger of ghettoization" or a fundamentalist drift toward a new marginalization and detachment from the public sphere in France. Capitalizing on the increasing awareness especially among younger Jews of their background and ethnic heritage, a variety of organizations have been founded to channel the revival movement into a direction consistent with the goals of Enlightenment. As early as 1967, Richard Marienstras (born 1928) founded the Le Cercle Gaston Crémieux [Gaston Crémieux Group] expressly to promote the idea of a culturally autonomous diasporic Judaism beyond the realm of religion. In his *Être un peuple en diaspora* [To Be a People in Diaspora] he offered a critique of the "mythe de la 'centralité' d'Israël" (1975, 53) [myth of the "centrality" of Israel], arguing that in the course of history, Jewish life in the diaspora had succeeded in surviving and prospering and has helped prevent the Jewish people from annihilation. The perils of assimilation, Marienstras suggested, have not endangered the common core of existence that Jews from all over the world continue to share—a core that he locates in Jewish memory and that does not require a nation-state as its base at all. The latter, he argued, has historically proven to be more vulnerable to destruction than small enclave-communities.

Other organizations followed suit, among them Liberté du judaïsme [Freedom of Judaism] in 1987, Albert Memmi's Association pour un judaïsme humaniste et laïque [Association for a humanist and secular Judaism], 1989, Centre juif laïque [Secular Jewish Center], 1989, Rencontre progressiste juive [Progressive Jewish Association], 1990, Association des étudiants juifs laïques [Association of secular Jewish students], 1991, and Gescher. Altogether, there are more than fifty Jewish organizations associated with the umbrella organization Conseil représentatif des institutions juives de France [Representative Council of Jewish Institutions of France]. The term "néo-associationnisme Juif" (1986, 150) [Jewish neo-associationism], coined by Claude Tapia, indeed fits the emergence of groups catering to specific understandings of Jewish identity.

Newly founded journals (*Combat pour la diaspora* [Battle for the Diaspora], *Traces*, *Pardès*, *Yod*,and *Les nouveaux cahiers* [The New Notebooks]) afford the various groups the opportunity to express themselves spontaneously and freely. Radio stations, like Radio J, Radio Shalom, Judaïque FM, or Radio Communauté are on the air twenty-four hours a day. Institutions and institutes have been established to allow for the systematic study of the past and present of Judaism. The Association pour l'Étude et la Diffusion de la Culture Yiddish [Association for the Study and Diffusion of Yiddish Culture] was founded in 1981, seminars on Jewish studies at the École des Hautes études en Sciences Sociales [School for Advanced Studies in Social Sciences] were established in 1982, and the Collège des Études Juives [School for Jewish Studies] was established within the Alliance Israélite Universelle [Universal Israelite Alliance] in 1984, with a newly renovated library on the rue La Bruyère to meet the needs of its many users. At the Sorbonne, a professorship for the study of Judeo-Spanish language and culture was established. Also worth mentioning is the cooperation between the Centre Rachi and the Université de Paris IV (1984), as well as the formation of the École des Hautes Études du Judaïsme in 1986 [School for Advanced Studies in Judaism].

These academic ventures reflect only one side of the new vivacity of Jewish life in France. Over the course of the last several decades, one could observe a "radicalization" (Gutman 1984, 95) of Jewish discourse that goes back at least to the alienation of French Jewry by Charles de Gaulle during the Six-Day War. The general's remarks provoked large numbers of Jews to express publicly their criticism of the government's reorientation of its Middle East policy in favor of the Arab states. From that point forward, Zionism advanced to the point of large-scale demonstrations on the streets of the French capital, which climaxed in 1976, when Henri Hajdenberg and his Renouveau juif [Jewish Renewal] organized the popular "Douze heures pour Israël" [Twelve Hours for Israel] attended by hundreds of thousands Frenchmen, among them Pierre Mendès France, Bernard-Henri Lévy, and Elie Wiesel.

This new assertiveness and political militantism were espoused by the very top levels of the Jewish organizations. The first meeting between a French prime minister and the president of the Conseil représentatif des institutions juives de France, CRIF [Representative Council of Jewish Institutions of France], the representative body of French Jewry, immediately after the election of Valéry Giscard d'Estaing heralded a new role for France's Jewish community organizations in national politics. With the rise of the New Right and Le Pen's nationalistic Front National [National Front], this assertiveness has grown even more and resulted in the foundation of Jewish organizations like the Union des étudiants juifs de France [Union of Jewish Students of France], which contributed to alliances such as SOS Racisme [SOS Racism], started in 1984, to support the fight against racism and anti-Semitism.

Glimpses of the Dark Past

A step back into the past can shed light on the evolution of the new attitudes among Jews in contemporary France. French Jews had responded with a sense of bewilderment and disbelief to the Jewish Laws passed in France, the *Statut des Juifs* [Statute of the Jews] of 1940, which excluded Jews from public service and robbed them of their rights and belongings. Yet in spite of the reprisals and deportations—almost a fifth of the approximately 330,000 Jews living in France were deported and 80,000 were killed[4]—the involvement of French

4. Approximately 80,000 of the 300,000 to 330,000 Jews who lived in France before the war (among them about 130,000 to 140,000 Jews born outside of France) were killed. 24,500 French-born and 56,500 Jews born outside of France were reported missing. Thus, 10 percent of the French-born Jews and 40 percent of the immigrant Jews became victims of the Shoah. See Klarsfeld 1983.

citizens in the persecution of their Jewish compatriots remained for many decades a taboo subject in postwar France. The shock of the Vichy years initially did not end the cultural invisibility and the attitude of *quant-à-soi* [keeping to oneself] that had been prevalent within French Jewry, generally viewed as one of the most acculturated diasporas.[5] It took the Jewish community several decades before it succeeded in reaffirming its "identity within French society" (Rousso 1991, 133).

Interestingly, the beginning of the demystification of the era of collaboration within the legal system, in the media, and in the field of historiography coincided with the beginning of a literary movement by the generations born after the Shoah. Rousso, born in 1954 in Egypt to Jewish parents, published his important study *Le syndrome de Vichy de 1944 à nos jours* [The Vichy Syndrome from 1944 to Today] in 1987. Robert O. Paxton, an American historian who looked at France as an outsider, gave the impetus for Rousso's research with his pioneering book *Vichy France and the Jews: Old Guard and New Order, 1940–1944*, published in 1972. The French translation in 1973 of this groundbreaking study, which was the first to include documents on collaborationist activities from German archives, was "not very well received" in France (Hoffmann 1995, ix).

Reminiscing about the end of the 1970s, when his professional interest in the Vichy regime began to develop, Henry Rousso states:

> During the course of my research I realized that this topic which had seemed to be so remote was in reality a very up-to-date one. An example: I studied in the Archives Nationales the documents of the era. Then I would go outside to purchase a copy of *Le Monde* where on the front page I found a polemics about the past of a collaborator, about the preparations for a trial. Then I realized that France, too, was still captured by the past; as they say in Germany, "that the past doesn't disappear" (1990, 105).

The events, which reminded the French public in general and its Jewish population in particular that the country's present was still a captive of the past, culminated in the 1970s, after de Gaulle had in 1967 publicly vented his suspicion that French Jews were unreliable patriots. The doubts of the general

5. The attitude of "quant-à-soi" was critically reviewed during the thirtieth Colloque des intellectuels juifs de langue française in 1989. See "Le 'quant-à-soi,' " in *Données et débats: Actes du XXXe colloque des intellectuels juifs de langues française* (de Fontenay 1991). See also the editor's introduction to Elisabeth de Fontenay, "On the *Quant-à-soi*" (Astro 1994, 217–24), which reminds the reader that this term also carries the connotation of "dignity" and "reserve."

about the loyalty of French Jews toward the French nation reminded them of their fragile status as citizens (Birnbaum 1995, 220). And it brought back the memory of the assumptions on which their citizenship had been founded. The Jewish historian Shmuel Trigano, one of the most prolific and controversial thinkers and activists among the members of the post-Shoah generations, relates de Gaulle's remark of 1967 back to the construction of the Jewish community as defined first by the emancipation in the French Revolution and then by the Napoleonic regime. When in 1791 the approximately 40,000 Jews living in France received French citizenship, they were acknowledged as individuals but had to leave behind any notion of belonging to a Jewish community. Jewish identity was from now on supposed to be based solely on religion, not on a shared culture or on a history of being a special people. Renunciation of Jewish identity was the price to be paid for emancipation. The Napoleonic model relegated the aspect of religion entirely to the private sphere, confining Jewish identity to the synagogue:

> as individuals they were expected to be citizens like everyone else, but collectively they were established as a "religious community."
>
> The problem with that was that it laid Jews' loyalty open to question: the idea of a "Jewish conspiracy" (the accusation that Jews maintained secret international links among themselves that were directed against their fellow citizens) became the basic prism of the antisemitism that emerged, contrary to all expectations, in republican France. (Trigano 1994, 181–82)

Four years after de Gaulle's remark, another head of state, Georges Pompidou, pardoned the collaborator Paul Touvier, who was responsible for killing Jews during the Vichy Regime. Valéry Giscard d'Estaing and Raymond Barre made statements that, according to many observers, verged on being anti-Semitic (Birnbaum 1995; Philippe 1981). Between 1978 and 1981, the Darquier de Pellepoix affair—concerning the former coordinator of Vichy's anti-Jewish program who was living in Spain and who had never regretted his actions and beliefs—came to haunt all those who preferred to think of French collaboration as merely a mishap of the past. The long-overdue indictment of a collaborator based on crimes against humanity sent the first legal signals that would make it more difficult to retain the myth of France as a society of resistance fighters. At the same time, however, revisionism began to strive for academic accreditation. The case of Faurisson, a university professor who in the respectable daily *Le monde* in 1975 denied the mass extermination of Jews, caused consternation especially among intellectuals. Yet the wave of Holocaust denial did not reach its climactic point until—as the historian Pierre Vidal-Naquet observed—the American series *Holocaust* was broadcast in 1979 on television. As the series reminded the general audience of the concentration camps, albeit in a highly sentimentalized fashion, terrorist acts painfully contradicted the assumption that militant anti-Semitism was a thing of the past. The bombing of the synagogue on the rue Copernic in 1980 and of Goldenberg's delicatessen on the rue des Rosiers in August 1982, as well as the desecration of the Jewish Cemetery in Carpentras in May 1990, were among the most brutal acts that shook France in the latter part of the last century.

The public deconstruction of the Vichy past came to a head when the country learned in 1994 about François Mitterand's friendship with René Bousquet, head of police under Vichy. The French people started to realize the implications of Mitterand's custom of sending flowers each year to the grave of Vichy's head of state Marshal Pétain (ostensibly to acknowledge the hero of World War I). The governments of Jacques Chirac and Lionel Jospin discontinued this gesture of their predecessor and instead officially acknowledged the involvement of the French in the persecution of Jews, followed in 1997 by words of regret by the French archbishop Olivier de Berranger.

Glimpses of New Beginnings

The myth of a solidly anti-Fascist past eroded only very slowly in the collective memory of the French nation. The participants involved in the debates on Jewish identity that took place shortly before and after the end of the war did not yet fully grasp the implications of the roundups and killings of French Jews for the rebuilding of the nation and its Jewish communities. These early postwar debates were shaped by the late Simone Weil (1909–43), the influential intellectual and leftist activist who had renounced her own Jewishness during the Vichy years and who came to embody the long-standing tradition of acculturation. She proclaimed Christianity a superior religion and took to the extreme Comte de Clermont-Tonnerre's famous assertion of 1791 that Jews should abolish their life as a community. Calling for the "total displacement of Judaism by Christianity's 'authentic' spirituality" (Nevin 1991, 246), her voice resonated among many Jews of the Republic as the enlightened claim of modern humanity and challenged them to attack the Vichy laws against Jews from a universalist and civil rights perspective, rather than from the perspective of victims of anti-Semitism.

While Simone Weil had fundamentally questioned the raison d'être of

Jewish identity, Jean-Paul Sartre immediately after the war doubted its substance. In his essay "Réflexions sur la question juive" [Reflections on the Jewish Question], written in 1944, the non-Jewish philosopher reduced Jewish identity to the anti-Semite's projection of the Jew: "c'est l'antisémite qui crée le Juif" (Sartre 1946, 185) [it is the anti-Semite who creates the Jew]. Remaining within the path of Jewish Emancipation through the French Revolution, Sartre had difficulties attributing to Judaism any substantive traits, appreciating its history, or imagining "any other goal for the Jew but total assimilation" (Suleiman 1999, 133). Though Sartre wanted to break the republic's silence about the fate of the Jews and certainly defended them publicly, his *J'accuse* failed to acknowledge that there are indeed forms of Jewish identity beyond what he had called the "inauthentic Jew," the Jews whose identity gets imposed on them by the anti-Semites. Sartre's plea for an "authentic" form of Jewish existence remained vague, with only social but no cultural, historical, or religious contours. He challenged the Jews to leave behind the optimism of rational Enlightenment and to accept instead their lot of martyrdom, the role of the pariah.

Sartre's argument—according to the American scholar Seth L. Wolitz, "the basis of most intellectual debate in France concerning the Jew and his representation for the next forty years" (1994, 123)—contributed yet another chapter to the history of French-Jewish relations in which the non-Jewish French could conceive of Jewish emancipation only as acculturation and without really grasping the dilemma this identification carries with it. In the wake of this school of thought, which over the course of centuries came to dominate Jewish life in France, the Dreyfus affair had been regarded by the vast majority of non-Jewish French citizens and French Jews as a mere anomaly. Similarly, there was a strong tendency among non-Jews and Jews alike to view the flare-ups of anti-Semitism in the 1930s and later even the deportations of Jews aided by French police in the same manner.

Not until the end of the 1950s did Jewish memory begin to contest unspoken assumptions of collective French memory and break the silence of France's involvement in the genocide. In 1956, *Nuit et brouillard* [Night and Fog] by Alain Resnais and Jean Cayrol reminded the audiences of the deportation primarily of resistance fighters and political prisoners, not without running into problems with the censors. In 1961, the year of the Eichmann trial, Frédéric Rossif's film *Le temps du ghetto* [The Time of the Ghetto] focused for the first time in French film history on the fate of the Jews. In 1959, André

Schwarz-Bart received the prestigious prix Goncourt for his epic novel *Le dernier des justes* [The Last of the Just], followed two years later by Anna Langfus for her *Les bagages de sable* [Suitcases of Sand]. Marcel Ophuls's documentary *Le chagrin et la pitié* [The Sorrow and the Pity]—interestingly a Swiss-German rather than a French production—was finished in 1969, but the officials in charge of programming prevented the film from appearing on TV until 1981.

The Moroccan-born historian Georges Bensoussan differentiates two more stages in the advance of collective Jewish memory. First, the Six-Day War, which initially had brought back the fear of genocide, elicited on French streets the first massive demonstrations in support of Israel, and Israel's victory strengthened the confidence of Jews in France. At the same time, the arrival of Jews from the Maghreb and the coming of age of the first generation of Jews born after the Shoah profoundly changed the demographics and with it the attitudes of the Jewish population in France. Then, in the late 1970s and early 1980s, Bensoussan argues, Jewish memory reacted assertively and aggressively to the advance of revisionism and anti-Semitism. Claude Lanzmann's documentary *Shoah* (1985), which was financed by the French Ministry of Culture, introduced a groundbreaking way of remembering the extermination of the Jews in the East. The trials of Klaus Barbie (1987) and of Paul Touvier—the first Frenchman tried for crimes against humanity—started to end a long history of legal amnesia.

Under de Gaulle, the deportees had hardly been mentioned during official commemorations and had been honored only occasionally and locally with monuments erected by municipal authorities or, in rare cases, by the state government. The new charter of the umbrella organization CRIF, ratified in 1977, explicitly stated for the first time in its history specific political goals, such as the condemnation of all forms of persecution and anti-Semitism as well as the full participation of Jews in French society. Organizations such as Fils et filles des déportés juifs de France [Sons and Daughters of the Deported Jews of France], founded in 1979 in the wake of Beate and Serge Klarsfeld's research, catalyzed a certain change in attitude among the responsible officials (Barcellini and Wieviorka 1995). A national holiday commemorating the victims of racist and anti-Semitic persecution, however, was not established until 1993, signed into law by President Mitterand, who at this point in time had not yet come forward about his own role as a young politician in the Vichy government.

Destroying the "master narrative" (Lyotard 1984) of France as a country innocent of collaboration and anti-Semitism, a critical discourse on Jewish memory emerged, acknowledging at its outset that "while memory of the past was always a central component of Jewish experience, the historian was not its primary custodian" (Yerushalmi 1982, xiv). According to Yosef Hayim Yerushalmi, who in 1982 bemoaned the absence of Jewish historiography, literature (and ideology) had assumed the role of shaping Jewish memory and of retrieving what had fallen by the wayside of history. Yerushalmi's charge (*zakhor*, or remembrance) was heeded by a growing number of historians, inspired by Klarsfeld's monumental *Le mémorial de la déportation des Juifs de France* [Memorial to the Deportation of the Jews of France], a huge volume published in 1978 that recorded the names and biographical data of 76,000 Auschwitz-bound Jews as well as the names of the German and French officials who ran the machinery of deportation. The documents disclosed in the book were immediately used as legal evidence in Nazi trials in Germany and other countries. The creation of the government-sponsored Mission Mattéoli [Mattéoli commission], which since 1997 has systematically investigated the spoliation of the belongings of French Jews during the war, marked the culminating point of this historical endeavor. In 1991, the Jewish historian Pierre Vidal-Naquet critiqued the role attributed to the catastrophe in Jewish historiography, and proposed a switch of paradigms:

> La mémoire n'est pas l'histoire: elle choisit, élimine par pans entiers les moments dont l'idéologie impose l'élimination (tout particulièrement, aujourd'hui, ces longues périodes de l'histoire juive qui n'ont pas été tragiques), annule le temps, gomme les évolutions et les mutations. (1991, 16)
>
> [Memory is not history: it chooses, and eliminates in broad strokes those moments upon which ideology imposes elimination (most strangely, today, these long periods of Jewish history that were not tragic), voids out time, erases evolutions and mutations.]

A New Generation Enters

Alarmed by the patterns of denial and by the attacks of anti-Semitism, uneasy with their parents' choice of acculturation, and encouraged by the attitude among the Jewish immigrants from the Maghreb, the post-Shoah generations set out to find their own position with respect to both gentile society and to the experiences and lifestyles of the older generations. They witnessed a societal process in which the arrival of immigrants from the former colonies and protectorates began to corrode the monocultural hegemony of *civilisation française*, irrevocably changing the face of the population. In 1977, President Valéry Giscard d'Estaing declared, "The time has come to state that there is no contradiction between being fully French and continuing to live according to local or regional traditions, customs or cultures" (Schnapper 1983, xlix). The new appreciation of regional concerns and minority traditions began to erode Jacobin French centralism, and the growing presence of Muslim immigrants challenged the notion of France as "the Church's eldest daughter," as a largely monoreligious—that is, Catholic—country. Ecological movements inspired by local constituents questioned the prevalence of national industrial interests. The adherence of the educational system to the principle of *francisation* came under fire both by immigrants and regionalists, and the universalist conception of the nation was undermined by the *nouveaux philosophes*, many of them of Jewish descent and anything but reluctant to use metaphors from the Hebrew Bible in their works. In 1981, "le droit à la différence" [the right to difference], a motto coined by regionalist forces, was promoted to a slogan of Mitterand's presidential campaign, and the question whether Jews should refer to themselves as "juif français" [French Jew] rather than as "français juif" [Jewish Frenchman] gained new meaning.[6]

To begin appreciating their ties to Jewish past and tradition, the young Jews, however, had to overcome barriers that had been set up not by the state but by their own reaction to the state. The political imperative of the rebellious era had been to put the cause of internationalism above ethnic (not to mention Zionist) concerns, leading many young Jews in Europe to ignore the little they knew about their roots. The initial wave of politicization in the late 1960s and 1970s had left little space for the exploration of ethnic, religious, regional, and cultural differences. After all, leftist doctrines insisted that any affiliation other than solidarity with the working class was tantamount to false consciousness, a remnant of bourgeois ideology. In his essay on the Jewish question, Marx himself had laid the infelicitous foundation of anti-Semitic thought on which some of his twentieth-century followers continued to build. Thus even the Six-Day War produced ambivalent responses among Jews who

6. See Halbronn 1996. Halbronn claims that such identificatory dilemmas are more or less unique to France.

often would turn away from what many of them perceived as Israeli imperialism. Daniel Cohn-Bendit, for example, remembers that during this event his Jewish identity simply "fell apart" (1975, 11).

In France as well as in England, Italy, and Germany, many young Jews would not reconnect to their ethnic and cultural heritage until after the student rebellion had reached its ideological climax and opened up discourses beyond the realm of class politics. The processes set in motion by the student rebellion, according to the Jewish writer Maurice Partouche, caused a "crise d'identité qui traverse l'Europe" (1982, 324) [identity crisis that runs throughout Europe] and affected the members of the 1968 generation, who mostly had been too young during the Algerian War, most profoundly. Cohn-Bendit, in retrospect, acknowledges the blindness of the Left when he states:

> L'extrême gauche, comme la gauche, a toujours répugné à se poser le problème de l'identité individuelle. Pour définir quelqu'un, on se réfère toujours à son appartenance de classe. Mais notre identité est le fruit de multiples expériences. (1975, 9)
>
> [The extreme left, like the left, has always been reluctant to face the problem of individual identity. To define someone, one always refers to his class. But our identity is the fruit of multiple experiences.]

Younger Jews became curious about the course Judaism took in the United States, where a multitude of voices had created different strands of Jewish identities and communities and had started to articulate publicly their concerns and attitudes. What earlier had been denounced as a category of the accidental and subjective now became celebrated as a particularity worth exploring. The path taken by historian Annette Wieviorka, born in 1948, is typical for the *retour identitaire* [return to the roots]: the daughter of nonreligious parents from Poland with Bundist convictions, motivated by a political agenda, spent a couple of years teaching in China at the height of the student movement and returned disillusioned and eager to discover her family's cultural and linguistic heritage, writing in 1979 an autobiographical book (*L'écureuil de Chine* [The Chinese Squirrel]) in which she reflected on the path her life had taken: "Je sentais confusément que j'avais trahi une judéité que je ne situais pas" (1997, 208) [I felt confusedly that I had betrayed a Jewishness that I did not situate anywhere]. After her studies of Yiddish in New York, she went on to publish *Les livres du souvenir* (1983) [The Books of Memory] with Itzhok Niborski, a study of books commemorating life in the shtetl before the

Shoah. A specialist on the Nazi persecution, Wieviorka became a driving force of the Mission Mattéoli. André Neher, one of the grand old men of Jewish thought and criticism in France, had commented on the first Colloque des intellectuels Juifs de langue française [Colloquium of French-Speaking Jewish Intellectuals]: "Longtemps, l'intellectuel juif a fait figure d'enfant perdu du judaïsme" (1969, 180–91) [For a long time, the Jewish intellectual has looked like the lost child of Judaism]. Not even ten years after the first gathering of this kind, the Jewish intellectual had returned home for good.

Shedding obsolete and stifling templates of identity, including Sartre's, and bidding farewell to the notion of the invisible Jew, a number of theoretical reassessments began in the late 1970s to explore the conditions of contemporary Judaism and the leeway available for identity negotiations. André Glucksmann categorically rejected Sartre's definition of the Jew in declaring "Ce n'est pas l'antisémite qui fait le juif" (1984, 172) [It is not the anti-Semite who makes the Jew], and Luc Rosenzweig juxtaposed traditional Jewish identity with a fundamental principle of the philosophical Enlightenment:

> Ce qui nous fait juifs, ce n'est pas le regard de l'autre, fût-il antisémite (et donc reconnaissant dans le juif une spécificité), mais bien cette impossibilité de se considérer comme un homme nouveau, ce refus d'un des axiomes de la modernité: être cause de soi-même. (1980, 11)
>
> [What makes us Jews is not the perspective of the other, be he anti-Semite (and thus seeking in the Jew a specificity), but the impossibility of considering ourselves a new person, the rejection of one of the axioms of modernity: being the cause of oneself.]

This aspiration to author one's own script of identity, to invent oneself, became the major objective of Rosenzweig's generation, which had grown up under a legacy of a silence that the perpetrators intentionally had spun around their crimes and that the survivors could not break because of the paralyzing effects of the trauma they had experienced and the feeling of guilt of having survived while their friends, family, and neighbors had been murdered. They had grown up in families that had been shaken and truncated by the genocide, in which the Shoah was not just a singular event but a continuing force of emotional destruction.

From the perspective of a Jewish child of survivors whose heritage goes back to Eastern Europe, Alain Finkielkraut attempted in *Le Juif imaginaire* (1980) to locate his own upbringing on the map of Jewish experience. The essay by the child of survivors accomplished at the level of identity discourse what the Six-Day War had done at the political level: it complicated, if not fractured, tendencies toward a mythologization of the Jew as the victim per se. In highly self-critical words, Finkielkraut took on the self-fashioning of young Jews who cast themselves in the tragic role of the victim, the outsider, the persecuted:

> I forged a tragic spectacle from the tragedy of my people, and I was its hero. In short, I played at being persecuted, and did so in the mode of pantomime or the purely ceremonious gesture that I carried off without actually compromising myself. I was a swashbuckler of the concentration camps—but why accuse myself? My date of birth alone explains this propensity to bombast. I was born too close to the Holocaust to be able to keep it from view, and at the same time I was protected by all the horror of this event from a renewal of anti-Semitism, and least in its organized and violent form. In a sense, I was *overjoyed;* the war's proximity at once magnified and preserved me; it invited me to identify with the victims while giving me the all but certain assurance that I would never be one. I had all the profit but none of the risk. I could, knowing my immunity, revolt against torture and fascism. (1980b, 19–20)

Finkielkraut's provocative exclamation "Jewishness is what I miss, not what defines me" (1980b, 38) from his 1980 essay recaptured a feeling that the novelist Georges Perec had expressed in his seminal piece "Ellis Island: Description d'un projet" [Ellis Island: Description of a Project] that had appeared in Rosenzweig's "Catalogue for the Jews of Today" the year before. Perec realized that his experience of being a French-born Jew of Eastern European origins who had survived persecution (he was born in 1936 and died in 1982) did not so much set him apart from the rest of society but rather apart from the experience of his own family. He had grown up with the feeling

> d'être quelque part étranger par rapport à quelque chose de moi-même, d'être "différent," mais non pas tellement différent des "autres" que différent des "miens": je ne parle pas la langue que mes parents parlaient, je ne partage aucun des souvenirs qu'ils purent avoir. (1979, 53–54)

> [of being somehow estranged from myself, of being "different," but not all that different from the "others" but rather from "my own people": I do not speak the language that my parents spoke, I do not share any of the memories that they may have had.]

Both born to Jews of Eastern European descent, Perec and the somewhat younger Finkielkraut looked at their ethnic heritage as an empty category rather than as the core of their identity, as a figment of the imagination in desperate need to be rediscovered and newly defined. Having grown up in the milieu of Eastern European Jews living in France, Finkielkraut paradigmatically challenged his peers to look for forms of self-definition appropriate for the post-Shoah period. Shmuel Trigano, born near Algiers and therefore in a context less affected than Europe by the Shoah, asked his coreligionists to assert consciously their Jewishness by returning to the Torah and to Jewish law.[7] The experience of their *naissance tardive* [late birth], of having been born after the war, preoccupies most of the authors of this generation and serves as one of the most crucial incentives for the act of writing as a means of self-exploration, as for example in Claude Gutman's (born 1946) *Les réparations* [Reparations], published in 1981:

> Je n'étais qu'un enfant de la paix né dans une drôle d'après-guerre. Comment aurais-je imaginé qu'ils en avaient exterminé des millions, qu'il en restait encore et que j'étais parmi leurs descendants, si proche? Comment imaginer que mes parents s'étaient embarqués sur un *Exodus* en partance et que j'étais né, au bout du voyage, en terre autrefois biblique, et britannique par mandat? Je n'avais connu que la paix. (1981, 11)
>
> [I was nothing but a child of peace born in the odd times after the war. How could I have imagined that they had exterminated millions, that some still remained and that I was among their descendants, so close? How to imagine that my parents had embarked on an *Exodus* about to begin and that I was born, at the beginning of the voyage, in a land once biblical, and British by mandate? I had never known anything but peace.]

The younger generations do not deny that the Nazi genocide is, to use a formulation by Robert Misrahi from 1963, the "*référence absolue* pour tout avenir possible," a "back-ground, ou le grund, de toute expérience et de toute conscience juives" (1963, 91) [*absolute point of reference* for all possible futures; a background, or the basis, for all Jewish experience and conscience]. Rather, they see in it the necessary but not the sufficient condition of their own situation. One finds this attitude uttered in emotional terms of anguish, like in rhetorical question of the main figure in Chochana Boukhobza's novel *Le cri* [The Cry]: "Vous croyez que le judaïsme se résume au nazisme? Au machiavélisme du système hitlérien? . . . Que nous, les vivants, sommes des

7. Triganos's complex position in the current French debate about orthodoxy is discussed in Shurkin 2000.

nécrophages?" (1987, 261) [Do you think that Judaism comes down to Nazism? To the Machiavellianism of the Hitlerian system? . . . That we, the living, are necrophagous?]. This attitude is also expressed in a manner that reflects the discourse of philosophical universalism, as in the words of Luc Rosenzweig that simultaneously document his generation's heritage of Enlightenment:

> Le spectre d'Auschwitz est présent, bien sûr, mais il fonctionne plutôt aujourd'hui comme une catégorie a priori de la connaissance, indispensable à tout juif qui pense le monde occidental, que comme un spectre à conjurer. (1979, 7)
>
> [The specter of Auschwitz is present, of course, but today it functions more like an a priori category of knowledge, indispensable to every Jew who thinks of the world in Western terms, rather than a ghost to ward off.]

This indebtedness to universalism must be taken into account when judging, for example, Arno Klarsfeld, the son of Beate and Serge Klarsfeld, for his behavior as a civil prosecutor in the 1998 war crime trial of Papon, the former secretary-general of the Gironde during the Occupation. The young Klarsfeld (born in 1967) upset many observers of the trial not only because he would arrive at the courthouse in roller blades and wear blue jeans under his lawyer's black robe. Most irritating to many was that at the last minute he introduced a plea for a lesser penalty than the life sentence for Papon that the prosecuting government authorities had sought.

But even as the self-styled *enfant terrible* that he presented himself as, he remains first of all the *enfant*, the child of his parents, carrying out the same mission that is driving their life. The end remains the same, it is just the means, or at least the gestures and manners of the younger, that differ. That pertains even to Arno Klarsfeld's literary pursuits: in his novel *Les dieux ne songent qu'à dormir* (1995) [The Gods Only Think about Sleeping], he features a young protagonist who exposes the plagiarisms of an Auschwitz novel by checking facts against the *Le mémorial de la déportation des Juifs de France*, written by the father of the author himself.

The children of the survivors, it seems, developed their manner in the school of antiauthoritarianism. And upon graduation, many went on to seek ways of leaving the persona of "imagined Jew" behind. Alain Finkielkraut moved on to dedicate himself to ethical aspects of Judaism, inspired by the work of Emmanuel Lévinas, one of the most important representatives of Jewish thought in the twentieth century. Shmuel Trigano went on to propose a kind of spiritual Zionism informed by traditional Jewish values. Still others have turned to documenting their perspective on the past of their Jewish families as well as of the Jewish ghettos they left behind and the Jewish communities in which they spent their formative years. They accomplish this as playwrights (like Liliane Atlan or Jean-Claude Grumberg), photographers (like Frédéric Brenner or Jacky Azoulay), as directors (like Dante Desarthe, Martine Dugowson, Emmanuel Finkiel, Jean-Claude Grumberg, Renaud Cohen, Charlotte Silvera, Steve Suissa, Yolande Zauberman, or Jean-Jacques Zilbermann, all following their older colleagues Claude Berri, Michel Drach, Michel Mitrani, and Moshe Mizrahi), or as artists (most prominently like Christian "Liberté" Boltanksi), but primarily as writers.

Demographic Shifts

Seth L. Wolitz was not exaggerating when he stated that "not since the Martin Buber–Franz Rosenzweig debates in Germany of the 1920s has there been anywhere, in the diaspora or in the land of Israel, such intense intellectual debate as in France to define and imagine the Jew" (1994, 134). There is no doubt that this debate as well as the *teschuva,* the reaffirmation of ritual and religion, would hardly have gained such momentum without the impact of Jewish immigrants from the Maghreb, who during the era of colonialism had retained a much stronger relationship toward the Jewish religion than had the vast majority of French-born Jews.

According to the historian Doris Bensimon, more than 240,000 Jews from North Africa immigrated to France between 1945 and 1975, peaking in the decade between 1955 and 1965 as a result of the independence of Morocco and Tunisia in 1956 and of Algeria in 1962. Approximately 500,000 Jews emigrated from these countries, leaving behind their Jewish communities, which, in some cases, like in Algeria, were almost entirely drained of members (Bensimon 1989). Since then, Jews from the Maghreb have constituted the majority of the roughly 600,000 Jews living in France and have been largely responsible for the re-Judaization of French Jewry in the 1970s and 1980s. The number of Jewish communities in France more than doubled during this time and quadrupled since the 1950s. The urban centers of Jewish life, which decades earlier had housed Jewish immigrants from Eastern Europe, like the Parisian neighborhood of Belleville, are now strongholds of Sephardic life. The suburb Sarcelles in the northern part of Paris has been nicknamed "little Jerusalem." The construction of most of the synagogues in the last decades can be traced to the Maghrebi influx, and most rabbis who have received their training in France since the end of the war are of Maghrebi origin. In the last few decades, the positions of the Grand Rabbin de France [Chief Rabbi of France] and the president of the Consistoire de Paris [Jewish Council of Paris] as well as of most of the local Jewish communities have been occupied by Sephardic Jews of North African descent who represent fifty percent of France's Jewish population. With the exception of Brooklyn, New York, there is hardly a place in the diaspora outside of France where these Sephardic and Ashkenazi Jews live in such close contact.

The attitude of the Maghrebi immigrants toward Jewish life in France can be traced back to the fact that they had not grown up under the Jacobin notion of cultural hegemony but rather within countries in which different ethnic, cultural, religious, and linguistic communities had learned to coexist with each other, especially in Morocco. Openly acknowledging their Jewishness at home, they brought with them a dedication to religious practice, Jewish law, and spiritual values and only gradually began to accept the state of Israel and the Shoah as important reference points of their identity (Bensimon and DellaPergola 1984; Abitol 1994). Shmuel Trigano remembers the experience of his "déracinement algérien" [Algerian uprooting] in 1962 as a

> cassure personnelle et culturelle. J'ai été jeté dans un monde que je ne faisais qu'imaginer à l'école en Algérie. . . . Puis, tout de suite après, de la découverte dans l'horizon de cette énorme et sombre bâtisse enfumée qui a pour nom Auschwitz. (Trigano 1984, 81)

> [personal and cultural fracture. I had been thrown into a world that I had only imagined at school in Algeria. . . . Then, immediately thereafter, the discovery on the horizon of this dark, enormous, smoking edifice called Auschwitz.]

Maghrebi immigration differed in many respects from the arrival of Jews from Eastern Europe that took place at the end of the nineteenth and beginning of the twentieth century. Unlike their coreligionists from Eastern Europe, the Jews from North Africa had been in intimate contact with French culture, history, and language long before their arrival in France. The educational level of the Jews especially from Algeria was quite high, and they successfully pursued upward social mobility by sending their children to institutions of higher education. Their familiarity with France dated back to their training in French schools (in Algeria) or in the schools run by the Alliance Israélite Universelle [Universal Israelite Alliance] (in Tunisia and Morocco), instilling in them an affinity to France that, with few exceptions, was stronger than their bond to the countries in which they had grown up. In 1870, the Décret Crémieux [Crémieux Decree] had turned all Algerian Jews into French citizens, setting the legal stage for acculturation but also for anti-Jewish agitation against them in Algeria.

In the two decades before and after the turn of the century, the French-born Jewish community had had a hard time absorbing and accepting the immigrants from east and central Europe, who, fleeing from pogroms and economic hardship, fundamentally changed the demographics and forms of institutional representation of French Jewry. The immigrants' open display of their ethnic heritage, starting with the Yiddish language, disturbed the French-born Jews who, as Israelites, were proud of the high degree of acculturation that afforded them societal acceptance, which they saw threatened by the arrival of mostly uneducated Jews from the East. The Vichy decrees affected Jews of non-French background living in France more severely than French-born families. According to the records gathered by Serge Klarsfeld, immigrant Jews were more exposed to persecution than those who had been born in France: "In other words, 10 percent of French Jews and 40 percent of immigrant Jews were victims of the genocide" (1983, 180–81).

Another immigration wave from the East arrived on the eve of World War II, cementing the demographic minority status of French-born Jews and adding to the tensions between these two groups (Hyman 1998). The anti-establishment thrust of the newcomers from the East was conjured up again by the post-Shoah generation. For example, when Luc Rosenzweig invited Wladimir Rabi (Rabinovitch), an activist, scholar, and critic born in turn-of-the-century Vilna (and father of the writer Anne Rabinovitch), to contribute to his "Catalogue pour des Juifs de maintenant," Rabi energetically demanded nothing less than the abolishment of the institutional structures of the official Jewish communities. In his eyes, they had failed to integrate the impulses coming from the new demographics:

> D'abord détruire tout ce qui est *establishment*. Car c'est dans l'*establishment* que se situe le centre même de toute la paralysie, de toute la corruption, de toute la dégradation. D'abord détruire. Ensuite, et des signes permettent de

> conjecturer le renouvellement, ensuite seulement viendra, pourra revenir le moment de reconstruire et de parachever un monde créé inachevé. (1979, 25)
>
> [Firstly, to destroy everything that is *establishment*. Because it is in the *establishment* that the very center of all the paralysis, all the corruption, and all the degradation sits. Firstly, destroy. Then, by signs that allow the envisioning of renewal, only then will come—will be able to come—the moment for reconstruction and the completion of an unfinished creation.]

It is obvious that history in general and Jewish history in particular has had a different impact on each of these groups. The Jews of the Maghreb were not affected by the Shoah the way the European Jewish communities were, even though the Vichy government relinquished the Crémieux Decree and made sure that its Statute of the Jews would be enforced in North Africa as well (Abitol 1983; Lasker 1994). Only the Tunisian Jews had to suffer German occupation in their home country. Arguably, the most significant experience of the vast majority of Jews from the Maghreb was not Nazi persecution, but expulsion from their home countries during decolonization (preceded in Morocco and Tunisia by anti-Jewish campaigns) and integration into French society. The world of Islam was much more familiar to the Maghrebi Jews than Catholicism. Immigration to France shattered their image of France as the homeland of equality and as the harbor of tolerance and changed their experience of being encountered by the Other: while in their North African homelands they had been easily recognized as Jews—and, if applicable, as French citizens—in France, they would now face discrimination not as Jews but, mistakenly, as Muslim immigrants. Neither the loyalty of the Maghrebi Jews to France nor their fast and successful socioeconomic integration into French society enabled them to cast off the stigma of the immigrant with relative ease—an experience initially felt even in interaction with the established Jewish community in France.

It is intriguing to see that the Jewish writers of Ashkenazi background have received important impulses from the works by peers whose origins go back to Algeria, Tunisia, Morocco, and even Egypt. The literary production of the latter, as will be discussed in the next chapter, began to flourish as a means of taking stock of the human costs of decolonization and of the price paid for a manifold—linguistic, ethnic, national, and social—experience of acculturation. Certainly, the Sephardic writers of Maghrebi background brought to their writing their love of the French language and their intimate familiarity with French cultural and literary tradition. But they also brought to it the notion that the idioms of their lost homes are worth being introduced into a French literature that hitherto had prided itself on its adherence to the Cartesian ideal of purity and clarity. Their willingness to enter the republic of letters without ignoring their complex national identities, their cultural, religious, and linguistic heritage very soon became matched by the readiness of their Ashkenazi peers to shed the persona of the Marrano and to address the French public with stories that speak to all aspects of Jewish life in France.

In 1996, Jacques Halbronn, historian and president of the Centre d'études et de recherches sur l'identité Juive [Center for Study and Research on Jewish Identity], suggested that "anti-Maghrebism" was about to replace the anti-Judaism in present-day France (1996, 65). The Algerian-born writer Marlène Amar describes in a passage of her novel *Des gens infréquentables* (1996) [Bad Company] this syndrome in an impassive yet moving way:

> La scène a lieu un matin au marché de Passy. C'est une grande halle aux lourds piliers de béton, couverte de bâches en plastique et éclairée au néon. Il est neuf heures. Il n'y a presque personne. Ma mère a un foulard sur la tête, noué dans la nuque comme les femmes le portaient là-bas. Dans les allées rectilignes, elle flâne un moment avant s'arrêter devant un étal de fruits et légumes. Derrière son comptoir, la marchande a les bras croisés. C'est une petite dame grasse, avec un longue jupe froissée. Ma mère dit qu'elle voudrait un kilo de pommes. La commerçante feint de ne pas entendre, regarde ailleurs. Doucement, ma mère répète. La femme se tourne alors vers elle, la toise longuement et dans un rictus découvrant une dentition jaune, lui crache qu'elle ne sert pas les Arabes. (1996, 89)
>
> [The scene took place one morning at the Passy market. It is a large hall with heavy cement pillars covered by plastic tarpaulins and illuminated by neon light. It is nine o'clock. There is almost nobody there. My mother has a scarf around her head, tied at the nape like the women wear it there. In the rectilinear aisles, she dallies a moment before stopping in front of a stall of fruits and vegetables. Behind the counter, the vendor has her arms crossed. She's a fat little woman wearing a long, wrinkled skirt. My mother says she would like a kilo of apples. The woman pretends not to hear, looks away. Softly, my mother repeats. The woman turns to her then, looks her slowly up and down, and, with a yellow-toothed grin spits out at her that she doesn't serve Arabs.]

At the beginning of the new millennium, the situation of the Jews in France is more complex than ever. As many of them perceive a pro-Arab tendency in the French government's foreign policy, they consider their own safety and security interests both at home and in Israel to be in peril. After the events of September 11, 2001, many fear that the Islamic fundamentalism spreading in France cannot be curbed simply by imposing sanctions to ensure the separation of state and religion. The debate started in 1989 that eventually lead to the prohibition of head scarfs in public schools hardly prepared the country for the extremist actions and anti-Semitic attacks that have made international headlines in the past few years. Political observers of all political, ethnic, and religious backgrounds were surprised that the anti-Semitism of the far right would find a comparably vicious counterpart in segments of the Islamic population of France.

2 Departures

"Qu'est-ce que la littérature juive?"

"Juif, le suis-je lorsque j'écris? En quoi cela consiste-t-il de l'être alors? Que signifie-t-il d'écrire en tant que Juif? Comment s'exprime, se manifeste l'être juif?" (Koster 1991, 137) [A Jew—am I that when I write? What does being a Jew consist of then? What does it mean to write as a Jew? How does Jewishness express and manifest itself?].

Serge Koster's intricate questions have been preoccupying writers and readers for decades. The American literary critic Elaine Marks, author of a study entitled *Marrano as Metaphor*, responded to them by suggesting that there is no such "thing as 'Jewish writing.' " For her, writing and style "are marked by historical moments and individual temperaments, positioning, and variations, not by race, ethnicity, class, or gender" (1996, 69).

However, Marks's book is concerned primarily with works by authors belonging to the generation of Cohen, Lévinas, and Sarraute. Over the course of the last twenty-five years, a new corpus of literature has emerged, and with it terms such as "jeune littérature juive" [young Jewish literature], "littérature des générations d'après" [literature of the post-Shoah generations], or "nouvelle littérature juive" [new Jewish literature]. Given the explicitly Jewish themes and positions explored in this new discourse, a formulation such as "Jewish presence in French writing" (Marks 1996, xvii) appears to be too tentative and cautious. And while in theory it may be the case that their kind of writing can be "echoed, imitated and assimilated by non-Jews" (1996, 69), one must realize that such attempts at appropriation have hardly made it onto the lists of the publishing houses. The case of *Fragments* (1995) [Bruchstücke], the fabricated memoirs of an alleged Shoah victim authored by Binjamin

Wilkomirski, indicates that the stylistic features of survivor literature can be imitated. Many a literary critic initially took the hoax for what it pretended to be. Even if one ignores for a moment Wilkomirski's intentional deceit, the question still remains as to what extent the discourses of Jewish persecution and of suffering indeed can be "assimilated" by non-Jews without transgressing a border marked vaguely yet definitely by terms like "authenticity" and "experience" and without raising difficult ethical as well as aesthetic questions.

There is no doubt that a critical argument cannot be based on ethnicity alone. There are many authors of Jewish descent currently writing in France who do not speak to Jewish issues or concern themselves with literary traditions of Judaism. For example, the novels by Emmanuèle Bernheim (born in 1955), which in the last few years have gained enormous popularity in France, do not represent any meaningful notion of Jewish writing. This is true, too, for the recent literary debut of Justine Lévy, the daughter of the prominent philosopher Bernard-Henri Lévy, who himself has been participating both in his critical work and in his fiction (*Le diable en tête*, 1984 [Devil on the Mind]) in the recent "pluralization of ways to be Jewish" (David 1993, 22) described in this book.

There is also no doubt that the terms "Jewish writing" and "French literature" are by no means mutually exclusive. Ruth Wisse has documented convincingly that the Jewish experience of linguistic acculturation has generated an "eagerness to master coterritorial cultures" (2000, 7). Jewish writers in the diaspora would find it difficult not to participate in the literary discourse of their native country. On the contrary, Jewish authors of the post-Shoah generations initially have to struggle to find their own voice in the concert of styles conducted overwhelmingly by non-Jewish writers.

"Jewish writing" is a highly diverse project that is anything but a static entity or the manifestation of a homogeneous school or movement. It has been shaped, as sketched out in the previous chapter, by a variety of historical, cultural, political, generational, and, last but not least, aesthetic factors and concerns. The American critic Robert Alter is right in emphasizing that a "simple formulaic key for identifying the Jewish character of all Jewish writers" (1994, 66) cannot be provided. And yet, as Wisse points out in her book *The Modern Jewish Canon*, "while the definition of Jewish literature is open to interpretation, its existence is not" (2000, 18), and one should like to add that the dilemma of definition and identification must not be perceived as a predicament in any way.

It does not make the job of literary critics any easier when they have to admit that the object of their inquiry eschews exact definition and easy categorization. Anyone working on aesthetic phenomena is familiar with the resistance of art to conceptualization and classification. This may also be why the most recent study of Jewish authors in France was offered not by a literary scholar, but by a sociologist who—as a student of Dominique Schnapper—approaches the works of the primarily older authors in their complex relationship to the prevailing societal discourses. Centering her subtle study around the concept of "identity," Clara Lévy has succeeded in identifying the Shoah as one of the dominating events in the life and works of the authors in this older generation. However, outside the social sciences, the concept of "identity" has lost much of the currency it held before poststructuralism started to register fundamental doubts about the notion of a coherent self and of a homogeneous and static core constituting an entity that harmonizes the tensions of contradictions at work.

Defining the literary endeavors of post-Shoah authors is even more challenging, because the theme of the Shoah is no longer a common denominator. But that contemporary Jewish writing is not "littérature du génocide" (Ruszniewski-Dahan 1999, 9) [literature of the genocide] does not mean that it is "imaginary Jewish writing," that is, defined only by what it is lacking, to apply Alain Finkielkraut's skepticism about a substantive definition of contemporary Jewish identity to this writing. Certainly, one can easily list statements by authors who speak eloquently about the vacuum of Jewish traditions and contexts that characterized their formative years. Many of the authors discussed in this book do have a stressed relationship to Jewish religion: their attitudes toward Judaism range from ignorance and indifference or even critique to various forms of piety and orthodoxy. Similarly, Jewish culture for many of them is hardly a point of reference and in very many cases not at all the context in which they have spent their formative years. Primarily the historical experiences of the Jewish people both in Europe and in North Africa as well as in the Near East in the course of the last twenty-five years have caused the younger generations of writers to revisit their attitudes toward Jewish culture and religion and thus their own understanding as Jews.

The scholar Alan Astro was the first to introduce contemporary French Jewish writing to English-speaking audiences. He used the term "minimization of Jewishness" (1994, 7) to describe the void of a vital Jewish cultural context experienced by Georges Perec. This lack informs the lives of many of the authors born after the Shoah as documented in a passage from Gérard Wajcman's novel *L'interdit* (1986):

> Éloigné d'une religion dont il n'avait jamais eu la tentation ni éprouvé le besoin, insoucieux des traditions, dans ce décompte négatif où, jusqu'alors, il avait mesuré son écart d'avec la vie juive, il reconnaissait au contraire le trait le plus certain de sa judéité. Cela semble un paradoxe. (1986, 221–22)
>
> [Far removed from a religion toward which he had never had any inclination nor felt any need for, indifferent to tradition—in this negative tally by which, until then, he had measured his distance from Jewish life, he recognized on the contrary the most certain trait of his Jewishness. That seemed paradoxical.]

Yet it is precisely this very vacuum that often provides the crucial stimulus for their writing, for their attempts to trace what the notion of "Jewish authenticity," discarded in the 1950s and 1960s, could possibly entail. They had to "reconstitute the past from stories rather than direct knowledge," as Geoffrey H. Hartman has pointed out, starting out not from within but often from a point beyond a life defined by Jewish culture, religion, and ritual (1994, 18).

The term "autojudeography," borrowed from Robert Ouaknine, a Sephardic author writing in French, may succeed in fending off the charge of essentialism most vehemently brought by the literary critic Itamar Even-Zohar, who in regard to debates about contemporary Israeli literature warned that "only a nationalistic Jewish approach, or a racist anti-Semitic one, or ignorance . . . would adopt the term 'Jewish literature' on the basis of the origin of writers" (1978, 80). "Autojudeography" directs the attention to the dynamics of Jewish writing that are predicated on a writer's Jewish affiliation but that are characterized by a paradoxical nature: it is a process that creates the *judéité* [Jewishness] of a text rather than being the product of the Jewishness of the author. Given the "trou de mémoire" [gap in memory], to quote the paradigmatic title of Koster's autobiography, this writing cannot be the reflex of the writer's Jewish background precisely because this background so often is missing: "Pas de généalogie, pas de racines, pas de lopin, pas de maison, pas de fibres juives. Pas de spoliation, puisque pas de possession" (Koster 1991, 87) [No genealogy, no roots, no plot of land, no house, no fiber that is Jewish. No plunder, because no possessions].

The dynamics of autojudeography, which in the next chapter will be discussed as an important form of autobiographical writing, leave it to the writers to contemplate what being Jewish could entail for them as *imaginative* rather than as *imaginary* Jews. The very concept of autojudeography points to the fact that the writers' self *(auto)* is the point of departure for their writing *(graphie)*. A majority of texts indeed are bound to the *auto*biographic experience of the authors, and, via writing, they uncover relationships toward the past and present of the Jewish people and their own family *(judéo)* that otherwise would have gone unnoticed and that now become embraced in their works.

It is worthwhile to look at the highly diverse expressions contemporary Jewish writing has been generating, including Eliette Abécassis's theological thrillers, Henri Raczymow's fictional recreation of Jewish resistance in the ghettos, Myriam Anissimov's biographies of Primo Levi and Romain Gary, Marco Koskas's portrayal of Yassir Arafat in his *Arafat, ou le Palestinien imaginaire* [Arafat, or The Imaginary Palestinian], Sylvie Weill's historical novel about the medieval rabbi Rashi, Gilles Rozier's Moses novel, Claude Gutman's novel about Shabbetai Tsevi, Patrick Modiano's documentary narrative about a victim of the Vichy roundups, Clément Weill Raynal's police novel about alleged resistance fighters in the French provinces, and Eric-Emmanuel Schmitt's double life of Adolf Hitler. The worlds of Maghrebian and Egyptian Judaism are being explored, as are the politics of past and present-day Israel, the tensions between Ashkenazi and Sephardic Jews in France, and the ideologies of anti-Semitism. The shtetl of Poland and Belleville, the *mellah* and the *hara* of the Maghreb, the offices of Parisian psychoanalysts, the gas chambers of the concentration camps, the Queen Mary heading for Europe in 1949, the immigration camps of Israel, and the vacation homes at La Baule are all featured among the settings, and so are the political circles of the Latin Quarter, the brothels of Cairo, the yeshivas in Brooklyn, Strasbourg, Paris, and Meah Shearim, and the coffee houses of Nabeul. All the literary genres are represented: children's books (like Claude Gutman's *La maison vide* [The Empty House]), theater comedies (like Marco Koskas's *Le roi des schnorrers* [The King of the Cadgers]) autobiographies, novels, parables, poetry, documentary texts, and detective novels among them.

Contemporary Jewish writing is an ongoing undertaking (rather than, for example, a literary "school" or movement) that revolves around not one but several focal points. One of them is what Maurice Blanchot calls the "désastre" [disaster], the event beyond experience (1986, 1), which calls for a notation fundamentally different from common forms of writing. Edmond Jabès's notion of Jewish writing represents another one, suggesting that Jewish writing is not a thematic discourse, but rather one that incessantly strives for the unspeakable, unsettling everything that has been said, including itself (1985, 28). The oeuvre of Kafka represents yet another focal point omnipresent in texts by younger authors, more so than the work of any other author, Jewish or non-Jewish. The Jewish religion and its texts and the proliferation of commentary feature in this constellation of foci as well, even if the forces of attraction emitted by the religious text have not yet been so strong as to produce a religiously committed work. Gil Ben Aych's *Le chant des êtres* [The Chant of Beings] (discussed in chapter 5) is the only text that stylistically displays the formal features Martin Buber once defined as characteristic of religious speech (1936). Yet the ironical structure of this novel by the Algerian-born writer at the same time insists on its secular and, in the end, philosophical nature.

It is remarkable that most of the concepts used in discussions about Jewish literature emphasize a communal notion. In this regard, Cynthia Ozick's idea of "liturgical literature" and the idea of a "minor literature" presented in 1975 by the psychoanalysts and critics Gilles Deleuze and Félix Guattari (in *Kafka: Pour une littérature mineure* [Kafka: Toward a Minor Literature]) converge even though they share no other features at all. The American Jewish writer and critic Cynthia Ozick suggested in an essay titled "Toward a New Yiddish" that only those literary productions will enjoy a lasting impact that are created by Jews and that are "centrally Jewish" or "liturgical" in the sense that "liturgy has a choral voice, a communal voice: the echo of the voice of the Lord of History" (1983, 169). For Deleuze and Guattari, it is a characteristic of minor literature that

> in it everything takes on a collective value. Indeed, precisely because talent isn't abundant in a minor literature, there are no possibilities for an individuated enunciation that would belong to this or that "master" and that could be separated from a collective enunciation. . . . what each author says individually already constitutes a common action, and what he or she says or does is necessarily political, even if others aren't in agreement. (1986, 17)

Deleuze's and Guattari's notion of a "collective enunciation" and Ozick's suggestion that the liturgical mode will be a new, a "*public* rather than a coterie form" (1983, 175) both attribute an immense volume to the voice of Jewish writing. The amplification of the individual's voice—Ozick uses the image of blowing the shofar, which is "heard far" (1983, 177)—to a larger, societal one has important consequences. It puts the writers in a peculiar position, threatening them with being perceived less as individuals than as members of a community, school, or movement just at a point when they are trying to find their artistic voices. What Deleuze, Guattari, and Ozick envision primarily as a positive feature, the writers may experience as a hardship. The pressure exerted by the political and the public may also stifle creativity and channel it onto the beaten path of the formulaic, which some authors have difficulties avoiding. Within the concert of the new appreciation of minority cultures and their productions, one easily ignores a feature that Richard Marienstras has called "monstrous": "La minorité . . . c'est un monstre. On la somme de produire sans cesse ses raisons de survivre. Qu'apporte-t-elle aux autres? Qu'a-t-elle à invoquer contre l'histoire qui la détruit? Contre le progrès qui la nie?" (1975, 62) [The minority . . . is a monster. They demand that it continuously demonstrate its reasons for surviving. What does it bring to others? What does it have to hold against the history that destroys it? Against the progress that negates it?]. Responding to these and the many other questions Marienstras raises is difficult enough an undertaking, but to realize that every sentence of a literary text will be read, willy-nilly, as a response to such questions can be a frustrating experience for a writer. The act of writing, in other words, takes place under conditions that potentially deprive the author of conditions of literary receptions enjoyed by nonminority writers. This restriction was felt and articulated in one of the first debates among Jewish writers in France, which raised the question of whether the possibility of Jewish writing is or is not predicated on a Jewish readership.

Literary Debates on Jewish Writing in France: 1965, 1982, and 1995

Over the course of the last several decades, writers have repeatedly engaged in debates about these questions. The concerns as well as the arguments raised in them have changed according to shifts in the self-perception of the writers involved in these debates.

In 1965, the Union des étudiants juifs de France [Union of Jewish Students of France] organized a roundtable discussion with Jewish authors to examine the status of Jewish writing in France.[1] The list of invited panelists—all belonging to the generation born before the war and, interestingly, most of

1. The proceedings of this event were documented in the journal *Les nouveaux cahiers*, which had been founded in the same year.

them born outside of France—seemed to allow the discussion to focus directly on the scope and the possibilities of Jewish writing, rather than first having to question the very existence of such a literature. And yet this very assumption turned out to be questioned by the participants after all.

Anna Langfus (born 1920), who had grown up in Poland, quite naturally identified a writer's relationship to Judaism with his or her relationship toward the Jewish religion: "Selon moi, il y a la langue et il y a Dieu. Tant que ces deux éléments seront absents, je ne crois pas qu'on puisse vraiment dire: voilà une littérature juive" (1965, 32) [For me, there is language and there is God. As long as these two elements are absent, I don't believe one could really say: here is a Jewish literature]. For her, there is no such thing as a contemporary Jewish literature, because it lacks the very core of Jewish writing of the past: a spiritual dimension in the service of the Holy One.

In opposition to Langfus, Piotr Rawicz (born 1919 in Llviv, then part of the Ukraine) separated creed from literature by insisting on the latter's independence as a "littérature juive de périphérie" [peripheral Jewish literature] and pointing to the long history of "cette littérature juive 'problématique' " (1965, 30) [this "problematic" Jewish literature]. In this view, the core of Jewish literature lies in refusal and resistance rather than in an unproblematic relationship with the Jewish religion or any other system of belief. Rawicz's position resembles in many ways what before him Isaac Deutscher had called the "Jewish tradition" of the "non-Jewish Jew." However, Rawicz insisted that this centrifugal gesture of refusal and opposition must not be confused with a gesture of suffering, which for him is the source of any creative expression and a feature of the human condition in general.

Arnold Mandel's position in a certain way mediated between Langfus and Rawicz. Perceiving Judaism as first and foremost a culture, "une manière d'être très profondément rattachée à une culture" (1965, 34) [a way of being very deeply attached to a culture], Mandel reminded his colleagues that any attempt to merge the space of literature with the realm of religion risks losing sight of the achievements and nature of cultural productions as such. Mandel acknowledged that it is impossible for him to write about "Pierre et Marie," that is, to write as a French gentile. His "emotional experience" is Jewish and does not allow him to write as, for example, a non-Jewish Alsatian, even though he was born in 1913 in Strasbourg and intimately familiar with this part of the country. Since the Dreyfus Affair, the situation of the Jewish writer has been an "absurd" one, a term that was very much in fashion in the philosophical debates of the time, based in the notion that the Jewish author cannot but accept his "Kafkaesque anxiety" (1965, 35).

Albert Memmi, born in Tunisia in 1920, offered yet another perspective on the questions at hand. As early as in 1957, this author of the fundamental critique *Portrait du colonisé précédé du portrait du colonisateur* [The Colonizer and the Colonized] had drawn attention to the linguistic dilemma faced by Maghrebian writers whose mother tongue was being imperiled by the cultural politics of the colonizer. In the context of the debate about a Jewish literature, he complained primarily about the lack of a common language, with Hebrew hardly being read and understood outside of Israel. According to Memmi's definition, a literary work can be called Jewish literature if it takes into account the author's Jewish background, his or her *condition juive*. However, in Memmi's view, the Jewish existence is primarily a condition of oppression, and given a readership disinterested in such an experience, Jewish writers find themselves stripped of a real foundation for their work. For Memmi, there is only one way out of this situation: Israel provides the sole basis for Jewish literature, because only Israel provides a language common to the authors and their Jewish readers, and only Israel allows for a Jewish identity beyond oppression and marginalization. In other words, there is no Jewish literature of the diaspora—a position that reflects Memmi's critical concept of the diaspora that he articulated in his *Portrait d'un Juif* (1962).

Speaking not as a writer but as a cultural critic, Richard Marienstras addressed the authors with a set of questions that were less concerned with the traditions of Jewish writing as with the writers' contribution to contemporary Jewry—a Jewry living in the diaspora:

> Les écrivains présents ont-ils un sentiment de responsabilité vis-à-vis d'un groupe juif vivant? Le souci de créer des "œuvres juives" est-il chez eux permanent? Souhaitent-ils, soit par leur œuvre, soit par une action individuelle, contribuer à la survie de ce groupe en tant qu'élément original au sein de la société française? (1965, 24)
>
> [Do current writers have a sense of responsibility toward a living Jewish group? Is their concern for creating "Jewish works" a permanent one? Do they wish, either through their work or by individual acts, to contribute to the survival of this group as the original element at the heart of French society?]

Marienstras is concerned with the stylistic concessions a Jewish writer has to make when writing for a largely gentile audience that is typically only partially, if at all, aware of the history and the experience of the Jewish people. Thus what in a different context could be presented through subtle allusions must instead be made very explicit, thereby limiting stylistic options and strategies. Each text carries a burden: it has to convey information about a past from which this literature issued. Writers are left with the task of *explaining* what they would prefer to *tell*. From this point of view, it is in the end the readership that prevents Jewish writers from writing Jewish literature.

Marienstras identified some commonalities in the works of the panelists: their works portray scenes of Jewish life from before the war and depict the values of intact Jewish communities before they were destroyed, thus eliciting a kind of nostalgic look back. "Cette littérature, donc, s'adresse aux vivants, mais elle se nourrit du passé" (1965, 23) [This literature, then, addresses itself to the living, but it is nourished by the past]. The Jewishness of these texts is attributed to protagonists who define themselves as Jews in a positive, substantive way solely in reference to the past. By contrast, their Jewish identity in reference to the present evolves primarily from a process of painful differentiation from their surroundings rather than from one of identification with them. Thus the literature mirrors the problems of being Jewish in postwar France, where the force of acculturation presents itself as both a menace and a temptation. As Jews in the present are less inclined to define themselves in reference to religious and cultural traditions, they draw instead on historical and societal notions.

Borrowing from the vocabulary of existentialism, Marienstras offered an alternative to these dominant patterns of identification and suggests that "une œuvre juive est un choix, ou une forme d'engagement vis-à-vis de la minorité à laquelle on appartient" (1965, 39) [a Jewish work is a choice, or a form of engagement with the minority to which one belongs]. Being Jewish and being a Jewish writer, then, is in the end a matter of "invention," an individual's choice undetermined by history and tradition. Marienstras's position is clearly indebted to Sartre's notion of authentification, and like Sartre's concept, is rather vague. Unlike Sartre, however, Marienstras suggests that it should be the task of the writer to help imagine what Jewishness could mean in an era that has witnessed the loss and destruction of Jewish heritage. To find a model for such an inventive power of Jewish literature, Marienstras pointed not to Israel but to the United States and works by such contemporary writers as Bernard Malamud and Saul Bellow.

Given that most of the writers had their national, cultural, and linguistic roots outside of France, the question of their status as "French writers" quite naturally is pressing. The Jewish philosopher Edmond Jabès, born in 1912 in Cairo, has in many of his books reflected on the complex relationship of Jewish writers to the French nation and the French language. In his last work, *Un étranger avec, sous le bras, un livre de petit format* (1989) [*A Foreigner Carrying in the Crook of His Arm a Tiny Book*, 1993], he compared the situation of the Jew to that of a foreigner. Reviewing the ways in which the venerable representatives of the pre-Shoah generations situated themselves with respect to French literature, the critic Clara Lévy in her study *Écritures de l'identité* [Writings of Identity] notes that most of them emphasize the uniqueness of their oeuvre instead of associating it with any particular literary movement of the time:

> Whether by self-inscription into the space of the book to the detriment of the space of literature (for Jabès), by feigned professional self-denial (for Cohen), by self-exclusion from the literary milieu (for Memmi) or by the militant demand for the creation of a new literary genre (Claude Vigée), the four best known contemporary Jewish writers in the French language are united by a common will to proclaim their singularity and their marginality within the literary realm. (1998, 111)

1982: A "Massive Symptom"

Inspired by the surprising success of Patrick Modiano, the growing reputation of Elie Wiesel, and the impact of the American-Jewish writers, in 1974 the journal *Tribune juive* [Jewish Tribune] dedicated an issue to Jewish writing in contemporary France. The journal interviewed seven writers and intellectuals, among them the well-known writers Albert Memmi and Arnold Mandel, as well as some newcomers like Myriam Anissimov and Albert Bensoussan. Still, most of the authors hesitated to acknowledge that they were part of a larger phenomenon of Jewish writing in present-day France, and only Albert Bensoussan—the youngest of all participants and the only Maghrebi-born among them—affirmed without reservation that such a "new French Jewish literature" indeed existed. Most of his colleagues instead continued to endorse the differentiation between French writers of Jewish origin and Jewish authors in the French language or insist upon the criterion of a Jewish language. However, the outlook on the future development of Jewish writing in France was much more positive and was contextualized within the early stages of a rediscovery of Jewish roots in general. Irène Kanfer, author and translator from the

Yiddish, observed astutely that some larger societal and international trends had begun to provide a "strong antidote" to the leftist preoccupation of many of the young Jewish intellectuals and writers. The pending bankruptcy of the governing political and social ideals, she predicted, would contribute to the spiritual awakening of those who would no longer ignore the anti-Semitism of countries that purportedly adhered to the doctrines advocated by the Left (Kanfer 1974).

Not even ten years later, Kanfer's prediction turned out to be true. In 1982, the editorial staff of the newly founded journal *Traces* dedicated an entire issue to what now was confidently perceived as the "symptôme massif" [massive symptom] of an emerging Jewish literature in France authored by post-Shoah writers, many of them Sephardic Jews of Maghrebi background.

The debate had come a long way from the very first explorations of the scope and nature of French-Jewish writing. Whereas the very existence of a Jewish writing in French was still a point of heated debate in 1965, it now seemed to be a given. And whereas at the roundtable in 1965 the sole endorsement of postwar Jewish-American writers came from the critic Marienstras rather than from any of the writers themselves, the reference to the scene of contemporary Jewish-American pop culture was now a given. The "Catalogue pour des Juifs de maintenant" was dedicated first of all to Woody Allen and the Marx Brothers, and only secondly to the French-language author Albert Cohen. Toward the end of the 1970s, the output of the École juif américaine was elevated to a topic of French literary criticism and discussed by the literary critic Rachel Ertel as an example of a minority literature. Ertel identified several of the important features of works by Bellow (who had received the Nobel prize for literature in 1976), Malamud, and Roth, whose major novels all had been translated into French. These features included the common background of the authors (mostly of Eastern European descent), primarily Jewish protagonists, themes of social criticism, and, reflecting the ambivalence of the condition of the Jew, a preponderance of satire and humor as narrative strategies. Ertel noted that although contemporary Jewish literature is highly complex and its texture not captured by "une définition unidimensionnelle" (1982, 91) [a one-dimensional definition], its existence cannot be doubted.

Ertel was the first to apply the notion of a "minor literature" to the comparative study of contemporary Jewish writing. Looking at Kafka writing in German as a Jew living in Prague, Deleuze and Guattari had coined the term "déterritorialisation" [deterritorialization] to describe a situation in which a major language, in this case German, is used by a minority in a territory where the major language survives only "for strange and minor uses" (1986, 17).[2] According to Deleuze and Guattari, the revolutionary force of minor literature derives from the attempt by the deterritorialized writer to instill this "paper language" with a "new intensity," to "arrive at a perfect and uniform expression, a materially intense expression" (1986, 19). Ertel sees deterritorialization as characteristic of the works of the Jewish writers from the Maghreb. And it is primarily their work that was discussed in the "Dossier: Littérature juive" [Dossier: Jewish Literature] of the journal *Traces*.

This issue of *Traces* also featured Janine Gdalia, then the editor of the series *Judaïques* [Judaics] published by the press *Lattès* and an affiliate of the Fédération Sepharde [Sephardic Federation]. In her contribution, she insists on a broad and inclusive description of the emerging Jewish literature in France and on a description that would take into account the multiplicity of voices both within this literature and within individual authors:

> Écriture juive? écriture de la différence, de la souffrance; marque d'une expérience multiple assumée ou héritée, symptôme d'une vision aiguë, aiguisée sur le monde, traces d'un regard parfois traqué, douloureux. L'écriture juive saurait rendre dans ses méandres cette expérience humaine faite de foi spécifique d'aspiration universelle, rendre compte de cette démarche qui, si elle n'est pas exclusive de l'homme juif, lui est tout de même très familière. (1982, 91)
>
> [Jewish writing? writing of difference, of suffering; the mark of an assumed or inherited manifold experience, the symptom of an acute eye, sharpened on the world, traces of an occasionally haunted, melancholy perspective. Jewish writing would know how to render in its meandering this human experience made of specific faith in a universal aspiration, to take account of this reasoning that, though it does not belong exclusively to the Jew, is all the same very familiar to him.]

For Gdalia, the most intriguing feature of this literature is a new interest in memory and the past. This fascination with the past is manifested in the phenomena of both the "nouveaux Ashkenazim" [new Ashkenazim] rediscover-

2. For a critique of the work of Deleuze and Guattari, see JanMohammed and Lloyd 1990 as well as Kronfeld 1997.

ing the *Yiddishkeit* their parents had left behind, and of young Sephardic writers looking back to the times when different cultures and ethnicities mingled in the cities of the Maghreb. She explains this historical curiosity as a response to the exhaustion of the great ideas and ideological projects that had governed the late 1960s and 1970s.

According to the critic Lazare Bitoun (born in 1944 in Casablanca), the works of the newly self-assertive French Jew removed the self-imposed invisibility of the literature by the Frenchman of the Israelite faith. There is no more *se faire oublier* [self-imposed forgetting], no more hiding behind *noms de plume,* no more writing solely for Jewish audiences. The new motto instead is "se faire entendre" [make oneself heard], to make oneself heard as participants of a highly heterogeneous literary project reflective of the diversity of attitudes prevalent among young Jews:

> La jeune littérature juive qui se manifeste aujourd'hui est sans conteste l'héritière de toutes ces tensions, elle est la croisée des courants culturels juifs et français, ashkénazes et sépharades, bourgeois, religieux ou militants. Elle les réunit ou s'y écartèle, mais elle crée en tout cas l'espace nouveau d'une expression originale; c'est de cette unité et de cette diversité qu'il faut rendre compte. (1982, 82)
>
> [Young Jewish literature that appears today is without contest the heir to all these tensions, it is the intersection of cultural currents: Jewish and French, Ashkenazi and Sephardic, bourgeois, religious, or militant. It unites them or is torn apart in the process, but in any case it creates a new space for original expression; it is this unity and this diversity that one must recognize.]

Bitoun, then a professor at the University of Paris VIII–Vincennes, observes that behind the many voices of contemporary Jewish literature there is, after all, one genre dominating the imagination of the young writers: most of their works are autobiographical in nature. He also perceives that they share a common point of departure, proceeding from the here and now of French society. According to Bitoun, differences within this "minority ensemble in a hegemonic language" (Raczymow 1982a, 77) arise with respect to the language. Whereas the French-born Jews have unhindered access to "correct French," the writers born outside of France display a bilingualism that comprises the French learned in French high schools abroad and Judeo-Arabic (and, one should add, Judeo-Spanish). This, Bitoun notes, has contributed enormously to the rejuvenation of the French literary idiom.

Serge Koster's contribution to the discussion is the exception that confirms what Bitoun perceived as the new rule. The writer and critic, born in 1940 in Paris, admits that he has difficulties accepting the designation "écrivain juif de langue française" [Jewish writer in the French language]. Instead, he sees himself primarily as an "écrivain français" [French writer], although he does not deny that his being Jewish may have an impact on his way of writing. Not living in a Jewish milieu, where he would perceive himself as an outsider, Koster calls himself a "Juif en négatif" [Jew in the negative] who is guided by the desire to "repérer la ligne de fissure" [situate the fault line] that separates his generation from the traditions of Judaism (1982, 97).

Shmuel Trigano may have had the profile of writers like Koster in mind when he expressed doubts about the validity of the "renouveau actuel de la culture juive" (1982, 97) [contemporary renewal of Jewish culture]. Trigano finds this to be a highly problematic phenomenon because the authors involved usually strive for a categorical fixation of Jewishness without being capable of imbuing it with a sense of authentic Jewish experience. The scope of the writing of his contemporaries, Trigano decreed, is limited on the one extreme by theoretical conceptualization and on the other by folkloristic trivialization:

> La tonalité de toute cette littérature, narrative ou essayiste, semble être cruellement dépourvue d'un souffle "juif," à moins que cela ne soit simulé dans un maniérisme gothique tout à fait abstrait et plutôt kitsch. Dans les récits romanesques, la dimension juive n'est présente qu'à titre de couleur locale. Les personnages n'ont que peu d'épaisseur juive existentielle. On ne lit pas la trace de leur judéité dans leurs gestes ou la texture de leur personnalité. La judéité n'est présente dans l'horizon qu'à l'état d'objet externe. Ce qui fait une situation littéraire "juive," ce devrait être quelque chose de plus que la manifestation objective du Juif: c'est son sens profond, sa structure, la nature de la langue. (1982, 94)
>
> [The tonality of this entire literature, narrative or essay, seems to be cruelly deprived of any breath of the "Jewish," except when it is simulated in a wholly abstract and rather kitsch gothic mannerism. In these romantic stories, the Jewish dimension is presented as no more than local color. The characters have only minimal existential density as Jews. One does not see a trace of their Jewishness in their gestures or the texture of their personalities. Jewishness is present in this perspective only as an external object. What makes a literary situation "Jewish" must be something more than the objective appearance of the Jew: it is its deep meaning, its structure, the nature of the language.]

The superficial approach to their subject matter that Trigano perceives in the fiction of his peers reflects the writers' estranged or at least distanced relationship to Judaism. According to Trigano, this tension manifests itself stylistically and formally in a predilection for the novel—a genre with roots not in the Jewish tradition, but rather in the French Enlightenment. In Trigano's view, contemporary Jewish writers are sacrificing their own cultural heritage as assiduously as their predecessors did.

Henri Raczymow looks at contemporary Jewish writing instead as "un phénomène constatable, répertoriable, statistique" [a perceivable, classifiable, statistical phenomenon] and does not hesitate to talk about a "naissance d'une 'École française du roman juif' " (1982a, 71) [birth of a "French School of the Jewish novel"]. While Raczymow, too, observes the lack of "une rhétorique, un maniement lexical, une rythmique qui puissent être tenus pour spécifiquement juifs, fût-ce en langue non juive" [a rhetoric, a lexical technique, a rhythm that could be held to be specifically Jewish, if in a non-Jewish language], he does not discount the authors' contribution to this "littérature juive d'expression française" (1982a, 72) [Jewish literature in French]. In addition to himself, Raczymow counts only Patrick Modiano—although he was born to a non-Jewish mother—among the French-born representatives of this enterprise and deems the Maghrebian writers to be the most promising proponents of this literature. Their common background of experience and the tension that they exhibit toward French ideology converge in a unique tonality: "toujours avec verve, humour, chaleur (ô Madame de la Fayette, ô Gide), de dire leur là-bas outre-Méditerranée" (1982a, 74) [always with verve, humor, warmth (oh Madame de la Fayette, oh Gide), to evoke their being from over there, across the Mediterranean].

With few exceptions, the native French authors born after the Shoah do not share their predecessors' feeling of not belonging to the tradition of French literature. Having grown up under the governing literary paradigms of postwar France, their struggle is one of finding their own voice apart from the stylistic trends of the time, of staking out a literary space suitable for their experience and background. There are, for example, authors whose work over time has shown a growing tendency toward Jewish themes and concerns, most prominently among them Henri Razcymow, or the lesser-known writer Catherine Axelrad (born in 1956). Axelrad's first novel, *L'homme au car VW blanc de ma jeunesse* (1988) [The Man with the White VW Bus of My Youth], reads like a typical contemporary narrative of female "sentimental education," whereas her following book, *La Varsovienne* (1990) [The Woman from Warsaw], presents the narrative of a young woman who must speak up when she hears her politically radicalized friends from the student rebellion downplay the Shoah: "Je n'avais pas été élevée dans le culte d'Auschwitz, loin de là, mais on ne fait pas l'Histoire en la niant" (1990, 87) [I had not been raised in the Auschwitz cult, far from it, but you don't make History by denying it]. Axelrad's next fictional piece, *Vies et morts d'Esther* (1993) [The Lives and Deaths of Esther], journeys into genealogical terrain by reconstructing the curriculum vitae of a Jewish ancestor. With this book, Axelrad takes a path taken by many of her peers that during the 1980s led them to conceptualize issues of Jewish history primarily by recounting the stories of parents and grandparents. The point of departure of this path toward re-Judaization had been the lack of, rather than the defining power of, a Jewish identity.

Only a few authors have addressed from the very beginning of their literary careers in their works the questions of what it meant and what it means to be Jewish in France. Certainly both Patrick Modiano and Myriam Anissimov found their voice immediately; their path toward Jewish writing is a comparatively direct one, and the concept of autojudeography does not apply to their literary projects. It is perhaps not by chance that both of these writers are among the older representatives of Jewish writing, born during the end or immediately after the end of the war. Their memory and formative years precede the political period that was supposed to erase ethnic and cultural differences in the name of a collective identity of a different, or Marxist, sort.

The critique of the Enlightenment, formulated in the 1970s and 1980s by the "new philosophers," also has left a mark on contemporary writing. The new appreciation of *différence* (and the advance of Derrida's notion of *différance*) went hand in hand with the devaluation of the very universalism that the Enlightenment had counted among its main achievements. With it fell the humanist pathos that still had permeated books like Albert Cohen's *O vous, frères humains* (1972) [Oh You, Human Brothers]. Cohen's tone of emphatic reconciliation even with the anti-Semites is foreign to the literary production of the younger authors. Rooted in Cohen's childhood experience, *O vous, frères humains* tells the story of a disillusionment with the French nation and of the psychological weight the pariah status exerts on the young protagonist, who had hardly any notion of his Jewish identity until he encounters anti-Semitism. The peculiar thing about this narrative of stigmatization is its elegiac tone—Cohen wrote the book in old age, "au seuil de ma mort" (1972, 22) [at the threshold of my death]. Moreover, Cohen conveys a salvational message to anti-Semites:

> Dites, vous, antisémites, haïsseurs que j'ose soudain appeler frères humains, fils des bonnes mères et frères en nos mères, frères aussi en la commune mort . . . êtes-vous vraiment heureux de haïr et fiers d'être méchants? Et est-ce là vraiment le but que vous avez assigné à votre pauvre courte vie? (1972, 208)
>
> [Say then, you, anti-Semites, haters whom I suddenly dare to call human brothers, sons of good mothers and brothers by our mothers, brothers also in death . . . are you really happy to hate and proud of being mean? Is that really the purpose that you have assigned to your poor, short life?]

Such a confident stance, perhaps the prerogative of the older Jewish author and the diplomat involved in international affairs, is uncomfortable for the younger writers in a climate of revisionism and political and terrorist anti-Semitism. Not only do they feel separated from Cohen's position historically but also stylistically: the rhetoric of emotional appeals employed in *O vous, frères humains* (which range from *megaloprepeia* to *epimone* and *epiplexis*) does not even recur as a quotation in the *ars poetica* of postmodernity. So deep is the hiatus between the generations that the younger writers, in no way spellbound by their predecessors, escape a Bloomian "anxiety of influence." Thus neither Kafka nor Proust nor Cohen and his peers exert a stifling influence on the young writers: not Kafka, because he was not a French author; not Proust, because he was not "really" a Jewish author; and not Cohen and his peers, because their position in history removed them from becoming objects of either literary patricide or beatification.

Perspectives from the Maghreb

As early as 1983, the critic Guy Dugas declared that the literary production of the Sephardic Jews never before had been so abundant and varied and that more than nineteen works pertaining to *littérature sépharade d'expression française* [Sephardic literature in French] had appeared within the last few years alone (1983, 11). In a volume on *Cultures juives méditerranéennes et orientales* [Mediterranean and Oriental Jewish Cultures], published in 1982 and focusing on contemporary Sephardic culture, some of these Maghrebian authors writing and living in France stepped forward for the first time to explore jointly and publicly the characteristics of their production. Under the auspices of the Tunisia-born Annie Goldmann, author of *Les filles de Mardochée: Histoire d'une émancipation* (1979) [The Girls of Mardochée: The Story of an Emancipation], Albert Bensoussan, Paula Jacques, Marco Koskas, Maurice Partouche, and Katia Rubinstein discuss how certain formative experiences were translated into the various idioms of their fiction.

Most of these authors left their home countries during their childhood and early youth: Paula Jacques left Egypt as a ten-year-old, Katia Rubinstein left Tunisia at fourteen, and Maurice Partouche left Algeria at the same age. Thus, they would become aware of the political developments that led to the independence of these countries and to the exodus of the Jews only from hindsight, when they were already living in France. In most cases, their memory relies heavily on the narratives of their parents and grandparents. Their works may be seen as a vehicle for collective memory, inherent in which is the danger of idealizing and stylizing the past. Indeed, this risk of mythologizing the *hara* of Tunisia and the *mellah* of Morocco, it turns out, is a matter of concern among these writers. At the same time, they also express their awareness that these spaces are vacant on the map of their non-Maghrebian readers' imaginations. The following passage from a story by Ami Bouganim, who was born in 1951 in Mogador, Morocco, and moved in 1967 to Paris, shows that these writers are not only looking back at the cultures to which they had to bid farewell, but they are also looking seriously at their audiences, who often seem better equipped to visualize the shtetls of nineteenth-century Poland than the life of Jews in twentieth-century North African societies:

> Les autres ne connaissaient du Maroc que l'allure blessée de leurs parents, leurs regards désamorcés, leurs souvenirs de vieux juifs. A certaines réunions, je leur racontais, à eux qui savaient mieux comment vivaient des Polonais dans un ghetto que des Marocains dans un mellah, Mogador. Je leur parlais de Rabbi Pinhas, de Rabbi Mard'haï, de Rahamim et de tous les autres. "Que sont-ils devenus? . . ." demandaient-ils. Je retraçais l'ambiance qui régnait dans la rue des Epices, dans les synagogues où les juifs s'éternisaient en cantiques parce que la prière se confondait avec le chant, dans le mellah, par journées de grandes rumeurs. (1981, 220)

> [The others knew nothing of Morocco but the wounded appearance of their parents, their drained looks, their old Jewish memories. At certain gatherings I recounted to them, to those who knew better how the Polish lived in a ghetto than the Moroccans in a mellah, Mogador. I spoke to them of Rabbi Pinhas, of Rabbi Mard'haï, of Rahamim and all the others. "What became of

> them? . . ." they asked. I explained the atmosphere that reigned on the rue des Epices, in the synagogues where the Jews carried on and on in hymns, because prayer blended into song, in the *mellah*, on the days of the great murmurs.]

The cultural background of their ancestors provides a more pronounced backdrop to their writing than does that of Jewish writers whose families had emigrated to France from European countries. The Tunisia-born Marco Koskas admits without hesitation that he is an "écrivain juif, d'expression francophone, avec un imaginaire totalement ancré dans la Méditerranée" (1982, 318) [Jewish writer who speaks French with an imagination completely anchored in the Mediterranean]. What surprised him upon his arrival in France was not so much the omnipresence of the Catholic roots of French culture, but rather the high degree of secularization that in France had its impact on Jewish communities: "La laïcité, c'est un climat qui peut être un climat littéraire sans racines, désaffecté et avec lequel je ne sens absolument aucune accointance" (1982, 318) [Secularism is a climate that can be a literary climate without roots, empty, and with which I feel absolutely no connection].

The writers gathered by Annie Goldmann see themselves as outsiders in more ways than one and as having—in the terminology of postcolonial theory—"hybrid" identities. That is, as immigrants they feel a friction that sets them apart from French society; as Maghrebian Jews, they feel estranged from the official institutions of the established Jewish community; as emigrants, they are separated from their countries of birth; and as members of the younger generation, they feel a distance from the Judaism practiced by their ancestors. The identification of the acts of reading and writing with praying, which was second nature to Marcel Bénabou (born 1939 in Meknès, Morocco), is unfamiliar to them, nor is their literary production driven by the hyperactive memory that Bénabou in his *Jacob, Ménahem et Mimoun: Une épopée familiale* (1995) [Jacob, Ménahem, et Mimoun: A Family Epic] acknowledges as the almost overpowering stimulus for his desire in his youth to write a book of the *mellah* in Meknès comparable to the grand masterpieces commemorating Jewish life in Central and Eastern Europe.

For the younger writers, it is their own condition of hybrid identities that makes up the core of their literary production. Katia Rubinstein uses the term "reassimilation" to conceptualize the trajectory of the work by her peers: "Le mouvement de création actuel s'ancre en même temps dans un mouvement de réassimilation de la culture juive puisque nous n'avons pas eu d'éducation juive" (1982, 328) [The movement of contemporary work is anchored at the same time in a movement of reassimilation of Jewish culture, because we have not had a Jewish education]. Their common background of having grown up in Mediterranean countries with Islamic cultures and of having experienced the rupture of emigration is the subject matter for their writing, thus enriching French literature with new subjects, figures, and stylistic forms. Indirectly contradicting Trigano's evaluation, they claim that their language is quite different from the conventions set by the long history of the French novel: "C'est une langue qui n'a pas la rigueur, la linéarité de la langue française. Il s'agit bien de la langue française, mais pas du style français" (Goldmann 1982, 316) [It is a language that doesn't have the rigor, the linearity of French. It is certainly the French language, but not the French style]. Although the majority of these authors grew up speaking French at home and studied French literature in North African *lycées*, they simply did not consider the language of Voltaire and Proust to be their mother tongue. Having encountered the French language outside of the national context in which it possesses the vitality and the validity of a lingua franca, they felt strongly attracted to this language. Rubinstein described this attraction as an erotic game in which the French language, as a temptress, promises more than it can keep. The first encounter is a kind of prelude or foreplay, followed by the anticipation of a blissful climax—that of philosophical abstraction:

> J'ai passé quatorze ans en Afrique du Nord, et nous étions tous les invités de la langue française de la même façon que Kafka disait qu'il était l'invité de la langue allemande. Ce qui définit la situation linguistique commune de tous les écrivains du Maghreb, c'est justement d'avoir été d'abord et avant tout les invités de la langue française. Quand on est enfant et qu'on est un invité, lorsque l'hôte est très beau, grand et blond, on l'aime et on l'aime passionnément. Ensuite cet amour de la langue française m'a conduite paradoxalement à vouloir la capter, là où elle se manifestait de la manière la plus éclatante. (1982, 322)

> [I spent fourteen years in North Africa, and we were all guests of the French language in the same way that Kafka said he was the guest of the German language. What defines the shared linguistic situation of all the writers from the Maghreb is precisely that: having been at first and foremost guests of the French language. When one is a child and one is a guest, when the host is very handsome, tall, and blonde, one loves him, and one loves him passion-

> ately. Then this love for the French language paradoxically drove me to a point where I wanted to capture it exactly where it displayed itself in the most dazzling way.]

Fascinated by the possibilities offered by the French language, Rubinstein eventually began to study philosophy, realizing after several years of teaching this subject that her attitude toward the language had changed profoundly:

> je me suis rendue compte, à l'usure, que ce langage philosophique qui représentait dans mon esprit l'essence même de ce que la langue française pouvait offrir de mieux ne remuait que du vent, et dans la conjoncture actuelle, ne sert jamais qu'à uniformiser toutes les créations qu'elles soient en transformant le travail littéraire en essais pseudo-philosophiques. (1982, 322)
>
> [I understood, after some time, that this philosophical language, which to me represented the very essence of the best of what the French language could offer, moved nothing but wind, and in the current situation served only to standardize all creation by transforming the piece of literature into pseudo-philosophical essays.]

An intriguing dynamic of linguistic acculturation thus becomes apparent: the desire to master a code that promises access to a cultural body eventually exercises a force that prohibits the use of any other means of expression. What initially felt like the power of seduction later becomes recognizable as an oppressive force to which the individual sacrificed her own linguistic heritage. As an act of resistance, these authors created a "mélange des langues, cette bâtardise des langues" (Partouche 1982, 329) [mix of languages, this bastardy of languages], which eschews the conventional insistence on stylistic purity. According to Françoise Lionnet's notion of *métissage*, this "macédoine de langues . . . une langue poétique complètement éclatée et très désordonnée" (Rubinstein 1982, 323) [mosaic of languages . . . a completely fragmented and disorderly poetic language] also renders justice to the Maghrebi writers' experience of a mutual contamination of different national, linguistic, ethnic, and cultural codes and practices.

The complexity of the situation becomes more evident when one considers that the lingua franca of their childhood homes, Judeo-Arabic or Judeo-Spanish, was hardly known to them as a written language. According to Guy Dugas, the ghetto has hardly ever been a literary space (1990, 136–40). Thus, these authors perceive French as the epitome of a literary language, cementing a difference between everyday and literary language that is more pronounced than what French-born writers may experience. In addition, their search for models of Judeo-Arabic or Judeo-Spanish writers whose international reputation would rival that of the older masters of Yiddish literature yields few results. Among the older Jewish authors from the Maghreb who had embraced French as the language for their writing, there was only Ryvel (pseudonym for Raphaël Lévy) and Albert Memmi. But with the exception of Marcel Bénabou (born 1939 in Morocco), there were hardly any younger or even post-Shoah writers and, aside from the 1928-born Algerian poet Myriam Ben, hardly any women authors at all to serve as role models for the many young female authors. For all of them, French literature would be at once a point of departure for their literary education as well as a critical point of reference for their literary creativity, which sometimes is difficult to contain within the "French French." A book written in Judéo-Espagnol, such as Marcel Cohen's *Letras a un pintor* [Letters to a Painter] from 1985, remains a rarity among the production of the Sephardic writers based in France.

When Henri Raczymow, the son of Polish immigrants, focused in his portrait of his peers from the Maghreb on the humorous and energetic diction of their writing, the limits of understanding that had restricted the reception of works by Maghrebian writers became all too evident. By contrast, Raczymow's older colleague Arnold Mandel was much more able to appreciate the peculiar situation of the immigrant writers, having himself been intimate with the situation of bilingualism in his youth: "En plus, tous ces jeunes écrivains sont intellectuellement des produits du lycée français avec son cartésianisme endémique. En tant que tels, ils sont aliénés par rapport à eux-mêmes" (Mandel 1980, 94) [Moreover, intellectually, all these young writers are the products of the French secondary school with its endemic Cartesianism. As such, they are alienated from themselves].

The feeling of alienation as well as what Raczymow had called the "schizophrenia" of having one foot grounded in universalism and the other in Judaism is one reason that the literary projects of the younger authors only rarely gain the dimensions characteristic of the grand historical narratives told by their predecessors. Instead, the literary explorations by the younger writers tend to be self-explorations, preoccupied with the problematic status of young protagonists who often are only slightly disguised alter egos of the authors. Their texts partake in the larger phenomenon of an identity discourse that opens up vistas on many dimensions of the self. Ethnicity and cultural heritage certainly figure prominently in this discourse, as do issues of gender, sexuality, nationality, and postcolonialism. One must also take into account the relatively young age of these authors in noting that they—with a few exceptions—have not created epics comparable in scope to *La mémoire d'Abraham* [The Memoir of Abraham] or *Le Messie* [The Messiah] by Marek Halter or *Le dernier des justes* [The Last of the Just] by André Schwarz-Bart that span Jewish history from its biblical beginnings to the catastrophe of the twentieth century. The narrower scope of the narrative projects by the authors of the more recent generations reflects their understanding of what it means to be a post-Shoah writer in France today. They do not offer the redemptive narratives that locate—as Saul Friedländer observed about Israeli literature until the 1960s—the history of the Jewish people within a larger mythical framework (1994). The recourse to biblical history does not provide them with the foil they need for their inquiries. Their interest concerns more recent layers of history: the points where the more immediate past of the family intersects with the one of the nation designates for them the coordinates where they begin to trace the formation of their own histories and identities. In this respect, the overarching category of the Jewish people recedes behind the category of the immediate family, which a generation trained by schools of Freudian and post-Freudian psychology dissect and scrutinize in search of their own genesis.

"A *New Jewish Affirmation*"

In 1995, Raczymow edited a special issue of the journal *Pardès* to scrutinize the current relationship between literature and Judaism from the wider perspective of European literature. The theoretical level of the individual contributions to this issue were even more sophisticated, including, for example, approaches informed by Lacanian psychoanalysis. The corpus of the authors discussed now comprised both members of a prominent league of contemporary French-Jewish writers and lesser known authors of the past, including André Spire, Armand Lunel, and Benjamin Fondane. The attention paid to Jewish writing of the past had increased; the search for predecessors whose works might shed light on the dilemma of the present turned out to be more successful than ever before. Also, the list of contributors had grown to include now-important post-Shoah writers such as, for example, Myriam Anissimov, Albert Bensoussan, Berthe Burko-Falcman, Norbert Czarny, Cyrille Fleischman, and Cécile Wajsbrot.

The older generations' concern about writing for a readership that is largely oblivious of Jewish traditions and the present shape of Judaism has been notably absent in the recent discussions. In the 1980s and 1990s, writers could count on a general awareness in the French population about Vichy's treatment of Jews as well as on a familiarity with the presence of Jewish life in France that in the 1960s was by no means a given. The question about audience has altogether disappeared from the debates, as if the fact that most of these writers have access to the major publishing houses and many are successful in winning literary awards has settled this issue for good. The large size of the cohort of Jewish writers may have been a factor as well—authors no longer feel that they are on their own or that they are the lone survivors of a group imperiled by extinction. The "massive symptom" diagnosed in 1982 had taken hold and resulted in an "affirmation juive nouvelle" (Raczymow 1995a, 10) [new Jewish affirmation].

However, a another notion to which the previous debates had alluded only in passing now is being articulated more fully. In a Europe recently troubled by refugees having to flee their countries due to fears of "ethnic cleansing," the notion of persecution is no longer unique to the Jewish experience. This awareness has consequences for the writer, as acknowledged by Clarisse Nicoïdski:

> On peut être clandestin, avoir été persécuté, parler plusieurs langues sans être juif! On peut être fils ou fille de tailleur, sans être juif! On peut considérer que l'écrit est le seul lieu d'existence possible, sans être juif! (1995, 281)
>
> [One can be living in the underground, have been persecuted, and speak many languages without being Jewish! One can be the son or the daughter of a tailor without being Jewish! One can consider writing the only place where existence is possible without being Jewish!]

This attitude is additionally a rebuttal to an earlier view sported in some intellectual circles in the mid-1990s that had risen to some prominence among literary critics—that of the identification of the Jew with the writer per se or that of the conflation "writing and Jew(daism) have become metonyms of one another" (Shapiro 1994, 183; Silverman 1999). Cécile Wajsbrot, born in 1954, renounced this mythologization by insisting "la littérature ne m'est jamais apparue comme un domaine spécifiquement juif, où une forme de judaïsme pourrait s'exprimer" (1995, 293) [literature has never appeared to me to be a specifically Jewish domain in which a form of Judaism could express itself]. In these years, the writers' self-perception shows a certain kind of demystification that aligns their tasks and positions with those of representatives of other minorities now persecuted. There is a desire to do away with patterns that, taken out of the context of the biographies of the older Jews, are in danger of becoming masks of stylization prone to hiding rather than to revealing the shape of contemporary Jewish writing. The aims and objectives seem to be set as "modeste et subjectif" [modest and subjective], to use a phrase by Cyrille Fleischman (1995, 259). Accordingly, larger issues such as the importance of religion as one of the foundations of Jewish identity and the role of Israel as the host country of Jewish literature, which were discussed amid controversy in the 1960s, barely surface at all thirty years later. Even the role of Yiddish as one of the *Ursprachen* of Jewish writing has become more or less a moot point, except for authors whose mother tongue is Yiddish, as in the case of Myriam Anissimov (who took the name Anissimov because the producer of a record she made considered her original name, Frydman, to be "too Jewish"). But Anissimov (the daughter of a Yiddish writer) realizes that melancholy surrounds Yiddish and that its days are numbered: "il sera comme un membre amputé dont on a conservé la mémoire sensorielle" (1995, 240) [it will be like an amputated limb in which one retains sensory memory]. Wajsbrot's experience reflects that of many authors for whom the Yiddish language does not have the intimacy it possesses for those who grew up speaking it. She acknowledges that she did not begin to understand Yiddish—the language of her parents and grandparents—until she began to study German in high school.

It comes as no surprise that none of the contributors to the discussions could offer a precise definition of contemporary Jewish literature. After all, given the wide differences in the voices involved as well as the rapid changes in the development of this young literature, such a definition remains beyond the realm of the possible. Much as Alain Finkielkraut and his peers came to realize that their quest for "authentic" forms of contemporary Jewishness will remain unfulfilled, the current debate has come to appreciate that the new vitality of Jewish writing will make it more difficult than ever to define its core. Rather than insisting on a sense of vague difference, Finkielkraut argued that Jewish identity after the catastrophe of the Shoah should articulate itself in the form of cultural production: "to make Jewishness something other than a title, an emblem, or a flamboyant form of ignominy; to transform a declaration of identity into a way of life; to substitute an active cultural experience for the coquettish presentation of the self" (1980b, 98).

Thus critics are well advised to consider the contours of post-Shoah Jewish writing rather than trying to pin down its necessarily elusive core. Indeed, by reading both the theoretical statements of the authors and their fictional works, themes, motifs, and stylistic forms, one discovers that there are many cores that are continuously shifting their form and their position. With regard to a literature that essentially is still in *statu nascendi*, one has to concentrate on the dynamics and movement that the works of fiction display and on the trajectory of the aesthetics that they encapsulate. Critical dissection and strict classification is a task best left to critics facing a corpus of a literature that has eclipsed its most lively and productive period. The increasing production by the younger generations merits thorough attention to individual forms of expression as well as to common concerns and strategies in the presentation of these concerns. A formulation by Albert Camus, which the organizers of the 1989 Colloquium of Jewish Intellectuals used to sum up the current state of Jewish life in France, may serve as a heuristic paradigm governing such an undertaking. The formula "solitaire et solidaire" [solitary and united] takes the individuality of any artistic expression into account without denying that the solitary work of writing always takes place in a realm that is larger than the piece of art itself and that it takes part in a discourse of which the author may or may not be aware.

After the Fires: Patrick Modiano

The appearance of Patrick Modiano's short novel *La place de l'étoile* in 1968 marks the first step in the coming of age of the literature by the post-Shoah generation. It is remarkable to see how Modiano entered the stage by shattering the conventions of emotional empathy, moral decorum, and political unambiguousness that had prevailed in the works of Modiano's predecessors. Modiano, born in 1945 in Boulogne-Billancourt, instead presented a highly ambiguous and sarcastic outlook on Jewish identity that blurs the borders between collaboration, fascism, and Jewishness; transgresses codes of literary decorum; and upends well-established notions of what Jewish life during and after Vichy had looked like. The critic Charlotte Wardi positioned the writers of Modiano's generation by comparing their tasks to those of the previous generation: "Pour leurs héros, il ne s'agit plus de s'intégrer à une civilisation fascinante, mais d'en faire le procès et de se situer par rapport à elle" (1981, 87) [For their protagonists, it is no longer a matter of integrating themselves into a fascinating civilization, but of putting it on trial and of situating themselves in relation to it]. The work of Modiano, however, shows that the younger writers have to settle their accounts not only with French society but also with their forebears and their relationship to the French nation.

In *La place de l'étoile,* the attribute "Jewish" awaits clarification in vain, and even the anti-Semites have difficulties identifying who is a Jew and who isn't. The boundaries between Jews and collaborators here become porous indeed, and the figure of the *Juif collabo* [collaborationist Jew] turns into the hero/anti-hero of a burlesque play of identities that is grounded in the unpredictable, the improbable, and, of course, the unpardonable. Modiano's protagonist Raphaël Schlemilovitch—a name that recalls Adalbert von Chamisso's problematic protagonist as well as a plethora of associations with the Yiddish term *shlemil*—wanders through the political landscape of a Europe beyond good and evil and through a literary landscape of styles, allusions, and quotations from Jewish as well as from anti-Semitic authors.[3] In *La place de l'étoile,* whose publication was delayed because of the Six-Day War, the vicissitudes of Europe before, between, and after the wars are captured in the form of a picaresque novel featuring a *schlemihl* who goes out of his way to offend friends and foes and with them expectations of personal, political, and philosophical decorum:

> Je me procurai deux tourne-disques. Pour composer mon *Requiem judéo-nazi* je fis jouer simultanément le *Horst-Wessel Lied* et l'*Einheitsfront* des brigades internationales. Ensuite, je mêlai à l'*Hitlerleute* l'hymne de la Thaelmann Kolonne qui fut le dernier cri des juifs et des communistes allemands. Et puis, tout à la fin du *Requiem,* le *Crépuscule des dieux* de Wagner évoquait Berlin en flammes, le destin tragique du peuple allemand, tandis que la litanie pour les morts d'Auschwitz rappelait les fourrières où l'on avait conduit six millions de chiens. (1968, 114)

> [I got myself two record-players. In order to compose my *Judeo-Nazi Requiem* I played the *Horst-Wessel Lied* and the *Einheitsfront* of the International Brigades simultaneously. Next, I mixed the *Hitlerleute* with the hymn of the Thaelmann Column, which was the last cry of the German Jews and Communists. Then, at the very end of the *Requiem,* Wagner's *Twilight of the Gods* evoked Berlin in flames, the tragic destiny of the German people, while the litany for the dead of Auschwitz recalled the pounds where they brought six million dogs.]

3. The literature on Modiano has traced these references minutely. See Avni 1994, Coenen-Mennemeier 1998, and Kauffmann 1984.

Modiano's novel eschews the logic of realist narratives. The units of time, place, and plot as well at the credibility of the individual characters have been tossed up in the air, creating a pandemonium over which Schlemilovitch presides, at various times, as a pimp, as a writer, as the Wandering Jew and the lover of Eva Braun, as a patient of Sigmund Freud, and as an adherent of Jean-Paul Sartre ("Jean-Paul Schweitzer de la Sarthe"). The Jew's alleged rootlessness, antipatriotism, and craftiness are exaggerated here to expose these elements of anti-Semitic propaganda in all their absurdity: Schlemilovitch is of Venezuelan and Greek descent, wants to enter the École normale as a "première phase d'assimilation" [first phase of assimilation] to eventually become "maréchal de France" (1968, 52) [marshal of France], and in the end is trying to settle in Israel where he will get mistreated by the Israelis. The nomadic restlessness of this Zelig-like figure extends to his literary position in history, where he situates himself simultaneously as a connoisseur of the Jewish tradition and as a lover of the anti-Semitic canon. Whereas he finds on the other side of the Rhine self-assertive literary ancestors and "plus fortes personnalités: Henri Heine, Marx-Ézéchiel, Franz Kafka" (1968, 29) [stronger personalities: Henri Heine, Marx-Ézéchiel, Franz Kafka], French cultural history offers a more problematic heritage that, however, Schlemilovitch scrutinizes in search of models:

> Après avoir été un juif collabo, façon Joanovici-Sachs, Raphaël Schlemilovitch joue la comédie du "retour à la terre" façon Barrès-Pétain. A quand l'immonde comédie du juif militariste, façon capitaine Dreyfus-Stroheim? Celle du juif honteux façon Simone Weil-Céliné? Celle du juif distingué façon Proust-Daniel Halévy-Maurois? Nous voudrions que Raphaël Schlemilovitch se contente d'être un juif tout court. (1968, 84)

> [After having been a Jewish collaborator, Joanovici-Sachs style, Raphaël Schlemilovitch plays in the comedy of "return to the earth," Barrès-Pétain style. And what of the dirty comedy of the militaristic Jew, Captain Dreyfus-Stroheim style? That of the shameful Jew, Simone Weil-Céline style? That of the distinguished Jew Proust-Daniel Halévy-Maurois style? We would like for Raphaël Schlemilovitch to content himself with being simply a Jew.]

Identification is a complex psychological process in which the images of the alter ego, of the Other, and of the foe become as influential as the positive models of loved ones. Neither Modiano nor his protagonist suffers from any "anxiety of influence." On the contrary, the novel welcomes both the Jew Marcel Proust and the anti-Semite Louis-Ferdinand Céline as "ghostwriters" for the story of Schlemilovitch's own life. They function as the godfathers for *La place de l'étoile*, a novel by an angry young man who makes his literary debut trying to outdo the grand names of a literary history that indeed has proven to be politically ambiguous over and over again. Shocking those who only reluctantly accepted the "retro style" he initiated, Modiano had his protagonist pose as a "juif antisémite" [Jewish anti-Semite], aiming to create "une Waffen S.S. juive et une Légion des volontaires juifs contre le bolchevisme" (1968, 26) [Waffen S.S. and a League of Jewish Volunteers against Bolchevism].

Certainly, there is—as Modiano stated almost thirty years after the appearance of the novel—an element of family history. And without a doubt, there are some biographical similarities between the author and his protagonist. Both were born in Boulogne-Billancourt, both have a father whose roots go back to Greece, and both have lived on the quai Conti in Paris. But it would be a mistake to conclude that the novel is an "imaginary autobiography" (Morris 1996, 22) even if Modiano once stated that the work on the book was based on the desire "d'élucider ma propre origine, une quête de mon identité" (Jamet 1975, 35) [to clarify my own origin, a quest for my identity]. Instead, Modiano merely uses bits and pieces of his own biography in his kaleidoscopic view of Jewish existence as an overdetermined construct consisting at once of contradictory theorems, falsities, myths, biographies of real people, and, sure enough, anti-Semitic projections. Literary materials—quotes, allusions, pastiches, and parodies—figure very prominently in this novel. Its author—a literary novice—recommends himself to his audience as a sovereign intellectual who is in absolute command of the cultural history of the "dark years" of Occupation and the complex developments that preceded them.

After all, Modiano's youthful tour de force was conceived during a period characterized by a lack of models and stylistic paradigms able to render justice to the attitudes of his generation's unique historical situation, since the history of French letters had left few traces of Jewish authors who strayed from the trampled path of acculturation. Entering the scene of Jewish writing in 1968, Modiano set foot into unknown territory to map the vicissitudes of a literary project that at that time seemed to have neither a past nor a present. In 1968, when even Georges Perec, undoubtedly the most experimental writer among the survivors, had not yet published his innovative works, the young Jewish writer departed from a vacuum.

Drawing the genre close to the territory of black comedy, Modiano—and later Pierre Goldman in his picaro novel *L'ordinaire mésaventure d'Archibald Rapoport* [The Ordinary Misadventure of Archibald Rapoport]—broke with the humorous and amusing quality of older writers like Jacques Lanzmann (born 1927), Joseph Joffo (born 1931), or Claude Berri (born 1934), and even went a step further than Romain Gary (born 1914) had done in his *La danse de Gengis Cohn* [The Dance of Genghis Cohn] of 1967. These authors permitted complicit laughter at their protagonists' pranks and elicited compassionate sympathy with the sorry fates they describe. Modiano and Goldman, however, shape their first novels to provoke irritation and impatience by writing about highly irreverent young Jews who resolutely take their fate in their hands. Modiano's Raphaël Schlemilovitch and Goldman's Archibald Rapoport, we will see, are extremists: one of them a notorious impostor and Nazi sympathizer, the other a hardened serial killer. If one wanted to look for Jewish authors who in the mid-sixties and early seventies published works of similar shock value, one would have to turn to the Budapest-born playwright George Tabori (born 1914) and the German Jewish novelist Edgar Hilsenrath (born 1926). Tabori's "Die Kannibalen" (1994) [Cannibals] and Hilsenrath's *Night* (1966) and *The Nazi and the Barber* (1971) both upset the aesthetic contracts of the postwar years, which had discouraged writers from addressing the Shoah by means of satire, parody, and black comedy.

Almost overnight, Modiano filled the vacuum of literary models with a multitude of literary references and stylistic innovations, for which he was rewarded with both the Prix Roger Nimier and the prestigious Prix Fénéon. But the courage and audacity that had led him in the grand opening of his career, regardless of responses from friends or foes, eventually were tamed. In retrospect, Modiano may have doubted whether his youthful iconoclasm would have a future—the later editions of the novel omit some of the original publication's most provocative passages!

Pierre Goldman's Not So Ordinary Literary Beginnings

The next steps in the formation of this literature show how tightly the literary projects of the young writers, at least initially, were interwoven with the politicization that drove the student movement of 1968. In 1975, the autobiography *Souvenirs obscurs d'un Juif polonais né en France* [Dim Memories of a Polish Jew Born in France] of the political activist and revolutionary Pierre Goldman appeared, followed two years later by his novel *L'ordinaire mésaven-*

ture d'Archibald Rapoport, which, like Modiano's *La place de l'étoile*, narrated the biography of contemporary Jewish identity in the form of a picaresque novel.

Goldman, born in 1944 to parents who had fought in the French resistance movement, had signed on as a student with Communist groups and in 1967 joined a Venezuelan guerrilla force. Sent back from Cuba to France to continue the revolutionary work at home, he lived in Paris the life of a political extremist and societal outcast (Friedlaender 1990). Goldman had a record of armed robberies and was sentenced to life imprisonment for a murder he did not commit. In prison, he completed his *licence* in philosophy and wrote his memoirs, in which he described his alienation from and by French society unequivocally:

> Je n'avais pas de preuve à donner—on me la demandait depuis toujours, en silence, depuis que j'étais né et bien que je fusse né, en France, en un temps où il m'était refusé de naître Français—je n'avais pas de preuve à donner parce que, profondément, je n'avais jamais été Français. J'étais seulement un Juif exilé sans terre promise. Exilé indéfiniment, infiniment, définitivement. Je n'étais pas prolétaire, mais je n'avais pas de patrie, pas d'autre patrie que cet exil absolu, cet exil juif diasporique. (1975, 56)

> [I did not have to prove that I was French—they had always been silently asking for proof, ever since the day I was born, despite the fact that I had been born in France at a time when I was not permitted to be born French—I did not have to prove that I was French because basically I had never been French. I was only an exiled Jew without a promised land. Exiled indefinitely, infinitely, definitively. I was not a working man, but I had no country, no country other than absolute exile, the Jewish exile of the Diaspora.] (1977a, 28)

The very beginning of Pierre Goldman's autobiography *Souvenirs obscurs* is exemplary in exploding the laws of autobiographical discourse: the vita told here from the outset is marked by the history of persecution. The narrator's first reflection shows him as a dead man, followed by the notion that his national and his ethnic affiliation are in conflict with each other: "Je suis né le 22 juin 1944 à Lyon, en France, en France occupée par les nazis (longtemps j'ai pensé que j'étais né et mort le 22 juin 1944). Je suis juif. Je suis d'origine juive et je suis juif" (1975, 27) ["I was born on June 22, 1944, in Lyons, France, in France occupied by the Nazis (for a long time I thought I was born and died on June 22,

1944). I am a Jew. I am of Jewish ancestry and I am a Jew" (1977a, 1)]. The account obeys the technical rules of legalistic writing, as it is a powerful document of self-defense in which the accused makes his plea to the French public. Goldman prefaces his autobiography with a long excerpt of the bill of indictment for his alleged murder of a pharmacist and his assistant on the rue Richard-Lenoir. The enumerative "Parcelles de mon enfance" [Pieces of My Childhood] that are encapsulated in his curriculum vitae prefigure the unique shape of Georges Perec's 1978 *Je me souviens* [I Remember], one of the most important documents of contemporary Jewish autobiographical writing (especially in its refusal to remember any events relating specifically to the writer's Jewish experience). Simply listing individual images of his childhood—all of which are introduced by the phrase "Je me souviens" [I remember]—Goldman provides in "Parcelles de mon enfance" a sparse and self-effacing record of memory, which in both form and substance suggest that a Proustian-style "search for a time lost" is no longer a narrative possibility for him and his generation of French Jews.

Goldman's "Curriculum" scrutinizes the police report of the alleged crime, and a chapter entitled "Le procès" reconstructs the trial during which Goldman was sentenced to life imprisonment (he was acquitted in a second trial). Undoubtedly, Goldman's allusions to Kafka—instantaneously noticed by his contemporaries and elaborated on by the Jewish critic, philosopher, and writer Hélène Cixous and the neo-Marxist critic Régis Debray[4]—were not merely literary but also existential in nature:

> On m'autorisera aussi à dire que j'eus l'impression de vivre une situation kafkaïenne: Juif et innocent, il m'arrivait de rêver que, libre, j'errais dans la ville, y rencontrais mes amis, sans pourtant cesser d'être, dans cette liberté rêvée, onirique, incarcéré. J'ajoute que j'entrepris la lecture du *Procès:* je ne pus la terminer, elle m'était trop douloureuse, j'en ressentais une intolérable angoisse. (Goldman 1975, 130–31)

4. See Cixous 1975a. Cixous reads Goldman's trial against the backdrop of her interpretation of Kafka's *Der Prozess* [The Trial], Régis Debray against the backdrop of his reading of revolutionary Marxism where Kafka, embodied by Goldman, appears "combattant de la Révolution mondiale en pleine paix bourgeoise" (Debray 1975, 13) [battling the worldwide Revolution in the midst of bourgeois peace]. Henri Raczymow in his recent book on the assassination of René Bousquet reintroduces the allusion to Kafka's *Der Prozess* when he talks about his own emotional involvement in the trial of Bousquet and, later, in that of Didier, who killed Bousquet before he was handed his verdict. See Raczymow 2001, 341–42.

> [I hope I may also be permitted to say that I had the impression of living in a Kafkaesque situation: a Jew and innocent, I sometimes dreamed that I was free, roaming the city, meeting my friends; although, in those dreams of freedom, I was still imprisoned. I will add that I started to read *The Trial:* I could not finish the book. It was too painful for me. It gave me an intolerable feeling of terror.] (1977a, 140)

His childhood, Goldman relates in the opening chapter, was "une longue rêverie inerte qu'anima, seul, le spectacle d'Auschwitz, d'Oswiecim, en Pologne" (1975, 32–33) ["a long inert reverie stirred only by the spectacle of Auschwitz, of Oswiecim, in Poland" (1977a, 6)]. Spending his boyhood summers in Poland, he learned about the brutal killing of his maternal grandparents—his grandfather was murdered by the Nazis while reciting the Psalms. In describing his emotional response as a child to these family stories told to the young Goldman by his mother, the author offers insight into the origins of the militant activism that characterized his political career, which began in the Sorbonne chapter of the Union des Étudiants Communistes [Union of Communist Students]:

> C'est en Pologne que je cessai de haïr la violence (mais je conservais toujours, en mon tréfonds, une répulsion rabbinique pour la force brutale). . . .
>
> En Pologne, je fus pris du goût de l'action, envahi du rêve et du désir de l'histoire, et je voulais que cette histoire soit de violence, m'y libérer de la meurtrissure d'être juif. (1975, 34)

> [It was in Poland that I ceased to hate violence (though in my innermost depths, I would preserve a rabbinical revulsion for brutal force). . . .
>
> In Poland I was seized with a taste for action, overcome by the dream of, the desire for, history, and I wanted it to be a history of violence, in which I could free myself from the pain of being Jewish.] (1977a, 8)

Souvenirs obscurs d'un Juif polonais né en France is the author's attempt to make sense of his own life by relating his actions as an adult to the beginnings of his life and to the fate of his family and people.

Yet, as a written document (Goldman's attitude toward the medium of writing is addressed in the next chapter), it first of all belongs to the genre of the confession and, as such, addresses a larger audience as well as a larger cause than just the story of the self. The book aims at revealing and condemning the legal system's anti-Semitism by alerting the public outside of the courtroom to the "fascist-minded enthusiasm" that prevailed during Goldman's trial. It attempts to create a public space that allows for the account of a Jew whose conscious desire to resist acculturation and integration into French bourgeois society led him to collide violently with the power centers of this society instead of settling passively on its margins. Thus, Goldman's autobiography, written in a spirit both defensive and offensive, stands as a modern *J'accuse* authored by the defendant himself as an outcry against his victimization. Indeed, his narrative is woven together by the causal psychology and milieu theory of naturalism, whose stylistic preferences it seems to share as well. Its reception, after all, showed that it was successful as a hybrid text, at once private confession and public pamphlet: the appearance of his *Souvenirs* prompted the authorities to grant Goldman a new trial, one in which he ultimately was acquitted from the murder charges. His assassination in 1979 by members of a right-wing commando group elicited an outcry by the public in general and a reevaluation of the dangers of anti-Semitism by French Jews in particular. For many of his peers, the murder brought to the forefront the issue of their own status and safety as outspoken Jews. Luc Rosenzweig responded by conducting a series of interviews with young Jews (later published as *La jeune France juive* [Young Jewish France], 1980). The autodidact Goldman was on the verge of being promoted to martyr for those who realized that they, facing the choice between their Judaism and the university, had chosen the latter (Rosenzweig 1994, 183–84). Rosenzweig's collection of interviews came to stand as a powerful homage to Goldman, not as a political extremist but as a persecuted Jew whose death told the story of France's inability to render justice to its Jewish citizens. In his preface, Rosenzweig, the son of German Communists, wrote:

> En tuant Pierre Goldman, ses assassins, quels qu'ils soient, ont tenté de mettre un terme définitif à une histoire que la France traîne comme un boulet: celle de la lâcheté collective d'un peuple qui accepte d'envoyer "ses" juifs à la mort. (1980, 9–10)
>
> [In killing Pierre Goldman, his assassins, whoever they were, attempted to put a definitive end to the history that France drags like a ball on a chain: that of the collective cowardice of a people who accept sending "their" Jews to death.]

Lazare Bitoun, in a first survey (1982) of this emerging Jewish literature, explains the impact of Goldman's life and memoirs by pointing to his rejection of the discourse of victimization and of the "mot israélite et sa connotation aigre-douce de la langue française" [word Israelite and its bittersweet connotation of the French language] as well as to Goldman's courage to replace it "par le mot Juif qui revendique et affirme une différence" (1982, 82) [with the word Jew that proclaims and affirms a difference]. And indeed, the traces of Goldman in the works of his peers are numerous, ranging from outrage about his assassins who remained at large[5] and Myriam Anissimov's dedication of one of her books to him to the book-length treatises by Hélène Cixous and Régis Debray. Jean-Luc Allouche has memorialized him in an autobiographical narrative as a Jew who—because he could never be assimilated—embodied the absolute stranger, the "lueur d'une dernière fraternité désespérée" (1983, 95) [light of a last, desperate fraternity].

Modiano's and Goldman's unique contributions to the emergence of this new literature can be explained in part by their relationship with the student movement. Neither of them was governed by the imperatives of the movement, which required its adherents to neglect, if not to forsake, those parts of their identity that were beyond the scope of proletarian politics. To be sure, Modiano's and Goldman's backgrounds, which provided such a buffer between them and the party lines of the student movement, could not have been more different. Goldman saw little value in the May 1968 events and instead sought to continue, as it were, the resistance of the Warsaw ghetto by the means of Latin American guerrilla warfare.[6] Modiano's background, on the other hand, featured a father who had led an obscure and politically dubious existence in the gray zone between conservatism and collaboration. In an early interview, Modiano reflected on the points of departure that separated his path from that of most of his peers: "Les jeunes se rebellaient contre le père parce qu'il symbolisait l'ordre. Mais quand le père ne représente pas l'ordre, tout se complique" (1969, 133) [Young people rebel against the father because he symbolizes order. But when the father does not represent order, things become complicated]. This statement also pertains to Goldman's relationship to his father's legacy, albeit in the opposite sense. Thus, in the late 1960s and early 1970s, neither Modiano nor Goldman had to fight off the self-imposed restrictions that prohibited so many of the members of the student movement from articulating themselves as Jewish intellectuals and writers.

5. Outrage at the failure to catch Goldman's murderers appears in Catherine Axelrad's novel *La Varsovienne* (1990).

6. See Auron 1998. Jean Paul Dollé in his biography *L'insoumis: Vies et légendes de Pierre Goldman* neglects this aspect of Goldman's Jewish background ("blessure de sa naissance" 1997, 161) in his interpretation of Goldman's turn toward violence.

At the end of the 1970s, several more powerful patterns were introduced to the texture of Jewish writing, complementing the picaresque-style novel and the autobiographical account. In 1979, Marco Koskas, who was born in Tunisia in 1951, published his novel *Palais Bounel* [Bounel Palace], which eschewed the stylistic paradigms set by the *nouveau roman* and instead picked up on the playful, nonlinear narrative and quasi-oral conventions of Arabic *khurafa* storytelling. Koskas's novel provided the overture for a number of novels by authors from France's former colonies and territories in which the authors would explore the former life in the Jewish quarters of their hometowns, the *hara* of Tunisia or the *mellah* of Morocco. These were also the settings of a series of more or less autobiographical accounts by women writers from the Maghreb, most prominently Annie Goldmann's *The Girls of Mardochée* and Katia Rubinstein's *Mémoire illettrée d'une fillette d'Afrique du Nord à l'époque coloniale* [The Illiterate Memoir of a North African Girl of the Colonial Era] both of which appeared in 1979 as well. The stylistic differences between the two books are striking: Goldmann links her account to the genre of testimony and organizes it as a progressive, multigenerational "Histoire familiale d'une émancipation" [family story of emancipation] that reads almost like a historical account. Rubinstein, on the other hand, loosely presents fragments and splinters from her childhood in Tunisia, intertwining allusions to the events leading to the country's independence and memories of the family's departure for Paris from the limited perspective of the child protagonist. Yet despite their different choices of narrative strategies, both authors partake in the aesthetic project of telling stories and writing history from a woman's point of view. They accomplish this by complementing their experience growing up as Jewish women outside of France with theoretical notions and insights of feminism, as the title of Rubinstein's book (an allusion to Simone de Beauvoir's memoirs) hints. Once French *écriture feminine* [women's literature] began to incorporate autobiographically informed discourses, it could turn toward these early texts by French women writers from the Maghreb for models.

After the Shtetl: Henri Raczymow's New Beginnings

The year 1979 is also the year in which Henri Raczymow's *Contes d'exil et d'oubli* [Stories of Exile and Forgetting] brought together the past of the shtetl and the present of the Belleville diaspora (the Parisian neighborhood populated by Eastern European Jewish immigrants) in a powerful literary tribute. Raczymow (born in 1948) began his literary career in 1973, but he published three novels before he wrote his first "Jewish" one. His first works did not speak to his cultural and ethnic background as an Ashkenazi Jew born in France after the war.[7] Also, these books were written in the governing stylistic paradigms of the time. Raczymow then came to realize that his—and his Jewish peers'—point of departure after all was a distinct one and that he would eventually have to address this in his writing. He also realized that the detached aesthetics of the new novelists hardly provided a fitting vehicle for what he had to say.

> Les théories des adeptes du *Nouveau Roman* me séduisaient. Ils se plaisaient à répéter que, dans leur travail, ils n'avaient rien à dire, qu'ils avaient à faire, à fabriquer des formes fictionnelles. . . . Ce que je devais comprendre par la suite, c'est que, précisément, je n'avais, sinon rien à dire (j'aurais pu dire, écrire, comme beaucoup, n'importe quoi), mais j'avais *à dire le rien*. Ce qui n'est pas la même chose. (1986, 177)
>
> [The theories of the disciples of the New Novel seduced me. They liked to repeat that in their work they had nothing to say, but things to do, that they had to create fictional forms. . . . What I subsequently came to understand, was that in fact, I did not have nothing to say (I could have said to write, as many do, no matter); but I had to *say nothing*. Which is not the same thing.]

Raczymow's formulation echoes a passage from Georges Perec's novel *W, ou le souvenir d'enfance* (1975) [W, or The Memory of Childhood] in which Perec (who was born during the war) had linked the purpose of his writing to the act of commemorating his parents who were killed by the Germans when Perec was still a young child:

> je sais que ce que je dis est blanc, est neutre, est signe une fois pour toutes d'un anéantissement une fois pour toutes. . . . je n'écris pas pour dire que je ne dirai rien, je n'écris pas pour dire que je n'ai rien à dire. J'écris: j'écris parce que nous avons vécu ensemble, parce que j'ai été un parmi eux. (1975, 59)
>
> [I know that what I say is blank, is neutral, is a sign, once and for all, of a once-and-for-all annihilation. . . . I am not writing in order to say that I shall say nothing. I am not writing to say that I have nothing to say. I write: I write because we lived together, because I was one among them.] (1988, 42)

7. See Astro 1994, Fine 1985 and 1988, and the dissertation by Dickstein 1997.

The "nothing" Raczymow has in mind is the lost world of Ashkenazi Judaism, which constituted the background of his family but from which he, the son of immigrant parents from Poland, had been shut off by history in general and family history in particular: "Mon père *déplaça* sa différence radicale (juive) en une différence moindre (communiste)" (1980, 91) [My father *displaced* his radical (Jewish) difference onto a lesser (communist) difference] casting a silence over the family's past as well as over the Shoah. Without any handed-down traditions and without any shared heritage or stories about the past, Raczymow had a "nothing" to deal with that only imagination and the writer's own research would be able to articulate. In the words of the critic Geoffrey H. Hartman: "The eyewitness generation expressed a return of memory despite trauma; this 'second' generation expresses the trauma of memory turning in the void, and is all the more sensitive, therefore, to whatever tries to fill the gap" (1994, 18).

Perec, although too old to be called a member of the "second generation," was facing this very point of departure in his "Ellis Island: Description d'un projet" when he in 1979 reflected upon the absent notion of his Jewish upbringing:

> Je ne sais pas très précisément ce que c'est
> qu'être juif
> ce que ça me fait que d'être juif
> c'est une évidence, si l'on veut, mais une évidence médiocre
> une marque, mais une marque qui ne me rattache à rien;
> ce n'est pas un signe d'appartenance,
> ce n'est pas lié à une croyance, à une religion, à une
> culture, à un folklore, à une langue;
> ce serait plutôt un silence, une absence, une question
> une mise en question, un flottement, une inquiétude:
> . . . .
> Je n'ai pas le sentiment d'avoir oublié,
> mais celui de n'avoir pu apprendre. (1995a, 58–60)[8]

8. Interestingly, this edition omits the words "à une histoire, à un destin," which were part of the original text printed as "Ellis Island: Description d'un projet" in Luc Rosenzweig's "Catalogue." The later edition continues by juxtaposing Robert Bober's (Perec's coauthor) Jewish upbringing with Perec's own experience.

> [I don't know exactly what it is
> to be a Jew,
> or what effect being a Jew has on me
> there's something obvious about it, I suppose,
> but it's a worthless obviousness
> that doesn't connect me with anything.
> it isn't a sign of belonging,
> it doesn't have to do with belief, or religion, or a code
> of behavior, a way of life, or a language;
> it seems more like a silence, a deficiency, a question,
> a questioning, a dubiousness, an uneasiness:
> . . . .
> I don't have the feeling that I have forgotten
> but that I was never allowed to learn.] (1995b, 60–62)

Hartman's colleague Marianne Hirsch suggested the neologism "postmemory" to identify the starting point of such authors as Perec and Raczymow. Postmemory is "distinguished from memory by generational distance and from history by deep personal connection," and its "connection to its object or source is mediated not through recollection but through an imaginative investment and creation" (Hirsch 1997, 22).[9] It is the lack of personal memory of the decisive events of twentieth-century Jewish history that prompted many Jewish writers to take up the pen in the late 1970s and early 1980s when the members of the older generations ceased being available as witnesses of the Shoah, of the Vichy era, and of decolonization. The work of the younger generation recreates history in lieu of memory rather than being based upon it. In this regard, Pierre Nora's notion that "generational memory is stocked with remembrances not so much of what its members have experienced as of what they have not experienced" (1996, 525) aptly describes the point of departure common to Raczymow and his peers.

In his *Contes d'exil et d'oubli*, Raczymow addressed this point of departure head-on. Matthieu Schriftlich, the narrator of the section titled "Préhistoire" [Prehistory], is disturbed by the "absence of memory," which drives him to urge his grandfather to tell him the tales of life in the Polish provinces before the war and to break the silence in which the past has been cast. The setting—

9. Hirsch, Hartman, and Fine all refer solely to Raczymow rather than acknowledging Perec's oeuvre, which predates Raczymow's essay and novels by several years.

Belleville in the 1950s—provides an apt location for Matthieu's reconstructing the collective saga of the shtetl, not least because this community, too, is about to be changed profoundly in the 1970s (with the arrival of the immigrants from the Maghreb), when the story is being told. The narrative construction of the *Contes* shields the text from the perils of folklorization and of nostalgic sentimentalism that the critic Régine Robin has identified as natural moments in any process of "re-establishing roots and lost identities" (1989, 129). Raczymow approaches the lost world of the shtetl via mediated citation and through the reappropriation of historical forms rather than directly. The tales told by the grandfather resemble patterns of Yiddish storytelling, which, according to David G. Roskies, one of the preeminent historians of this art, is characterized by the "illusion of live speech," created "by turning to the monologue," and by the way it decenters "the world of tradition by favoring outcasts, deviants, children, and women" (1995, 295). Moreover, the intricate narrative rhythm of the *Contes d'exil et d'oubli* echoes the cyclical character of Jewish time: the continuous repetition of certain reflections harking back from Belleville to prewar Poland creates a circular notion of time that eschews the idea of historical progression.

The narrative questions whether the tales told here are true, whether the towns can be found on any map at all, and whether the lake in which the Jews from the area allegedly had been thrown really existed. Raczymow, after all, is a postmodern author well aware of the epistemological limits of the historical account and the "mémoire trouée" [spotty memory] of the dying witnesses, and he points out that all the proper names he has noted down are, after all, just words, linguistic matter of principally dubious referentiality. It is a book written, to use the title of a book by the literary critic Robert Alter, "after the tradition," following tradition while being aware of its loss. The very name of the narrator, Matthieu Schriftlich, indicates the mediated character of the stories shared by him. "Schriftlich" in German means "written," and with this choice of name the author subtly alludes to the need to fix in writing what orally would get lost with the death of the people who have been informing Matthieu Schriftlich's accounts. The biblical stories that recur in the tales by the elders and the stories from the shtetl share the same fragile status: "Et comme la Prise de Jéricho me semble proche dans le temps à côté de nos histoires fantaisistes d'une Pologne non moins mythique" (1979, 99) [And how the Capture of Jericho seems to me near in time to our fantastic stories of a Poland no less mythical].

"Among Jews," David G. Roskies stated in regard to Yiddish storytelling, "the best that could be hoped for was a tale of averted disaster" (1995, 186). Commemorating in literary form this feature of the Yiddish narrative, Jewish writers of the younger generation cannot avoid addressing the disaster that is responsible for the end of the literary culture to which they feel indebted. Raczymow does so rather subtly; both the Shoah and the deportations from France are mentioned more or less in passing and in code. The reason for this taciturn manner of historical referencing may lie either within the conventions governing Yiddish storytelling or within a realism that takes into account the reluctance of many Jewish immigrants from Eastern Europe to give up even after the roundups and deportations their belief in the great French nation. In an essay from 1980, Raczymow juxtaposed his parents' fascination with French civilization with his own experience of growing up as a Jew in the Fourth and Fifth Republic—an experience he calls "schizophrenic" because he was no longer able to reconcile contradictions in the way the previous generations had managed their striving for acceptance and acculturation. The admission of this schizophrenia for him was not only the first step toward overcoming it but also the condition for writing:

> La culture, la langue, la littérature que je connais le moins mal ressortissent à la civilisation française. C'est un fait. Mais un autre fait reste incontournable: ce sont des gendarmes français qui vinrent chercher certains des miens, des nôtres, et les expédièrent on sait où. Entre ces deux faits également vrais et qui me déterminent entièrement, comment choisir? Je ne choisis pas. Je fais avec. Une chose est désormais claire en tout cas. Nous avons trop longtemps vécu sur le mode schizophrène, dans l'impossible ubiquité qui voulait qu'on eût un pied ici et un pied là, un pied dans ce qui nous restait de judéité, honteuse ou refoulée, un pied dans une universalité illusoire, qu'on la nomme francité ou internationalisme: ce ne sont qu'artefacts. La judéité ne peut plus être je ne sais quel "supplément d'âme"; elle sera, elle est ce par quoi l'Histoire, et mon histoire, prend soudain, enfin, un sens. (1980, 93)
>
> [The culture, the language, the literature that I know the least inadequately come out of the French civilization. This is a fact. But another fact remains unavoidable: it is the French gendarmes who came to find some of my people, of our people, and sent them you-know-where. How to choose between these two equally true facts which shape me entirely? I don't choose. I work with both. After that, one thing is clear in any case. We have lived too long in the schizophrenic mode, in the impossible ubiquity that would have us

with one foot here and the other there, one foot in what we have left of Jewishness, shameful or repressed, and one foot in an illusory universality, whether one calls it Frenchness or internationalism: those are nothing but artifacts. Jewishness can no longer be some sort of "supplement to the soul"; it will be, it is the thing by which History, and my history, takes on suddenly, finally, a meaning.]

The Predicament of "Naissance Tardive": The Daughters of Myriam Anissimov and Dominique Garnier

Like so many books by authors born during or immediately after World War II, both Myriam Anissimov's and Dominique Garnier's first novels (*Comment va Rachel?* 1973 [How Is Rachel?] and *Nice, pour mémoire,* 1980 [Nice, for Memory]) are dedicated to the parents of the authors. Anissimov's novel commences with the announcement of the death of the protagonist's father. Her book is very bleak, telling the story of a young woman who finds happiness neither in her lower-class family home, nor in marriage, nor with the lover for whom she will leave her husband. Taking place entirely in the realm of the private, *Comment va Rachel?* has no ambition to place the vita of the young Jewish heroine into a larger societal or cultural context in order to explore whether her tribulations have a dimension beyond the subjective and the accidental. Only very occasionally does the novel make allusions to the sufferings of the Jewish people in the twentieth century. During her childhood, Rachel would hear her father, a tailor struggling to make ends meet, decry anti-Semitism, while her peers in school blame her for killing Jesus. Yet such notions remain in the background of the vignettes that Anissimov presents from the life of a young woman who slides into a state of severe emotional disorder and utter despair that, so it seems, were brought upon her by a love life that is anything but fulfilling and by a general feeling of profound humiliation.

In this troublesome emotional context, a photograph remembered by the protagonist takes on a curious role. It shows a group of women smiling sadly in the Warsaw ghetto. Rachel has known this photo since her childhood, but in her current situation it gains new importance as she reads in the sad smile of the women an awareness of their fate: "Elles sourient, elles attendent. Elles savent qu'un jour ce sera fini" (1973, 143) [They smile, they wait. They know that one day this will be finished]. The first-person narrative does not allow for any explanation linking the situation of the women in the ghetto to the one of the protagonist. However, the arrangement of the flashback at a point in the narrative when Rachel herself becomes aware of the hopelessness of her own—comparatively trivial—circumstances and condition is telling in itself. It is a problematic point in a first novel that Alain Finkielkraut called the "roman de l'étoile jaune" [novel of the yellow star], perhaps because it dramatizes the life of the protagonist according to the sufferings inflicted on the previous generation.[10] The author, born in 1943 in a refugee camp in Switzerland, struggles in her first novel to find a language capable of relating the crisis of her protagonist's love life to her own or her parents' suffering as persecuted Jews settling after the war in France.

This irritation arises from the incongruity between the conditions suffered by the inhabitants of the ghetto, whose personal lives were extinguished by the means of mass persecution, and the state of the woman who, after a difficult childhood, encounters betrayal and humiliation in her private life. The suspicion that such a comparison risks trivializing the pain of the persecuted certainly is eased when the readers learn at the end of the book that the protagonist is considering suicide by turning on the gas. In any case, the strength of Anissimov's *Comment va Rachel?* rests in its very outspoken presentation of the sexual and emotional relationship between men and women from the point of view of the woman by stripping from this favorite theme of French literature the illusion of an equal distribution of roles and power between the sexes. In this regard, Anissimov's book also is an intriguing complement to the American Jewish novel of the 1960s and 1970s, putting on a map crowded with sexually obsessive middle-aged men the life of a young woman. Anissimov's protagonist is not at all troubled by the intellectual minds and the sardonic attitudes of her American peers. Hers is a life of passivity and depression to which the men she has encountered have contributed their share. Unlike Rachel, the heroines of Anissimov's later books will take control of their lives and actively face up to the challenges of their surroundings, examining the discourse of victimization equipped with a historical perspective and sharp intellectual acumen.

Dominique Garnier, born in 1954 in Nice, renders the portrait of Noémi, a young woman who comes to Nice in order to trace the paths her mother,

10. Marc Elikan stresses the agreement rather than the differences between Anissimov's and Finkielkraut's position (Elikan 1995).

Sarah, and her grandmother, Mamele, took trying to seek refuge during the Occupation in *Nice, pour mémoire* (1980) [Nice, for Memory]. Garnier works with the technique of narrative withholding to keep the readers in suspense about her heroine's quest, her feelings, and perceptions. Abrupt segues interlock Noémi's story with that of her mother, sometimes fusing them such that the readers can no longer distinguish whether the text is referring to Sarah in 1940 or to Noémi in 1980. The signs emitted by the city, too, are ambiguous, and the protagonist perceives some of them (advertisements displayed on the streets) as traces of the Occupation period (racist slurs) rather than belonging to the present. The entire setting is literally about to be shaken up by a catastrophe, although the tremors foretelling a major earthquake that could level Nice ultimately remain without consequences. With the notion of an earthquake that frightens all inhabitants, the novel alludes to parabolic narratives that—like Camus's *La peste* [The Plague]—speak about Fascism without naming it. *Nice, pour mémoire* shows a society in flight (reminiscent of the exodus in 1940) in which Noémi moves around like a dispassionate observer troubled not by the peril of a coming natural disaster but disturbed by the aftershocks of a catastrophe that the official seismographs never seem to register.

Whereas the fiction of Myriam Anissimov centers on the experience of being "torturé par sa propre mémoire" (1973, 35) [tortured by her own memory], the novel of Dominique Garnier is built on the memories of others: "Non pas des souvenirs. Je n'ai pas de souvenirs" (1980, 91) [No memories. I have no memories]. She tries to explain herself to a young German fellow whom she has met during her stay. Eventually, the conversation takes a turn that points directly to the situation of the generations born after the Shoah:

> —Depuis un mois je parcours la ville. Les rues me parlent. Les maisons, la mer, le soleil, les odeurs, et jusqu'à vous, tout me rappelle que quelque chose s'est passé. Mais quoi? Moi, Noémi Fogelman, sans souvenirs je crois, je ne suis pas. Ce sont . . .
>
> —Qui? murmura Hans tendu vers son secret.
>
> —Ce sont les souvenirs d'une autre. (1980, 91–92)

> [—I have been walking the city for a month. The streets speak to me. The houses, the sea, the sun, the smells, and, up until you, everything reminds me that something has happened. But what? Me, Noémi Fogelman, I think, without memories, I don't exist. These are . . .
>
> —Who? Hans murmured, drawn to her secret.
>
> —These are the memories of another person.]

This past of which the young woman knows so little (she had never known Mamele and her fate will remain unknown to her) nonetheless exerts its power on Noémi, who at once seems paralyzed and driven by it to uncover whatever is hidden beneath the layer of silence and ashes. Noémi is unable to distance herself from the fate of her maternal ancestors until the end of the novel, when she learns that the earthquake is not going to happen after all. The critic Claire Gorrara reads the last line of the novel—"Plus rien que le bruit de ses pas" (1980, 139) [No more than the noise of her footsteps]—as a subtle announcement of the beginning of a new phase in Noémi's life where she is "freed from her obsessive concern with Sarah's past" (Gorrara 1998, 116). Apocalypse averted, history does not seem to repeat itself after all, thus opening up a space beyond the past.

Annie Goldmann's Family Saga of Emancipation

Pierre Goldman's hyperbolic reading of family history led him to interpret Jewish identity in his books as a summons to militant action and resistance directly related to the political history of the Jewish people, whereas the notion of Jewishness in Anissimov's first novel consisted of the narrative of a tragedy, in the story of victimization of a female biography suggestively placed in the history of the victimization of the Jewish people. However, there is another pattern that allows for the creation of a sense of continuity between the self and the parent's past—a notion of continuity that in the eyes of Annie Goldmann is one of progression and liberation.

Goldmann's *Les filles de Mardochée: Histoire d'une émancipation* [The Girls of Mardochée], published in 1979, signals already in the subtitle its narrative thrust: "Family story of an emancipation." The term *émancipation* evokes both the history of Jewish emancipation and the struggle of the women's movement for recognition—as a book on the female ancestors of Annie Goldmann, it shows where and when these two notions of gaining independence and acceptance did or did not correlate with each other.

The author, born Annie Taieb in 1931, began working on her saga of three generations of women from Tunisia as early as the 1960s by interviewing her grandmother Élise, who was born in Tunisia a few years prior to the French occupation. The book's design reflects Goldmann's wish to give voice to the accomplishments and independence of the various women in her family, beginning with Élise's reminiscences and followed by excerpts from an account by Élise's oldest daughter, who, born in 1890, trained to became a lawyer. Concluding the book is a chapter that shows how the author inscribes herself into this reconstructed legacy of political and female emancipation set up by her grandparents, who fostered the family's integration into modern society by leaving behind many of the ghetto's constraints. In the short preface to her book, Goldmann sketched out its intent and method:

> Ce livre est un simple témoignage. Ni retour au passé ni nostalgique attendrissement. Il m'est paru, simplement, qu'une trace devait être conservée, à travers quelque existences particulières, du cheminement d'une, puis de deux, puis de trois générations dans un certain contexte: la Tunisie de la fin du XIXe siècle et de la première moitié du XXe. Il est fait à partir de documents de première main qui ont le mérite, la saveur et l'incomplétude de la spontanéité. (1979, 9)
>
> [This book is a simple testimony. Neither a return to the past nor a nostalgic softening. It seemed to me, simply, that a trace should be preserved, through some particular existences, from the progression of one, then of two, then of three generations in a certain context: Tunisia at the end of the nineteenth century and the first half of the twentieth. It is made from firsthand documents that have the merit, flavor, and incompleteness of spontaneity.]

Les filles de Mardochée is an early example of an oral history project undertaken to conserve a past about to vanish in front of a young generation that strives to ascertain a family background of emancipatory achievements ignored by the annals of official history. Aware of the perils of stylization and sentimentality inherent in such a project of family narratives, Goldmann is also careful to avoid any simple deterministic patterns in placing her own attitude toward Judaism within the multigenerational context. Escaping the chauvinistic rule of her father, she went to Paris to study and settled there for good in 1956 (where she later married the sociologist and critic Lucien Goldmann). Here, she realized that she had for many years neglected her roots in "culture juive orientale" (1979, 124) [oriental Judaism] entirely. And yet, the student of psychology and sociology even during the era of Jewish revival in the aftermath of Maghrebian immigration to France holds on to her belief that the *hara,* the world of the Jewish ghetto in which her grandmother had grown up, is a place uninhabitable by young people:

> Même en tant que Juive, je ne pense pas que le recours au passé, à la fidélité à des formes de pensées figées, soit une manière d'assumer sa judéité dans le présent. . . .
>
> Je n'ai reçu aucune éducation religieuse et j'ignore tout des rites et des

> dogmes juifs. J'ai longtemps ignoré l'histoire même du peuple juif; par mon éducation et ma curiosité intellectuelle j'ai très tôt été confrontée à d'autres systèmes de pensée. Or qu'est-ce qu'être Juive? Marx disait que voir passer un Noir dans la rue et dire que c'est un Noir ne signifie rien car ce pourrait être un chef de tribu ou un esclave. Pour moi, paradoxalement, ce qu'il y a de juif en moi est justement ce qu'il y a de plus universaliste dans la pensée juive. (1979, 124)
>
> [Even as a Jew, I don't think the return to the past, with loyalty to frozen forms of thought, is a way to come to terms with Jewishness in the present. . . .
>
> I have not received any religious education and I don't know anything about Jewish ritual or dogma. For a long time I didn't even know the history of the Jewish people; because of my education and my intellectual curiosity I was confronted very early on with other systems of thought. And yet what is it to be Jewish? Marx said that to see a black man pass in the street and say that he was black means nothing because he could be the chief of a tribe or a slave. For me, paradoxically, the parts of me that are Jewish are precisely the most universalist elements of Jewish thought.]

A return to the beginnings, Goldmann states unequivocally, is not possible and not even desirable: this is one of the insights of her account that goes back to the past of a female legacy of "essayer de faire sa vie" [trying to make her life] beyond the conventions of religion and society. Following the path of secularization that her ancestors had paved, Goldmann in the end embraces the universalism promoted by her French education while trying to marry her ethnic background with the challenges set forth by the liberation movements in the aftermath of 1968. Working in the trajectory of the *femmes de plume* [writing women] of her family, her next book, not surprisingly, was a study on feminism and Judaism.[11] Guy Dugas's observation that the succession of generations within a family is "a special means of accessing the roots of identity" (1990, 153) can be aptly applied to Goldmann's work as well, as long as one emphasizes that this process also entails acts of disassociation for which the previous generations at times provide the foil.

The beginnings of Jewish writing after 1968 are marked by the works of agnostics who only rarely had been exposed to the religious practices of Ju-

11. See Gdalia and Goldmann 1989.

daism. Their Jewishness or *judéité*, to use the terminological differentiation offered by Albert Memmi in his *Portrait d'un Juif* [Portrait of a Jew] in 1962, intersects historically, but hardly religiously or culturally, with the rich traditions of Judaism. For the Ashkenazi writers, the Shoah—or more precisely, their parents' experience of the Shoah—is one of the focal points of their fiction. Whereas the writing of the former generation of Ashkenazi Jews was primarily a literature of the genocide, the literary production of the succeeding generation finds its impetus in the past of its parents. Henri Raczymow's springboard is a time "d'outre-mémoire, . . . préhistorique" (1979, 103) [beyond memory, . . . prehistoric], but his subject matter as well as the genre he chooses—the *yizker bukh*, the book commemorating life in the Jewish ghettos of Poland—are borrowed from the world of an earlier generation. Pierre Goldman crafts accounts of contemporary Jewish resistance to fight the fallacies of the Israelites and most expressively shatters the notion of Jewish invisibility. Myriam Anissimov, on the other hand, portrays the children of the victims as incapable of action and caught between the guilt of the survivors and the lack of identificatory models for resistance. She describes in her first book the syndrome of "telescoping," that is, the emotional handing down of traumatic experiences from family members, preoccupying many authors for years to come. In her later work, Anissimov powerfully reverses the psychological effect described at the beginning of her career and instead follows the imperative of remembering the family lost to the Shoah. Standing outside of the context of both victimization and resistance, Patrick Modiano rejects all of the official models of Jewish identity and instead has his Jewish antihero infiltrate the cultural and literary monuments of French anti-Semitism. While their ideological agendas could not be more different, Modiano's protagonist shares with Goldman's ruffian a combative tone of self-assertion. Self-assertion—albeit of a very different kind—also is the driving force of Annie Goldmann's genealogical inquiries and of her search for a female legacy of emancipation from misogynist beliefs that will allow the author to articulate her own position within Judaism. Maghrebi-born women writers like Katia Rubinstein, Nelcya Delanoë, Chochana Boukhobza, Paule Darmon, and Marlène Amar later joined Goldmann in her attempt to stake out a literary space for a negotiation of their female identity as Sephardic Jews in postcolonial France without succumbing to the temptations of acculturation or of nostalgia for the lost world of Maghrebi Judaism.

3 Assertions

Autojudeographies

The opening sentences of the autobiographical account written in 1979 by Robert Ouaknine (born in 1950 to Moroccan immigrants) illustrate the circumstances under which many of the young Jewish authors set out to write:

> Une annonce dans "Libé" invitant à l'écriture; une occasion de fouiller, de retrouver une histoire, de régler un vieux compte, du genre "la différence que je revendique, d'où elle sort?" Pourquoi m'affirmer juif alors que je ne pratique plus depuis longtemps, que je n'ai aucun lien avec la communauté et qu'Israël reste quelque chose de lointain (même si mes contradictions passionnées ne me permettent pas une position claire sur la question. Et pourquoi après tout en aurai-je une?). Pourquoi ne pas écrire ces choses qui sont mon histoire? D'écrire, je suis passé à rechercher, puis à confronter. J'ai montré le premier texte que j'avais écrit à ma mère et à mes frères. On en a discuté, longuement. Il est vite devenu prétexte, à dialogues, reproches, explications. Avec le passé de silence qu'on se traînait, l'occasion était trop belle pour ne pas la louper. Moments intenses d'échanges, de remise en cause, ne réglant rien mais montrant des possibilités de rompre ce silence familial étouffant, négateur. (1979, 123)
>
> [A notice in "Libé" soliciting contributions; an opportunity to search, to recover a story, to settle an old account, of the genre: "from whence does it come, this difference that I declare?" Why affirm that I am Jewish when I haven't practiced for a long time, when I have no ties to the community, and when Israel remains something far away (even if my passionate contradictions don't allow me to have a clear position on the question. And why, after all, would I have one?). Why not write about these things that are my history? From writing, I moved on to searching, and then to confronting. I

> showed the first text that I had written to my mother and my brothers. We discussed it for a long time. It rapidly became a pretext for dialogues, reproaches, explications. Given the silence of the past that one drags along, the opportunity was too good not to miss. Intense moments of exchange and of calling things into question don't settle anything, but show the possibilities for breaking this stifling, negating family silence.]

This passage exemplifies how the turn toward Jewish writing after 1968 responded to the call to revisit a particularity hitherto kept hidden. In this case, the call had been issued by Luc Rosenzweig, who was soliciting contributions to his "Catalogue pour des Juifs de maintenant" with an ad placed in *Libération*. Just a few years earlier, at the peak of the student movement, such an acknowledgment of Jewish difference, or of contradictions governing personal identity, would have been decried as sheer private indulgence. These statements now stand as a prelude to Ouaknine's reconstruction of an autobiography that admits how complex identities actually are and rejects the imperative to subsume everything under an overarching political agenda. The act of writing as a "search for a time lost" recognizes the author's Jewish heritage as the formative context of his biographical development, in which his ancestors naturally play a major role. The pun of Ouaknine's title, "Autojudéographie" [autojudeography], elicits different associations. It suggests that the author's autobiography is essentially a Jewish one, that his Jewishness may have been created by himself, and that his very act of recording his life as a Jew is what "makes" him a Jew in the first place. But the neologism may also allude to the contradiction of recording a biography that to a certain degree has already been written for him. "Autojudeography" indeed is an apt term to describe the dynamics of an important part of contemporary Jewish writing. It is the act of writing, more than the fact of ethnic belonging, that creates the unique attitude toward Judaism and the Jewish people displayed in the works of these young generations of authors. The proclivity toward the autobiographical *(auto)* and the self-reflexive preoccupation with the nature of writing *(graphie)* provide the narrative frame within which the notion of Jewishness *(judéo)* appears.

Writing his autojudeography, Ouaknine has to take into account that the power of his authorship regarding his biography ends where his family heritage begins: his own autograph, so to speak, bears the mark of his Jewish heritage. And yet, without his act of writing it, the text would not exist as a record, and the author would not be able to face up to it. The American anthropologist

Jonathan Boyarin formulates the situation of this generation as follows: "Seeing ourselves as pre-placed and placing ourselves within the tradition, we are also cognizant of the demands expressed by Walter Benjamin's dictum that 'in every era the attempt must be made anew to wrest tradition away from a conformism that is about to overpower it' " (1996, 35–36). Georges Perec elaborated once in an interview on the relationship between his writing and his Jewishness in a manner that illuminates the concept of autojudeography:

> Je crois que j'ai commencé à me sentir juif lorsque j'ai entrepris de raconter l'histoire de mon enfance et lorsque s'est formé le projet, longtemps différé, mais de plus en plus inéluctable, de retracer l'histoire de ma famille à travers les souvenirs que ma tante m'a transmis. Cette recherche de mes racines, qui m'a depuis conduit vers de nombreux chemins que je n'ai pas fini de parcourir, m'a fait, je crois, prendre conscience de cette appartenance à une culture fondée sur l'exil et sur l'espoir, sur l'effacement et sur le recommencement. (1979, 9)
>
> [I think I began to feel Jewish when I took on the task to tell the story of my childhood and when the plan, long postponed, but increasingly inevitable, took shape, to trace the history of my family through the memories that my aunt had passed on to me. This search for my roots, which has since taken me down numerous paths that I haven't finished following, made me, I think, become aware of this belonging to a culture founded in exile and in hope, in obliteration and new beginning.]

The "tradition" with which Ouaknine's "Autojudeography," the autobiographical writing of Georges Perec, and the fiction of many of the authors born after the war struggle is the vacuum of a tradition that consisted of silence. In 1969, Perec in his lipogrammatic novel *La disparition* [The Disappearance] marked this silence with the omission of the letter "e" throughout the entire text. The rationale of this kind of "writing of the self," or what in French is called "écriture de soi," is neither "art for its own sake" nor "art in the service of therapy," as is so often found in the post-political era. Instead, it aims to strengthen the bonds with the past, with forms of Jewish life lived by the previous generations, and it succeeds in supplementing the nation's collective memory with fragments of the lost Jewish memory. To do so, it has to interrupt the silence that has imperiled efforts to hand over traditions and share stories about the past within this most basic form of the Jewish community. This literature attempts to reassess what it means to be Jewish after the fires by affirming its affiliation to its people. Writing turns out to be one of the essential means of this affirmation, and as such has to start puncturing the conforming silence of the established community, be it the community of the family or the community of French postwar Jewry. Concerning the "scandale de leur silence et de mon silence" [scandal of their silence and mine], Georges Perec emphatically declared in his *W, ou le souvenir d'enfance* (1975) [W, or The Memory of Childhood] that his writing and the memory of his parents (whom he had lost early in his childhood) merge to an inseparable unit: "j'écris parce qu'ils ont laissé en moi leur marque indélébile et que la trace en est l'écriture: leur souvenir est mort à l'écriture; l'écriture et le souvenir de leur mort et l'affirmation de ma vie" (1975, 59) ["I write because they left in me their indelible mark, whose trace is writing. Their memory is dead in writing; writing is the memory of their death and the assertion of my life" (1988, 42)].

In the preface of his study *Les Juifs, la mémoire et le présent* [The Jews, Memory, and the Present], historian Pierre Vidal-Naquet confirms that the phenomenon of "autojudeography" is not at all confined to the writing of fiction or autobiographical writing:

> Assez paradoxalement, je dirai volontiers que c'est moins parce que je suis Juif que j'ai écrit ces pages que l'inverse: c'est en écrivant ce livre, et quelques autres travaux, que je suis devenu Juif, Juif de volonté si l'on veut, ou Juif de réflexion. (1981, 11–12)
>
> [Paradoxically enough, I will readily say that it is less because I am Jewish that I have written these pages than the opposite: it is in writing this book, and a few other works, that I became, as one might say Jewish, Jewish by will, or Jewish by reflection.]

The act of writing ensures that the individual's desire for autonomy does not go unfulfilled: the writer's Jewishness is not a given—especially in regard to the "spotty memory"—but the result of a process of personal self-assurance and of historical reappropriation in which the writer voluntarily embraces the power of the principles of filiation and affiliation. It is a paradox that challenges the authors to reflect upon these dynamics in their narratives.

Writing with the Body: Pierre Goldman's Fiction of Autobiography

The inclination of the young Jewish writers to address the very act of writing as part of its own discourse is present perhaps for the first time in the work of

Pierre Goldman. From the outset, Goldman's *Souvenirs obscurs* serves the purpose of self-explication. The text is occasioned by the need to defend itself and the author, and it reflects on the nature of this need by articulating the special context from which this peculiar defensiveness emerges.

In Goldman's autobiographical account, the apologetic drive owes its force to the author's obligation to explain to the prosecutor and to the nation at large how he has arrived at his current situation: "Pour écrire ce texte, j'ai dû surmonter le dégoût d'écrire. J'ai dû surmonter le dégoût de cette affaire: le dégoût qu'il y soit encore publiquement question de moi" (1975, 19) ["To write these lines, I had to overcome my repugnance for writing. I had to overcome my repugnance for this affair, a repugnance for continuing as a subject of public discourse" (1977a, xxi)]. For Goldman, the political activist and guerrilla, writing brings with it assumptions that run counter to his life of clandestine warfare for the sake of the oppressed. Writing implies the notion—problematic for him—of the supremacy of reflection over acting, and of the public persona over the anonymous combatant.

> Ce qui me retenait d'écrire, c'était la sensation qu'il s'agissait d'un acte obscène où je risquais d'être aimé ou haï publiquement, possédé, la sensation, homme public, d'être le masculin, ainsi, d'une femme publique. (1975, 32)
>
> [What held me back from writing was the feeling that it would be an obscene act, that I would be loved or hated—possessed—in public, the feeling that, as a public man, I would be the masculine equivalent of a prostitute.] (1977a, 6)

This statement enlists Goldman in the long-standing tradition of anti-intellectualism, employing misogynist imagery (the writer as prostitute) to devalue the potency of the writer as an "homme public," now cast as a male prostitute. Thrown into jail and thus forced to renounce, at least temporarily, his active life, Goldman can no longer choose between the alternatives of the *vita activa* and the *vita contemplativa*. He uses the time in prison to study philosophy and to write his account, in which the statement quoted above appears in parentheses as a complete non sequitur. At the very end of the last chapter of the autobiography, titled—alluding to Kafka —"Le procès," Goldman returns to the nature of his undertaking and his concern about the act of writing:

> J'ai déjà dit l'aversion que m'inspirait l'acte d'écrire et d'être l'objet et le sujet de cette écriture. Une autre raison m'avait toujours interdit d'écrire: je

voulais écrire ma vie dans la vie, l'y inscrire, qu'elle soit un roman. Elle ne le fut pas et de l'avoir écrite sans la romancer ne la transforme pas en roman. Au terme de ce récit, je devrais me tuer, expier ainsi cette révélation où j'ai dû m'écrire afin de sauver ma vie d'une accusation fausse et infamante. (1975, 279)

[I have already spoken of the aversion I felt for the act of writing, for being the object and subject of that act. There was something else that had always prevented me from writing: I wanted to write the story of my life by living it, to inscribe it on life itself, to make my life a novel. It was not a novel, and to have written it without fictionalizing it does not transform it into a novel. At the end of this narrative, I ought to kill myself and by so doing, expiate this self-revelation that I have had to make in writing in order to save my life from false and shameful accusation.] (1977a, 134–35)

Goldman dismisses writing as a hyperbolic gesture of existential heroism that he must renounce when self-justification becomes necessary. His rejection is not confined to these grounds, however. Subscribing to a combative tradition of political resistance that goes back to his parent's fight against Fascism, Goldman favors stronger weapons than the pen and wants to fight for the sake of the oppressed rather than just for his own skin. In prison, however, he is left with the pen and preoccupied with the defense of his own life.

Whereas the autobiography is a written form of self-defense, a counter-dossier to the one provided by the government, Goldman's novel *L'ordinaire mésaventure d'Archibald Rapoport* [The Ordinary Misadventure of Archibald Rapoport] is a form of fictional resistance to the image of the acculturated Jew. The autobiography's juxtaposition between writing and acting is at play here, too. And yet, Goldman is writing the novel as a writer, no longer as an imprisoned guerrilla. His protagonist Rapoport, however, has pushed the *vita active* of the guerrilla-turned-author to the very extreme:

Il avait toujours connu le désir endeuillé d'écrire et, parmi les raisons qui avaient empêché qu'il le fît, il y avait surtout la sensation qu'écrire était une lâcheté, une façon d'assouvir désirs, fantasmes et rêves dans une fiction substitutive, au lieu de les accomplir. J'aime trop vivre, disait-il, pour pouvoir écrire (j'écrirai quand je ne banderai plus, disait-il aussi). Et la publicité de l'écriture, qui abolit l'anonymat, supposait, lui semblait-il, le désir terrifié d'échapper aux signes funèbres de la solitude. Mais il n'écrirait qu'au moment où il serait dans une confrontation inévitable et cristalline avec la mort—qui inclurait une contemplation constante—il écrirait quand sa vie

> consisterait exclusivement à mourir, il ferait seulement le récit de sa vie et son livre ne paraîtrait qu'après qu'il eût, lui, disparu: il avait décidé qu'en vertu des multiples articles du Code pénal relatifs au châtiment du meurtre, il serait condamné à mort et exécuté. (1977b, 62–63)
>
> [He had always had the mournful desire to write, and, among the reasons that had prevented him from doing so, there was most of all the feeling that writing was an act of cowardice, a way of fulfilling desires, fantasies, and dreams in a substituting fiction instead of accomplishing them. I like living too much, he said, to be able to write (I'll write when I can't get it up any more, he also said). And the publicity of writing, which abolishes anonymity, presupposed, it seemed to him, the terrified desire to run from the gloomy signs of solitude. But he wouldn't write until the moment when he was in an inevitable and crystalline confrontation with death—which would include constant contemplation—he would write when his life consisted exclusively of dying, he would tell the story of his life and his book would appear only after he had himself disappeared: he had decided that, by virtue of the multiple articles of the penal code applying to the punishment of murder, he would be condemned to death and executed.]

This construction reveals the extremism in the design of this figure who also is the offspring of members of the resistance movement, whose commitment to putting their lives in the service of a cause grander than their own existence has left their child an orphan. Rapoport decides to become a murderer in order to become a writer, and to be executed in order to be read, thus turning upside down the therapeutic or ersatz function of writing, and reversing fundamentally the situation that had caused Goldman to write his autobiography. Initially, Goldman had set out to write to defend himself against murder charges; two years later, he creates in Rapoport a literary *alter ego* who sets out to kill in order to support his desire to ensure "qu'on sût ce qu'il avait été. Il désira qu'on le connût, enfin, après sa mort" (1977b, 62) [that it be known he had been. He wanted to be known, finally, after his death]. The chain of events that had led to the celebrated accomplishments of the resistance fighters is no longer intact for a member of the post-Shoah generations. Rapoport is trying in vain to commit acts of resistance upon which he can mount a claim for glory and for an afterlife in literature.

Rapoport's tattoo, discovered by an officer during the physical examination following his surrender, represents for him the only appropriate—that is to say existentially based and physically manifest—form of writing: "Je suis un écrivain qui n'a jamais écrit, dit Rapoport, mais j'ai écrit ces lignes sur ma chair car je suis mon propre livre" (1977b, 129) [I am a writer who has never written, said Rapoport, but I have written these lines on my flesh because I am my own book]. Unlike the numbers that the Nazis burned into the skin of their victims, Rapoport's tattoo is self-inflicted—he is the author of a text that marks his own body, his own life: writing and living have become identical as writing (the medium of the life of contemplation) and the body (the medium of the life of action) are no longer separated.

This notion of *autography* in Goldman's novel provides a radical counterpart to his *autobiography*. Ultimately, after having escaped imprisonment for his senseless killings, Rapoport sets out to write in the conventional way, separating his *vita* from his life. The excerpts that the readers get to see bring back images of the young outlaw Goldman's early days of combat in the Antilles. After all, as an author Rapoport accepts that writing, although always trotting behind life, can offer salvation and rescue, and it can save "des images perdues et elle sauve des expériences, les élève au-delà de l'absurdité, du désespoir où le mutisme les ensevelit" (1977b, 186) [lost images and it saves experiences, lifts them up out of the absurdity, the despair, or the silence that shrouds them]. Committing the memories of his youth to paper, the hero dies crying, thus freeing himself from the literal magical spell that had kept him from showing any signs of human emotion. Autojudeography here has a redemptive effect because it restores the outcast to the covenant of his people and allows him to state, as his last words, that he was a good Jew. Writing in the face of death not only saves the memory of Rapoport's troubled life under the spell of the Shoah from vanishing into silence but ultimately, it also saves him as a Jew and as a human being.

Writing the Silence: Gérard Wajcman and the Prohibition of Speaking

In the wake of the often misunderstood dictum by the German philosopher Theodor W. Adorno that to write poetry after Auschwitz is to commit an act of barbarism, it has been argued that language lacks the power to express the horrors of the persecution, and that imagination fails to render a just impression of the pain suffered in the camps. While Adorno's statement of the early 1950s "has been appropriated without reflection or context by the very culture industry he so vigorously attacked" (Ezrahi 2000, 142), it may even have had a muting impact on post-Shoah writers (at least of the German language) who had grown up as students of an *ars poetica* that questioned the mimetic powers of language to express the horrors of the past.

Adorno himself came to define his position later more precisely, influenced not least by the literary accomplishments of certain writers: "I have no wish to soften the saying that to write lyric poetry after Auschwitz is barbaric; it expresses in negative form the impulse which inspires committed literature. . . . it is now virtually in art alone that suffering can still find its own voice, consolation, without immediately being betrayed by it" (1977, 186). Adorno warned that "turning the suffering into images" cannot render justice to the experience of the victims, regardless of how stark and uncompromising these images are. Favoring instead the aesthetics of stylization, he surmised that for example the late, extremely sparse poetry of Paul Celan indeed was able to "articulate unspeakable horror by being silent" (Adorno 1984, 444). Silence itself may be the most appropriate response to the incommensurability of the Shoah. Celan, who after the war had settled in Paris and had become (not unlike Heinrich Heine a century earlier) a champion of French letters, committed suicide in 1970—an act that has been seen as the existential radicalization of his poetry's tendency toward *Schweigen*, silence.

For the younger writers, the question of how to represent the unspeakable in language poses itself as a set of several questions. How can one write poetry after Celan's monumental poem "Todesfuge" [Death Fugue], which stands out as a literary monument imbued with the authority and authenticity reserved for works by the artists who had experienced the suffering in the camps? How can one not try to represent, if not the unspeakable of the disaster, then at least the unspoken—that is, the parents' silence with respect to their past? How can one continue the project of Jewish literature without addressing the Shoah, and yet how can literature continue without the representation of the Shoah becoming the dominant mode? Is the Shoah really an event that effaces the imagination of the artist—and, finally, does it really lie at the core of the contemporary undertaking of Jewish writing? Such questions in mind, the young protagonist of Agnès Desarthe's *Les peurs de conception* (1992) [Fears of Conception] self-critically takes measure of her own and her generations' literary powers, suggesting that she is "certainement pas assez poète pour arriver à la cheville d'Anne Frank" (1992, 19) [certainly not enough of a poet to hold a candle to Anne Frank].

Gérard Wajcman's novel *L'interdit* (1986) is undoubtedly the most experimental novel written in the aftermath of works by older authors such as

Georges Perec and Serge Doubrovsky. (The title of the novel allows for a wide range of English translations, including "The incapacitated," "The interdiction" or even "The taboo.") Wajcman, born in 1949, presents a text that consists almost entirely of footnotes by an anonymous editor commenting on the main body of text, which is not printed on the pages. The first 247 pages are blank except for footnotes that over the course of the book give the reader an idea of what may be happening in the missing main narrative. Toward the end of the book, the notes reveal that the protagonist, who seems to have suffered from amnesia, had discovered his Jewish background while on a trip to Venice. The rediscovered identity presents itself to the protagonist—to whom, as the title suggests, access to his roots has been forbidden—first of all as a state of isolation and loneliness:

> Les juifs étaient nés de la disparition d'un peuple. . . . S'il n'y avait pas un peuple, s'il n'y avait pas une véritable unité, aucun ne pouvait être un juif parmi d'autres, avec les autres: il devenait Le juif, portant seul la charge de vivre pour tous, parce que simplement le hasard avait voulu que lui soit vivant, parce qu'il était seul. (1986, 222–23)
>
> [The Jews were born from the disappearance of a people. . . . If there wasn't a people, if there wasn't a real unity, there could be no Jew among other Jews, with the other Jews: he became The Jew, carrying alone the challenge of living for all, simply because it had chanced that he be living, because he was alone.]

Having visited the ghetto and the synagogue, he retreats more and more from the world, locking himself up in his hotel room. Self-effacement seems to follow the effacement of memory manifest in the blank pages of the book. An allusion to Serge Klarsfeld's *Le mémorial de la déportation des Juifs de France*, in which the bottom of the pages remain blank to denote silence as the proper reaction to the listing of the names of the deportees displayed on the individual pages, sets off a chain of reflection on the protagonist's relationship toward language and silence. Remembering that his parents used to speak Yiddish with each other, he slowly begins to gain more access to his past, thus allowing him to begin writing and to begin talking about himself. The editor notes: "Ce silence qui l'avait envahi était peut-être une condamnation pour n'avoir pas su faire bon usage de la parole, par lâcheté, impuissance, par peur" (1986, 233) [This silence that had invaded him was perhaps a condemnation for not having known how to use words well, out of cowardice, weakness, out of fear]. A few pages later in the book, the main body of text suddenly appears, rendering the comments superfluous; their narrative stance has switched from the third-person commentary to a first-person explanation—which, now that the narrator has begun to author his own text, is no longer necessary.

The narrator-protagonist reminisces on the genesis of his aphasia and finds in his inability to understand his parents' Yiddish conversation the origin of his failure to enter the realm of language. He conceives of this inaccessibility of the native tongue of his parents as an initial "interdiction." Moreover, perceiving Yiddish as a language that is about to become mute due to the lack of speakers, he goes on to speculate "ce qui s'est passé dans le Ghetto par exemple n'est sûrement pas sans rapport avec ma mutité. Être silencieux, ce serait ma façon d'être juif" (1986, 255) [what happened in the Ghetto, for example, is certainly not without bearing upon my muteness. To be silent would be my way of being Jewish].

Wajcman's *L'interdit* speaks not only about an interdiction perceived by the protagonist in his childhood but, more generally, about a prohibition imposed on the Yiddish language by the history of persecution. The identification of Judaism with Yiddish that the book suggests in central places shows to what extent this work is rooted in the Ashkenazi understanding of Judaism, ignoring the Sephardic tradition as well as the experience of North African Jews affected by the Shoah in a different manner. The book seems to advance the therapeutic optimism of a recovery from the loss of memory and language due to a confrontation with a linguistic *Urszene* that enables the narrator to reconstruct his identity, which until then had existed only in snippets of notes and comments. He recovers his lost self, which is manifest first of all in language as an essential feature of the lost community of Jews. According to the narrator, like language, silence, too, always refers to a community of speakers:

> Ce silence, c'est la langue des morts entrée en moi, un silence qu'elle creuse profond, dont elle m'entoure et qui dit "nous." Elle disait "nous" naguère, mais je ne l'entendais pas—le nous des disparus dont, tant que je croyais parler, je ne savais pas être. Mais moi aussi, déjà, j'étais un disparu. Le silence enfin vient le dire dans ma bouche. J'étais une photographie, muette, d'un absent. Toujours j'avais été. Le silence prononce mon absence, il me donne une place, dans le temps. Je n'y ferai plus obstacle. (1986, 267)
>
> [This silence is the language of the dead that has entered into me, a silence that this language pushes in deep, with which it surrounds me and which says

> "we." It used to say "we," but I didn't hear—the we of the disappeared whom, as much as I believed I spoke for, I did not know how to be. But I, too, I was already one of the disappeared. The silence finally came into my mouth to say that. I was a mute photograph of somebody who wasn't there. I had always been. The silence declares my absence, it gives me a place in time. I will not put up any obstacles.]

The end of the book imparts a sense of pathos that integrates the untold and forgotten story of the persecuted to this autojudeography par excellence. In the muted space of Gérard Wajcman's book, contemporary Jewish identity is predicated solely on the fate of the persecuted, on the lost language of a vanished world. This identification leaves no options for the offspring of the survivors but to model their own understanding of what it means to be Jewish on the fate of those who perished in the Shoah. The desire of the young to give their lost elders a voice is a paradoxical undertaking, as it requires an act of enunciation to make the silence audible: at the very moment the narrator has articulated this insight, he has to end his narrative.

Writing vis-à-vis the Silence: Amar's *Des gens infréquentables* and Boukhobza's *Les herbes amères*

In Marlène Amar's *Des gens infréquentables* [Bad Company], the narrator recreates the short life of her cousin Samuel, with whom she had lost contact upon her arrival in France. The story "commence par un silence" (1996, 21) [begins with silence], which is broken only when the narrator begins to inquire about Samuel's fate and with it the experience of her family at large. To break the silence and to understand, she becomes a journalist and poses questions until her family members begin to talk—to talk about persecution in the pogroms of the Arabs, the emigration from the North African desert, the humiliating experience of the immigrants, the abuses suffered by the Ashkenazim, the fallacies of remigration, the spaces, smells, views, people, and feelings left behind. It is the self-imposed task of the young woman to get people to speak who have not shared any of these stories before:

> Ma mère, elle, ne parlait pas. Lorsque je la questionnais, elle disait qu'elle ne savait pas ou qu'elle ne se rappelait plus. Longtemps, j'ai cru qu'elle avait vraiment tout oublié.
>
> Le silence a duré des années. (1996, 22)

> [My mother did not speak. When I questioned her, she said that she did not know or that she no longer remembered. For a long time, I believed that she really had forgotten everything.
>
> The silence lasted for years.]

Once she begins to talk to her daughter, cruel images of pogroms back in Algeria are conjured up that the narrator records almost impassively. Family history is recorded against the matrix of larger historical events, and the reader is introduced to "ce peuple perdu désormais dans une France trop grande" (1996, 20) [these people who now have gotten lost in a France too large] and whom nobody would approach, as they are considered "bad company."

Amar's task is a twofold one: she sets out to create a picture of a people and their history that the French audience needs to acknowledge and to appreciate. And she creates, as a record for and of the family, a picture album of a family dispersed by the events of decolonization. The act of enunciation has two different audiences, one public and anonymous, the other private and intimate. This doubling reflects the personal experience that these two domains cannot be kept separated.

Chochana Boukhobza, born in 1959 in Tunisia, does not at all revisit the sites of her ancestors and seems to draw much less than Amar from the experience of her own life. And yet in her work, as in Amar's, silence functions both as a motif and a motive.

In her novel *Les herbes amères* (1989) [The Bitter Grasses], the girlfriend of Marc, a young man who will eventually die in an accident, charges that "Marc est mort à cause de ce silence" (1989, 161) [Marc died because of this silence]. Marc has never had a chance to learn much about his family's past: he is the son of a woman who is living in a ghetto of her own sufferings, where she compares the stomach cancer that is about to kill her with the lethal force of the Nazis. The son becomes a painter who covers his canvas with black paint and who only rarely (and then incoherently) talks about the

> mémoire vide, du silence des parents, d'un nécessaire combat. La déportation d'Auschwitz pour sa mère, la résistance pour son père. Il confondait les époques, cherchait des dates, des noms, et les joues entre ses mains, répétait qu'il oubliait tout, ne retenait rien, pas même l'histoire familiale. (1989, 96)

> [empty memory, of the silence of the parents, of a necessary struggle. The Auschwitz deportation for his mother, the resistance for his father. He conflated the eras, sought the dates, the names, and, his face in his hands,

repeated that he forgot everything, retained nothing, not even the family history.]

When his mother, a survivor of Auschwitz, protests his attempt to make a sketch of her face, Marc has to defend himself by explaining to her that painting is his way of narrating ("raconter" [to tell]). She reacts with anger: "Déchire, mon fils, ça ravive trop de douleurs et d'humiliations" (1989, 131) [Tear it up, my son, that brings back too much pain and humiliation].

Boukhobza succeeds in naming the most important reasons for the silence of the victims, which after the war met uncannily with the silence in which the perpetrators were trying to hide their guilt. As a way of protecting their fractured selves from the pain evoked by remembering the trauma of persecution, many of the survivors indeed remained silent and would relate neither to the public nor to their children what they had been through. Afraid that the public would turn away from their stories, and also anxious not to burden their children too heavily with their accounts of the horrific past, survivors found themselves in the end even more isolated. In 1979, Bruno Bettelheim, in his afterword to Claudine Vegh's book *Je ne lui ai pas dit au revoir* [I Never Told Him Goodbye] introduced Helen Epstein's volume *Children of the Holocaust* to the French public. Epstein had in the same year familiarized the American audience with the immense emotional impact that the traumatic experience of the survivors had on their children.[1]

In the case of Marc, the sole link between the mother and her surroundings, the silence is nearly suffocating. Not unlike the protagonist of Anissimov's first novel, this young Jew, too, suffers from a past that was not his own but nonetheless affects his entire life. In Marc's philosophy, Marxism, the leading source of understanding the world, fails because it does not recognize that Auschwitz is in the center of a universe devoid of the sacred. Obsessed with an "esthétique d'un combat permanent, d'une vigilance quotidienne" (Boukhobza 1989, 100) [aesthetic of permanent struggle, an everyday vigilance], he joins a terrorist group. Marc eventually dies in an accident after yet another silence is broken for him: he learns that the man whom he had known as his father—the same man who had pretended to be a heroic member of the

1. Two years later, Nadine Fresco's influential study "La Diaspora des cendres" (1981) described from a psychoanalytical perspective the dilemma of not being able to talk about losses while being at the same time entirely preoccupied by them.

Jewish resistance—was living a lie. In reality, this man was the brother of the man whom Marc's mother had married before the war but who later disappeared. Returning from Auschwitz, Marc's mother imposed the identity of her husband upon the brother, and with it she imposed a "silence" to keep this exchange a secret. Marc learns about the lie just prior to his lethal accident. Whether his death was really a suicide is left open.

Boukhobza clearly borrows elements from melodrama, such as the female protagonist's attempt to improve her station in life by allying herself with a lover, sudden changes of fortune, and a tragic ending that thwarts the hero's effort to leave the fate of her family behind. Yet Boukhobza skillfully manipulates these generic traits by employing them in a narrative that goes beyond the realm of psychological sentimentalism. A peer of Marc's mother points to the lassitude of the survivors to explain why a man would give up his own life to live his brother's, and suggests that Marc suspend judgment in light of the immense hardship and existential losses the returnees had to face. He also refers to Jewish law according to which a man takes the place of his dead brother, thus introducing a notion that is even more foreign to the atheistic son. Another religious explanation is offered at the end of the novel when the old man sketches out "en termes bibliques" [in biblical terms] the possible reasons behind a life that indeed seems unjust. This episode transposes the narrative, which up to this point had been primarily psychologically informed, to a level that suggests an interpretation beyond the ones to which the young protagonists themselves have access, without, however, requiring them to subscribe to the powers of tradition and religion.

The figure of Marc, too, gains narrative weight during the course of the novel: with the revelation of the family plot, he is no longer a rebel without cause. His death, the exact circumstances of which remain unclear, can be read psychologically as an overreaction to the disclosure that leaves him in a state of betrayed trust and disappointment. Yet it also shows how difficult it is to continue the narrative of the ones born after the Shoah once a legacy of heroic resistance becomes shattered and ancestors thought to be brave heroes reveal themselves as weak human beings.

Writing a Way out of the Silence: Cécile Wajsbrot's *La trahison*

"La France ne sait pas affronter son histoire" (1997, 59) [France doesn't know how to face its history]—this line from Cécile Wajsbrot's novel *La trahison*

[Treason] places the discourse of silence within the political discussion about the country's difficulty in confronting its past. The plot takes place in the early 1990s and features an encounter between a twenty-eight-year-old Jewish woman, Ariane, who is working on a history of French radio broadcasting, and a legendary seventy-year-old radio news anchor, Louis. Ariane realizes early in her interviews with Louis that he has been guarding all his life a secret from his past, and she tries to get him to reveal to her what he has been hiding.

Unlike Anissimov in *Comment va Rachel?* or Boukhobza in *Les herbes amères*, Wajsbrot, who was born in 1954, employs language that has a distinct societal dimension and that goes beyond the private and psychological experience of the protagonists. She uses her lonely heroine Ariane to articulate a general critique of the nation's inability to break the silence that for so long hid the responsibility of French citizens in the persecution of their Jewish compatriots. This critique is cast in terms that point to the larger context of the country's inability to mourn.

> Ainsi voyait-elle sa vie comme un effort, une tentative permanente de se dégager de cette histoire qui l'emprisonnait, la guerre et la déportation, l'attitude des uns et des autres, et qui l'empêchait de se sentir vraiment chez elle dans un pays où elle était pourtant née, à cause de la collaboration, de la dénonciation, mais aussi à cause du silence qui se prolongeait aujourd'hui, à cause de cette volonté farouche de détourner les yeux, de poser le regard ailleurs, à cause de la reconstruction qui avait eu lieu sans faire place nette, sans déblayer, mais sur les ruines, directement, comme à Varsovie, lui avait-on raconté, un nouveau quartier s'était édifié sur les ruines de l'ancien ghetto sans qu'ils aient pris la peine d'en faire disparaître les fondations puisqu'il fallait que ce soit vite fait, si bien que ce nouveau quartier était plus élevé d'un mètre que le reste de la ville et que cette dénivellation marquait à la fois la volonté d'oubli et l'impossibilité de l'oubli. C'était toute France qui s'était reconstruite avec ce mètre de décalage que les gens feignaient d'ignorer mais qu'ils ne pouvaient pas ne pas remarquer. (1997, 114)
>
> [Thus, she saw her life as an effort, a permanent attempt to disentangle herself from this history that imprisoned her, the war and the deportation, the attitude of "us" and "them" that prevented her from feeling really at home in a country where she had in fact been born, because of the collaboration and the denunciation, but also because of the silence that continued today, because of that fierce desire to turn the eyes away, to look elsewhere, because of the reconstruction that, instead of making a clean slate, of clearing things

> away, had taken place directly on the ruins, as in Warsaw, where, they had told her, a new neighborhood had risen up on the ruins of the old ghetto without them having taken the trouble to remove the foundations, because it all had to be done quickly, even though this new neighborhood stood more than a meter higher than the rest of the city, and this difference in height betrayed both the desire to forget and the impossibility of forgetting. All of France had reconstructed itself with this meter of displacement that people pretended not to see, but that they could not help noticing.]

Over long passages, Wajsbrot's book reads like a story that could turn into a romance (which it will not do, after all)—without pushing sentimentality into self-complacency, but by observing how the past penetrates private realms of the present and how difficult it is to pull history out into the public realm. Ariane's insistence finally makes Louis talk—but before this can happen, he has to remember.

Wajsbrot's book succeeds in showing that the return of the repressed indeed haunts everyday life, and that the act of remembering seeks a place within everyday life that is sheltered from the eyes of the Other, in this case Ariane. Louis tries to find in his sister a person who would listen to his attempts at reconstructing his and his anti-Semitic parents' failure forty years earlier to rescue his Jewish girlfriend Sarah, whose relatives fell victim to the Velodrom d'Hiver roundup. Contrasting the biography of someone who was too weak to help a victim during the Vichy years with the biography of someone who grew up as the daughter of former victims, Wajsbrot considers the effects of two-sided amnesia. In Louis she portrays a man who was incapable of leading a full life after the war because an important piece from the puzzle of his past remained missing. Louis is ambivalent about Ariane's vexing questions, responding in a guarded and defensive manner. And yet he apprehends that the answers to these questions can alter who he has become.

La trahison does not feature a protagonist who has committed heinous crimes or who has acted out of anti-Semitic motivations. In Wajsbrot's almost conceptual juxtaposition between the perpetrators and the victims, Louis stands between the extremes. His inability as an adolescent to convince his parents to hide a Jewish girl with whom he had a complex love affair is a narrative construction that allows the author to sketch out a scene of reconciliation. Eventually, Ariane will show her understanding for Louis's failure. However, the novel insists that Louis's honest and remorseful confrontation with his behavior of the past is a prerequisite for such understanding—and that understanding will not be granted when such confrontation is missing, as in the case of Louis's sister. Writing here becomes identical with modeling a rapprochement between those who in the past stood on opposite sides, by outlining what steps need to be taken. Toward the end of the book, this message is also cast in political language as Ariane reflects on the fiftieth anniversary of the raid in the Vélodrome d'Hiver. She expresses her belief that the country is about to recover its memory, "lentement, avec réticence, mais un peu plus qu'avant" (1997, 178) [slowly, with reluctance, but a bit more than before]. Here at the last it becomes evident that Wajsbrot is writing in the tradition of a humanism that is not without echoes of the existentialist notion that people, in certain situations, can make choices that change their fates.[2] The readers learn that Louis had joined the resistance after he had witnessed Sarah's deportation. The author introduces him after all into the social contract on which postwar France wanted to erect its future as a nation.

Writing Against the Silence: Myriam Anissimov's *Sa Majesté la Mort*

> J'écris ces lignes pour que Samuel soit à nouveau parmi nous. Que nous puissions imaginer ses mains saisissant l'archet et le violon. Ces pages sont la tombe que je lui ai construite, alors que ses assassins voulaient que sa mémoire soit à jamais effacée. (Anissimov 1999, 278)
>
> [I write these lines so that Samuel will be amongst us again. So that we can imagine his hands seizing the bow and the violin. These pages are the tomb that I built for him, though his killers wanted his memory to be erased forever.]

Anissmov's *Sa Majesté la Mort* [His Majesty, Death], published in 1999, is dedicated to the endeavor of remembering, via writing, a family genealogy endangered by the peril of becoming "illisible" (1999, 15) [unreadable]. Reconstructing the past by searching for photographs and documents, by reading letters, and by listening to the stories of her mother, the author-narrator faces an almost insurmountable challenge:

> La presque totalité des membres de notre famille avait disparu avant ma naissance. Ils étaient nés à Szydlowiec, une petite ville de Pologne, proche de Radom, où les Juifs avaient été séquestrés par les Allemands, avant leur déportation et leur liquidation dans les chambres à gaz du camp d'extermination de Treblinka, en 1942. (1999, 13)

2. See also Wajsbrot's portrait of Thomas Mann in her novel *Mariane Klinger* (1996).

> [Almost all of the members of our family had disappeared before my birth. They were born in Szydlowiec, a little town in Poland, near Radom, where the Jews were sequestered by the Germans before their deportation and liquidation in the gas chambers of the Treblinka extermination camp in 1942.]

Whereas many of Anissimov's previous works had been based largely on autobiographical materials, *Sa Majesté la Mort* does not pretend to be anything other than a memoir. As such, it offers the reader a kind of contract that, according to the literary critic Philippe Lejeune, confirms to the reader that the author, narrator, and protagonist are identical and engage in proper self-representation (1975). Yet the autobiographical contract between author and reader does not promise that the "I" of the text will evade the power of the narrative, which transforms the self into a narrated figure unable to escape the dynamics of the narrative, resulting in semantic instability and ambiguity. The first-person narrator of the book finds herself confronted at the outset with a genealogical gap that only her writing and the research informing her writing can bridge. Naming in the most concrete manner possible what happened in the past is the initial step the book takes. Thus, the name of the concentration camp in which members of her family had been killed becomes immediately superimposed on the geographic location of the family's origins. The date of their murder is the first one mentioned, preceding the birth of the author-narrator by one year. Anissimov sets a stage for the narrative by pointing out from the very beginning that this stage once was populated and is now hauntingly vacant.

The narrative continues by naming the steps that marked the journey from the village to the concentration camps, minutely presenting the titles and German words officially used in signifying the various parts of the camp and its staff. This opening passage builds toward a stark juxtaposition between the perspective of the Jews who were killed in the camp and the life enjoyed by the Germans who were running the extermination site. It culminates in a short excerpt from an interview the commander of the camp gave to an English journalist while in jail in postwar Düsseldorf. In this excerpt, the former commander remembers joyfully the efforts to embellish the camp with flowers and gardens: "C'est difficile de décrire ça maintenant avec exactitude, mais c'était devenu réellement beau" (1999, 14) [It's difficult to describe it now exactly, but it became really beautiful].

Not to comment on this statement is a powerful comment in itself. The unmediated switch of perspective from the Jews who are getting undressed for the gas chambers to the unrepentant commander who is marveling about the flower arrangements on the grounds is a comment in itself. Within the first page, a *lieu de mémoire*, a site of memory, has been created in which no reconciliation will take place, as it is still inhabited by remorseless perpetrators whose lack of humanity has not been and will never be recuperated. Anissimov takes up the challenge of representing the Shoah head on, not shying away from what many see as the central, yet ultimately unachievable task of contemporary art. Her opening signals that she will not fall silent in the face of this challenge; instead, she will render justice to the victims of the Nazi genocide.

Sa Majesté la Mort continues to intertwine the narratives of the parents and grandparents with stories from the life of the author. Anissimov creates with her book a forum on which she stages crucial moments of her own life, asserting her own presence in this book of family remembrances. Switching back and forth between scenes from the ancestors' lives in Poland and the survivors' lives in French exile and vignettes from her own early childhood hiding under the auspices of a Protestant nun, Anissimov carries on a narrative that she had begun to tell as early as 1992, in *Dans la plus stricte intimité* [Family Only].

The book is, in some sense, a commissioned piece, instigated by the author's mother: "Elle décida alors que je serais la dépositaire de sa mémoire, de celle de tous les siens; les vivants et les morts" (1999, 15) [She decided that I would be the guardian of her memory, of the memory of all of her people; the living and the dead]. The daughter does not reduce her own role to that of an archivist, but instead establishes from the beginning her own place in the history of the family and in history at large. And yet the vectors of Anissimov's prose always pull the narrative from the present of the years 1997 and 1998 back toward the past where she discovers, among other things, fragments of the Yiddish language, which she claims as her own. "Écrivain yiddish de langue française" [A Yiddish Writer in the French Language] is the title of an essay in which Anissimov proudly accepts a linguistic legacy on which many of her books reflect melancholically. The "langue hybride" [hybrid language] of her work, the author assumes, results from the "terreau fécond du conflit entre le français et le yiddish" (1995, 239) [fertile compost of the conflict between French and Yiddish]. And yet, while Yiddish does present an important linguistic and cultural backdrop for Anissimov's books, one can hardly trace in them any elements reminiscent of the traditions of Yiddish storytelling. Neither the *Aggadah* nor artistically rendered—and therefore secularized—forms of traditional folk narrative are present in her work, and neither are anecdote, parody, and parable forms in which this author is interested. Her art of storytelling—unlike the work of Alain Gluckstein, Cyrille Fleischman, or Henri Raczymow—puts imagination into the service of historical reconstruction rather than allowing it to follow the path of "creative betrayal" that, according to the literary historian David G. Roskies, modern representatives of Yiddish storytelling have taken. Anissimov's work is geared toward the autobiographical while constantly searching, like a historian, for the traces of the lives of her ancestors, as if neither of these stories could be told separately.

Writing On: Alain Gluckstein's Grand Old Men

Alain Gluckstein's *Nos grands hommes* [Our Great Men], which appeared in 1997, is a highly complex novel, concerned, like many of the stories by the somewhat older Cyrille Fleischman, with the past and the present of Yiddish literature. Like Fleischman, Gluckstein addresses the demise of this part of Jewish writing with a sense of humorous and at times melancholic nostalgia. Fleischman's story "Le petit bureau d'à coté" [The Little Office Next Door] features an episode from the life of a Yiddish writer whose work is finally being translated and reviewed in a French journal, though unfortunately—and to the writer's vivid irritation—in the same issue that will include his obituary.

Unlike the short story writer Fleischman, however, Gluckstein uses a grand design for a novel with an intricate and constant shift of narrative perspectives and forms, including excerpts from texts of various genres. It self-reflexively enters into a dialogue with both the art of Yiddish storytelling and the genre of the *yizker bikher*, memory book, authored by survivors of Polish communities and aimed at preserving the memory of life before the destruction. To this dialogue Gluckstein, born in Paris in 1960, brings a postmodern interest in playing with traditions and in mixing genres.

Nos grands hommes, Gluckstein's second novel, pays homage to Berl Louson, a former jeweler, who followed his wife's plea and became a writer at a point when "la littérature yiddish avait autant besoin de ma plume qu'un squelette d'infirme d'un cautère sur sa jambe de bois pourrie" (1997, 7) [Yiddish literature needs my pen about as much a disabled bag of bones needs a cauterization on the rotten wood of his peg leg]. Writing in the 1980s in Paris,

Berl acknowledges that his narrative does not follow the chronology of events because it is overburdened by history:

> nos juifs pieux, mais d'autres juifs également, et spécialement moi, Berl Lourson, qui n'arrive jamais à replacer les événements, au moins les événements récents, dans une chronologie vraisemblable, comme si tout s'écrasait, pour finir, de mon existence, événement sur événement, tous mêlés, comme les cuillerées de terre qu'on jette dans la fosse au cimetière. (1997, 253)
>
> [our pious Jews, but other Jews too, and especially I, Berl Lourson, who never manage to put events—at least recent events—into a plausible chronology, as if everything from my existence splattered down in the end, event upon event, all mixed together, like the handful of earth that they throw in the grave at the cemetery.]

The association of writing and dying is by no means an extraordinary notion, but it persists through the entire novel. Berl reminisces about life in the Polish shtetl where he had lived with relatives and friends before leaving for France. He describes the dying immigrant community in Paris of the seventies and eighties and its cultivation of its Bundist heritage of revolutionary Jewish politics organized around the meetings of the "Amsterdamer-Bund." Berl and his friends, mostly writers who only rarely manage to focus their imagination on the present, engage in debates about the possibilities and impossibilities of continuing the tradition of writing in a language that is about to disappear. The miraculous earlier survival of Yiddish during Chmielnicki's violent pogroms becomes the topic of one of the many stories told in the book. Berl presents himself first as the author of a novella in Yiddish that in 1938 had some impact on a very small group of readers, and as a man who after the war dreamed about finishing the immense project of a Yiddish-language encyclopedia. This undertaking had been discontinued after the two volumes on the entry "Jews" had appeared during the war.

Nos grands hommes is the ironic swan song of a milieu in peril of becoming unintelligible even to itself, which is accessible to outsiders only via an appendix. This text is the "Petit lexique facultatif établi par Rita Glik et destiné à l'intelligence de l'ouvrage appelé 'Nos grands hommes' " [Useful vocabulary gathered by Rita Glik and intended for the comprehension of the work called "Our Great Men"] and its author is Berl's daughter, herself a writer. The alphabetically arranged dictionary introduces historical and cultural terms such as "Golem" or "Guéfiltè fish" to the readers whose knowledge of Jewish traditions, *landsmanshaftn*, and the history of Jewish life in prewar Poland may be limited. Yet the dictionary is also a pastiche of the kind of reading aids that one finds in many books by contemporary Jewish authors, as its fictitious compiler included terms such as "Jews" and the name of the fictitious Polish hometown of her father in the appendix.

Interrupting the flow of the narrative are long excerpts of Berl's story "Le Braque de Chmielnicki" [The Hound of Chmielnicki] and excerpts from various additions to the "Yisker-bou'h de Kulichow"—[*Yizker-Bukh* of Kulichow], the book of commemoration prepared by several members of the Amsterdamer-Bund on their hometown—as well as the "Curriculum secret de Lazare Glik" [The Secret Résumé of Lazare Glik], about which the narrator says: "Un jour, vous aussi vous aurez besoin de Lazare le faussaire (quatrième édition)" (1997, 159) [One day, you too, you will need Lazare the counterfeiter (fourth edition)]. With the inclusion of "The Hound of Chmielnicki," the novel incorporates a historical narrative that features the life of a medieval rabbi, whereas the *yizker-bukh* addresses Jewish life in Poland in the first part of the twentieth century. The "secret résumé" renders the biography of Lazare Glick, Rita's future husband, a child of French and Polish Jews who was born, "comme tout le monde, en 1946, un 1er janvier, quelque part à l'est de l'Oder" (1997, 159) [like everyone else, in 1946, one January 1st, somewhere east of the Oder].

At the end, while the old narrator Berl burns a Yiddish-language manuscript by one of his deceased friends because it had resisted all his efforts to decipher and understand it (and because it had made him fall asleep), a younger generation nevertheless continues in the literary traditions of Judaism. Berl's adopted daughter Rita, an orphan from war-ridden Indochina, has authored a novel, "Guéfiltè Nem" [Gefilte Nem], from which *Nos grands hommes* includes an "excerpt." ("Nem" is a Vietnamese fish dish!) Rita's novel offers glimpses of a New Jersey community of survivors deprived of real ties to the Old World, troubled that their offspring may never be able to offer them more than a *kaddish* over their graves.

The autojudeography of Lazare Glik elevates the association of death and literature to yet another plane. Lazare's secret curriculum vitae recounts the chapters in the life of a young Jew who during the late sixties had remained a distant observer of his comrades' terrorist fight against the establishment, contentedly printing editions of *L'enfant juif* [The Jewish Child] on the press owned by his benefactor. At one point, this young man sets out to make a modest living by saying the *kaddish* at funerals in Bagneux cemetery. He has bigger ambitions, however, and embarks on a project of "l'embaumement littéraire" [literary embalming] of decrepit Jews:

> J'allais faire une œuvre pie, pie et rentable: je proposerais à chacun d'eux une belle biographie, écrite en bon français, reliée pleine peau, et que pourraient consulter leurs enfants et leurs petits-enfants, et les enfants de leurs petits-enfants, pour les siècles des siècles, et rien ne s'entendrait tout à fait de ce qui avait fait leur vie—le genre de *kaddish* avec lequel on pouvait mourir en paix. (1997, 220)
>
> [I would make a pious work, pious and profitable: I would offer to each of them a fine biography, written in good French, leather-bound, which their children and their grandchildren, and the children of their grandchildren could consult for centuries to come, and nothing would be precisely understood about what had made their lives—the sort of *kaddish* with which one could die in peace.]

A phantasmagorical encounter with the Golem, whose presence in the cemetery has been often speculated about, eventually forces Lazare to confront his own mortality and to sit down to write the account of his own life, the "secret résumé."

Gluckstein thus proffers a huge canvas of Jewish characters who cannot help but see themselves as members of a vanishing people, and who therefore are all in one way or another involved in documenting the Jewish life of earlier times. The narrator's dream that he will be the last Jew on earth is an indicator of the gloomy mood penetrating the novel. Another indicator is the gloomy definition of the Jews as a people who differ from others not because of their faith, their values, or their language, but because of their susceptibility to suffer from a certain illness that turns them into a "conservatoire humain de la maladie de Gaucher" (1997, 123) [human reservoir for Gaucher's illness]. *Nos grands hommes* is a melancholic piece of literature written by one of the youngest authors of this "new Jewish literature." Gluckstein treats his figures with loving respect and avoids any notion of tragic apocalypse, even when he has his narrator Berl confess laconically that he is editing the "*yisker-bou'h* de ma vie sans ordre" (1997, 254) [*yizker-bukh* of my life without any order], the written memorial of his own life. "Pas de nostalgie, Berl, surtout pas de nostalgie" [No nostalgia Berl, above all no nostalgia], advises one of the writers in the novel, the author of the manuscript *Nos grands hommes* who is an ardent opponent of the "commémorations dont nos sociétés juives se montrent si prodigues" (1997, 22) [commemorations with which our Jewish societies show themselves to be so extravagant].

Consciously avoiding any inclination toward the sentimental, the novel displays an appreciation of Jewish literature by the older generations as an aging project. The novel produces quite a humorous effect through its awareness of its own successful and creative perpetuation of a tradition to which it is about to bid farewell. The book comments on the end of a tradition by using the very means that once had established this tradition itself: "Parody," according to the scholar Ken Frieden "in particular, was integral to the rise of Yiddish fiction" (1995, x), and parody, one now can add, is integral in the kaddish for Yiddish fiction. Gluckstein playfully draws on central motifs and aspects of Jewish folklore and history using the wheeling and dealing of the Amis de l'Amsterdamer-Bund [Friends of the Amsterdamer Bund] as a microcosmos that also speaks to the current interest in writing Jewish history and literature. This interest has been growing in the last years, even though the motives and incentives have varied from generation to generation. One of the shtetl-immigrant writers in the novel cuts off his ties to the past so completely after the war that he dispenses with his Jewish name as well as his accent and his devotion to motifs of Jewish life in the East. Instead, he embarks on an illustrious career as a writer of indistinguishable ethnicity and interest. The novel does not condemn such a life of literary acculturation, but it places assimilation in a rich context of highly hybridized, yet highly creative emanations of the cultural productions of Jews. After all, it even alludes to the power of handed-down forms of Jewish narratives on non-Jews, as the work *Guéfiltè Nem* by Berl's Asian-born daughter Rita documents. Her son, the narrator mentions at the end, has grown up speaking some Yiddish, though it is very reminiscent of the German he has been learning in high school. Kenneth Avruch's suggestion that contemporary diaspora Judaism is made "not of tradition, but of traditionalizing" undoubtedly reverberates in this grandfather-grandson constellation.[3] Pointedly, the novel ends with the picture of the aging Berl and his grandchild visiting a cemetery together, capturing generational continuity against the backdrop of a site of memory devoid of any life.

3. Quoted in Boyarin 1991, 158.

Writing or Praying?

In Jewish history, the act of writing is inseparably intertwined with religion. Harold Bloom once stated that the Jewish people, known to be the people of the book, "*were* a text-centered people, perhaps as much as any people ever has been. If we still *are* a people, it can only be because we have some texts in common. Culture in our context broadly must mean literary culture, if by 'literary' one means biblical and post-biblical *written* tradition" (1985, 109). It is very much the post-biblical *secular* written tradition that contemporary Jewish literature accepts as a common point of reference, rather than turning toward the biblical tradition for literary or spiritual inspiration. This reluctance to use the Torah as "hypotext" (Genette 1982), as a point of departure for literary explorations, is hardly surprising considering the highly secular nature of artistic production since the Enlightenment. Anna Langfus has found few students among succeeding authors: Weil's *Les vendanges de Rachi* [The Grape Harvests of Rachi] and Gutman's *La folle rumeur de Smyrne* [The Mad Rumor of Smyrna] thematize the lives of prominent Jewish religious figures, yet they do this via the distancing mediation of historical narratives. Only Gilles Rozier's *Moïse fiction* [Moses Fiction], which appeared in 2001, leaves this self-imposed generic framework behind to create a much less authentic picture and a highly subjective image of a biblical figure: in the novel's stream of consciousness, Moses appears in all the fragility and loneliness that God cannot ease for him.[4]

How closely contemporary secular writing approaches the religious tradition without ever merging with it can be seen in a poem by Emmanuel Moses:

> "Deutéronome, 25, 17"
>
> Rappelle-toi le goût de
> L'écharde.
> Les taches de cire
> Devant la mer
> Qui ne voit pas.
> L'odeur d'arêtes
> Et de toile. (1989, 68)

4. See also Eric-Emmanuel Schmitt's *L'évangile selon Pilate* (2000).

["Deuteronomy 25:17"

Remember the taste of
The splinter.
The drops of wax
Before the ocean
Which does not see.
The smell of fish bones
And of canvas.]

The poem invokes a moment of great historical significance by generating a poetic image to complement what the Torah presents only as a very brief reminder of Amalek's massacre of Jews during the Exodus. The poem opens with a quotation from the Torah passage to which its title refers so directly—"Rappelle-toi" [Remember]—but it goes on to display a very different movement, one that neither identifies the torturer of the exhausted Jews nor even points to the accusatory tone of the biblical passage. Rather, it recreates the historical event as a highly elusive moment, fixating physical sensations and reflections tied to the event in nature imagery. An anonymous voice commemorates the moment; its request to remember may be directed to the Jewish people—as in the Torah—or may be intended merely for the individual whose soliloquy we are witnessing.

The Torah offers a report of the killings, adding that once the Jewish people have reached the Promised Land, they must not forget to erase the memory of Amalek. Emmanuel Moses's poem complies with the imperatives of Deuteronomy 25:19: "you shall blot out the remembrance of Amalek from under heaven. Do not forget." The poem does not speak of Amalek directly; his name has indeed been eradicated from memory as it is not mentioned in the poem. And yet, the poem does heed the imperative of *zakhor* by claiming, as the title indicates, to take the place of the passage of the Torah to which it refers. The poem achieves its aim precisely because it recreates lyrically the imperative of blotting out a remembrance of the enemy of the Jews without forgetting "it"—an event no longer accessible in the language of the Bible and in modern times replaced by the memory of the Shoah to which this text ultimately refers.

One cannot call Emmanuel Moses (born 1959 in Casablanca) a religious author, even if "Deuteronomy, 25, 17" is not the only poem by Moses that engages in a dialogue with the Hebrew Bible. Considering his poetry as a whole, one realizes that this author turns to Jewish religion the way he turns to Greek Antiquity or to the Christian Middle Ages. Moses's collection of poetry (*Métiers*, 1989 [Professions]) is not a reflection of the indifference of contemporary secularism toward religion. The eclecticism of the book, in which Judaism is present without Moses's having allotted it any special place or exclusive status, shows that contemporary Jewish literature can freely draw on the religious tradition as one reservoir among others of religious images, ideas, and cultural traditions. We see Judaism here as part of a heritage that the poet has stripped of any claims for exclusiveness and that he instead uses, like the *bricoleur* described by Roland Barthes, in an endeavor so heterogeneous that believers may find it blasphemous.

While the demographic phenomenon of the "newly observant Jew" (Schnapper 1983) has not yet produced a convincing literary expression of its own, the emergence of this type has appeared in literature, even if displaced into circumstances well beyond the French nation:

> Je ne suis pas chrétien; j'appartiens à une communauté de juifs religieux qui vivent en marge, à contre-courant de la société actuelle, et que l'on appelle les hassidim. En tant que juifs, par une tradition millénaire, nous sommes voués à transcrire les paroles et les faits importants pour que perdure la mémoire. C'est pourquoi je vais accomplir mon devoir et écrire cette histoire dans sa vérité et son exactitude. Ce qui est mon but ici.
>
> Je dois dire tout d'abord que les hassidim ne cherchent ni à convaincre ni à convertir les peuples. Ainsi, je n'écris pas pour être lu; j'écris pour conserver la vérité des faits et la pérennité de la mémoire. C'est pour elle que j'écris et pour la postérité: c'est par mes pères et les pères de leurs pères que j'ai appris qu'il fallait consigner et conserver secrètes dans un petit coin du monde les choses et les pensées, non en vue de l'actualité et des lecteurs présents, car nous avons une vocation monastique et vivons à l'écart de tous, mais pour les lecteurs futurs, les générations à venir qui sauront découvrir et comprendre: découvrir nos secrets et comprendre notre langue. Je n'écris pas pour moi, car l'écriture n'est ni un exutoire ni un épanchement impie et païen. Pour moi et pour les miens, l'écriture est sacrée, elle est un rite auquel je me donne presque à contrecœur, avec le goût du devoir. C'est ma façon de prier; de chercher le pardon; de sacrifier. (Abécassis 1996, 21–22)
>
> [I am not Christian; I belong to a community of religious Jews who live on the margins, against the stream of contemporary society, and they are called the Hassidim. They are dedicated by ancient Jewish tradition to the tran-

> scribing of important words and events, to keep their memory alive. So is my duty and aim here: to tell this story with truth and rigorous accuracy, to tell what happened.
>
> But first I should say straight away that the Hassidim do not seek to persuade or convert people. I write, not in order to be read, but to preserve the truth of events in perpetuity. I write for posterity: I learned from my fathers and their fathers' fathers that events and thoughts must be preserved and hidden in a small corner of the world, not for present-day readers, since we live a monastic life, away from society, but for future generations who will discover our secrets and understand our language. Writing is not a mere outlet for me, but a sacred ritual, which I embark upon almost unwillingly, as a duty. It is my way of praying, of seeking forgiveness, of making a sacrifice.] (1998b, 9)

In *Qumran*, Eliette Abécassis's young narrator Ary Cohen faces no easy task. An orthodox Jew and the son of a prominent Israeli archeologist, he is becoming involved in the struggle to rescue one of the legendary Dead Sea Scrolls that had been discovered at the Qumran site, a few miles south of Jericho, in 1947 and was lost several years later. The events surrounding the lost manuscript take place in 1999 (the novel was published in 1996), and Ary's report describes, among other events, mysterious murders (crucified Bible scholars), the involvement of international secret services, lessons in the history of Jewish sects, and love affairs with students of anti-Semitic Bible experts.

While dealing with mundane and secular events and figures, the narrator continuously makes use of narrative devices of religious provenance. One passage of the long novel gives an introduction into the Hebrew alphabet and the meaning of the individual letters according to the Kabbalah. References to the origins of Jesus, to his relationship to the Essene sect, who may have been the authors of the Dead Sea Scrolls, and to the world of contemporary Hassidic Judaism are more than just historical window dressing in a novel whose central issue is the rise of Christianity from Jewish roots. Yet Abécassis frames her voluminous novel in a manner that capably embraces her epic-scale material. The titles of each of the eight chapters refer to one of the scrolls and quote passages from them in their epigraphs. In the last two chapters, she replaces Ary's first-person narrative entirely with the text of the scrolls. Ary, the scribe, has done his duty and withdraws behind the sacred texts. At the same time, Abécassis's novel is a highly ironic text, and the deference of her narrator toward orthodoxy is not at all shared by the author, who as a "scribe" also does not subscribe to Ary's credo of the writer's role. Abécassis, a teacher of philosophy born in 1969 and now a celebrated writer, has set up a design that exposes the tensions between Christianity and Judaism, and portrays them as manipulative—and murderous—forces in a suspenseful religious thriller. She surprises the readers of her crime novel over and over with her speculations about the motives of the individual players, among them the Vatican, scholars, businessmen, and theologians. She leaves no ploy of the genre unused to sustain the readers' suspense during long conceptual passages addressing Christological debates or the historical formation of Judaism. *Qumran* is a best-selling novel based on impressive erudition, dealing with some of the burning issues of Christian and Jewish belief, yet it is anything but a religious novel.

The question of whether Jesus was a member of the Hebrew sect of the Essenes is at the core of the theological discussions and motivates the players, who variously insist on this relationship or—like the Christians—try to prevent any evidence that could strengthen the idea of such ties. Ary, who has reversed his father's path from religion to the secular world of science to attend a *yeshiva*, unwillingly becomes involved in the search for the missing manuscript. His education in the background of the battle over the ancient scrolls, decried by some Christians as a medieval fabrication, will also become the reader's education in the complicated subject matter. During his struggle to find the lost manuscript, Ary even kills a rabbi who is later revealed to have been the Wicked Priest. The outcome of Ary's pursuit of the truth eventually substantiates his belief in the power of the word in a way not even he could anticipate. The novel seems to suggest that the pious young student, returning to the Qumran caves where he finds the last descendants of the Essenes, will soon emerge from the ancient site of Jewish faith at the shore of the Dead Sea as the messiah the scrolls have prophesied.

The strange dating of the beginning of the plot in the year 1999 allows for such a future chronology of events, and retrospectively makes the elevated tone of his self-pronouncements understandable as a token of his chosen status. After all, the narrator had already insisted in his prologue that the notion of the present is unknown to the Bible, which instead merges the past with the future. In this sense, his account also possesses an almost cyclical quality, ending with the fate of the newly initiated Ary as a member of an ancient sect of the Jewish people: "Il y a deux mille ans débuta une histoire qui changea la face du monde une première fois, et une seconde fois, il y a cinquante ans maintenant, lors d'une surprenante révélation archéologique" (1996, 21) ["Two thousand years ago a story began which changed the face of the earth, and again for a second time fifty years ago, thanks to an amazing archeological discovery" (1998b, 9)]. Time, the narrator wants to demonstrate, is not a linear dimension, but rather manifests itself in abrupt jumps relating distant events to each other; clearly, this is an understanding of time not as secular history but, as the German-Jewish philosopher Walter Benjamin showed, as a messianic *Heilsgeschichte* (that is, a history that provides salvation) ignored by profane history. Benjamin was also the one who introduced the notion of archeology to the study of history and memory, insisting that remembering can reveal layers of the past; that memory is like a field in which an archeologist digs for sedimented strata of previous cultures. Indeed, Abécassis links the messianic return of the savior in her novel to an archeological discovery uncovering the ongoing presence of the Essenes' past in the seaside caves and with it the hope for deliverance that Ary had studied in the ancient texts.

Writing in the vein of Umberto Eco's intellectual detective novels, Abécassis uses the eloquence of biblical scholars in *Qumran* to familiarize her readers with the textual universe of contemporary theology, which, not unlike the fate of the protagonist, harks back to ancient beginnings. In *L'or et la cendre* [Gold and Ashes], her second novel (1997), Abécassis continues to work with a similar technique of marrying the suspenseful to the learned; this time, however, she shifts the setting of the conflict between Jews and Christians to France and Germany in the year 1995. In this novel, too, she poses the fundamental philosophical question about the existence of origins and their comprehensibility to the human mind. This time, however, it is not the authorial origin of a document that is at stake, but the origin of evil as such. Abécassis's protagonists debate the anthropological, theological, and historical reasons for the Shoah, creating a vast picture of the positions that have been presented on these laden issues over the last decades. Her essay *Petite métaphysique du meurtre* (1998) [A Short Account of the Metaphysics of Murder] reads like a philosophical guidebook to her fiction. The essay summarizes the positions by post-Shoah theologians like Emil Fackenheim and Richard Rubenstein on the possibility or impossibility of believing in God after the camps, but also references the historical debates prompted by the revisionist views of the German Ernst Nolte.

The alter ego protagonists of her second novel are a historian and a journalist—not by chance both members of writing professions. For Abécassis, writing is the endeavor par excellence to penetrate Jewish history, as it participates in the constant annotating of and commentating on the textual processes that have influenced the course of the Jewish people. This also explains why the plot devices Abécassis created in both her detective novels center around texts: in *Qumran* around the scrolls, in *L'or et la cendre* around a lost little brown book which may or may not have contained a revelation of the origin of evil. Interestingly, in both cases the writers of these ominous documents of central importance to the fate of Judaism remain anonymous. Dramaturgically, they are props, and yet they ultimately do refer to the importance attributed to the *sefer*, the written text, in Judaism and in Jewish history. The absence of the scroll and the brown book in the novels creates severe difficulties for the protagonists, all caused by interruptions of the textual criticism (reading, understanding, interpreting) of these documents. Their absence also constitutes a breach between the previous generations, which had access to these documents, and the ones who were born later, whose fate continues to be affected by words they have not had a chance to read. The younger characters pursue these words, in search of salvation, at the cost of their lives.

Writing by Dictation: Colette Fellous's *Rosa Gallica*

> Écris écris maintenant ce qui trotte ici, dans cette chambre et jette-le dans ton dictionnaire si tu veux mais à mon avis c'est une histoire que tu as inventée, tu n'iras jamais au bout de tes mots car tu n'as pas encore compris que j'étais moi-même ton dictionnaire et que tous les mots que tu portais depuis toujours, c'était en moi que tu les avais recueillis, la première fois. Écris donc sous ma dictée, et dis-leur surtout que je suis née loin d'ici. (Fellous 1989, 141)
>
> [Write write now what is scurrying about here, in this room, and put it in the dictionary if you want but in my opinion it's a story that you made up, you will never go to the limit of your words because you haven't yet grasped that I myself was your dictionary and that all the words you ever carried, you gathered from me the first time. Write then according to my dictation, and above all, tell them that I was born far from here.]

This narrative, it seems, has been set into motion by its object, the narrator's mother, who at the end of her life urges her daughter to put her story down in writing. In a hospital room, she asks her daughter to be her voice, to articulate not just the stories that made up the mother's life but also nothing short of the truth of that life itself: "Mais ce n'est pas du tout une histoire, c'est une vérité, une pure" (1989, 28) [But it's not at all a story, it is a truth, a pure one]. The narrator's task is an impossible assignment, as she knows that there are no facts but only stories about facts, that pure truth is beyond the writer's capacity. She knows that putting her pen to paper will transform her mother's life; that it will be an act of "l'inventer pour toujours" (1989, 13) [creating for eternity].

And yet, this assignment is by no means the only unusual feature of the relationship between mother and daughter in Colette Fellous's *Rosa Gallica* (1989). At the very start of the novel, the narrator confesses that she always had been aware of the task of "d'écrire ma mère" (1989, 21) [writing my mother]. In her eyes, her account of her mother's life is a gift to be returned, part of an exchange in which the daughter merely reciprocates for what she had received from the mother:

> elle m'ayant donné la langue et moi lui traçant le dessin de ses jours, surtout prends soin de ne rien trier, parle aussi des malheurs que des petites joies, des bêtises que des grands rires et même ce qui n'est pas très beau à dire, n'hésite pas, va dans la vérité, tu passes trop de temps à rédiger ton dictionnaire, occupe-toi plutôt de ta maman et dépêche-toi quand même, que j'en profite un peu, tu sais bien comme dans la vie il est si vite trop tard. (1989, 21–22)
>
> [she having given me language, and I tracing out for her the sketch of her life, above all take care not to pick and choose, speak of the pains as well as the little joys, the foolishness as well as the laughter, and even of that which is not very pretty to say, don't hesitate, go into truth, you spend too much time writing your dictionary, busy yourself instead with your mum and hurry up, so that I can enjoy it a little bit, you know how in life it so quickly becomes too late.]

Equipped with her mother tongue, the narrator is supposed to use language to mirror her mother's everyday life so that the core of this biography can become visible within it. At no point does the mother mention an anonymous audience as the envisioned readership of this account. There is no reader, and, one is tempted to say, there is no writer at work either, since the mother does not want her portrait reflected through someone else's lens. In passages like the one quoted above, the seeming disappearance of the narrator with regard to her object becomes traceable: the voice of the mother intercepts the narrator's voice with directives that will turn out to be impossible to follow. The daughter-narrator thus faces a mission that she cannot carry out but that she cannot simply abandon, because her narrative is, after all, a token of her love.

Fellous, born in Tunisia in 1950, has her narrator approach the double-bind situation of being a writer who composes as well as constructs a story as opposed to a secretary who merely takes dictation. She achieves this balance of acting as agent and scribe by incorporating her mother's voice into her own, blending her own and her object's perspective, in a way letting the other speak for herself. The daughter's appreciation of the linguistic gift she has received from her mother leads her to measure words carefully and precisely and to explore the historical semantics and the shifts in the meaning of terms she uses. The proximity of related terms in various languages such as French, Arabic, and Hebrew becomes a subject of her writing as well because her mother would have preferred the two latter ones as the lingua franca of the story of her life. Examining semantic and morphological connections between these languages is the narrator's homage to a person who grew up speaking Arabic rather than French.

As a novel, *Rosa Gallica* situates the narrative of the mother in a sphere beyond history and official politics where the personal is the dominant category. In her novel *Midi à Babylone* [Noon in Babylon], Fellous powerfully raises questions about persecution of the Jews ("Mais dites-moi, savez-vous au moins où sont passés tous les corps qu'on a brûles? . . . Regardez vos archives, s'il vous plaît, aidez-moi à retrouver" (1994, 60) [But tell me, do you at least know where all the bodies that they burned went? . . . Look at your archives, please, help me to find them]. The story of her mother, however, remains without such a dimension. It even does away with the laws of chronology. It relates via associations often trivial moments whose importance can only be grasped from within the texture of the mother's life. From the outside, these details must remain banalities. There is no attempt to turn the few biographical moments to which the account keeps returning into a suspenseful plot, or to suggest a movement, a rhythm, or a certain tension to accommodate the reader. There are deep fears of death and the anxiety of illness that repeatedly punctuate the narrative and the narrator's conscience as a girl and adolescent.

In her memoir *Avenue de France* (2001) [France Avenue], Fellous remembers that in 1967, arriving from her native Tunisia in Marseille, she found herself faced with the question "la littérature est-elle un art ou une arme?" (2001, 52) [is literature an art or a weapon?]. Her works show that she has not succumbed to the fallacy of this alternative. Pursuing instead literature as a poetic form of remembering intimate experiences, she has turned writing into a political gesture by bidding farewell to the activist concept of the political that was dominant in the late sixties.

What renders the account of the ordinary life recounted in *Rosa Gallica* extraordinary is not the depth of reflection or the exceptional nature of experiences, but the mother's almost poetic and sometimes hermetic diction, which is echoed in the narrator's language and which culminates at the end of the novel. With a long monologue, possibly uttered just before her death, the mother urges her daughter one last time to record her account of her life, and this time the novel documents nothing but this monologue. The narrator has resigned herself to the role of scribe, and as a scribe she becomes the medium to pen the *écriture automatique* [automatic writing] of the mother's last soliloquy. The vision-like delusions that the narrator writes down meet with the readers' compassion for a woman who at the end of her sufferings deliriously finds in her daughter the voice for her messianic hope of giving birth to the child of a prince, suggesting the notion of a future, of a new life.

When the authors born after the Shoah and their protagonists pick up the pen to engage in the act of writing, they have to face up to the very blank page that initially confronts every writer. Yet theirs is the blank page of effaced memory that awaits their attempt to articulate what otherwise would forever fall victim to the "univers concentrationnaire" [concentrationary universe], a term David Rousset (1946) coined in his account of being an inmate of the Buchenwald camp. Unable to indulge—like some of their non-Jewish peers—in the luxury of nonreferentiality or of an imagination unhindered by the weight of history, these authors speak of the pain suffered by their kin and of the indifference exhibited by their non-Jewish compatriots. In this respect, the stage onto which these writers enter already has been set. On it they confront the challenge of having to create narratives that can bear the tension between a history that forces its way into their imagination and a present that must not be overpowered by the experience of the past. Regardless of whether they narrate their own biographies within the parameters of *écriture de soi* [autobiographical writing] or whether they sketch the lives of young protagonists against the backdrop of fictional worlds, these authors cannot but punctuate their accounts with the diacritical marks impressed upon them by the past. In the words of Deleuze and Guattari, the cramped space of minor literature "forces each individual intrigue to connect immediately to politics. The individual concern thus becomes all the more necessary, indispensable, magnified, because a whole other story is vibrating within it" (1975, 17).

For Ouaknine, interrupting the silence with his own voice opened up both a new approach toward the autobiographical and a dialogue in his family. Other writers sought to establish such a dialogue with the French public at large—in Wajsbrot's case for didactic, in Goldman's for didactic as well as for existential reasons. And whereas the works by Anissimov, Czarny, Fellous, Wajsbrot, and others tell stories in order to prevent life stories from falling prey to silence, the detective novels by Eliette Abécassis and Clément Weill Raynal (*Le tombeau de Rachi*, 1997 [The Tomb of Rashi]) approach the unspoken by uncovering the bodies lying beneath a blanket of silence with which others have tried to cover up their heinous crimes.

4 Filiations

Family Portraits of the Artists as Young Jews

> Je ne puis jamais être en effet juif tout seul, si coupé que je sois de la communauté ou même de ma famille. Si je me veux juif, il faut bien que je me rapporte à une généalogie, à une histoire passée, présente, peut-être même future. (de Fontenay 1991, 184)

> [Indeed, I could never be a Jew alone, so cut off as I am from the community or even from my family. Choosing to think of myself as a Jew, I need to relate to a genealogy, a history of the past, the present, and maybe even the future.]

The Jewish philosopher Elisabeth de Fontenay points to the importance of the family as a microcosm of the Jewish community and as a necessary (and possibly even sufficient) communal context for the individual to live as a Jew. This position, by no means novel, reverses Sartre's definition of Jewish identity. Here Jewish identity is predicated on a community of Jews rather than of anti-Semites. This definition is also an attempt to overcome the quandaries that result from the common definitions of Jewish identity as a religion, a race, or an ethnicity. Suggesting instead "filiation" and "affiliation" as the defining principles, de Fontenay wants to allow as much space as possible for the idea of an autonomous, self-determined embrace of an individual's Jewishness: "Si je me veux juif" (1991, 183) [If I choose to think of myself as a Jew].

The notion of affiliation as a relationship to a historically perceived or simply presently defined community, and the notion of filiation as a genealogically defined relationship, leave it up to individuals to scrutinize their families to determine exactly what their relationship to Judaism and the Jewish people looks like and what "filiation" entails for them. De Fontenay's construction is a precarious one because one obviously does not choose the family to which one belongs, but one can (she and the writers of the younger generations insist) choose whether one would like to follow the models provided by one's family. This choice may be limited in real life; in the realm of imagination, however, it is limitless.

It is this ambivalent relationship of the younger Jews to their predecessors that troubled Luc Rosenzweig. In the preface to his *La jeune France juive* [Young Jewish France], he reflected upon the difficulty in mediating between the desire for individual and autonomous designs of life and the established facts of filial bonds and ethnic identity. For Rosenzweig, too, Jewishness is generated first of all, if not solely, within the family, because there are no societal entities beyond the familiar realm that could assist the family in this function. Nonetheless, this power of the family is problematic:

> Car il faut bien se rendre à l'évidence: il n'y a qu'une chose qui fabrique des juifs d'aujourd'hui, les familles juives. Quel que soit le lieu où l'histoire les a déposés, quelle que soit leur attitude vis-à-vis de la religion ou de la politique, ces familles juives marquent les enfants qu'elles produisent d'une empreinte que tous les polissages scolaires ou sociaux ne parviennent qu'atténuer faiblement. (1980, 11)
>
> [Because one really must face the facts: there is only one thing that makes Jews today, Jewish families. No matter where history has placed them, no matter what their attitude toward religion or politics, these Jewish families mark the children that they produce with a mark that educational or social polishing can tone down only minimally.]

The family's unique role thus becomes a potentially overwhelming factor in the formation of the offspring. Its power threatens to deprive the young of the freedom of self-determination that Rationalism provided the modern individual: "Ce qui nous fait juifs, ce n'est pas le regard de l'autre . . . mais bien cette impossibilité de se considérer comme un homme nouveau, ce refus d'un des axiomes de la modernité: l'être cause de soi-même" (1980, 11) [What makes us Jews is not the perspective of others . . . but the impossibility of considering ourselves a new person, the rejection of one of the axioms of modernity: being the cause of oneself]. Rosenzweig's already mentioned insistence on the principle of autonomy as the framework of the modern individual and de Fontenay's reminder of the principles of filiation and affiliation as the frameworks outside of which Jewish identity cannot emerge allude to the antipodes that delineate the narratives of contemporary Jewish writing. Colorful family tableaux provide the backdrop for books as different from each other as Pierre Goldman's novel about the orphan Rapoport and Annie Goldmann's saga about Jewish women in the Maghreb. The family serves both as subject matter and potential readership, and becomes a potential impediment (due to its proclivity to keep things unarticulated) as well as a *conditio sine qua non* for these writers, for whom the family is a source of knowledge, information, and insight that they need to tell their stories. Genealogy provides a legacy to fall back on or a tradition to strike out from. It emits forces of attraction as well as repulsion that keep the offspring captivated and bound to the family as the first segment of the Jewish community he or she encounters. If the family is missing, as in the case of families murdered by the Nazis, the space left painfully vacant must be filled by projections.

Examining what exactly the notion of filiation entails is one the motivating forces in Patrick Modiano's oeuvre, and it has been a preoccupation of many of the younger authors for reasons identified by Robert Ouaknine in the opening of his autojudeography. The book that Annette Kahn, daughter of a Jewish resistance fighter, wrote as a journalist for *Le point* on the Klaus Barbie trial, is yet another example of how the dynamics of autojudeographic writing reconstitute filial bonds to confirm, in the end, the affiliation with the Jewish people. Kahn (born in 1941 in Saint Etienne) was a young child when her father Robert died as one of the last victims of Klaus Barbie. Kahn states in the preface that she "had no real memory of him" (1991b, 11).[1] *Why My Father Died: A Daughter Confronts Her Family's Past at the Trial of Klaus Barbie* (1991) was commissioned by an American publishing house; as Kahn uses the assignment to cover the trial for her own "work of mourning" (Freud 1917), her writing delves into the memory of her father further than ever before. Thus, in the epilogue she can exclaim that the work on the book has changed her profoundly: "As for me, I have come out of the Barbie trial a different person. Thanks to the trial, and to this book, I have finally gotten to know my father. I have taken the faint memory of a man, a mere fistful of dust, and lent him substance" (1991b, 238).

In one of the chapters, Kahn talks about her mother's silence she had encountered as a child and later as an adolescent who was afraid that she would have to listen to her mother's stories about her and her husband's past. Cover-

1. The French version of Kahn's book, *Robert et Jeanne à Lyon sous l'Occupation* (1990), differs in several respects from the English edition. On Kahn, see Gorrara 1998, 117–20.

ing the trial, Kahn for the first time in her life begins to approach her mother, "determined to make her speak," while feeling that she is becoming her mother's torturer. In her following book, *Personne ne voudra nous croire*, 1991 [Nobody Will Believe Us], Kahn refers to the children's complicity in their parents' silence as the point of departure of her new interest in documenting the testimonies of survivors, "afin que ces voix nous survivent à jamais" (1991a, 8) [so that these voices outlive us forever]. Kahn has put her writing in the service of preserving the memories of a generation of witnesses who, as Elie Wiesel indicated in his testimony at the Barbie trial, are about to perish: a form of affiliation initiated by the act of revisiting her filial bonds against the backdrop of judicial writing.

One extreme of the literary reaffirmation of the filial principle pushes autojudeography to a point where the "auto" dissolves into the biography of the father to cement the author's Jewishness. Following a trajectory set up by Albert Cohen's *Le livre de ma mère* (1954) [The Book of My Mother], which memorialized the mother as the guardian and guiding force of a childhood to which Cohen looks back full of melancholy, Pierre Pachet's *Autobiographie de mon père* [Autobiography of My Father] (written in 1985 and published two years later) fuses the voice of the son, the narrator, with that of the father. Born in 1937, Pachet looks back on experiences different from those of his younger colleagues whose formative years fell in the period of postwar reconstruction. Unlike him, they learned to look at the institution of the family as well as at the politics of Jewish communities with empathetic rather than critical eyes. Pachet acknowledges the book's mission to continue the narrative, if not the life, of the deceased father:

> La parole de mon père mort demandait à parler par moi, comme elle n'avait jamais parlé, au-delà de nos deux forces réunies. Elle me niait, me demandait mon aide pour se consacrer à elle-même, et je voulais cela (c'est pourquoi je n'apparais presque pas dans ces pages).
>
> J'avais cette voix en tête, je n'avais même qu'elle. Elle était en moi la voix la plus spontanée.
>
> "J'avais cette voix en tête": folle présomption. J'ai cru et voulu l'avoir. Je me suis accroché à cette illusion pour la transformer en projet, et m'y enchaîner. J'ai voulu être l'héritier. (1987, 5)

> [My dead father's voice demanded to speak though it had never spoken, beyond our combined strength. It repudiated me, demanded my help to in

order to devote itself to itself, and I wanted that (that is why I almost never appear in these pages).

I had this voice in my head, I in fact had nothing but that. It was the most spontaneous voice in me.

"I had this voice in my head": foolish presumption. I believed I had it and wanted to have it. I clung to this illusion in order to transform it into a plan, and go on with it. I wanted to be the heir.]

This passage from the author's preface points to the inherent contradiction in the narrative design of an "autobiography" of a father authored by the son. This construction is set in motion by the paternal voice that summons the son to function as its medium of articulation, very similar to the mother-daughter relationship in Colette Fellous's *Rosa Gallica*. Pachet plays with the rhetorical convention of invocation, which has the writer appeal to the muses for inspiration, and has the ghost of the father seek in his son a voice of identification.

Anne Rabinovitch and Alain Fleischer follow to a certain degree Pachet's paths of filial admiration. Rabinovitch (the daughter of Wladimir Rabi) does this in a most subtle manner: in her fiction, the father is ubiquitous and constantly referred to in allusions, but he never appears as a figure. Conversely, in Alain Fleischer's short autobiographical pieces, the father's presence emerges as the image the son faces looking into the mirror of the autobiographical text:

> J'ai mis longtemps à reconnaître mon père, longtemps à déceler en quoi j'étais absolument son fils, son descendant dissemblable, longtemps à faire la part du ressemblant dans la dissemblance, longtemps à me voir en lui, à le voir en moi, longtemps à l'aimer peut-être, longtemps à remonter le fil des mots jusqu'à lui dans cette langue commune, le français, maternelle, pour moi, étrangère jusqu'au bout pour lui, longtemps avant de parler avec lui, de jouer avec lui, longtemps avant de m'approcher autrement qu'avec crainte de cet étranger taciturne, farouche, pudique, longtemps non pas à réduire son étrangeté, son *étrangèreté*, qui restèrent entières, mais à quitter, pour aller vers lui, le monde de référence, le monde familier, le monde familial. (1999, 235)
>
> [I put a lot of time into recognizing my father, a long time into figuring out in what respects exactly I was his son, his dissimilar descendent, a long time taking account of resemblance in dissimulation, a long time seeing myself in him, seeing him in myself, a long time loving him perhaps, a long time tracing this line of words back to him in this shared language, French, maternal for me, as foreign as possible for him, a long time before speaking with him,

> playing with him, a long time before approaching otherwise than with fear this taciturn stranger, fierce, prudish, a long time not to lessen his strangeness, his *foreignness*, which remained whole, but to leave behind, in order to go toward him, the world of reference, the familiar world, the familial world.]

The son's cautious rapprochement to his father is a step toward a declaration of love for a man and his idolatries. A lover of books by the anti-Semite Louis-Ferdinand Céline and of pork *charcuterie*, the atheist immigrant from Hungary has impressed on his son the notion that contradictions and inconsistencies are features of a biography to be cherished and valued rather than to be ignored or ironed out. With regard to the father's nonconforming way of being Jewish, the son responds by drawing the lines of his own position somewhat closer to tradition: "Je me sens peut-être encore plus juif que mon père" (1999, 244) [I feel perhaps more Jewish than my father]. Fleischer's portrayal of his father occupies virtually the entire space of his two "Autobiographical Fragments." Whenever the son appears in this or other autobiographical sketches by Fleischer, he does so in his relation to the father whose iconoclasm appears to be a key to Fleischer's aesthetics. Being, aside from Wajcman, the only author among his peers to share Georges Perec's taste for stylistic innovation, Fleischer (born in Paris in 1946) shows in his writing that he partakes both in Jewish and non-Jewish traditions and that his imagination is as much intrigued by secular French history and everyday life as it is by obscure tales surrounding Talmudic libraries. With respect to the breadth of his literary settings and styles, he is very much the son of Jewish modernism and its eclectic ability to amalgamate materials, notions, and traditions of very different provenance, similar indeed to his father's ability to cross boundaries.

Nonetheless, a critical rather than an identificatory perspective informs the exploration of the filial link to the Jewish past and to Judaism in the majority of contemporary texts. Patrick Modiano, Antoine Spire, Nickie Golse, Marco Koskas, Chochana Boukhobza, Gilles Rozier, and others take to task father figures who, in making their life choices, went down paths that appear to their children as historical dead ends. Guided by the desire of self-determination identified by Rosenzweig, autojudeography scrutinizes filial bonds and ancestral models to establish a form of Jewishness the authors can consider appropriate for their own lives.

The Color of the Dark Years of Occupation: Patrick Modiano's *Les boulevards de ceinture*

La place de l'étoile had formed the shrill overture to an oeuvre in which the father-son relationship and the cultural place of Jews during the Occupation are recurring themes. Modiano—son of a (non-Jewish) Belgian actress and a Jew whose roots go back to the Italian-Jewish community of Thessalonika and who in the Occupation had taken advantage of the collaboration—here renders a colorful portrait of a problematic father figure. In *La place de l'étoile*, the protagonist's father managed in 1944 to sell the forêt de Fontainebleau to the German occupiers and presents himself all the while as a role model to his son. Psychoanalytic readings of the texts have succeeded in discovering a pattern of son-father identification that goes far beyond the patronymic suffix of the protagonist's name, Schlemilovitch.[2] Modiano's second novel, *La ronde de nuit* (1969) [Night Round], features a double agent working for both the Resistance and Vichy who nevertheless remains an exemplary son to his mother, the only person he cares for in the world.

In *Les boulevards de ceinture* (1972) [Ring Roads], Modiano sketched, in a style more reminiscent of the minimalism of the *nouveau roman* than of his first novel, the fragile relationship between a father and his son. During the years of the war, the almost nonexistent bond between the two threatens to deteriorate from indifference to lethal intent. The Algerian-born Chalva Deyckecaire has broken off communication with his French-raised son for reasons that remain unknown both to the seventeen-year-old son and the reader. Why his black-marketeer and forger father would throw him in front of a metro train also escapes the understanding of the son, who is incapable of penetrating the wall that the father has erected around himself. Ten years after the incident, which the son survived, he begins his search for his father, eventually finding him shortly before the end of World War II in an underworld of former foreign legionnaires, profiteers, blackmailers, and collaborators. In this circle, Chalva, who will not recognize his son, barely scrapes by and is hardly being taken seriously by anyone around him. When the son becomes aware of the anti-Semitism of this milieu, his attitude toward his father turns from pity to solidarity with the weak man. In the heat of passion and desperation, the son kills one of the anti-Semitic agitators. During this act of violence, he ad-

2. See Chasseguet-Smirgel 1988.

mits openly both the Jewish descent of the father as well as his relationship to him, crying "C'EST MON PÈRE" (1972, 185) [THIS IS MY FATHER]. After fleeing the scene of the crime together, father and son again lose sight of each other. In the end, the son will be left only with a photograph to remind him of his father, who stands in the picture among his shady former comrades. The book ends with the advice of a bartender to whom the son has shown the photograph and who vaguely remembers the fate of the people in it. He would do better to think about his future than to pore over faded photographs, the barman laconically opines.

Modiano himself has commented on the symbolism of his protagonist's filial quest and its pathetic outcome, not by pointing to the double binds of Jewish existence during the Occupation in particular but by referring to the dissolution of ethical models in general:

> Ce père minable et fantomatique que recherche le narrateur peut être le symbole de beaucoup de choses. Symbole de l'effritement des Valeurs (avec un grand V), de la disparition de tout principe d'autorité et de toute assise morale, etc. . . . toutes choses qui étaient liées à l'image traditionnelle du Père. (1972, 2)
>
> [The pathetic and ghostlike father sought by the narrator can be the symbol of many things. Symbol of dissolution of Values (with a capital V), and of the disappearance of any principle of authority and of all ethical foundation, etc. . . . of everything traditionally linked to the image of the Father.]

For Henry Rousso, Modiano's early novels, which in France signaled the start of a *mode rétro*, are reflections and acknowledgments of the difficulties encountered by the parent generation in holding on to their integrity while living under the occupying forces: "Comment faire mieux trente ans plus tard?" (1987, 152) [How to do better thirty years later?]. Yet Modiano's novel also testifies to the desire of the children to learn more about the stories of those who happened to be Jewish during the war and who happened to find themselves giving in to the temptations of collaboration. Thus, the proclamation of Chalva's son in the decisive moment of murder is a revealing speech act indeed, for he does not declare "I am his son," but rather "THIS IS MY FATHER." Whereas the son would have posited himself actively within the relationship in the first formulation, in the latter he is present only indirectly via a possessive adjective. The son, who remains nameless during his entire narrative, did not avoid facing his father's dilemma, nor did he refrain from defending the honor of a broken man with whom he does not want to identify himself. Modiano's novel similarly accepts the burden of a legacy without proclaiming that legacy as its own. One may wonder whether the search for the father in France of the 1970s and 1980s would have gathered all its momentum without Modiano's powerful contributions to this part of the collective memory.

In one of Modiano's more recent books, he reconstructs painstakingly the fate of a Jewish girl who was deported from Paris to Drancy in 1942 while at the same time adding to the puzzle of his own autobiography. *Dora Bruder* (1997) is a documentary narrative that connects moments from the lives of Modiano and Bruder, older by twenty years, despite the fact that the two have never met or known each other. Coincidences between their lives stirred Modiano's curiosity and led him to search the archives and municipal registers for traces of Dora's existence. It seems as if the story of the unknown Jewish woman enabled the author to acknowledge moments of his own biography that he, at least at the beginning of his career, had carefully protected from the public: "En écrivant ce livre, je lance des appels, comme des signaux de phare dont je doute malheureusement qu'ils puissent éclairer la nuit. Mais j'espère toujours" (1997, 43) [In writing this book, I send out signals, like a lighthouse beacon in whose power to illuminate the darkness, alas, I have no faith. But I live in hope (1999, 35)]. Modiano's attempts to shed light into the gray areas of the past concern both the disappearance of Dora Bruder, who had lived in parts of Paris the author knew well, and segments of his own biography.

For example, *Dora Bruder* offers the key to an important episode at the end of *Les boulevards de ceinture*, in which the son voluntarily climbs into a police van with his father without knowing where this journey will end ("Rue des Saussaies? Drancy? Villa Triste?"). In *Dora Bruder*, we learn about a similar trip in a Black Maria, but this time the trip, for which the son had not volunteered, ends at the police station, where father and son will be cross-examined because the father had neglected to pay child support for the son. Modiano records how hurt he felt by his father's complete indifference toward his presence during this ride and goes on to provide yet another key to his first novel, *La place de l'étoile*, and with it to the raison d'être of his writing in general:

> Et cela me semblait d'autant plus injuste que j'avais commencé un livre—mon premier livre—où je prenais à mon compte le malaise qu'il avait éprouvé pendant l'Occupation. J'avais découvert dans sa bibliothèque,

> quelques années auparavant, certains ouvrages d'auteurs antisémites parus dans les années quarante qu'il avait achetés à l'époque, sans doute pour essayer de comprendre ce que ces gens-là lui reprochaient. Et j'imagine combien il avait été surpris par la description de ce monstre imaginaire, fantasmatique, dont l'ombre menaçante courait sur les murs, avec son nez crochu. . . . Moi, je voulais dans mon premier livre répondre à tous ces gens dont les insultes m'avaient blessé à cause de mon père. Et, sur le terrain de la prose française, leur river une bonne fois pour toutes leur clou. (1997, 72–73)
>
> [And I felt the injustice of that all the more since I had embarked on a book—my first—in which, putting myself in his shoes, I relived his feelings of distress during the Occupation. A few years earlier, among his books, I had come across certain anti-Semitic works from the forties, books that he must have bought at the time in an effort to understand what it was these writers had against him. And I can well imagine his surprise at the portrayal of this imaginary, phantasmagoric monster with clawlike hands and hooked nose. . . . As for me, I wanted my first book to be a riposte to all those who, by insulting my father, had wounded me. And, on the terrain of French prose, to silence them all and for all.] (1999, 57–58)

The biography of Dora Bruder, it turns out, is simultaneously a portrait of the artist as a young man who, had he been born a few years earlier, likely would have shared her fate. It is a book that compares the author's position in history with those of the victims of the Shoah and of the war, of whom Dora is just one example among many, but nonetheless worthy of all the research the author can possibly undertake. The lives of four poets—the Germans Friedo Lampe and Felix Hartlaub, and the Frenchmen Roger Gilbert-Lecomte and Maurice Sachs—likewise arouse Modiano's interest because of the date of their death: "Beaucoup d'amis que je n'ai pas connus ont disparu en 1945, l'année de ma naissance" (1997, 100) ["So many friends whom I never knew disappeared in 1945, the year I was born" (1999, 81)]. Modiano, who at the beginning of his career as a writer had his protagonists hide themselves in an endless charade of changing identities, almost thirty years later retrieves in minute detail the little evidence that exists to help identify and particularize figures from the past. Without his efforts, these figures, such as Dora Bruder, his father, and many others commemorated in this book, would have been forgotten forever. Whereas his earlier works had mingled fictional characters with those of his own family, *Dora Bruder* juxtaposes documentary materials about men and women previously unknown to the author with personal memories of real relatives. The text thus reads as the precise mirror image of the books that made the young Modiano the avenger of his estranged father. In this mirror the picture of the family has changed and now includes adopted members, hence the word "Bruder"—from the German "brother"—in the title.

Pierre Goldman's Good Jewish Son

In jail, Pierre Goldman had written his autobiography *Souvenirs obscurs*, which was a somber response to an unfounded criminal charge and to a courtroom atmosphere that he considered racist. Acquitted and released from prison, he wrote his novel *L'ordinaire mésaventure d'Archibald Rapoport*, which is a hyperbolic response to the anti-Semitic projection of the Jew as the criminal subverting the *Grande Nation* and a written fantasy of his indomitability. The book also documents his longing to participate in, if not to create, a work of historiography that would redeem the humiliations suffered by the Jewish people. Whereas his autobiography had fought for personal redemption in an almost legalistic manner, his novel evokes nothing less than a mythopoetical framework:

> Quand l'indicible, enfin, sera gouverné par les écorchures invisibles de la transparence, quand l'écorce brûlée des évidences illuminera le règne opaque de la douleur normale, les chroniqueurs de la malédiction, qu'ils soient bénis, diront, s'ils disent encore, l'histoire sans fin d'un Juif étrange qu'attendait l'échafaud. (1977b, 11)
>
> [When the unspeakable, finally, is taken over by the imperceptible scratches of clarity, when the burned surface of the facts illuminates the opaque reign of normal sadness, the chroniclers of the curse, let them be blessed, will tell, if they are still speaking, the endless story of a strange Jew who waits for the scaffold.]

The beginning of Goldman's novel reads like the opening of a mystical, archetypal narrative that introduces the reader to the sufferings of a hero of special status and singular nature. Goldman's novel appeared in 1977, shortly after his release from prison and two years before he was killed by members of a right-wing group. Although both books bear titles that put them into the tradition of the picaresque, the difference between the narrative styles employed at the beginning of the curriculum vitae and of the novel show that Goldman will take full advantage of the inventive license granted to the fiction writer. The tradition of the picaro allows for a hyperbolic treatment of the fate of a hero who is a member of the underprivileged class; we follow him as he weathers the upheavals of historical events, sometimes outwitting fate through his ingenuity and naïveté. The image of torment sketched out in the opening of Goldman's novel places the story of the hero in a large, universalizing frame as part of a long history of the anonymous foreign Jew on the verge of the forgotten and unspeakable. Again, hyperbolic embellishment and the humorous effect created by the contrast between the humble status of the protagonist and his heroic deeds are generic traits of the picaresque novel, as are overnarrating, grandiloquence, and, for that matter, the sudden shifts in the protagonist's fate.

Goldman's *L'ordinaire mésaventure* continues by describing the circumstances surrounding the birth of the protagonist, Archibald Rapoport, shortly after the heroic death of his father, an active member of the *résistance*. His mother introduces the newborn to the long and unending chain of suffering inflicted on the Jewish people. To commemorate his father's martyrdom, she puts her child under a magical spell: he can never laugh or cry; his father's martyr-death will prevent him from giving in to the weaknesses of a normal human life. The rift between this mock-autobiography and Jean-Jacques Rousseau's *Confessions*, the archetype of French autobiographical writing, could not be broader. Whereas both Rousseau and Rapoport take up the pen to depict their misfortunes at length, Rousseau, writing within the cult of sensibility, declares at the outset that he is a person of early and deep passions who as a child already "tous les sentiments m'étaient déjà connus" (1973, 37) [had felt everything]. The emotional framework bestowed on the young Rapoport is the very opposite.

Had the mother's spell failed to impress the sufferings of the Jewish people upon the newborn, her next act certainly would have succeeded in doing do so: immediately after her child's birth, she kills an S.S. officer visiting a nearby brothel with a knife normally used to circumcise Jewish boys, thus plunging her infant permanently into a family history of militant action and extremism. Within the first two pages of the novel, the stage upon which the protagonist will lead his life is set: he will grow up among Jewish partisans, be educated by a former prostitute, and find comfort and inspiration by socializing with other outcasts such as homosexuals, political extremists, and transvestites. In postwar France, the spell cast by his mother becomes the boy's mission as he follows his parents' path, fueled by a strange fascination with violence first encountered while watching the Algerian war unfold. Driven by his disgust for "pouvoir colonial" [colonial power], Rapoport will join various liberation movements, ultimately transforming himself into an outlaw.

Goldman's novel is a remarkable examination of the motivations and confinements of an extreme life experienced—and released—in the realm of imaginary deviance, rather than in reality. Goldman has historical discourse intersect with sexual discourse in a most peculiar way: the mother's killing of the Nazi officer with the knife used in circumcision is juxtaposed with the scene of the protagonist's circumcision by his aunt in a manner that carries provocative sexual undertones. Foucault's notion that "généalogie . . . est donc l'articulation du corps et de l'histoire" (1971, 154) ["genealogy is situated within the articulation of the body and history" (1984, 83)] appears here in extremely combative forms: as the corporeal resistance of the genealogical bond against the power of history (for which the mother, to be sure, eventually will have to pay with the loss of her life) and as the sexualization of the body in an almost carnevalesque confirmation of the genealogical principle. The partisan spirit of Rapoport's family embraces acts of political as well as sexual dissidence: in this respect, the sexual initiation of the adolescent protagonist by his prostitute aunt complements the ideological legacy of his parents. Thus, Goldman's protagonist does not revolt against a code of behavior set by his predecessors by leading the uninhibited sexual life of an enfant terrible. On the contrary, even in this respect he behaves very much like a dutiful son inheriting a family tradition of sexuality, unconcerned by the plea for libidinal constraint.

In yet another aspect of loyalty to family traditions, Goldman stuns the reader with the father-son relationship that informs the entire biography of Rapoport. The author constructs a system of filial symbolism in which a messiah (Rapoport's father) dies, leaving his son (Rapoport) to redeem his family and the Jewish people killed by the Nazis:

> et Archibald Rapoport voulut pleurer, ne pleura pas, murmura mon Dieu mon Dieu je ne crois pas en toi et son murmure devint une psalmodie où il invoquait son père Chmoul et il disait Chmoulek mon père ô mon père je t'en supplie délivre-moi de cette douleur qui couvre ma chair et mes viscères mes os mes nerfs et me brûle comme une peau d'angoisse pérenne délivre-moi rends-moi à la vie je suis un mort vivant qui meurt sans vivre. (1977b, 120)
>
> [and Archibald Rapoport wanted to cry, did not cry, murmured my God my God I do not believe in you and his murmur became a chant in which he in-

> voked his father Chmoul and he said Chmoulek my father oh my father I beg you deliver me from this sadness which covers my flesh and my intestines my bones my nerves and burns me like a perpetual skin of anguish deliver me give me to life I am a living dead who dies without living.]

Rapoport utters his Christ-like plea after he has committed several murders. He believes himself to be insane and is pondering suicide. As the "juif maudit," he had been charged with an impossible mission. The personal and the political become fused and confused in this unrealizable quest, just as Jewish Messianism and the tradition of the imitation of Christ become conflated in the syncretic passage just quoted. To place oneself in the position of God's son is the ultimate form of autonomy permissible within the realm of religion: proclaiming oneself a direct offspring of the Eternal One is an unmistakable act of self-filiation rivaled in its hubris only by patricide. But then, who will kill God if he is the embodiment of the resistance fighter?

Goldman's protagonist Rapoport pushes his mission to the extreme of lonely guerrilla warfare; in a similar fashion, the author himself ultimately pushes his literary mission beyond the picaresque in an attempt to create a novel about Jewish life not at the margins of society—and literary history—but far beyond them. To find models for his societal heretic, Goldman looks to the black masses imagined by the (Catholic) decadent Joris-Karl Huysmans and draws on the Marquis de Sade, Antonin Artaud, and Jean Genet for inspiration, all of them authors who, like his protagonist toward the end of his life, were driven to experience physically the connection between the realms of writing and of extreme corporeal sensations.

Both Patrick Modiano and Pierre Goldman describe seemingly infinite trajectories of filial loyalty in their narratives, trajectories borne out by protagonists who, rather than simply fulfilling the missions handed down to them by their parents, execute the orders of their forebearers in the most extreme manner possible: they are enfants terribles precisely because they are such loyal children. "Les jeunes se rebellaient contre le père parce qu'il symbolisait l'ordre. Mais quand le père ne représente pas l'ordre, tout se complique" [Young people rebel against the father because he symbolizes the establishment. But when the father does not represent the establishment, things become complicated], Modiano once stated in an interview,[3] and the mother of Goldman's antihero Rapoport at one point suggests, "les Juifs sont le peuple de

3. See Texier 1969.

la fidélité absolue absolument infidèle" (1977b, 23) [The Jews are the people of absolutely disloyal absolute loyalty]. Self-commentary and fictional speech here provide convex images of filial relationships held together by the adhesive powers of obedience *à contre cœur*.

Shock the Israelite: Antoine Spire's *Le silence en héritage*

From the beginning, Jewish writers have been intent on tackling the question of what it means to be Jewish after the Shoah in a country whose population still is predominantly Catholic and that only recently has shown signs of appreciating other cultures and religions. Imagining answers to these questions, their texts express their attitudes toward the French nation, an important concern especially for the authors who have immigrated to France, but one also raised by the offspring of French Jewish families who had seen their countrymen participate in the roundups during the Vichy Regime.

The question of how their parents and grandparents have been living as Jews in France or as French Jews during and after the Occupation, however, presents another focal point of contemporary Jewish writing. The very possibility of the project of acculturation becomes material for the literary examination of the biographies of the preceding generations of Jews. The slightly nostalgic or at times sentimental tone to be found in many a text describing the intact Jewish lives and communities of the prewar era has no parallel whatsoever in Antoine Spire's exploration of the type of the "convert":

> Enfant de "convertis," je souffre d'un effet à retardement de ce que les juifs ont subi, non pas que je me glisse complaisamment dans la peau d'une victime, mais je sens peser sur ma conscience le silence de ceux qui n'ont pas pu regarder de face le Moloch. (1988, 187)
>
> [As a child of "converts," I suffer the belated effect of what Jews have endured, not that I slide complacently into the skin of a victim, but I feel weighing on my conscience the silence of those who could not look Moloch in the face.]

Le silence en héritage [The Silence in Heritage], which appeared in 1988, offers the most extreme case of the drama of separation and of the tensions that the dynamics between children and parents can take on. Spire, a former editor in chief of *Le matin* and contributor to the weekly program *Voix du silence* [Voice of Silence] on the radio station France Culture, prefaces his novel with a quote from the Book of Ezekiel (18:2): "Les parents ont mangé des raisins verts et les dents des enfants en ont été agacées" [The parents ate green grapes and the children's teeth were irritated]. It was not by chance, the readers will eventually learn, that Spire chose a saying of a prophet who predicted the reconstruction of the destroyed temple. The underlying tension of the novel—the discontinuity between parents and children—has thus been prefaced in religious terms, authorizing the critical attitude of his young protagonist against the Israelites, embodied in his own parents. The first-person narrative features the story of the forty-year-old son Serge, who was born in France during the first years after the end of World War II. Organized as a confessional monologue, the account of his life nevertheless reads primarily as a *J'accuse* directed at his father's past. During his studies at the École normale supérieure on the rue d'Ulm, Serge's father had converted to Catholicism under the influence of his classmate Simone Weil and her charismatically presented critique of Judaism. Serge will have to struggle with his father's decision for the rest of his life, since he sees in it a betrayal of the family's past and the origin of his own pathogenesis. He remembers how as a child he had envied friends who had grown up within a home of intact bonds with Judaism: "C'est sans doute au contact de Sarah que le judaïsme m'est apparu comme quelque chose de plus que l'héritage de la persécution ou la fidélité à cette loi dépassée que mon père avait voulu remplacer" (1988, 19) [Without a doubt, it was under the influence of Sarah that Judaism appeared to me as something more than the legacy of persecution or loyalty to the outdated law that my father had wanted to replace].

Serge's career and the foundations of his world become shattered when he has to face the consequences of a violation of ethical and procedural medical standards while helping a young woman after her abortion. His actions cause the woman's death and leave him in an almost hopeless psychological state, which he perceives against the backdrop of Kafka's novels. Spire, however, directs the vagueness of Kafka's powerful existential metaphors of persecution to point to the estrangement of contemporary Jewish existence. Serge's "fall" and subsequent run-ins with the law appear to be symptoms of his inability to find his own identity, a process that has been aggravated by his family's turn away from their roots out of self-hate and inferiority complexes. The narrator-protagonist at one point even reaches for a comparison to Kafka's Gregor Samsa to acknowledge to himself his state of growing desperation and separation from reality.

Only reestablishing the link to Judaism that had been severed by his parents seems to offer him comfort and rescue. In jail he finds consolation even in the memory of the gravest parts of Jewish experience: "Une image m'a beaucoup aidé, c'est celle du camp de concentration. Je pensais à mon oncle qui y est mort, à ceux qui étaient des amis proches de ma famille et qui y avaient disparu" (1988, 56) [One image helped me greatly: that of the concentration camp. I thought of my uncle who died there, of those who were close friends of the family and who disappeared there]. Without going so far as to compare himself with the inmates of the camps, he does see himself within a continuous history of suffering by the Jewish people and thus turns to the Bible for help. Facing his trial, he prays with his friend and lawyer David, son of German-Jewish émigrés, who has managed to maintain the ties to his people's heritage and who introduces Serge to the ethics of Judaism and its conception of the law. In the successful public figure David, Serge finds an alter ego who aggressively and intelligently pursues his ambitions without, however, compromising his beliefs or his heritage:

> Comme si ce fils de juifs étrangers presque ignorés par la société française avait une revanche à prendre et qu'il était, pour ce faire, disposé à tous les compromis, comme s'il synthétisait à lui seul ces siècles d'histoire juive qui avaient transformé des parias de la société française en israélites respectables, fiers de leurs décorations et de leur guerre de 1914, prêts à tout pour s'assimiler et être considérés comme de bons bourgeois français. (1988, 37–38)
>
> [As if this son of Jewish foreigners almost unknown to French society had a revenge to take and as if he had been, in order to accomplish it, open to every compromise, as if he gathered into himself alone the centuries of Jewish history that had transformed them from the pariahs of French society to respectable Israelites, proud of their honors and their 1914 war, ready to do anything in order to assimilate and be considered good French bourgeois.]

The protagonist eventually learns to accept why decades ago people like his father left their Judaism behind and embarked on the experiment of conversion, just as he learns to recognize the luxury of his own position, granted to people only in specific historical circumstances. He is a reader of Elias Canetti, William Styron, and Myriam Anissimov, and entirely aware that his situation is by no means a unique one. On the contrary, Serge is highly conscious of himself as part of a group. Long passages of the book read like an essay on the struggle of Jews born after the Shoah to situate themselves within the history of Judaism and within the history of their families, conscious of the fact that they must often choose between the missions dictated by these two contexts.

> Il est souvent de bon ton de se moquer du retour au judaïsme d'une génération qui s'est précipitée dans la foi religieuse après avoir épuisé les joies amères des idéologies. Comme d'autres je me cabre sous l'injure de "juif imaginaire" et je veux moi aussi passer de l'ostentation à la fidélité. Je ne veux pas dynamiter les croyances d'hier. Seulement les relativiser. (1988, 191)
>
> [It is quite common to mock the return to Judaism of a generation that rushed into religious faith after having exhausted the bitter joys of ideologies. Like others, I balk at the insult "imaginary Jew" and I too want to move past ostentation to loyalty. I do not want to dynamite yesterday's beliefs. Only to relativize them.]

Serge turns to psychoanalysis, where he faces aspects of the familial bonds that had been unknown to him before, working especially toward a new understanding of the relationship to his mother. Yet the novel does not end by celebrating identity politics in the shadow of the power of history and society, even though Serge's move away from the master narratives of his rebellious youth has imbued in him a deep suspicion toward any system of belief or ideology. Even when his thoughts are occupied more and more with his childhood and past, he remains aware of the societal dimension of his quest and critically scrutinizes France's failure to rid itself of its mythical relationship to history:

> Mensonge que le cri de Jacques Chaban-Delmas à la barre du procès Barbie affirmant que la résistance était "une," que jamais, au grand jamais les libérateurs de la France ne s'étaient affrontés! Mensonge aussi que le silence obsédant de tous ces Français sur leurs abstention ou refus de résistance. Mensonge encore cet unanimisme de façade qui brosse le tableau d'une France gaulliste pour mieux cacher les camps de Gurs, de Rivesaltes, d'Aix ou de Drancy. (1988, 185)
>
> [A lie, the cry of Jacques Chaban-Delmas in the witness-box of the Barbie trial declaring that the Resistance was "one," a lie that the liberators of France never, never ever confronted! A lie too, the haunting silence of all the French upon their abstention or refusal to resist. Another lie, this facade of unanimity that paints the picture of a Gaullist France the better to hide the camps at Gurs, Rivesaltes, Aix, or Drancy.]

For the first time in the novel, the narrator-protagonist's full name—Serge Aaron—appears, set against the backdrop of the names of the perpetrators and collaborators. At the end of his account, Serge has managed to accept his failure and his fate, and has found the courage to rework the foundations of his life. When he ultimately decides to tell his mother about his decision to return to Judaism, she in turn surprises him with her confession that she, too, is about to take this path. Leaving behind the conceptual tone that has dominated long stretches of the book, the novel here embraces an almost symbolic notion of reconciliation between son and mother as the guarantors of the continuity of the Covenant within the family. Stepping out of the lawless and fatherless order of his youth, Serge finds in the newly restored ties to his mother a way back to the roots of his existence and to his people, thus undoing the tragedy imposed on the family by Simone Weil's misguided rationalism.

Expelled from Paradise: Nickie Golse's *Dans le jardin de mon père*

Nickie Golse sketches in *Dans le jardin de mon père* [In My Father's Garden], published in 1980, an even more complicated relationship between parents and children, examining how the forces of attraction and repulsion play out once the tensions have been transposed into the arena of the erotic. In Spire's novel, the family romance, to use Freud's notion of the child's imaginary restructuring of the relationships in the family, remained hidden underneath the surface. In Golse's book, however, it unfolds into a full-fledged family novel.

According to Freud, the desire to understand the life of the father by reconstructing it meets the daughter's need to transfer her love for the father, the first libidinal object, to other males. Anne, the protagonist and first-person narrator of Golse's novel, mourns the death of her father, Jacques, surprising the reader with her confession that she herself, rather than her mother, had been her father's true love. His death in 1978 becomes for her the occasion to settle her accounts with her mother, whom she holds responsible for the family's "déjudaïsation" (1980, 27) [de-Judaization] and thus for her father's unhappy life. For the adolescent Anne, her father's demise began when Jacques, a Polish Jew of little means, was introduced into her mother's well-to-do Parisian family, and with it into the acculturated establishment, whose arrogance, in Anne's eyes, is compensation for Jewish self-hatred:

> Comment s'y prit-elle pour rencontrer cet homme de trente ans, socialiste sans le sou, on n'a jamais voulu me l'expliquer . . . Comment Henri Meyer, son père, mon très cher Papy, patriarche argenté des tempes au portefeuille, francisé depuis le xviiie siècle, assimilé au point de déplorer l'indépendance d'un Maroc où il n'avait jamais mis les pieds, comment cet homme accepta-t-il pour gendre un "métèque," un "rastaquouère," jamais le mystère ne m'en fut révélé . . .
>
> C'est par ces termes en effet que mes grands-parents désignaient tout juif vivant hors d'un territoire idéal délimité par une ligne de métro imaginaire: Porte de Champerret, Miromesnil, Opéra. . . . Les habitants de cette cité dans la cité, aux conditions supplémentaires d'être français depuis au moins deux générations et d'exercer une profession "convenable" (médecin, avocat, financier, grand commerçant), avaient l'illustrissime honneur d'être des "Israélites." Pour les autres, les proscrits, les maudits, les réprouvés, on disait "juifs"! (1980, 27–28)
>
> [How she met this thirty-year-old man, a penniless socialist, they never wanted to tell me . . . How Henri Meyer, her father, my dearest Papy, patriarch silvered from his temples to his wallet, French since the eighteenth century, assimilated to the point where he deplored the independence of a Morocco that he never knew, how this man accepted for his son-in-law a dirty immigrant, a con man, that mystery was never explained to me . . .
>
> It is with these words in fact that my grandparents referred to every living Jew outside of an ideal territory bordered by an imaginary metro line: Porte de Champerret, Miromesnil, Opéra. . . . The inhabitants of this city within the city, with the supplementary qualifications of being French for at least two generations and of practicing a "respectable" profession (doctor, lawyer, banker, large-scale merchant) had the illustrious honor of being "Israelites." For the others, the outcasts, the damned, the banished, one said "Jews!"]

Anna's overwhelming pain about her father's death is an expression of the identification of the daughter, who had grown up without access to the traditions and the religion of Judaism, with her father, who fell victim to the mother's obsession with being accepted as a real French citizen.

The second chapter, however, casts light on the Lerbaum family from the perspective of Geneviève, the mother, who addresses her daughter in a letter that will reach its addressee much later in the book. This letter contains the story of a young woman who yearned to resist the pressure of her own parents and their social ambitions. Marrying a goy was not an option for her, even though her Jewish admirers all bored her. Her alliance with the poor tailor Jacques was a gesture of protest that would eventually take a disappointing turn: even as he climbed industriously within the social hierarchy of the family, Jacques quickly began to neglect his wife and children and to pursue lovers. Rejection and despair would later drive Geneviève into the arms of a former admirer, the non-Jewish Maxime, with whom she eventually conceived a child—Anne—whose paternity she revealed to no one.

In the following chapters, the narrative reaches a point where the family tragedy turns into melodrama: without Geneviève's knowledge, Maxime becomes Anne's lover. The dialogue between Anne and Maxime juxtaposes the life of a "juive inauthentique" [inauthentic Jew] and her "souffrances de déracinée" [uprooted suffering] with the experiences of her Jesuit-raised lover (1980, 168). Maxime even ventures to say that he would gladly have traded ten years of his excellent education for the experience of having lost a granduncle in Auschwitz. This may be meant to reveal the naïveté of a goy in dealing with the aftermath of the Shoah, but it also reflects a certain naïveté of the author in dealing with the subject matter of Christian-Jewish relations.

In a manner comparable to Antoine Spire in *Le silence en héritage*, Nickie Golse wrestles with the phenomenon of a legacy betrayed. In both cases, the misery of the youngest generation relates back almost causally to the misdeeds of a family patriarch who broke the covenant of his ancestors. The family drama that these authors unfold, clearly influenced dramaturgically by French classicism and its proclivity toward the design of Greek tragedy, tell the stories of offspring whose access to Judaism has been hindered by their rebellious turn away not from tradition but from their fathers' hubris. In the case of Golse's novel, there is a bitter lesson to be learned: against the daughter's will, the acculturated ways of the mother prove more formative than the heritage of the alleged father. Sharing in a certain manner the fate of her mother, Anne eventually marries, following not the call of her heart but the call of convention: only an ethnic, not an emotional bond draws her toward her fellow student Olivier. Anne indeed will depend on the mazel tov that seals her marriage and ends the novel.

Despite of the sentimentalism of Golse's novel,[4] one has to give the author credit for doing away with the monovocal mode characteristic of most of

4. The critic Gérard Valbert instead sees "l'art de se moquer de soi" [the art of mocking oneself] at play (Valbert 1980, 55–56).

the novels of young Jewish authors. The heteroglossia of *Dans le jardin de mon père* allows for a multitude of insights and the refraction of various attitudes and opinions within one narrative—a design that Golse uses to juxtapose sexes and generations as well as religions and ethnicities. She displays the painful process of re-Judaization and the emergence of a new Jewish identity within a societal constellation of opposing forces that all have their pull on the protagonist as she tries to find her own way back to the roots of her being.

The prevailing narrative design of the 1980s and 1990s does not display such a polyphonic structure. Authors in this period are primarily concerned with subject matter taken from their own experience, and the questions of identity formation they pose are too close to their own perspectives to provide scope for the surplus effect gained from switching between interior and exterior points of view. Such projects of working through the personal—even if their nature and impact are by no means confined to the individual who is articulating them—rarely allow for the luxury of narrative energies spent on a diversity of voices. Where the aesthetic discourse of minorities aims at defining the particular against the backdrop of society at large, forms of aesthetic concentration and segmentation offer themselves as appropriate means to measure the distance between the self and the Other. Especially when this difference is great, the choice of the monological narrative most adequately reflects the social estrangement of the protagonist.

Identification with the Dead: Henri Raczymow's *Un cri sans voix*

Many of the texts by the post-Shoah writers document a desire to uncover modes of Jewish existence that can take the place of the Israelite—a Jewish identity that no longer seems tenable after Vichy. In Claude Gutman's *La maison vide* [The Empty House] (a novel for young adolescents that first appeared in 1989), the fifteen-year-old protagonist rebukes his father retrospectively for having held on to his belief in France until his compatriots deported him. The son challenges the paternal denial of reality and the assimilationist credo of "quand on est en règle, on n'a rien à craindre" (1993, 13) [when one obeys the rules, one has nothing to fear] by blurting out, "Pourquoi tu n'as pas résisté, juste un peu?" (1993, 44) [Why didn't you resist, just a little?] The children of the victims sought a more combative model of Jewish identity to prepare themselves for the struggles to come; after all, one did not want to find oneself running into yet another "erreur historique" [historical error]. Historiography provided them with access to the legacy of Jewish resistance fighters who appeared to fill this vacuum (for example, *Il était des femmes dans la Résistance . . .* [There Were Women in the Resistance . . .] from 1978 by the Jewish novelist and historian Ania Francos, who was born during World War II).[5] However, in order to appropriate it for the present, this legacy first needed to be redefined. Pierre Goldman had the mother of his protagonist Rapoport choose the knife used for circumcisions to carry out her act of resistance, simultaneously initiating her son into an ethnically defined legacy of fighting against oppression. The fight against Fascism thus becomes a paradigmatically Jewish form of resistance, an alternative to becoming consumed by overriding ideological (that is, communist) concerns. Rapoport is thus spared the difficulties that trouble the children of the Israelites, although he will fail to find a way to carry out his mother's mission in postwar France.

Henri Raczymow tackles another set of generational dynamics. The notion "un juif polonais ne reconstitue pas sa généalogie" (1982b, 9) [a Polish Jew does not reconstruct his genealogy] frames his *Rivières d'exil* (1982) [Rivers of Exile]. In this three-generation novel, Mathieu, a writer, tells the story of his grandparents, Polish Jews who settled in France in the 1920s. Mathieu is driven to look behind the absence of his own genealogy, the "white page" of his family's past, which in the world of the writer symbolizes both the prerequisite for, and the anxiety about, the act of writing. His obsessive drive to address this absence, Mathieu says:

> est plutôt le désarroi d'un archéologue désarmé et quasi sans repères. Alors, à côté du "site" sans vestiges, du "site" rendu à son désert premier, il reconstitue, fruit de son imagination plutôt que sa connaissance, un tracé d'hypothèses, les pointillés d'une fabulation plutôt que d'une mémoire. (1982b, 10)
>
> [is more the confusion of a disarmed archeologist without any landmarks. When, beside the "site" devoid of remains, the "site" reduced to its initial wilderness, he reconstructs, more from his imagination than his knowledge, a map of hypotheses, the dotted lines of a confabulation rather than a memory.]

5. Francos in her prologue points to the reemergence of anti-Semitism in France (as well as to the death of the German RAF terrorists in 1977) as one of the reasons for her research (Francos 1978).

Mathieu, who shares his name and his interest in family matters with narrators in other works by Raczymow, may very well be a stand-in for the author himself. His point of departure is certainly representative of the situation of many of his peers, who as writers have to fill in with their research and imagination what the "transmission d'une mémoire familiale" (1982b, 10) [transmission of family memory] failed to hand down.

A good part of Raczymow's subsequent work has been guided by the technique described in the passage quoted above. *Un cri sans voix* [A Voiceless Cry], published in English as *Writing the Book of Esther,* is the most remarkable piece of his oeuvre. Here, Raczymow deals with the obsessive efforts of a young Jewish woman to find in the history of her people models for identification that her own family could not provide. It shows how the desire to inscribe oneself into a history of activism can turn lethal, especially if the objects of identification themselves have paid for their struggle with their lives.

Raczymow prefaces his novel with a powerful quote from the autobiography of Pierre Goldman: "Longtemps j'ai pensé que j'étais né et mort le 22 juin 1942 . . . Je n'avais pas l'âge de combattre, mais, à peine en vie, j'eus l'âge de pouvoir périr dans les crématoires de Pologne" (1985, 9) ["For a long time I thought I was born and died on the twenty-second of June 1944 . . . I was not old enough to fight, but as soon as I saw the light of day, I was old enough to have been killed in the crematoriums of Poland" (1995c, n.p.)]. This aptly describes the dilemma that Goldman himself had tried to solve by aligning himself with the political terrorists of the 1970s. Esther, the main character of *Un cri sans voix,* feels equally compelled to devote her life, spared by the accident of her late birth from extermination in the camps, to the cause of resistance. Born in 1943 to Jews who had resettled from Warsaw to France, Esther commits suicide in 1975 by turning on the gas in her kitchen. In 1982, prompted by newspaper reports that compare the invasion of Lebanon by the Israeli army with the Wehrmacht's invasion of Poland and the conditions in occupied Beirut with those in the Warsaw ghetto, Mathieu Litvak, Esther's brother and the narrator of the novel, finally breaks the family's silence about Esther's tragic end.

Mathieu begins to view his sister's life in a new light, grasping that it was the Shoah that was responsible for Esther's death rather than a mysterious disease. Esther had attributed special, existential, significance to the fact that her birthday coincided with the day of the uprising in Treblinka: "Je suis née le 2 août 1943 en France. Mais c'est à Treblinka, ce jour-là, que j'aurais aimé mourir, que j'aurais dû mourir" (1985, 14) ["I was born on August 2, 1943, in France. But it's in Treblinka that I would have liked to die, that day, that I should have died" (1995c, 4)]. The readers will later learn that Esther had an aunt who had been deported in 1942 and was murdered—with whom Esther shares her name. With her grandmother Raisl, who was killed in Treblinka, she shares her middle name, Rose. Without ever having had a chance to meet either of these women to whom she has developed strong emotional ties, Esther takes on their legacy. Her position in her family is a precarious one for which Raczymow creates an intricate metaphor. Not infrequently, parents in families injured by the Shoah would unconsciously associate their children with the family members they had lost, imagining the lives of the children as continuations of the lives of the dead.[6] In this case, however, it is the daughter, Esther, who points to the losses in her immediate surroundings with her own life—and death. Pursuing resolutely her identification with the dead, she kills herself:

> Puis la naissance de Mathieu, après la guerre, agrandit le cercle de famille. Le cercle de famille élargit le trou en son milieu. Le cercle de famille décrivait le pourtour d'un trou. Un trou que rien ni le temps ne combleraient . . . plus le cercle s'agrandissait, plus le trou, au centre, s'élargissait. Un jour, il deviendrait vaste comme la mer. Alors peut-être ne le verrait-on plus, tant il serait vaste. Peut-être, songe Mathieu, Esther s'est-elle tuée pour faire en sorte que le cercle cesse de s'agrandir, que les bords du trou se resserrent, qu'on n'oublie pas qu'il y eut, qu'il y a encore là un trou. Qu'une génération entière de Juifs est née de ce trou, de cette mer-là. Qu'elle dut, autrement que d'autres, apprendre ou réapprendre à respirer. (1985, 195–96)

> [After the war, the birth of Mathieu expanded the family circle. The family circle enlarged the hole in the middle. A hole that nothing, not even time, could fill . . . The greater the size of the circle, the larger the hole in the middle. One day it would become vast as the sea. Then perhaps it would no longer be visible. Perhaps, thinks Mathieu, Esther killed herself to prevent the circle from enlarging, so that the perimeter of the hole would recede, so that we wouldn't forget that there was, there still is, a hole. That a whole generation of Jews was born of that hole, that sea. That this generation, unlike the others, had to learn or to relearn how to breathe.] (1995c, 185–86)

6. For the impact of the Shoah on the following generations, see Hass 1990.

Un cri sans voix succeeds in describing in a most subtle manner the breakdown of familial relationships in the aftermath of the Shoah and the various attempts at repairing and healing them. A complex play of changing perspectives and the multilayered characterization of the narrator produce effects of both empathy with and estrangement from the heroine, whose brother Mathieu is a loyal chronicler as well as a distant observer. His is the attitude of a Jew born after the Shoah who is therefore, according to the survivors, incapable of understanding what had happened: "tu ne peux pas comprendre. Tu es né après, toi" (1985, 212) ["you couldn't understand. You were born after the war" (1995c, 202)]. Mathieu has learned to suspend judgment and to withhold commentary on the stories he hears about his sister. Yet while he is aware that the past cannot exert on him the crushing power that killed his sister, he is also aware that he cannot simply ignore the void left by her death. He decides to write the novel about the Warsaw Ghetto on which Esther presumably was working before her suicide. This text constitutes the first part of *Un cri sans voix,* which focuses on the life of the young Esther and her artistic ambitions during the family's time in the ghetto. As author of this novel, which sometimes features Esther as the first-person narrator, Mathieu wants to pay homage to his sister by fulfilling her last wish: he wants to give her, in literary form, the death that she had been longing for in vain during her life. In the novel, resistance fighters surround Esther, exploring different ways of fighting and saving their people. Mathieu shares with his readers the knowledge that his sister had stared incessantly at a photograph featuring a group of resistance fighters; his novel amplifies the historic photo to an imaginary portrait that now includes Esther herself.[7]

In the second part of the novel, Mathieu describes his sister's life in Paris

7. In his novel *Quartier libre,* Raczymow has a woman whose brothers had been denounced and killed by French collaborators articulate her bitterness concerning the impotence of the resistance: "Car qu'ont-ils fait, elle se demande, tous autant qu'ils sont, fort de leurs décorations, de leurs médailles et de leur titres de gloire, pour sauver Heinz, son frère, et Rywka, la mère de son mari, et tous les autres? . . . Lui-même, Étienne, a-t-il parcouru le moindre millimètre en vue d'empêcher sa propres mère de partir pour Beaune-la-Rolande? Sa résistance, à quoi, tout compte fait, a-t-elle servi?" (1995d, 13–14) [Because what have they done, she asks herself, for all that they are, strong by their decorations, their medals, and their glorious titles, to save Heinz, her brother, and Rywka, the mother of her husband, and all the others? . . . Étienne himself, had he moved even a millimeter in order to prevent his own mother from leaving for Beaune-la-Rolande? What, in the end, had his resistance served to do?]

after the war and his ambivalent relationship with her. Her bouts of depression, her attempts to identify in her attitudes and even in her choice of clothing with the inmates of the ghettos had alienated the younger brother from this highly talented young woman who had always been closer to the hearts of their parents than Mathieu. By accentuating the stressed bonds between the siblings, the book eschews the danger of becoming merely a hagiography or overly simplifying the figure of Esther. Simultaneously, it renders a complex portrayal of life in the ghetto by depicting the ghetto as a *lieu de combat*, the site of the intense struggle of the Jewish resistance, as well as a space poisoned by the complicity of the *Judenräte* and their collaboration with the Nazis. Mathieu, more distanced both in age and in attitude from the Jewish plight in the ghetto than his sister, is a critical reader both of Esther as an imaginary Jewish resistance fighter, to allude to Finkielkraut's notion of the imaginary Jew, and of what appears to him as the inability of so many Jews to fight against their lot:

> Esther, Mathieu ne l'aimait pas. D'elle, il ignorait tout. Ou peu s'en fallait. Il ne la connaissait pas. Quelque chose en elle ou en lui l'empêchait de pouvoir et vouloir la connaître. Les années qu'elle avait de plus que lui, peut-être. Ou bien, qu'elle soit née pendant la guerre faisait qu'il la projetait du côté de ses parents et de leur génération. Du côté de la préhistoire. Ce n'était pas simplement que cette période l'ait précédé, il se trouvait surtout et en outre qu'elle avait été unique dans toute l'histoire de l'humanité. . . . [Mathieu] ne voulait plus en entendre parler. Et le dégoût que sa sœur provoquait en lui, il comprit plus tard, durant l'été 1982, que l'époque même de sa naissance en était la cause et la seule cause. Mais pourquoi ce sentiment de honte? Cela tenait-il à ce que les Juifs avaient été les artisans mêmes de leur propre extermination? Faites-vous recenser comme Juifs, leur dit-on. Et ils accourent se faire porter sur les listes, se faire apposer la marque juive sur leurs papiers d'identité. (1985, 140–41)[8]

> [Mathieu did not like Esther. He knew nothing about her. Or very little. He didn't know her. Something in her, or in him, prevented him from knowing or wanting to know her. Perhaps because she was older than him. Or perhaps

8. Mathieu even includes the German Jews in his critique: "les Juifs allemands auraient été nazis comme les autres Allemands si les nazis n'avaient été antisémites" (Raczymow 1985, 140–41) [The German Jews would have been Nazis like all the other Germans if the Nazis had not been anti-Semites].

> the fact that she was born during the war made him cast her on his parents' side and the side of their generation. On the prehistoric side. It wasn't only because this period had preceded him, but also because it had been a period unique in all of human history. . . . He didn't want to hear about it anymore. And he understood later, during the summer of 1982, that the disgust that his sister provoked in him was due, and due only, to the period of her birth. But why this feeling of shame? Was it because the Jews had masterminded their own extermination? Have yourself registered as Jews, they were told. And they eagerly inscribed themselves on lists, had the Jewish mark stamped on their identity papers.] (1995c, 130–31)

In Esther's judgment only the victims are allowed to speak the unspeakable by articulating their experience of suffering: "Les autres, et surtout ceux nés après la guerre, qu'ils se taisent, se taisent. Leur parole est obscène, impudente" (1985, 129) ["The others, especially those born after the war, should keep quiet, be silent. Their words are obscene, impudent" (1995c, 119)]. Her story then is a tragic one also because she imposes on herself the verdict of silence, depriving herself of the possibility to capture the nightmares of the past in works of the imagination. It seems as if Esther has to die because she cannot save herself by speaking. Mathieu, on the other hand, decides to write both about life and death in the ghetto and about the life and death of his sister, and this decision must be read as Raczymow's programmatic stance in the aesthetic debates of the possibility of representing the Shoah. His move to speak for her is a conscious transgression of one of the most powerful aesthetic verdicts issued by a variety of historians and philosophers after the Shoah, among them Saul Friedländer, who posed the problem in the following way: "Does an event like the 'Final Solution' allow for *any kind* of narrative, or does it foreclose certain narrative modalities?"[9] The anthropologist Inga Clendinnen recently challenged the theoretical assumptions behind the idea that the Shoah is an incomprehensible experience, a "singular category of one" (1999, 88), and instead insisted that literature—as long as it avoids simplifications and the notion of closure—indeed is capable to represent it: "Writers must destroy silence in order to represent it" (1999, 177).

Raczymow's *Un cri sans voix* displays an acute consciousness of the perils of the banalization of evil to which many forms of depicting the disaster are prone. The book poses the question of how to deal with the horrors of the past

9. Friedländer quoted in Clendinnen 1999, 17.

by juxtaposing Esther's identificatory reembodiment of history (as the most extreme form of representation) with her brother's reimagination of it, which he authors as a last honor paid to Esther. His account destroys the silence (as Esther's suicide is her reenactment of the silence of the victims) by trying to demystify it. Death, he speculates, is a form of keeping your secret, even if you have nothing to hide.

But the book also provides an aesthetic maxim according to which the author has to remain a distance to the Shoah and its victims as every form of identification fundamentally imperils—that is the fate of the writer Esther—the very undertaking of writing. And while Raczymow continues in his fiction to draw closer to the experience of the victims, his narrator, Mathieu, at the end of the book instead wants to consider the case of the Esther, the escaped victim, closed for good. Writing about Esther as well as Esther's story, he has separated his own attitude toward the past of the Jewish people from Esther's. The trajectory of this separation continues. He wants to spare his children the burden of his people's and his family's past:

> Mon enfant, du passé, sera épargné. Il n'en portera nul stigmate. Ce sera vraiment un enfant d'après. Entre la guerre et lui, une génération aura grandi, un espace qui l'aura préservé comme d'une souillure abominable. Jamais je ne lui parlerai d'Esther. Son nom sera tu. Mon livre l'aura effacé. . . . Aucune filiation d'Esther à cet enfant. Sinon ce livre, peut-être. Mais un livre, rien de plus. (1985, 213–14)

> [My child will be spared the past. He won't carry its stigma. He'll really be an *afterward* child. Standing between him and the war would be a new generation, an interval of space that could protect him as if from a horrible taint. Never will I talk to him about Esther. Her name will be dead. My book will have blotted her out. . . . No direct line ("filiation" in the original—author) from Esther to this child. Except maybe through this book. But only a book, nothing more.] (1995c, 203–4)

Thus, *Un cri sans voix* ends with a gesture of resignation since, after all, one cannot ward off the past by recounting it.[10] For the sake of his son's future, Mathieu wants to reestablish the taboo that the family had erected around the death of Esther and that Mathieu himself had torn down with his account, the

10. Fine talks about Mathieu's "exorcism" (Fine 1985, 121–36). See also her seminal essay "The Absent Memory" (Fine 1988).

secret of her life, which, guarded by her suicide, he may never penetrate. And yet, Mathieu, too, knows that from now on Esther's fate can no longer be wrapped in silence since there is a book that will commemorate her life: "Mon livre l'aura effacé. Il fallait des mots, curieusement, pour cela. Des mots, et non du silence" (1985, 214) ["My book will have blotted her out. Oddly enough, you need words for that. Words, and not silence" (1995c, 204)]. There is the strong desire to replace the power of family ties by the power of the book, by the imaginative testimony that can substitute the forces of identification governing the family with the play of identification, with the cathartic power of literature. This force is so strong that neither Mathieu nor the readers ultimately can be sure that Esther wasn't just a figment of his imagination.

In this respect, Raczymow's book also has to be appreciated as a Purim story, as a very powerful contribution to the revisitation of this part of the biblical canon. The allusions to the biblical figure of Esther allow Raczymow to place the story of the modern Esther in a complex historical context of resistance to anti-Semitism. The reference to the original Esther, however, also embraces the notion of the vagueness of historical knowledge as well as of the question of authorship because Esther, according to tradition, is the author of the Book of Esther. However, *Un cri sans voix* does not share the optimism of the Book of Esther, and instead of telling a story of success and an end of suffering, it tells the story of continuous suffering, which, interestingly enough, juxtaposes the old imperative of *zakhor* with a new one. Mathieu's insistence upon blotting out the memory of his sister is, after all, a curious reversal of the command to blot out the memory of Amalek, the enemy of the Jews, in Deuteronomy 25:19. Thus, the narrator's attitude toward the past appears to be no less problematic and extreme as his sister's, albeit for different reasons. Raczymov drives his novel to a point at which Mathieu finally ask the question "Si je suis devenu nazi?" (1985, 212) ["Have I become a Nazi?" (1995c, 202)], and he leaves it up to the readers to judge how the narrator has managed to deal with the predicament of his kin.

Myriam Anissimov's *Dans la plus stricte intimité*

With her book *Dans la plus stricte intimité* (1992) [Family Only], Myriam Anissimov challenged herself to render a portrayal of a relationship between a Jewish woman, Hannah, and a Christian nun, whom Hannah calls her mother, because in her childhood she had spent months under her care. On the surface, this constellation seems to allow for an autonomous creation of filial ties on the part of the daughter in front of her "two mothers." And it seems to allow for Judeo-Christian reconciliation or at least a rapprochement between the two faiths. Yet, vis-à-vis the nun's affiliation with a church that Anissimov eloquently condemns for its involvement in the Shoah, there remains no doubt in the protagonist's mind about whose child she really is.

The relationship with the nun, based on Anissimov's own experience of hiding for several months in Switzerland as a child while a member of a Christian order lovingly cared for her, has implications for the architecture of the autobiographically informed novel. This book, too, is an attempt to recover the family's past "pour ne pas éprouver une effroyable solitude" (1999, 30) [in order not to feel a dreadful solitude], as Anissimov writes in *Sa Majesté la Mort*. As such, it must tell how Hannah, whose family suffered severe losses in the Shoah, can sustain such an intimate bond to a non-Jewish woman, a member of the very church that history has shown to have been an accomplice in the persecution of Jews. The tensions governing the narrative run between different people and different creeds, between victims and persecutors, yet the narrator never pauses to emphasize these differences despite the feelings she continues to harbor toward Sister Blanche. Attending the memorial service for the nun, Hannah cannot help reviewing in her mind the history of the church's anti-Semitism, beginning with the synod of Elvira in 306 through the cross erected by the Carmelites in Auschwitz. Quotes from Luther's tirades against the Jews are juxtaposed with the priest's sermon on love and understanding. The next jump cut in the narrative—a favorite technique of the author—abruptly transposes the locale to Birkenau's railroad ramp, visited by Hannah and her partner. Yet this sudden transition does not interrupt the narrator's chain of thought, which chronicles the steps that led the Catholic Church into complicity with the Nazis. There is no doubt that among today's Jewish writers in France, Myriam Anissimov is the most engaged in reminding the reader of exactly what happened in the past. Her insistence may be explained not least by the author's age and thus her own experience of growing up with the perils of persecution.

The narrator ventures to rescue the memory of Sister Blanche by separating her from the institution to which she had devoted her life. While the priest eulogizes the many virtues of the nun, the narrator maintains that Blanche's commitment to the church had been built on very fragile grounds after all: Blanche had once revealed to her charge that she had entered the order only because of a banal childhood promise. With this knowledge in mind, the narrator can forgive what in principle she ought to condemn. Thus the task of reconciling the tensions brought into the architecture of the family portrayal by the presence of the Christian nun becomes more feasible. After all, the title of the novel, *Dans la plus stricte intimité*, stresses the exclusiveness of blood bonds, and indeed, it is primarily concerned with the narrator's own family. Hannah reminisces about childhood hours spent in her erudite grandfather's library and the Yiddish writers surrounding her father, but she also records the diverse facets of her cousin Benjamin's burlesque life as the family's black sheep.

The title also alludes to the many funerals attended by Hannah over the course of the narration. This reference, in addition to the descriptions of the visit of the death camp, gives the book a solemn tone from which only Benjamin's comic adventures offer occasional respite. Hannah's and her mother's common search for the tomb of her grandmother in the Jewish cemetery in Metz is one of the main threads of the narrative, and their ultimate success provides the kind of closure that most Jewish families in the last century were unable to achieve. But this ending does more than just provide closure to the narrator's and her mother's quest: it also reaffirms the bond of the family proper with respect to the task of sorting through the complexities of manifold filial relationships. The search for the lost tomb ends with a kaddish offered at the grandmother's grave and the granddaughter's feeling that her ancestor's soul has taken clandestine possession of her. In the light of such strong bonds tying the family together, the lot of Sister Blanche indeed vanishes into the background, while the lives of those remembered only from old photographs reenter the stage.

Norbert Czarny's *Les valises*

In his novel *Les valises* [The Suitcases], Norbert Czarny, born in 1954, takes up a challenge quite different from Anissimov's. Neither of these two authors conceals the many similarities between the fictional figures and their own relatives, and they both end their books with scenes at the graves of their grandmothers. And yet, stylistic differences abound. The irreconcilable tone that permeates Anissmov's look at the horrors of the past is foreign to *Les valises*, which appeared in 1989. The book is devoted to the life of the narrator's deceased grandmother, Mémé, who figured as a central, even legendary presence in her grandson's life. Accordingly, a sentimental and forgiving mood dominates from the beginning. The book opens with the assertion that Mémé's life has been an exceptional one—after all, she managed to escape the roundups of the French Jews in 1942 by hiding: "L'Histoire et ses grands acteurs n'avaient aucune prise sur Mémé" (1989, 49) [History and its great figures had no claim whatsoever on Mémé]. Where Anissimov has the names and cruel deeds of the perpetrators memorized, as it were, her younger colleague Czarny first of all has to consult the annals to provide the historical dimension for a life that seems to have taken place "hors de l'Histoire" (1989, 71) [outside of History].

Unavoidably, commemorative writing verges on hagiography, and the author of *Les valises* is well aware of this generic inclination as he reconstructs the grandmother's journey. His account follows her from her childhood as an orphan in imperial Vienna to her marriage in Lemberg and her eventual arrival in France where, for a short and remarkably murky period of time, she worked in the barracks of the German occupiers. It remains the narrator's retrospective task to mediate between the particularities of Mémé's position in a history of which she had never been aware and the historical processes that shifted the centers of power from France to Germany and back. The narrator has to diminish the elliptical character of the grandmother's memory, conveyed to him through numerous conversations, hints, and allusions, by submitting it to comparison with the grand historical narratives. Czarny indicates, in a boldly frank narrative move, that his narrator is not in immediate possession of the necessary historical knowledge to fulfill this task, that he needs to turn to the wartime annals to research adequately the facts behind Mémé's story: "Beaucoup plus tard, essayant de mettre de l'ordre dans ma mémoire (les souvenirs de Mémé m'appartenaient déjà, comme le pot à lait et les plantes), j'ai consulté un livre d'Histoire" (1989, 45) [Much later, trying to put my memory in order (the memories of Mémé already belonged to me, like the milk jug and the plants), I consulted a book of History].

The most challenging part of the narrator's endeavor, however, consists of reconciling a tension that runs through the middle of his family, between the grandmother on one side and his father on the other. The conflict concerns the question of whether the past may be continuing in the present; the different generations find different answers to this question, which becomes crystallized in the German nation. Mémé annually retreats to the Bavarian spa town of Rosenheim, to which the father objects categorically because the town is renowned for its annual gathering of former members of the S.S. Only at the end of the book does the narrator reveal that his father had been in a concentration camp, using the same tone of nonchalant resignation that characterizes his accounts of Mémé's life:

> Ainsi, avant d'avoir un passeport français, il avait eu, grâce à son avant-bras gauche, un papier d'identité. Dépouillé de son nom et de toute famille, après un voyage en train qui l'avait ramené au sud de sa ville natale, il avait reçu un numéro. (1989, 158)
>
> [Thus, before having a French passport, he had had, thanks to his left forearm, identity papers. Robbed of his name and of all family, after a train ride which took him south from his native village, he received a number.]

These attitudes toward Germany reflect the characters' attitudes toward the perils of anti-Semitism and, more generally, their understanding of history and power. The father perceives former perpetrators crossing his path when he finds himself on a street in Germany where he and his son are exploring the history of their people. The son, however, is trying to hold on to the impression his grandmother had instilled in him of a Germany that is "paisible, amnésique et joyeusement tournée vers le futur" (1989, 71) [peaceful, amnesic and joyously turned toward the future]. The narrator's inclination to side with the grandmother's attitude reflects his generation's position, which scrutinized the parents while looking at the grandparents with empathy and melancholy for an innocent world before the Fall.

Neither Mémé's obliviousness toward the malevolent powers at large nor the overestimation of their danger is a possibility Czarny's narrator can accept. He eventually settles the dilemma of determining which of the two sides he will choose by youthfully shifting the emphasis of the narrative away from this center of tension. *Les valises*, it turns out, chronicles as much the older generations' wanderings through twentieth-century European history as it documents the younger generations' need to understand the journeys of the ancestors in order to help them figure out why they are where they are and who they are. Glancing into the pasts of their families, they find their own reflections as if they were looking in old mirrors: blind spots abound, waiting to be filled in with images created by memory as well as by the powers of imagination.

"The Deflowered Family Story": Gilles Rozier's *Par-delà les monts obscures*

> Mon père avait fini de mourir. . . . Je voulais qu'il raconte, qu'il me transmette quelque chose d'une vie longue et discrète. Il m'aurait donné les mots de cette existence, je les aurais portés en héritière jusqu'à ce que la mort me déshabille à mon tour. Mais j'étais arrivée trop tard. (Rozier 1999, 11)
>
> [My father had finished dying. . . . I wanted him to talk, so that he would transmit to me something of a long and quiet life. He would have given me the words of this existence, I would have carried them as an inheritance until death undressed me in turn. But I had arrived too late.]

The opening of Gilles Rozier's *Par-delà les monts obscures* [Beyond the Dark Mountains], which appeared in 1999, projects the narrator in a position directly opposite to the stances taken by the narrators of Fellous's *Rosa Gallica* or Anissimov's *Sa Majesté la Mort*. However, all three novels share a historical point of departure marked by the fading presence of the grandparents and parents of the young writers. After all, it is one of the most essential features of the situation of young Jews writing in the 1980s and 1990s that they are working at the historical moment when the survivors are about to cease living. The death of their elders and the awareness that their own generation is the last one to have enjoyed direct contact with the survivors are essential points of departure for the literary endeavors of the younger writers.

What the outsider may consider a mere demographic phenomenon many writers experience as a very personal and even existential incentive to commit the experiences of the preceding generation to literary memory. The process of literary commemoration, however, has its own dynamics, which can resist original intentions; further, the process is often built on the fragile ground of difficult relationships handed down in a manner that mixes figments and fragments of remembered exchanges. Catherine Axelrad's *Vies et morts d'Esther* (1993) [Lives and Deaths of Esther] tells the story of Esther, the grandmother of the narrator, Catherine, who is loosely modeled on the author herself, leading in the end to a surprising reflection on exactly this act of storytelling. As Catherine pieces together family documents and recalled conversations about the anti-Semitism of her grandmother's Polish homeland and her experience living under a false name in occupied France, the historical events that marked Esther's Jewish identity emerge as important. Yet they are not the dominating episodes in their account of her life, which first of all celebrates the formation of a personality despite all these societal impediments. The narrator ends her sober reconstruction of Esther's life with a retrospective observation, introducing herself to the stage to evaluate her own performance as a biographer.

> Trois mois plus tard j'ai commencé à raconter sa vie, à l'encre bleue sur un papier brouillon rose où les mots se déformaient, absorbés comme par un buvard, dans un texte que je voulais froid et impersonnel (toute cette histoire ne me concernait en rien, et je n'étais pas de ceux qui règlent leurs comptes par écrit) mais dont le ton, en réalité sifflant et hargneux, m'a sauté aux yeux à la première relecture. Incapable de comprendre, ni de supporter, l'image que le papier rose me renvoyait, j'ai rapidement rangé, égaré puis définitivement perdu ce récit écrit il y a dix ans, dont seul le titre me revient aujourd'hui: *Vies et morts d'Esther*. (1993, 122)

> [Three months later I began to recount her life, with blue ink on coarse pink paper upon which the words lost their shapes, absorbed as if by a blotting sheet, in a text that I wanted to be cold and impersonal (this whole story did not concern me at all, and I was not one of those who settle their accounts by writing) but of which the tone, in reality hissing and aggressive, jumped out at me upon the first reading. Impossible to understand or to bear, the image of the pink paper came back to me; I quickly put away, mislaid, and then definitively lost this written narrative ten years ago, and only the title comes back to me today: *Lives and Deaths of Esther*.]

In retrospect, the text that she started to write a few months after her grandmother's death does not show the expected sovereignty of a biographer employing the means of distancing and objectivation. Instead it reveals, contrary to her own initial assumption, that the narrator has been engaged in the reconstruction of the facts and data at an emotional level as well. The act of reconstructing the past of the Jewish ancestors turns out to be a process with unexpected consequences: in Axelrad's case, it brings to light a type of relationship whose existence had previously gone unnoticed.

Let us return, however, to *Par-delà les monts obscures* (the title is borrowed from Sholem Aleichem), by Gilles Rozier. Rozier was born in 1963 in Grenoble and works in the Paris-based Yiddish library Bibliothèque Medem. This slim novel is also part of the considerable number of books by Jewish authors of the postwar generations that tell the tales of missed encounters between children and their parents and of the various hindrances separating the times before and after the war. What sets Rozier's novel apart is the fact that it follows a pattern of biographical writing that aims to surprise readers with the presentation of unexpected insights into facets or facts of the portrayed life. *Par-delà les monts obscures* is a revelatory text that describes a woman in her fifties who returns from Israel after her father's death to expose the history of her family. Here, too, a veil of silence has been protecting the pain of the survivors, and has unwillingly added to an early estrangement between parents and children. These circumstances impel the narrator to state at the outset, "J'étais née dans une famille où le passé avait été trop cruel pour qu'on eût la grossièreté de le faire partager" (1999, 12) [I was born into a family in which the past had been too cruel for anyone to be so rude as to share it]. And yet in the last analysis, she considers this suffering incomparable to the pain of being left in the dark about the mysterious things that happened in the past. As she and her sister put their deceased father's belongings into order, the narrator finds among his papers, more or less by chance, a notebook, which she instinctively decides to hide. Her instincts also tell her that her father's notes must be of a highly intimate nature and that filial loyalty would prohibit her from violating the sanctity of the journal. However, the terms she uses to indicate how she feels compelled to open it relate her curiosity back to the silence in which the father had wrapped the past: "Mais je ne parviens pas à me taire" (1999, 61) [But I could not manage to be quiet]. Indeed, she goes on to admit that she even begins to enjoy the act of violating the sacred convention of the privacy of the dead, as if she were taking revenge by forcing her entrance into the "histoire familiale déflorée" (1999, 62) [deflowered family story].

The language of the journals puts up a certain resistance against the daughter's force, since the father, a former inhabitant of the German-speaking part of Lemberg, had written his notes in his mother tongue, which his daughter had never learned. Thus, translating them is a laborious task of uncertain outcome; the daughter must fill in some lacunae that she cannot understand fully although she keeps insisting, almost defensively, that she has not added or invented anything at all. The secret that her reading reveals concerns the nature of her father's early relationship with his brother and provides a key to the daughter's understanding of her own upbringing as an unwanted girl and of her relationship with her sister. The secret is by no means related to the family's Jewish heritage, although the narrative eventually turns to Sholem Aleichem's "The Little Redheaded Jews," from which it borrowed its title and motto, for an interpretative framework.

By showing the daughter's tribulations in approaching the hidden layers of family relations, Rozier has her learn to recognize how, over the course of the years, her relationship to her parents and her sister, and also to her husband, have been petrifying. Her confrontation with her father's youthful obsession with his brother will become a stepping stone for a liberation that has already begun to change her attitudes toward her surroundings. Finally, the costs she had to pay in her youth for having been born the superfluous daughter rather than the wished-for son have been made clear to her. One desire, however, will remain unfulfilled: that of living her life without the demons of her parents and her sister, in whose towering shadow she has spent her youth, a life "par-delà les monts obscurs" [beyond the dark mountains]. The narrator borrows this metaphor from Sholem Aleichem's satirical novella that deplores the miserable existence of the "petits hommes rouges" [little red men], Jews who live shut off from Jewish traditions and therefore from truth and happiness. But the narrator does not subscribe to the rewards promised in Sholem Aleichem's story about the return from the Diaspora to the Jewish homeland because she has met there not an entire people but only one person, her husband. Staying in France rather than in Israel, she settles among the "little red Jews" with whom she shares the strongest of all bonds, a common language, which Israel, the "pays des surhommes juifs" (1999, 53) [nation of Jewish supermen], could not offer her.

Working in dialogue with Sholem Aleichem's narrative, as it were, Rozier's short novel occasionally takes recourse to Christian metaphors and acknowledges the vicissitudes of the Diaspora and the existential choices entailed in living there even as the last member of a family. And yet, precisely by alluding to Sholem Aleichem's novella of the lost tribes of Israel as his novel's hypertext (Genette 1982), Rozier succeeds in presenting an intimate awareness of the imperative of the *teschuva*, the reorientation toward the Jewish homeland, as the dilemma of his narrator. In this respect, *Par-delà les monts obscures* may be read as a statement of resignation, one that replaces the high hopes for a better life in the homeland with the notion of coming to terms with oneself and one's heritage—not because of one's surroundings, but despite them.

Family Ties of No Importance: Agnès Desarthe's *Un secret sans importance*

Agnès Desarthe's second novel, *Un secret sans importance* [A Secret of No Importance], poses the issue of paternal filiation in a very different manner. There are secrets, hidden actions, and clandestine events at play here as well, yet they have little in common with the silence that reigns in the worlds of many of the fictional families created in contemporary Jewish writing.

Un secret sans importance received widespread attention and was awarded the Prix du Livre Inter when it appeared in 1996. It is a remarkable piece in many respects, mapping the paths of six Jews whose lives intersect in an almost haphazard and even mystical manner. The milieu is the social circles of Parisian intellectuals, among them the linguist Émile who is falling in love with his young neighbor Violette, Émile's friend Dan whose observant wife Sonia is about to die of cancer, and the young student Gabriel who may be Émile's son. The novel's title refers to the motto that reads—together with its slightly altered version at the very end of the book—like a manual to the rather undernarrated text: "Chacun pense avoir un secret. Pour certains, c'est une douleur, pour d'autres, une joie. C'est toutefois sans importance, car, un jour ou l'autre, une main indifférente, tombée mollement du ciel, les moissonnera" (1996, 11) [Everyone thinks he has a secret. For some, it is pain, for others, it is a joy. It is in any case unimportant, because one day or another an indifferent hand, softly fallen from the sky, will harvest them]. The constellation of characters promises a larger tableau of contemporary Jewish life than offered in many of the more monovocal narratives that feature the formative years of protagonists outgrowing their childhood homes. Family relationships undoubtedly are of importance in this group portrait, but Desarthe manages to complement the family aspect by weaving a subtle net of relations and associations beyond the realm of the family. Instead of the principle of critical filiation, it is an almost unconscious and in the end metaphysical form of affiliation to an invisible community that brings these people together.

In the core of the vignettes of different notions of Jewish life, Desarthe places Sonia, invoking with this figure a notion of religiosity that almost never enters the agendas of writers of non-Sephardic origin. Describing the funeral of Sonia, the author includes a Jewish mourning prayer as well as an excerpt from the "Song of Songs" and mentions that both of these religious texts were met with the laughter of some of the younger attendees of the funeral. The attitude toward religiosity is not at all confined to such quotations. It figures prominently in the portrayal of characters who, like Sonia, had been brought up by Orthodox families to guide their own families in this tradition or who, like Violette, have been tested in their belief (Violette's husband died in the Yom Kippur War while she was pregnant with their child). Desarthe dedicates long passages to characterizing Sonia's intimate relationship to God, whom she continues to trust even though her illness will take her away from her many children. And there is Gabriel, the student of linguistics, who recalls how while growing up in his grandfather's house he had been introduced only to the austerity of the Hebrew Bible. While there are moments in the novel when the existence of God is cast in terms derived from the history of French philosophical inquiry, a mystical sphere surprisingly opens up after Sonia's death: as an angel, she will clandestinely improve the lives of the people surrounding her. In the light of such religious mysticism, the novel's closing lines now read as a positive counterpoint to the motto of the novel: "C'est toutefois sans importance, car, un jour ou l'autre, une main attentive, tombée doucement du ciel, les moissonnera" (1996, 210) [It is in any case of no importance, because one day or another an indifferent hand, softly fallen from the sky, will harvest them].

Desarthe, born in 1966 in Paris, in the script for the film *Cours toujours* (1999) [English title: *Dad on the Run*] succeeded in sketching the religious contours of contemporary Jewish life in France in a humorous and lighthearted manner. In her novel *Un secret sans importance*, she experiments with the notion of characters who, after their deaths, continue to have access to the world of the living, toying with the models set up by Cocteau and Sartre. Desarthe has Sonia arrange the promising life of the handsome Gabriel, who, due to her intervention, will never learn whether Émile indeed is his father. Émile's paternity remains a secret without importance in a world where for a few decisive moments Sonia's benevolent spirit has the chance to put the lives of her friends and acquaintances on the right track "avant de filer vers l'au-delá" (1996, 210) [before heading toward the beyond]. Sonia's intervention preserves Gabriel's autonomy by keeping the question of whose son he is open, creating an extreme countermodel of filiation to Violette's case. The deaths in Violette's family following the killing of her husband have had a disastrous effect on her emotional life; she now requires constant medical supervision. At her mother's funeral, she jumps resolutely into her open grave. In the end it will be Sonia whose benevolent hand will guide Violette to leave France for Israel and escape the temptation to give in to Émile's courtship. Sonia's intervention seems to suggest that sometimes distance from the overwhelming fate of the family is achieved not with therapy but the hand of God.

Desarthe alludes to her characters' family backgrounds only subtly, in short flashes of memory that punctuate their everyday activities. Many of them, we learn, are immigrants or children of immigrants. Sonia spent her early childhood in Warsaw, and her husband Dan remembers how his own mother, beaten almost to death by a German soldier before being thrown onto the train, had fixed her gaze on the young child Dan "comme pour imprimer dans sa chair un dernier message. '*Vis!*' " (1996, 143) [as if to imprint onto his flesh a last message. "*Live!*"]. Violette, too, perceives her own position within her surroundings as marked by difference, or more precisely by the trace of a difference that her mother, an immigrant to France, had instilled in her. This element of foreignness surfaces primarily in Violette's use of French, which as a child she never spoke with her mother: "à flanc de coteau, il y avait des cailloux et beaucoup de poussière. *à flanc de coteau.* Elle n'avait jamais employé cette expression. C'était tellement français. Comme si elle n'y avait pas droit" (1996, 46) [On the side of the hill, there were pebbles and lots of dust. *On the side of the hill*. She had never used this expression. It was so French. As if she didn't have the right]. Violette's reminiscences from childhood return to her the sentiments of estrangement that had set the world of the family and the outside world apart from each other. Among these is the memory of being introduced to the history of the Jewish people by a puppet, operated by her father, whose voice the young Violette would recognize in the puppet's historical narrative. This flashback to her initiation into Judaism within the family becomes juxtaposed with the image of the puppet now sitting on her night stand, "muette depuis plus de vingt ans" (1996, 46) [mute for over twenty years].

The attention Desarthe's character pays to tone and register of speech—after all, both Émile and Gabriel are trained linguists—suggests that there are secrets hiding between words, behind expressions, and within sentences. "La moindre conversation recelait des trésors, pour peu que l'on prît la peine de l'écouter" (1996, 192) [The shortest conversation would contain treasures, if one just took the trouble to listen], Gabriel muses, having spent a good part of his adult life taping random conversation he overhears on the streets of Paris. It is in this spirit that the book is written, although the mystical dimension of Sonia's angelic good deeds adds a transcendental element, which provides relief and reprieve but no revelation. It could be read as a continuation of the ventriloquist's tales Violette heard in her childhood or as a tale in which Sonia's unfaltering faith proves strong enough to guide her friends and acquaintances through the perils of moments in their lives when they were about to fail. In the wake of Jewish religious thought, *Un secret sans importance* hints at the existence of secrets beyond those of which we are aware and that give us cause for either pain or joy.

Avenging the Parents: Eliette Abécassis's *L'or et la cendre*

If we search for authorial voices that are critical of the elder generation for their return to Judaism, very few books come to mind, among them Chochana Boukhobza's *Un été à Jérusalem* [A Summer in Jerusalem] (which will be discussed in the next chapter) and a scene in Emmanuel Moses's *Papernik* (1992). Moses, who was born in 1959 in Casablanca and has lived in Paris since 1986, is an Israeli academic who can see in his father's religiosity only a pathetic substitute for dealing with the pain caused by the death of his other son. Interestingly, *Papernik* is also the only novel of the 1990s written with the tradition of American-Jewish writing of the 1960s and 1970s in mind; it reminds the reader of the early work of Philip Roth, transposed into an Israeli setting. The middle-aged protagonist spends a large part of his time thinking about women and sex, and the remainder thinking about Israeli politics. Clearly, this atheist has little patience for a father who in his old age begins to study scripture to find solace.

Eliette Abécassis's first novel, *Qumran*, is charged with theological debates and at the end suggests an unusual continuation of the tradition of religious practice in contemporary Israel. In accordance with the biblical manner of presenting genealogical relationships, at the beginning of the book the protagonist traces his family tree all the way back to Abraham, presenting an almost page-long list of names of sons and their fathers. For the devout Jew, the self is first and foremost an entry in a record that contains the names and deeds of all one's forefathers.

In Abécassis's second novel, *L'or et la cendre* (1997) [Gold and Ashes], it is again a generational relationship that determines the plot; this time, however, she explores the relationship between a father and his daughter. This long novel is also a thriller with theological and historiographical dimensions, this time rendering an intimate picture of a family imploding due to the forces exercised on it almost fifty years earlier by Nazi perpetrators. Mr. Perlman had to bear the loss of his parents and siblings, but would never share his thoughts and feelings with his children, among them the young sculptor Lisa, who puts the dilemma of her own formative years in a succinct question: "Comment peux-tu faire ta crise d'adolescence et te révolter contre un père qui était à Auschwitz et qui ne s'en est jamais remis, parce que l'on ne peut pas s'en remettre?" (1997, 186) [How can you have your adolescent crisis and revolt against a father who was at Auschwitz and who has never recovered from it, because one can't recover from it?]. Yet it is the silence rather than the suffering of her parents that infuriates her. Whereas the former is foreign to her, the latter is part of her own experience, the decisive moment in the history of her people and her family and the decisive motive for her actions: "Je crois que je fais partie de leur souffrance, c'est ma communauté" (1997, 103) [I think I take part in their suffering, it is my community]. Lisa is a highly articulate woman who surrounds herself with journalists, artists, intellectuals, and historians to debate the planned Berlin Holocaust Memorial, the presence of Carmelite nuns on the site of the Auschwitz camp, the canonization of Maximilien Kolbe and Edith Stein, the role of Swiss banks in the war, and above all, the theology of evil. In her Marais apartment, she vents her rage against a God who did not stop the gassing of six million Jews and who—if he existed—deserved to have suffered in Auschwitz as well. There are few authors whose work is as clearly located within the aftermath of a spirit handed down from the Enlightenment as Abécassis's—a spirit of dialogical exploration of truth, of mutual illumination of opposing attitudes toward the grand questions of life.

L'or et la cendre is a dense novel with an international cast of characters all tied to each other by a mysterious and horrifying incident. This event leaves a prominent Berlin theologian dead, his body cut in half, and results in criminal trials that turn over many stones in the biographies of prominent French politicians with hitherto hidden Vichy connections. The plot is suspenseful but deliberately slowed down by the intense discussions in which the characters are constantly involved; a love story between the non-Jewish narrator and Lisa is meant to enrich the otherwise highly intellectual relationship between the figures. Lisa turns out to be as challenging and difficult as a lover as she is a daughter, scorned by her mother Mina—a professor of theology and author of several books on the Shoah—for her desire to marry a goy, Raphaël. As a sixteen-year-old, the Polish-born Mina had fought for the cause of her people in the resistance, and she insists that the Jewish heritage cannot and must not be abandoned: "Juive inauthentique qui tente en vain de se renier, mais juive quand même dans l'oeil de l'autre, juive confirmée par la conscience ou la condescendance antisémite" (1997, 197) [Inauthentic Jew who tries in vain to deny herself, but Jewish even so in the eye of the other, confirmed Jew by the anti-Semitic conscience or condescension].

In the end, these maternal worries seem unfounded, since there is reason to believe that Lisa did not enter her relationship with Raphaël in good faith and that, moreover, she actually was involved in the brutal killing of Schiller on the fifth anniversary of the liberation of Auschwitz. When their child dies a mysterious death the same day Lisa's father dies, Raphaël kills Lisa, assuming that she murdered both the child and Schiller as an incomprehensible, excessive act of revenge. The eventual psychological deterioration of Raphaël will turn out to be just as perplexing as the character of Lisa, whose bonds to the fate of her family appear to be incomprehensible.

In a manner comparable to the ending of *Qumran*, the closure of this novel suggests that the burden of history and the weight of the theological and philosophical questions pondered by the characters are too heavy for them to bear. The dissolution of personality—which in the case of *Qumran* took on historical-biblical and, in the case of *L'or et la cendre*, pathological-criminal dimensions—must not be read as the resignation of an author who does not know how to tie the ends of her complex narratives together. The protagonists may be able to solve the hideous crimes, remnants of the horrors of a past that refuses to go away, but afterwards they simply are not able to continue living their lives. Truth, Eliette Abécassis knows from the philosophy of the Enlightenment, is a category indispensable to human nature. But as a student of the *Dialectics of Enlightenment*, she also knows that truth, even if it were attainable, does not arrest the process of a virtually infinite inquiry, which reveals that even good will gives birth to evil.

An alter ego Lisa Perlman can be found in the protagonist of Thierry Gandillot's thriller *L'héritage Windsmith* (1996) [The Windsmith Legacy], who is also driven to restore the honor of a father and a family violated by the Nazis. As an adolescent, Raphaëlle Weissberg witnessed her entire family's deportation by the Germans. After the war she learns that the Nazis did not honor a deal they had offered to her father, according to which the Germans were supposed to spare the family in exchange for their extensive collection of paintings, hidden in their castle in the Dordogne. Juxtaposed with their fate is the biography of an American, Windsmith, an influential art collector and powerful mastermind whose dubious roots, as the novel exposes gradually, go all the way back to a Nazi past. Windsmith had managed to hide his links to the Nazis until the fall of the Berlin Wall opened access to archives on the East and with them his past. The paintings stolen from the French Jews seem to have passed through his hands. The core of the character constellation mapped by the novel is made up of the children of the generations immediately affected by the war—between them, the reconciliation that had eluded their parents and grandparents seems possible. Raphaëlle, an art historian, is determined to find the paintings that were stolen from her father, and with them those who eventually took advantage of the stolen collection. Meanwhile, Léo, the grandson of Windsmith, is able to accept her claims, from which his grandfather had run away all his life. Ultimately, the novel resolves the plot by pointing the finger not so much at Windsmith as at a former Nazi living in Salzburg who never had confronted his own guilt. By this time, however, the focus of the conflict has long been shifted away from contemporary France to the shores of the New World and back again to the mountain country of which Hitler had been so fond. Raphaëlle's choice not to kill the unrepentant Nazi who is responsible for her family's suffering at the end of this *roman noir* speaks of her humanity and forgiveness, which shine brightly against the backdrop of all the old scoundrels she has had to fight. Gandillot is not Jewish, and one wonders whether *L'héritage Windsmith*, if written by a Jewish author of his age (he was born in 1955), would have ended with a similar tone of reconciliation.

Literary Plea for a Different Father: Marco Koskas's *L'homme de paille*

Generations are tied together by memory, and memories can provide the close tie of mutual respect and consideration but also a strangling grip that can hold a generation hostage in a place hard to escape. Pierre Nora recognizes this power of generations to stake out places in which old and young need to meet if they want to appreciate each other as legitimate members of the same family, group, community: "generations are powerfully, perhaps even primarily, fabricators of *lieux de mémoire*, or mnemomic sites, which form the fabric of their provisional identities and stake out the boundaries of their generational memories. These mnemonic sites generate or become charged with unfathomable powers of symbolic evocation . . . The exploration of a generational memory begins with an inventory of these sites" (1996, 526).

In the case of young authors from the Maghreb, Nora's image "lieux de mémoire" needs to be understood quite literally as a space, but one to which these authors often have access only through memory or—even more indirectly—through the recollections of others. The desert metaphor that scholarship has suggested is a critical means to understand the francophone literature of the Maghreb[11] thus should in these instances be read more radi-

11. See, for example, Dugas 1990.

cally as a metaphor of the vacuum that often occupies the sites at stake here; the inventories are sparse because not very much has been transmitted between the parents and their children who grew up elsewhere.

The uprooting of families during the years of the Fascist regime created gaps in the biographies of those who had to flee and find refuge elsewhere, leaving marks on the offspring of these immigrants. The refugees' children would not always be able to understand the cultural and linguistic ties that had defined the lives of their parents. Several decades after the end of World War II, decolonization brought new experiences of displacement for other groups of Jews from culturally, politically, and historically very different parts of the world. Such experiences eventually would rejuvenate and enrich Jewish life in France, even if many of the more recent immigrants, Sephardic Jews from North Africa, regarded the French Ashkenazi community with a certain resentment. Later on, the difficulties of understanding each other would cause fractures even in the families of the immigrants themselves, when their offspring, who had spent their formative years in France rather than in the home countries of their parents, shed their commitment to the ways and beliefs that were second nature to their elders. "Non, tu ne vois pas! . . . Tout a été si facile pour toi!" (Boukhobza 1996, 123) [No, you don't see! . . . Everything was so easy for you!], cries the father in Chochana Boukhobza's *Pour l'amour du père* [For the Love of the Father], reproaching his daughter, who cannot accept his attitudes toward the new Diaspora, attitudes that still bear the stamp of having had to leave Tunisia and start all over again, as an outsider and a social nobody in France.

Marco Koskas's *L'homme de paille* (1988) [The Straw Man] is one of the most moving literary documents by the children of immigrants from the Maghreb, dedicated to the plight of those who arrived in France after the turmoil of the wars of independence. Unlike his first book, *Palais Bounel,* which owed its style to North African traditions of oral storytelling, this novel is a tightly organized first-person narrative. In the novel, a son remembers the pathetic life of his father, who had arrived with his family in France in 1964 only to die shortly after, in the "terre de liberté et de civilisation" (1988, 25) [land of liberty and civilization]. What is striking about this narrative is the frankness with which the son confesses his overriding feelings of shame and embarrassment about his father. "Ce pauvre type" [this poor guy], as the son refers to him, a man of little means and bad luck, left his small coffeehouse in Tunisia to settle in France, where he found work as an assistant in a barbershop. Twenty-three years after his death, his son sets out to come to terms with the life of this man and with the feelings he had toward him as a child. The father's death was experienced with relief among his relatives, and a tacit silence about the deceased lasted almost two decades, almost as if such a silence would be able to extinguish the memory of him, a loser in life by most standards.

L'homme de paille presents the story of this man who dies at only fifty-four in an entirely unsentimental and unsparing way, in which his shortcomings as a father, a husband, and a businessman outnumber his lovable features. As part of this frank reckoning with his father's character flaws, the narrator remembers how in the decades since his death he had felt compelled several times to embellish his father's legacy retroactively through writing. In fact, his turn to literature was itself caused by the lasting impact his father had on him:

> On n'en a plus parlé jusqu'à ce que je me mette à écrire un roman. C'était une saga, un roman des origines, qui s'inspirait de la véritable histoire de ma famille. Du moins la famille de ma mère. La fiction me permit de refaire vivre mon père, de le réinventer comme j'aurais aimé qu'il fût, et de le faire mourir à mon idée: il fondait comme neige au soleil. C'était une métaphore du silence qui avait suivi sa disparition. . . . Il est présent dans tout ce que j'écris. Je n'écris peut-être que pour lui redonner sa chance. En écrivant, j'essaye probablement de faire mieux que lui. Mais je lui ressemble trop, comme disent les gens de ma famille, pour y arriver. (1988, 12)
>
> [There was no more talk about it until I set about writing a novel. It was a saga, a novel of origins, which was inspired by the true story of my family. My mother's family, at least. Fiction allows me to make my father live again, to reinvent him as I would have liked him to be, and to make him die according to my idea: he would melt like snow in the sun. It was a metaphor of the silence that had followed his disappearance. . . . He is present in all that I write. I write perhaps only to give him another chance. By writing, I probably try to do better than him. But I resemble him too much, as the people in my family say, to achieve that.]

The entire book is an anti-novel of the immigrants' nostalgia for the life they had left behind in their homelands. Its author is a formerly dutiful child who has finally cast away the bonds that had forced him to offer his parents' generation what they desired, the redemption they could not find in their new surroundings. As such, it is a bitter book that breaks the "silence" in which the narrator's father had enclosed himself—a common element of the syndrome from which so many immigrants would suffer—to call openly the difficult, hidden family issues by their names. Interestingly, in this family of seven, it is the mother, the descendent of a family much wealthier than the father's, who has usurped the power of enunciation. (She, however, uses her voice primarily to vent her anger about her lot, living in an arranged marriage with a man of no social standing or ambitions.) When the narrator tries to surprise her with news of the book that he has just finished, she pretends that she, too, has written one, thus reminding her son that "la parole était le monopole" (1988, 28) [speech was the monopoly] of her. Instead of being proud of her son's accomplishments, the mother is vexed: "L'idée qu'un de ses enfants brise la malédiction de l'échec équivalait à déjouer le destin fatal qu'elle nous avait fixé" (1988, 30) [The idea that one of her children might shatter the curse of failure amounted to an evasion of the fatal destiny that she had fixed for us].

The son does not ignore entirely the difficulties his father had to face during his lifetime. There are certain physical ailments that, according to the narrator, are frequent among North African Jews, and conditions for Jews in Tunisia have worsened after the country's independence, endangering their right to due process because of their ethnicity. But none of these things add up in the son's mind to mitigating circumstances that could outweigh his disappointment with a father who, not unlike the one in Modiano's early novels, does not live up to his child's expectations. The son's narrative is one of painful memories and of a long process of disillusionment, which did not end after the arrival in France. When his family arrived in Paris from Tunisia, the father, who had emigrated several months before, forgot to pick them up at the train station.

There is little closure at the end of *L'homme de paille*, but there remains the narrator's determination that he will not alter his account, even though "la tentation est grande de revenir en arrière, de retoucher le portrait indécent" (1988, 128) [the temptation to go back and retouch the indecent portrait is great]. Told in a manner reminiscent of the new novelists, Koskas's novel leaves the reader with the sympathetic desire to defend the poor Jewish immigrant against his chronicler, especially during an episode near the end. Shortly before his death, the narrator's father begins to sing aloud in Arabic, vexing the neighbors of his sterile suburb and embarrassing members of his own family, who do not want to be perceived as different, Maghrebi, Jewish. Whereas the father has no difficulty admitting who he is and where he is from, his son is haunted by the fear of becoming identified with his father. He is afraid, for instance, to be addressed by him, since his father's voice would destroy his efforts to keep his background invisible to his non-Jewish French peers:

> Au lycée j'avais eu tant de mal à expliquer que je n'étais ni français ni espagnol ni arabe ni rien de tout, que je craignais de voir mon père ficher par terre cette identité mystérieuse rien qu'en m'adressant la parole. (1988, 49)
>
> [In high school I had so much difficulty explaining that I was not French nor Spanish nor Arab nor anything at all, that I feared seeing my father drive into the earth this mysterious identity simply by speaking to me.]

Like a convex mirror, this scene turns Jean-Paul Sartre's conception of Jewish identity as a reflex of the anti-Semite's glance upside down. The son can no longer avoid being defined as the Other once his father has addressed him in front of everyone as a Jew from North Africa. As long as his father is alive, the family's heritage can assert its hold over the son at any time, which explains the son's relief when his father suddenly dies of leukemia.

Even then, however, the position of the son remains fragile; envisioning his father as a straw man leaves him alone with the challenge of asserting himself as a man, as a Frenchman, and, possibly, as a Jew. To learn what any of these notions might entail, he has to look outside the circle of his family and explore their possibilities in his writing. His struggle for autonomy has run into the wall of filiation. Breaking through it requires courage and the powers of imagination.

The Berlin-born writer Barbara Honigmann, who has lived in Strasbourg for almost two decades, asks in her autobiographical essay "Selbstporträt einer Jüdin" [Self-Portrait of a Jewish Woman] why so many Jews of her generation have remained for such a long time "Kinder unserer Eltern" (1999, 11) [children of our parents]. For Honigmann, the reason is a simple one: it was more difficult for the children of Jews to elude the history and the stories of their parents than it was for their non-Jewish peers.

The history of persecution, discrimination, and exile indeed has had a most powerful impact on filial relationships. The children would eventually recognize that they had to reckon with the stories told—or not told—by their parents, challenging their own understanding of what it means to be a Jewish citizen in contemporary France. Questioning first the myth of a postwar France born out of the ashes of resistance to Fascism and later, following decolonization, the notion of a tolerant society that treats all its subjects equally, the younger generations of Jews discovered the humiliation imposed upon their forefathers and parents by their gentile compatriots both on European and North African soil. In their writing, they create a fictional space where all the contestants and generations meet again; they create a forum to readdress the unarticulated issues of their own coming of age, a stage where the family drama of their youth can be recast, altered, and sometimes resolved through the power of retrospective understanding. In their scripts for the encounters between old and young, they negotiate between their desire for an autonomous notion of the self and their recognition that the formation of the self takes place in an intergenerational process in which ethnic givens have to be reconfigured constantly.

Setting their portraits of young Jews against a backdrop of family histories, writers feature the children as relentless critics tearing apart the decisions made by the elders (as in the novels by Antoine Spire, Patrick Modiano, Marco Koskas, Nickie Golse). Or they place them harmoniously amid their parents to show that despite the predicaments of history, the power of the Covenant remains as strong as the family contract (Myriam Anissimov, Norbert Czarny). Remembering the unrecorded fates of the victims and articulating what rests behind the silence of mute immigrants are a fictional means to re-member, so to speak, truncated families. To create narratives that reinvest a family legacy of resistance with new meaning is a way of doing justice to the past, even if these narratives (like those of Pierre Goldman or Eliette Abécassis) show how difficult it is to keep in sight what it means to do justice to the present and to the self under the weight of these legacies.

5 ⊸ Displacements

Geographies of Lost Innocence: Jean-Luc Allouche's *Les jours innocents*

Alain Finkielkraut coined the term "the novel of dis-apprenticeship" (1980b, 89) to describe the experience of the children of Jewish immigrants who came of age in the 1970s only to realize that they are at home neither in a Jewish community that may have been part of their parents' experience nor in gentile society. Not only the country their parents left behind but also the culture that now surrounds the child have an identity less recognizable than expected: "Both his point of embarkation and the land of his homecoming—his community's Jewishness, and France as one nation indivisible—have together disappeared from the map. If they can be found, it's only as remnants" (1980b, 90).

Jean-Luc Allouche's *Les jours innocents* (1984) [The Innocent Days] documents the enthusiasm with which the younger generations had turned their backs to countries—in Allouche's case, Algeria—that they had perceived as "une marche d'empire, trop étroite" (1984, 18) [the country bordering the empire, too narrow]. They would come to realize that their new home offered them an "espace intermédiaire" (1984, 36) [intermediary space] beyond the "âpreté" [bitterness] of Africa but also that this space was inhabited by the specter of anti-Semitism ready to rise out of the interaction between people that the newcomers would perceive as superficial.

But despite the complicated courses of these passages narrated by the younger authors, the majority of their texts do not subscribe to the parents' and grandparents' nostalgia for the Jewish communities or the countries of origin left behind. This characteristic certainly sets them apart from previous generations of authors, whose texts, according to Clara Lévy, "sont imprégnés d'une forte nostalgie à l'égard de temps et de lieux disparus" (1998, 55) [are impregnated with a powerful nostalgia with regard to times and places that have disappeared]. Instead, the "narrative of displacement" has created what Stuart Hall, the British sociologist of the postcolonial black diaspora, has called an "imaginary plentitude" (1990, 236): "The diaspora experience as I intend it here is defined, not by essence or purity, but by the recognition of a necessary heterogeneity and diversity: by a concept of identity which lives with and through, not despite difference; by *hybridity*. Diaspora identities are those which are constantly producing and reproducing themselves anew, through transformation and difference" (1990, 235). This notion of embracing the new diasporic experience and of creating a perspective that is neither blind to the places left behind nor to the space now inhabited informs the majority of texts surveyed in this chapter.

Jean Allouche (born in 1948 in Israel and currently an editor of *Libération*) states quite categorically in his account of immigrating to France as a twelve-year-old boy how little he cared about leaving:

> la folie du désert, la nostalgie d'une terre fichée en chair comme une inguérissable blessure, la halte précaire, le cimetière des éléphants, le camp de fortune de gens qui n'avaient plus le courage de rebâtir une vie, la lente dégradation de la tribu, l'épuisement, la coupure, le fiel des jours qui passent sans espoir alors que ceux d'hier furent de miel, le ressassement, l'hystérie des soirs où le pain n'a plus de goût, où le vin est amer, le chant éteint, le feu étouffé sous la cendre. (1984, 24)
>
> [the madness of the desert, the nostalgia for a land marked in the flesh like a permanent wound, the unsafe bus stops, the elephant cemetery, the makeshift camp of people who no longer had the courage to rebuild a life, the slow deterioration of the tribe, the exhaustion, the rupture, the bitterness of days passing without hope while those of yesterday make honey, the brooding, the hysteria of the evenings when the bread no longer has a taste, when the wine is bitter, the song dead, the fire choked beneath the ashes.]

Allouche's younger colleague Gilles Zenou (who was born in 1957 in Morocco and died in 1989) provides a similar diatribe against his county of origin, Morocco, when in his novel *Mektoub* (1987) he has the young Emmanuel—a Jewish Candide of frivolous adventures and of a tragic ending—look forward to moving to Strasbourg to attend a yeshiva. The tirade is caused partly by the young man's boredom with the Moroccan provinces and their backwardness—“ville visqueuse, ville close, ville morte” (1987, 49) [sticky city, enclosed city, dead city]—partly by his weariness with a small Jewish world subjugated by constant angst, “la peur du rabbin, la peur du voisin, la peur de l’Arabe, la peur du roi Mahmoud VI” (1987, 50) [fear of the rabbi, fear of the neighbor, fear of the Arab, fear of King Mahmoud VI]. In his curriculum vitae, this “résident temporaire” [temporary resident] notes “Refus d’être juif” [Refusal to be Jewish] under the rubric of “Délits ou crimes” [Crimes Committed] and “Être juif à perpétuité” [To be Jewish forever] under the rubric of “Condamnations” [Penalties Served] (1987, 174).[1] In Zenou’s *La désaffection* (1990) [Disaffection], Emmanuel has in the protagonist Elie a counterpart who leaves behind his meaningless existence in a small French town to become a writer in Istanbul. Regardless of their individual cultural and geographical coordinates, Zenou’s protagonists are driven by a decisionism that echoes Camus’s existentialism (and, in the case of *Mektoub*, Gide’s *L’immoraliste* [The Immoralist]) and haunted by the notion of the absurd. For Elie, his wanderings provide the external conditions for his writing, which is driven by the desire of self-determination: “J’écris pour naître à moi-même” (1990, 102) [I write to be born to myself].

Writing as a form of self-conception is part of the dynamics of autojudeography. In the works of the Sephardic authors who arrived in France following their parents’ exodus from the Maghreb or who were born in France after decolonization, this self-conception appears in the form of a metamorphosis that the members of these generations underwent upon their arrival in the modern Western world, and that they try to understand through their writing. In the case of Allouche, who came from a very observant home, the dynamics of autojudeography entail the process of initially loosening the ties to the family’s practice of Judaism. Whereas the older ones respond to Ashkenazi rites prevalent in France in the 1950s and 1960s by rapidly establishing the religious and cultural infrastructure to accommodate their Sephardic heritage, the belief system of the younger ones often suffers its first fissures upon encountering a different form of Judaism. This experience as well as the influence of the philosophical paradigms governing the education provided by the schools puts an end to the “jours innocents” [innocent days]. Arnold Mandel’s

1. Zenou’s works undoubtedly partake in the “dialogue with Death” that Judith Klein sees (following Serge Moscovici’s reading of Ryvel) as a common denominator of Jewish-Maghrebi writing. See Klein 1998, 53.

insistence on looking at the young French Jewish writers as intellectual products of the "lycée français avec son cartésianisme endémique" (1980, 94) [French school with its endemic Cartesianism] thus needs to guide the reading of the works of their Sephardic peers as well in order to understand that they, too, "sont aliénés par rapport à eux-mêmes" (1980, 94) [are alienated from themselves]. Ami Bouganim, for example, is not only the author of a collection of colorful fables revisiting the lost world of the *mellah*, but also of a book analyzing the intersection of religious and philosophical discourse. Gilles Zenou, a student of Rabat's Lycée Descartes, submitted to the Sorbonne (Université de Paris-I Panthéon Sorbonne) his thesis on the "Phénoménologie de la condition juive en France et en Allemagne, au XXe siècle" [Phenomenology of the Jewish Condition in France and in Germany in the Twentieth Century]. Jean Allouche, for his part, recounts how the impact of the humanities professor came to replace the power of the rabbi as the formative experience of schooling succeeded in displacing the world of Judaism altogether: "le lycée devenait une Athènes aux fastes intellectuels si éclatants qu'elle en éclipsait la Jérusalem terne de mon logis" (1984, 32) [the high school became an Athens of such sparkling intellectual feasts that it eclipsed the dull Jerusalem of my home]. The French diaspora became the setting of a process of de-Judaization from which many children of immigrants would not recover until they managed to gain some distance from the domination of Western universalism and secular rationalism.

Allouche, in a search for "un autre Dieu que les petites divinités" (1984, 54) [a God different from the lesser divinities], bids farewell to Paris, the capital of the political, for Jerusalem, the capital of the religious. At this point, his account also leaves behind the first-person narrative and switches to the third person—a form of narrative distancing reflective of the distance that separates the author from Orthodoxy. The sojourn to Israel does not succeed in undoing this detachment. The first person does not reappear until the last section of the book, which recounts the visit to his native Algeria.

Algeria, he has to acknowledge, is no longer an inhabitable diaspora for the Jews. In Constantine, all the sites of religious practice have been erased, his "Jérusalem d'enfance est désolée et ravagée" (1984, 141) [childhood Jerusalem is desolate and ravaged]—pictures of devastation that resemble the ones offered by the Cairo-born writer Paula Jacques in her novel *L'héritage de tante Carlotta* (1987) [Aunt Carlotta's Legacy] describing the tragic end of Egyptian Jewry. These are all images depicting the destruction of yet another temple, though Allouche's melancholy is evoked not by the thought of the lost *hara* but by the fact that he, unlike his predecessors, has only the French language to articulate his feelings toward the new Algeria and to the painful history of the destruction of Jewish sites. Whereas his ancestors employed their mastery of "toutes les louanges de la Terre sainte" (1984, 131) [all the praises of the Holy Land] to celebrate the beauties of Israel and to espouse the laws of Judaism in their book, Allouche has been robbed by the diasporic experience of the possibility to write in any language other than French. Thus, his book is a manifestation of the autojudeographic point of departure:

> Le mien respire l'exil, parce que nous sommes dépouillés de notre héritage, projetés en d'improbables enracinements, précaires, dangereux, dérisoires. Fils de nous-mêmes, engendrés dans les tours et détours de la dispersion, détachés de la tutelle bienveillante, protectrice et exigeante de nos ancêtres. (1984, 131)
>
> [Mine breathes of exile, because we are robbed of our heritage, cast upon improbable roots, precarious, dangerous, laughable. Sons of ourselves, fathered in the twists and turns of the diaspora, separated from the beneficent, protecting, and demanding guardianship of our ancestors.]

Allouche's *Les jours innocents* originates in a Cartesian desire to find through the self-reflective act of writing a foundation of the self, framed, after all, in quotes from the Hebrew Bible and from the Talmud that introduce the individual segments of the book. The Talmudic tale that Allouche has chosen as the book's motto comments on the task of the scribe who, according to Rabbi Meïr, is charged with an assignment that will result in the destruction of the entire world if it is carried out the wrong way. Such a profound impact, *Les jours innocents* concedes, is reserved for a venerable religious tradition of Jewish writing to which some of the younger authors look back with curiosity and even with awe. No longer does the fate of the world or the fate of society depend on a correct form of written discourse. Allouche, however, does know that at least the future of the Jewish community continues to depend on a truthful record of its past that only writing can provide.

"Couscous Literature": Gil Ben Aych's Literary Voyages

"Contemporary francophone authors of the Maghreb," Valérie Orlando observes in her study *Nomadic Voices of Exile*, "do not draw from French or Arab cultures alone to write their narratives. Their literary force is a multiplicity that includes interaction between the two" (1999, 53). And, one would like to add, some of them do draw very consciously from the linguistic repertoire of the languages of both their childhood homes and of their diasporic life in France. Gil Ben Aych, who was born in 1948 in Algerian Tlemcen, reflects upon the relationship between nomadism and the linguistic equipment with which he navigates his exilic existence in "Ma langue" [My Language], a short essay published in 1978. The French-language author explores the dilemma of the immigrant writer for whom French is not the lingua franca despite his philosophy training at the Sorbonne. He has been taught the French language and has learned Arabic, but the "juif-parlé algérien" (1997, 12–13) [Algerian spoken by the Jews] is the language of his childhood and his family, whose disappearance he is witnessing and whose vestiges he is trying to save in his work.[2] Concluding that he does not really know in which language he writes, Ben Aych describes a situation of linguistic displacement and border-crossing that has left him without a language of his own: "Je ne sais. Mais je sais. Toute langue m'est étrangère" (1997, 13) [I don't know. But I know. Every language is foreign to me].

Ben Aych, who left Algeria with his family in 1956, has written and published all his books in French, and yet, as he acknowledges in his essay, he just translated them from the languages in which he thinks. This process of translation, however, does not filter out all the remnants of the languages the author has been exposed to. Thus his books offer a stylistic homage to the linguistic and cultural worlds of characters whose ties to Algeria remain strong. In his first novel, *L'essuie-mains des pieds* (1981) [The Hand-Towel for Feet], the linkage concerns culinary customs, which—as the literary historian Guy Dugas has pointed out—allude to deep memories residing in the body, connecting sensual experiences from childhood with the sphere of the family and the home (Dugas 1990, 148).[3] *L'essuie-mains des pieds* is organized as the account of a young boy, Nanou, in chapters that all bear the names of culinary dishes. From the perspective of an eleven-year-old narrator, odors and meals have the same relevance as the lot of relatives who are trying to get their feet on the ground in Champigny. Hélène Gans Perez, born in 1944 in Marrakesh,

2. Ben Aych's essay "Ma langue" was first published in *Les temps modernes* (1978).

3. See also Hazan-Aramar 1987, Cohen-Azuelos 1999, and, from the point of view of ethnography, Bahloul 1983.

makes ample use of Moroccan recipes in her book *Marrakech la Rouge: Les Juifs de la Médina* (1996) [Red Marrakesh: The Jews of Medina]. In the case of Ben Aych's Nanou, it is primarily his nose that helps orient him in his unfamiliar surroundings: "Dans la cuisine de tata Marthe ça sentait toujours la même odeur" (1981, 45) [In aunt Marthe's kitchen it always smelled the same]. Religious rituals as well as shared meals remain the last bastion of a family life threatened by the realities of the new diaspora. Sketches full of humor and affection show how the world of food and eating instinctively remains the yardstick for quality of life in a society in which the father struggles to keep the family above water with his small grocery store—and in which no one has higher ambitions. The mother reacts to ner new neighborhood with the suspicions of a person who has grown up poor in an agricultural society:

> Quel beau quartier . . . quel!!! . . . c'est ça qui compte tu crois, d'abord j'vais t'dire une chose, va voir la première épicerie sur quoi on va tomber et on va voir rien que les fruits et légumes va voir voilà ch't'en prie regarde tu crois je parle pour rien, regarde rien que des aubergines c'est des aubergines ça . . . c'est pas des aubergines . . . ratatinées et rabougries. (1981, 43)
>
> [How nice a neighborhood . . . how nice!!! . . . that's what counts, you think, well first I'll sure tell you something, go take a look at the first produce shop you find and you'll see nothing but fruits and vegetables, go take a look, there you have it I ask you, look, you think I speak for no reason, look there, nothing but eggplants, those are eggplants . . . those eggplants aren't . . . shriveled and stunted.]

Ben Aych's *Le voyage de Mémé* (1983) [Mémé's Voyage], recounts for the young reader how the grandmother of an immigrant family traveled by foot the long distance between Paris and the suburb of Champigny. His *Le livre d'Étoile* (1986) [The book of Étoile], presented as an oral narrative by the same grandmother, Étoile, recapitulates her journey from Algeria to France, capturing in long passages the breathless *parlando* of the old woman persuaded by her children to leave her home country. Imitating the associative, redundant, and ungrammatical patterns of spoken language, the author disappears behind the voice of the old, Arabic-speaking Jew whose diatribes against the Western industrialized world toward the end make way for a stream of consciousness recording the pain inflicted on her by exile:

> couscous noir, Versailles, rue Truffaut, soleil, Myriam, Déborah, Estelle, rue des Dames, shabbat, le bouillon, le thym, la semoule, le kiddouch, le mosseh,

> la radio, alors, est-ce qu'il est bon, il est très bon ma fille, que Dieu vous garde et que vous nous fassiez souvent des couscous aussi bon et encore longtemps. (1986, 172)
>
> [black couscous, Versailles, rue Truffaut, sunshine, Myriam, Deborah, Estelle, rue des Dames, shabbat, the broth, thyme, semolina, the kiddush, the mosseh, the radio, then, is it good, it is very good my daughter, may God protect you and may you often make us couscous this good for a long time to come.]

Le chant des êtres [The Chant of Beings], Ben Aych's most mature book (published in 1988) employs language that evokes the liturgical notion of religious discourse: "Simon était juif et devint autre. Comme devenir autre c'était l'être déjà, Simon devint ce qu'il était. Simon devint, fut et sera. Un être autre. Un être, un autre. Soit un être. Simon est" (1988, 13) [Simon was Jewish and became an other. As if becoming an other was to be that already, Simon became what he was. Simon became, was, and will be. A different sort of being. A being, an other. Though a being. Simon is]. Such linguistic experimentation, merging the opaqueness and circularity of biblical speech with the rigid diction of philosophical discourse, is an apt approach to the novel's topic and to the conflicting attitudes of some of the main characters. The book's focus is the thirteen-year-old Simon, who is pondering his relationship to God as he approaches his bar mitzvah, while two uncles of the same name—one a staunch communist, the other a pious believer—each try to exert their influence on him.

The setting again is Champigny, in the 1960s; the overall mode of the narrative again is characterized by humorous contemplation. The associations of the names allude to the bonds of family legacy, and to the notion that the three of them together present the wide spectrum of Sephardic Judaism in France. The teachings of the two uncles provide their young nephew with insight into the nature of "being," both in its spiritual and its material sense. Meanwhile, they offer the readers insights into the relativism experienced in the French diaspora, in which some of the immigrants' attitudes mirror those of the French natives:

> En France aussi, les adultes parlaient du passé, l'Algérie, comme d'un paradis, y compris ceux qui l'avaient quittée depuis longtemps, et du futur—Israël pour certains ou une meilleure situation sociale pour d'autres—comme d'un paradis. Mais le présent était toujours dur et difficile. Sujet à soucis. Or,

> Simon avait remarqué que les Français disaient toujours que la France c'était mieux "avant"—quand elle était moins moderne—ou qu'ailleurs, à la campagne notamment, la vie y était moins dure et moins difficile, plus agréable. Mais le présent était toujours dur et difficile. (1988, 16)
>
> [In France too, the adults spoke of the past, Algeria, as a paradise, including those who had left it long ago, and of the future—Israel for some, or a better social situation for others—as a paradise. But the present was always harsh and difficult. Subject to worries. And yet, Simon had remarked that the French always said that France was better "before"—when it was less modern—or that elsewhere, especially in the countryside, life was less harsh and difficult, more pleasant. But the present was always harsh and difficult.]

The parallelism in the narrator's choice of words underlines the idea that nostalgia is evoked not only and not primarily by the experience of immigration but by any notion of change, including the loss of the premodern and preurban form of community witnessed by the French. "*Nostalgérie*" [nostalgeria], the mourning for the lost home and country, is a sentiment that belongs to the world of the adult but is foreign to the young. Their attitude encompasses a very different stance to the notion of the past in general and of Jewish history in particular. Whereas the Jews, according to Simon, have a complicated past, a "passé composé," which is constructed by an element of the past and one of the present, the French enviously dwell in the realm of a simple past, the "passé simple" that distinguishes confidently and straightforwardly between yesterday and today.

Gil Ben Aych's double entendre alludes to which large extent the experience of the Jewish immigrant is informed by language. For the older immigrants, this is cause for struggle; for Simon it is cause for a playful exploration of his own position as a young Sephardi of Maghrebi origin who feels set apart from the gentile French people, the Jews of Ashkenazi background, and, to a lesser degree, from his older family members. The awareness of this manifold difference manifests itself in Simon's attitude toward the language spoken in his new surroundings in general—"un mélange de français approximatif pour colonisé (entendu autour de lui) et de français correct (appris à l'école)" (1988, 57) [a mixture of the approximate French spoken by the colonized (and heard around him) and correct French (studied at school)]—and in the milieu of the immigrants in particular—"un arabe idiolectal de Tlemcen, judéo-algérien local" (1988, 57) [an Arabic idiolect of Tlemcen, the local Judeo-Algerian]. The carefully crafted stylistic layering of the narrative and its self-conscious examination of linguistic differences, etymological histories, and shades of usage point to the protagonist's appreciation of nuances that Simon—and the idiom of the text—pushes to the extreme of a language of his own: "Simon était nuancé. Par les langues. C'est dans ces conditions que Simon commença de forger une langue: une langue qui ne fût ni l'arabe, ni l'hébreu, ni le français. Une langue. Sa langue. La langue de Simon" (1988, 57) [Simon was nuanced. Through languages. It was in these circumstances that he began to craft a language: a language that was not Arabic, not Hebrew, not French. A language. His language. The language of Simon]. *Le chant des êtres* thus presents a stylistically unique piece of prose that at times is lyrical and at times liturgical and in which references to Heraclitus, Marx, or Jahwe can coexist just as the notions of the love story, the family saga, and the linguistic lecture become interwoven into a text whose title suggests that a plurality of existences and identities together can craft one harmonic discourse.

Of Palaces and Ghettos: Marco Koskas's and Ami Bouganim's Art of Memory

While the chapter headings of *L'essuie-mains des pieds* read like the menu of a multicourse meal, there are no means of external organization whatsoever that could guide the readers through *Palais Bounel* (1979), the first novel of Marco Koskas (born in 1951). Turning the structure of Georges Perec's *La vie, mode d'emploi* [Life: A Manual], which had appeared just the previous year, into pure chaos, *Palais Bounel* is the almost anarchic tale of a multistory tenement building owned by the Bonan family in Nabeul. Perec had explored the metaphor of a jigsaw puzzle in the preface to his voluminous book about life in the building on Rue Simon-Grubellier, which was published with three indexes to make the hundreds of stories related to its inhabitants accessible. The gestalt of Koska's novel, in contrast, appears like a multicolored rug in which the many tales and anecdotes from the everyday life of the large Bonan family and their employees have been tightly woven together, enmeshing the inside of the tenement building with the world outside. The spatial sense offered by *Palais Bounel* thus differs profoundly from the "closed conformism of the cubes in Ryvel's *hara*," although the works of the Tunisian writer Raphaël Lévy (1898–1972) have had a strong impact in many respects on Koskas's literary fashioning of oral storytelling (Roumani 1984, 261).

Compared to the sophisticated narratives offered by Koskas, the structural conventionality of a novel like Monique Zerdoun's *Rue de la Mémoire fêlée* (1990) [Cracked Memory Road] renders the memory of the Jewish world of the Maghreb in a sentimental and naive manner: "Le Grand Rabbin hochait doucement la tête en caressant sa barbe" (1990, 145) [The chief rabbi gently nodded his head while stroking his beard]. Koskas avoids the effect of the picturesque by shattering the illusion that this world is easily accessible to the outsider. In his cacophony of stories and voices, the chronology of historical events such as the occupation by the Germans or the Bizerte crisis has been splintered and interspersed with stories about the fates of the inhabitants of the house. In the end, however, the historical realm powerfully marks the everyday life of the Bonan family: following Tunisia's independence and the new nation's suspicious attitude toward Jews, most of them depart for France, leaving behind only one family member to board up the houses. Thus, only a faint optimism reminds the readers of the larger humorous nature of the book, in which the messianic shimmers for a short and fleeting moment:

> Il était une fois une rumeur qui se répandit dans le pays en même temps qu'une nuée de parachutistes français tombait du ciel sur Bizerte avec, paraît-il, dans leur barda une bible juive et sous leur casque une calotte de prières comme on en porte dans les synagogues. (1979, 216)
>
> [Once there was a rumor that spread through the country at the same time as a swarm of French parachutists fell from the sky onto Bizerte with, it appeared, Jewish bibles in their baggage and prayer caps like those worn in synagogues under their helmets.]

Ami Bouganim's *Récits du Mellah* [Stories from the *Mellah*], which appeared in 1981, consists of forms of oral communication found in the Jewish ghetto of Mogador. The lives of the families portrayed are devoted to a piety far removed from the notion of studied religiosity of European provenance. Bouganim, born 1951 in Mogador, handles the symbolism with a certain naïveté, which, given the author's training as a philosopher in France prior to his aliyah to Israel, is actually a sophisticated literary construct. Figures and narratives from the Bible frame the individual stories, reflecting the strong religious ties of Bouganim's characters, who, however, never join any schools of orthodoxy.

Bouganim alludes indirectly to his impetus for telling stories when he has one of his characters voice vexation about his gradual loss of memory, which threatens to erase irrevocably the world of the ghetto. Like Marlène Amar,

Bouganim wants to provide answers to those whose curiosity has been raised and whose pride in their Sephardic heritage will not be relinquished:

> Les autres ne connaissaient du Maroc que l'allure blessée de leurs parents, leur regards désamorcés, leurs souvenirs de vieux juifs. A certaines réunions, je leur racontais, à eux qui savaient mieux comment vivaient des Polonais dans un ghetto que des Marocains dans un mellah, Mogador. Je leur parlais de Rabbi Pinhas, de Rabbi Mard'haï, de Rahamim et de tous les autres. "Que sont-ils devenus? . . ." demandaient-ils. Je retraçais l'ambiance qui régnait dans la rue des Epices, dans les synagogues où les juifs s'éternisaient en cantiques parce que la prière se confondait avec le chant, dans le mellah, par journées de grandes rumeurs. (1981, 220)
>
> [The others knew nothing of Morocco but the wounded appearance of their parents, their drained looks, their old Jewish memories. At certain gatherings I recounted to them, to those who knew better how the Polish lived in a ghetto than the Moroccans in a mellah, Mogador. I spoke to them of Rabbi Pinhas, of Rabbi Mard'haï, of Rahamim and all the others. "What became of them? . . ." they asked. I explained the atmosphere that reigned on the rue des Epices, in the synagogues where the Jews carried on and on in hymns, because the prayer blended into the song, in the mellah, on the Days of Distress.

In the narrative geography of the *Récits du Mellah*, secular France hardly appears at all. After all, it was to Israel that the vast majority of Moroccan Jews emigrated, while France became home to only a small elite. When the young protagonist of "Le fils du serpent" [The Son of the Snake] is forced to encounter the French world after his family moves into the French quarter of his hometown, he reacts with self-pity built, however, on the sands of self-irony:

> Malheureux Fils du serpent! Arraché à son milieu naturel, exilé à l'autre bout de la ville, dans une rue où les juifs se saluaient en français, s'interpellaient en français, jouaient en français. Un serpent, jouer à la marelle! Quelle acculturation! Il frôlait les murs, incapable d'articuler sa langue. Car le Français m'intimidait, moi, juif du mellah parmi les juifs parvenus qui mangeaient du pain beurré ou même du pain avec du chocolat. Comme elles étaient aériennes, ces petites filles à chaussettes blanches qui lorgnaient mon béret avec dédain! Je ne pouvais même pas les insulter, elles ne comprenaient pas le judéo-marocain. Alors, avec quelques bambins immigrés, nous leur jetions des pierres pour nous venger de notre dépaysement, troublions leurs jeux,

> balançant des souris mortes entre les pieds des demoiselles qui détalaient, paniquées et éhontées. . . .
>
> Peu à peu, néanmoins, je me mis à jouer à la marelle. Avec les fillettes. Je m'intégrais, lentement mais sûrement. Il m'arrivera même de goûter à du chocolat. Pire, je tombai amoureux. (1981, 211)
>
> [Unhappy Son of the snake! Snatched from his natural habitat, exiled to the other end of the city, on a street where the Jews greeted each other in French, called out to each other in French, played in French. A snake, playing hopscotch! What acculturation! He slunk against the walls, incapable of speaking his language. Because French intimidates me, me, a Jew from the *mellah* among established Jews who eat buttered bread or even bread with chocolate. How ethereal they were, these little girls in white socks who eyed my beret with disdain! I couldn't even insult them, they didn't understand Judeo-Moroccan. So, with several immigrant kids, we threw stones at them to avenge our disorientation, interrupted their games, chucking dead mice at the feet of demoiselles who bounded away in panic and shame. . . .
>
> Little by little, nevertheless, I began to play hopscotch. With the little girls. Integrated myself, slowly but surely. It even happened that I tried some chocolate. Worse yet, I fell in love.]

A bigger surprise, however, awaits him in Israel, where the son of the serpent (a name borrowed from the Talmud), who has succeeded in resisting his father's wish to become a rabbi, encounters, unexpectedly in such surroundings, the perils of contemporary *laïcité*. He now turns into an advocate of a notion of religion that he brings from Morocco's ghetto:

> Le serpent s'était mu en panthère noire qui braillait l'hébreu avec un accent oriental, scandant des slogans dans les rues de Jérusalem contre la ségrégation entre communautés, contre l'aliénation culturelle des juifs originaires d'Asie et d'Afrique, contre la déségrégation sociale et spirituelle des Marocains, contre le désenchantement messianique qui déversait les filles du mellah sur les trottoirs de Tel Aviv. (1981, 219)
>
> [The snake had metamorphosed into a black panther who yelled out Hebrew with an oriental accent, chanting slogans on the streets of Jerusalem against the segregation of communities, against the cultural alienation of Jews from Asia or Africa, against the social and spiritual desegregation of the Moroccans, against the messianic disillusionment that poured the girls of the *mellah* out onto the sidewalks of Tel Aviv.]

With its many portrayals of outsiders, its ironic look at rabbis, its fondness for the improbable, and its evocation of the oral narrative aesthetic,

Bouganim's *Récits du Mellah* appears as a bridge toward the tradition of Yiddish storytelling. The readers encounter in his second book a similar narrative world, equally focused on a small and well-defined community. Bouganim, currently the pedagogical director of the Alliance Israélite Universelle, left Morocco in 1967 for Paris, where he spent two years before settling in Israel. His *Le cri de l'arbre* [The Cry of the Tree], published in 1983 in Israel, depicts the mood among North African immigrants in the Promised Land and shares with the earlier book its lightheartedness and playfulness. Although the book is prefaced by a motto from the Talmud, narrative references to religion have lost their importance even as the biblical image of the crying tree arches over the entire narrative. Tensions between the life in the *mellah* the immigrants left behind and the *ma'bara,* their camps in Israel, occupy the minds of the characters, who are shown as members of a vivacious community, perturbed regularly by smaller quarrels.

> Une dispute éclate chaque jour dans cette réserve de Juifs aigris qu'est une ma'bara. Une femme marocaine roue de coups un enfant yéménite, un voyou irakien risque sa main dans un corsage tunisien, un fonctionnaire roumain traite un malabar tripolitain de "sale frenk," et c'est l'incident qui tourne à la querelle. Accusés de fourbir leurs légendaires couteaux, les Marocains houspillent les Yéménites qui aussitôt se départent de leur non moins légendaire bonhomie. Les Irakiens, sanglés dans leurs légendaires pyjamas, dénoncent la légendaire manie cleptomane des Roumains. Oubliant leurs lointains et communs ancêtres, ils vouent leurs proches ancêtres respectifs aux gémonies terrestres et célestes. Les querelles domestiques sont âpres entre ces déshérités de la terre promise. (1983, 64)

> [A dispute broke out every day in the reservation for embittered Jews that is a *ma'bara.* A Moroccan woman beats up a Yemeni child, an Iraqi lout risks his hand in a Tunisian blouse, a Romanian functionary calls a Tripolitan Malabar a "dirty Frenchman" and that is the incident that becomes a quarrel. Accused of polishing their legendary knives, the Moroccans scolded the Yemenis who immediately abandoned their no less legendary good humor. The Iraqis, engirthed by their legendary pajamas, denounced the legendary kleptomania of the Romanians. Forgetting their distant common ancestors, they subjected their respective immediate ancestors to earthly and heavenly disapprobation. Domestic quarrels are bitter between these disinherited peoples of the Promised Land.]

What keeps this colorful community together is their status as outsiders in a country run by Ashkenazi Jews, who treat the immigrants of non-European origin like second-class Jews and third-class citizens, simply ignoring their needs and rights. Life in the Promised Land has not turned out remotely like the immigrants' visions back home. The shifting politics of identity have twice worked against the immigrants, who in Morocco were perceived primarily as Jews and who now, in Israel, are perceived as Arabs. In one of the key episodes of the book, the author compares the gaze of an Ashkenazi official staring down a Sephardi petitioner to the gaze of the anti-Semite now turned against a Jew of lesser means. The arrogance of the political establishment and the obliviousness of the Begin government toward the situation of the new arrivals in the end elicits acts of resistance from the inhabitants of the *ma'bara*. The novel casts these actions in religious terms and suggests that they are inspired by the hope for a "Messie-philosophe" ["Messiah-philosopher"].

Whereas in his first book Bouganim mentions the realm of politics and the events leading the French protectorate to independence only in passing, his second novel is an eminently political text. *Le cri de l'arbre* chronicles the changes in the attitude of the Sephardim toward the government of the state of Israel; in hindsight it can be read as a *vademecum* to the history of the political upheavals of the 1980s and 1990s.

While the narrative pauses several times to comment on the difficulties the immigrants face with the Hebrew language and on the disadvantages caused by this deficiency, it also plays with the inclusion of Judeo-Moroccan idioms. Anything but defensive about their introduction into this French-language novel, Bouganim toys with the supremacy of pure French when he suggests in a footnote that some of these expressions represent valuable additions to the French language. These words and phrases ought to be considered by the Académie Française, he says, since the French genius had failed to forge such idioms. The book's playful self-referentiality does not concern only the matter of language but also the nature of language altogether. Paying homage in a footnote to Albert Cohen as the ultimate voice of Jewish writing, the author admits how much he—and some of his characters—are indebted to this "père-auteur" (1983, 91) [father-author]. Structurally, however, the differences between Bouganim's book and the works by Cohen are significant. Self-mockingly, another footnote suggests the term "littérature couscous" [couscous literature] to describe the interlacing of different narratives and different modes of speech that characterize *Le cri de l'arbre*. The fact that all these comments are offered in footnotes to the main text mischievously introduces an additional stylistic layer to the book, a dimension of critical and literary discourse, thus undermining its original appearance as a work crafted solely from passion for a certain ethnic heritage.

Postcolonial Anti-Memoirs: Katia Rubinstein's Anything-but *Mémoire illettrée*

Among contemporary Sephardic authors of Maghrebi background, Gil Ben Aych, Marco Koskas, Ami Bouganim, and Katia Rubinstein have made the most radical use of mixing and amalgamating different linguistic and literary codes and conventions. Building on the concept of "transculturation," while challenging the ideas of "acculturation" or "assimilation," the literary critic Françoise Lionnet has advanced the notion of *métissage* to describe postcolonial cultural productions that appropriate the French language to create a "vehicle for expressing a hybrid, heteroglot universe" (1995, 13). This universe is characterized by reciprocal influence between the paradigms of French literature and the literary and linguistic traditions that are part of the native culture of the writers. Among the essential effects of literary *métissage* is that it "de-exoticizes the non-West" (1995, 5), that it breaks down the hierarchy between the dominant culture and the colonial subject and instead incessantly renegotiates their relationship.

Mémoire illettrée d'une fillette d'Afrique du Nord à l'époque coloniale (1979) [The Illiterate Memoir of a Little Girl from North Africa in the Colonial Era] by Katia Rubinstein manifests this form of crossing linguistic, stylistic, and literary borderlines in a variety of ways. Rubinstein (born 1944 in Tunisia) intersperses the narrative of a young girl, Kadem, who describes her upbringing in the old harbor neighborhood of Tunis, with expressions, songs, and idioms of Judeo-Spanish, Arabic, and Italian origin. These languages constitute linguistic markers of identity that accompany the narrative through Kadem's arrival in France in 1959 and her return to Tunis-Carthage sixteen years later. At the same time, the readers find clippings from local newspapers scattered through the main narrative (at the book's outset, juxtaposing the history of celebrating July 14th in Tunisia with the family's celebration of Yom Kippur). These articles underscore the importance of the regional and the immediate vis-à-vis the struggle of the colonial power, France, to keep its grip on Tunisia, as they chronicle this process step by step.

One of the most intricate passages of the memoir speaks to the dissolution of linguistic borders in the narrator's mind as she peruses a copy of Lautréamont's *Les chants de Maldoror* [The Songs of Maldoror], found by chance in a Parisian bookstore. Rubinstein quotes Lautréamont's stanzas first in Arabic before rendering the French original, thus surprising French readers with an effect of cultural estrangement. For the narrator, of course, her mental translation represented just the opposite, an act of intuitive appropriation of the avant-garde of French culture into her own, personal realm of reference.

> ya chab, enti elli taabet min awjaa kawya,
> ech quoun elli tadda alik, ma najemchi nati
> ism lahal jarima ! miskin enti ! kaddach tit'alam !
>
> Adolescent, qui venez de souffrir des douleurs
> cruelles, qui donc a pu commettre sur vous un
> crime que je ne sais de quel nom qualifier!
> Malheureux que vous êtes! comme vous devez souffrir!
>
> Emerveillée par ce que je lisais, je ne me rendis pas tout de suite compte de l'étrange phénomène qui se produisait alors, car ce que mes yeux me donnaient à lire en français, mon esprit l'entendait en arabe.
>
> Le cœur battant, j'ouvrais et refermais le livre avec fébrilité et inconséquence, le manipulant dans tous les sens, comme si j'avais à identifier l'objet que j'avais entre les mains. (1979, 303–4)
>
> [Adolescent, who has just suffered pain
> so cruel, who then was able to commit against you a
> crime that I do not even know how to name!
> Unhappy one that you are! how you must suffer!
>
> Filled with wonder by what I read, I did not immediately become aware of the strange phenomenon that then arose, because what my eyes to me gave to read in French, my mind heard in Arabic.
>
> My heart beating, I opened and closed the book feverishly and fecklessly, manipulating it in every sense, as if I needed to identify the object that I had in my hands.]

The fifteen-year-old girl from Tunis recognizes herself in the cantos of the Comte de Lautréamont (who was fourteen, only a year younger than Kadem, when he was sent from his hometown in Uruguay to France) as they speak to the emotional world of the young newcomer to Europe. More importantly, the poems reflect in some passages an anarchic use of language that only the surrealists of a much later period would appreciate. Kadem had just enjoyed throwing her vocabulary notebooks into the rain:

> Je rirais, joyeuse de voir les mots ainsi déboîtés, écartelés, dispersés, désarticulés, ne sachant plus où donner de la tête, entre mon estomac, ma rate, mon foie, ma vésicule biliaire, plus de vocabulaire, plus de grammaire, plus rien que des lettres et au mieux des syllabes, leur équipée échevelée à travers mes humeurs, et dans la frénésie destructrice et désordonnée, l'ivresse, nocturne, chaotique, bachique. (1979, 302)
>
> [I laughed, overjoyed to see the words disconnected, quartered, dispersed, wrecked, no longer knowing where to give the lead, between my stomach, my spleen, my liver, my gall bladder, no more vocabulary, no more grammar, nothing anymore but letters and at best syllables, their wild escapade through my humors, and in the destructive, disordered frenzy, intoxication, nocturnal, chaotic, bacchic.]

The dissolution of language Kadem experiences here has many resonances in *Les chants de Maldoror,* originally banned in France, as it does, albeit to a different degree, in passages of the *Mémoire illettrée.* The entire book can be read as a provocative dialogue between cultures (French and Tunisian, Arabic and Jewish, Jewish and French, and so forth), between manners of composing autobiographic texts (the memoirs by de Beauvoir, by Memmi, and by Rubinstein), and between languages and literary conventions. The literary critic Ora Avni reads Lautréamont's prose poem (in itself a mixing of genres) as a poetics of reading that favors the image of a circuitous path leading the readers to the text, and as a poetics of anti-Romanticism that rewrites the canonical texts of its period. Following this reading, Rubinstein's memoir can be acknowledged as a form of autojudeography that rejects an easy, direct understanding of the narrator's life by challenging readers to reread the conventions of contemporary French autobiographical writing against the matrix of the poetic and anarchic work by this author from Tunis.[4]

The points of reference are not only Simone de Beauvoir's *Mémoires d'une jeune fille rangée* [Memoirs of a Well-Behaved Young Girl], the canonical women's autobiography published in 1958, but also Albert Memmi's semi-autobiographical text *La statue de sel* (1953) [The Salt Statue]; both de Beauvoir and Memmi received, as Rubinstein did, training in philosophy. Rubinstein's family background is not unlike Memmi's, but the differences of gender and generation are substantive indeed. Memmi addressed in his *Portrait du colonisé précédé du portrait du colonisateur* (1957) [The Colonizer and the Colonized] the linguistic dilemma of the colonized writer dominated by

4. See Avni 1984.

the power of the French language. *La statue de sel,* however, is written in a French that has erased almost completely any references to the linguistic world of the *hara* that Rubinstein so emphatically reintroduces into French literature. Rubinstein, one could say, is an ardent student of Memmi who takes the teacher's nativism more seriously than Memmi did himself. And unlike de Beauvoir's memoir, Rubinstein's autobiography emphasizes its perspective from outside France, from outside the educated Catholic bourgeoisie, and from outside the centers of the intellectual debates. In striking juxtaposition to both texts, Rubinstein's *Mémoire illettrée* presents a "messy" narrative, which violates literary codes and stylistic conventions as well as expectations of how a woman may speak about her body.

Like many of her compatriots, Rubinstein stresses the disappointment of encountering a France very different from the myth of the tolerant nation welcoming everyone to a life of freedom and equality. In her letters, Kadem decries France's "arrogance sèche et creuse, intolérance, mesquinerie, sophistication sournoise. On aime l'exotisme, et l'enjouement qu'il suscite" (1979, 289) [dry and shallow arrogance, intolerance, meanness, sly sophistication. They like exoticism, and the lightheartedness it supports]. And she expresses her astonishment about the "Juifs blonds" [blond Jews], who, in contrast to the "Juifs noirs" [black Jews] of North Africa, have cut their ties to the Jewish religion so irrevocably that their observance of Jewish holidays and rituals has lost its meaning entirely. The author prefaced her memoir with a quote from André Schwarz-Bart's *Le dernier des justes* (1959) [The Last of the Just], in which a long introduction presented the genealogical lines that linked the protagonist Ernie, living in the second half of the twentieth century, back to his ancestors in the tenth century. Rubinstein borrows the justification of Schwarz-Bart's narrator for copying the book of his family—a book that ends with an evocation of the suffering in the concentration camps. The family book as retold by Rubinstein mentions the horrors of the Shoah only in passing, when she remembers the disappearance of an aunt from Paris during the war. Kadem's mother only has a few laconic words for the aunt's fate: "pourquoi y faisaient les Allemands?, elle sait pas ézactement-ézactement; d'après elle, y sont beaux et forts mais y z'ont la méchanceté dans le sang!" (1979, 43) [why did the Germans do that?, she didn't know ezactly-ezactly; according to her, they're fine and strong but they've got nastiness in their blood!]

Thus, Rubinstein's memoir also engages in dialogue with the Jewish literature by Ashkenazi writers and their emphasis on the Shoah as the dominant event in Jewish history. Schwarz-Bart framed his *Le dernier des justes* with references to the oppression of Jews: the pogroms of York in 1185 and, almost 800 years and 400 pages later, the Nazi persecution. In the family book of the Jews from Tunis, it is emigration to France rather than the Shoah that interrupts lives and disperses families. The five segments of the book follow the girl's path from the realm of the family to the courtyard of their apartment building, from school to the city and eventually to Paris. Here, she realizes the costs her family has to pay for her restless curiosity, which even France will not be able to pacify.

"The Impossibility of Acting French Without Liking Ham"

Contemporary francophone authors of North African, Caribbean, and Asian background have generated a literature that testifies to the tribulations of immigration and to the difficulties of acculturation and social acceptance. The realities of displacement in the aftermath of decolonization and of exilic life in present-day France, experienced by people of diverse national, ethnic, and religious backgrounds, have created a context in which the fate of the Sephardic Jews arriving in France is just one example of many demographic shifts announcing the advent of globalization. Thus, the notion of the Jew as the embodiment of the person without a fatherland, inhabiting the margins of society in which he functions as the Other per se, meets with competing images, among them the "boat people" from Asia, the Muslim immigrants from the Maghreb, and the refugees from the Balkans haunted by the terrors of "ethnic cleansing."

The writing of the young Jewish authors and philosophers has in one way or another commented on the fate of all of these groups—most notably Gluckstein in his *Nos grands hommes*, where an orphan from Indochina is adopted by Ashkenazi parents and grows up to carry on the tradition of Yiddish writing. Hybrid identities (the writer Salim Jay, for example, is the son of a Jewish mother and a Muslim father) have come to inhabit spaces whose cultural overdetermination the term diaspora can grasp only vaguely. Hybrid positions have rearranged demarcation lines, crossing the borders of ethnicity, religion, and national identity. In the heated debates of 1989 surrounding the *Affaire du foulard*—questioning whether schools should allow Muslim girls to wear head scarves—Alain Finkielkraut and several other Jewish intellectuals insisted on the state's right to uphold the secularism [*laïcité*] of the public schools by forbidding members of minorities to display signs of their ethnic or religious adherence.

The literary explorations of the younger Sephardic writers overlap partly with those of (non-Jewish) writers belonging to communities that share with the Maghrebi Jews the experience of displacement, even if the concrete circumstances differ from each other. One of the commonalities concerns the portrayal of the lot of the older generations. For the members of the younger generations of Ashkenazi descent, the silence of their parents was a major incentive to turn to the medium of literature. It is a very different silence that the offspring of the Sephardic immigrants from the Maghreb encounter when facing the experience of their parents, and yet this silence, too, is one of the moving forces and major themes in their writing. In *L'homme de paille*, Marco Koskas uses the term "mutisme" [silence] for the emotional syndrome with which many of the first-generation immigrants responded to the difficult transition from their home countries to a society that was indifferent, if not hostile to its newcomers. "Entre nous que de silence, que de déserts, que de cicatrices" (1990, 46) [Between us nothing but silence, but deserts, but scars], reminisces the narrator of Gilles Zenou's last novel, *La désaffection* [Disaffection], about the relationship to his father, a weak man haunted by fear, pained by an illness his family was too embarrassed to face, and able to teach his son only one thing: "l'art de la fugue, l'art de l'effacement" (1990, 47) [the art of the fugue, the art of effacement]. In Chochana Boukhobza's novel *Pour l'amour du père* [For the Love of the Father], silence continually shuts down the dialogue between thirty-eight-year-old Alice and her father, an immigrant from Tunisia:

> Ce silence, pour Alice, ressemble au ciel de Paris. Il en a la couleur, la texture. L'air gris de la ville plane dans la maison, hiver comme été. Les années passent, il fait toujours gris, il fait toujours triste. Le père n'arrive pas à guérir de la Tunisie, il passe son temps à comparer, il compare la saveur des fruits qu'il a mangés là-bas avec ceux qu'il achète sur le marché de Clichy; il dit qu'au soleil la vie était plus facile, qu'elle avait du goût, que la pauvreté était légère à supporter. A Paris, celui qui manque de quelque chose, répète-t-il, est dans la détresse. La ville est trop grande, l'homme n'y a point de voisin et sa vie est dure. Il dit, la France est un pays où les vieux habitent seuls, sans leurs enfants; il dit, dans ce pays, les jeunes parquent leurs parents dans des asiles. Il dit qu'il a peur de l'avenir. Il ne dit pas qu'il craint que ses cinq enfants ne l'abandonnent, mais c'est comme s'il le leur criait.

> *Ana barani*. Je suis un étranger.
> Quand le père parle, sa parole est étouffante.
> Alice, à cause de la parole du père, n'a pas eu d'enfance. (1996, 10–11)

> [This silence, for Alice, resembles the Paris sky. It has its color, its texture. The gray air of the city hovers in the house, winter and spring. Years pass, it is still gray out, the weather is always sad. Father cannot get over Tunisia, he spends his time comparing, he compares the taste of the fruits he ate there with those he buys at the Clichy market; he says that in the sun life was easier, it had more flavor, that poverty was easy to endure. In Paris, he repeats, the man who wants for something is in distress. The city is too big, a man has no neighbors and his life is hard. He says, France is a country where the old live alone, without their children, he says, in this country, the young park their parents in homes for the elderly. He says he is afraid of the future. He does not say he fears that his five children will abandon him, but it is as if he cries out to them exactly that.
> *Ana barani*. I am a foreigner.
> When the father speaks, his words are stifling.
> Alice, because of the father's words, did not have a childhood.]

His daughters, having grown up under the European paradigms of psychology and self-awareness, have no difficulty diagnosing their father's inability to articulate his feelings as a "pathologie fréquente chez les immigrés" (1996, 45) [pathology often found in immigrants]. The father, in contrast, is not able to distance himself from his experiences and emotions or to gain a cognitive or even political understanding of his situation as an immigrant relegated to the very bottom of the social ladder. The offspring of the survivors of the Shoah have difficulties filling the ellipsis of their parents' discourse because the experience of the camps simply defeats the powers of imagination. The offspring of the immigrants, in contrast, struggle to grasp the situation of their elders. Often, the first-generation immigrants left their home countries too early in their lives to understand fully what their families left behind; for them, the customs and social realities of modern Europe are closer than life in the *hara* or the *mellah*.

It is not by chance that the protagonist of Boukhobza's *Pour l'amour du père* is a lawyer who works for the poor and underprivileged. Having witnessed the very beginning of her father's "drame de l'exil," when a ring he wore as a last memento of his deceased wife disappeared into the pockets of a Tunisian customs official, Alice later trained to become an attorney in order to fight the arbitrary violence of the state. (Similarly, the son of the title character in *L'homme de paille* thought about entering the legal profession as he foresaw the need to prevent his father from going to jail.) Alice's choice of profession is analogous to these authors' decision to pick up the pen and write about the tribulations of immigrants. This decision to write, however, does not result in sentimental texts of monochromatic defense for the ways of their parents. *Pour l'amour du père* speaks in highly critical terms about the tyranny of a father upon his family and the pain he, the "Oriental," inflicts on his children with his intolerance. With the distance from the patriarchally organized societies of North Africa, Boukhobza has also gained insight into the mechanisms of families governed by paternal authority. Her writing emerges from a feminist position that lets her protagonist doubt for the greater part of the book whether she, considering her own childhood experience, ever wants to have children. Among her sisters, disappointment with the institution of marriage is common. One of them has fled from the authoritarian family into the yoke of an unendurable marriage, and another one has been forced out of the house because of her love for a non-Jew. The father's experience of exile, the book shows, is a tragic one, yet the fate of his daughters and their suffering due to the conventional roles attributed to women are brought into the foreground of the narrative. Like many of the younger francophone women writers from North Africa, Boukhobza dismantles the drama of exile to show that it is part of a larger family drama that has many more victims rather than one (male) tragic hero.[5] The family's shared experience of living in France does not provide enough of a common basis for all its members to emphasize solidarity with each other over the bonds they share with people from the outside.

Alice is working on behalf of the Kurdish people, and the novel identifies her as a Jew outside her family's realm only when she meets Saïd, a Tunisian expatriate who is not Jewish. Boukhobza does not dwell at all on the tensions between the Arabic world and the Jews, which are mentioned in the dialogues between Saïd and Alice, but instead goes on to underline the common ground shared by both of them. Saïd sums up these commonalities in the following way: "Mon père était au FLN. Il a pris les armes pour chasser les Français. Et moi, j'aime Paris, ses rues, ses bars, l'alcool. Tu saisis le paradoxe?" (1996, 103) [My father was in the FLN. He took up arms to chase away the French. And me, I like Paris, its streets, its bars, alcohol. You grasp the paradox?] The core

5. See Cazenave 2000, 200.

of the generational divide between the immigrants and their children, it turns out, is not unique to the Jewish families from North Africa, who, as recognized in their literature over and over again, often are mistaken by the French for Muslims unless they directly identify themselves as Jews. And the experience of being the offspring of the generation that first came to France provides grounds for a solidarity between Arabs and Jews that is stronger than the old divide between these two peoples.

The figure of Alice as a lawyer fighting for the rights of all foreigners in France thus mirrors the mission of the author—to present the case of immigrants in the aftermath of decolonization and on the threshold to globalization rather than a new version of the old image of the "Juif errant" [wandering Jew].[6] Boukhobza's peer Colette Fellous offers in her *Avenue de France* (2001) a prayer to preface the account of her and her family's journey from Tunisia to France:

> C'est une prière qui aimerait épeler l'histoire d'un siècle non seulement dans cette région du monde, Tunisia North Africa, mais aussi dans tous les autres pays tissés de cabrioles, migrations, déplacements, illusions, glissements, métamorphoses, collages, paradoxes, clans, réseaux, rivalités, colonisations, grands cauchemars organisés, abandons, rêves de tous les jours, servitudes volontaires, hallucinations en tout genre. (2001, 24)
>
> [It is a prayer which would spell out the history of a century not only in this region of the world, Tunisia North Africa, but also in every other country woven of capers, migrations, displacements, illusions, slippings, metamorphoses, collages, paradoxes, clans, networks, rivalries, colonizations, great organized nightmares, abandonments, everyday dreams, voluntary servitudes, all sorts of hallucination.]

Like many other children of the era of postcolonization, Fellous, too, acknowledges that the story of her coreligionists from the Maghreb is just one among many narratives of displacement—a narrative in which the common experience of becoming and remaining unsettled overrides the ethnic and religious differences between Jews and other groups forced from their homes. This embracing of the fate of all the troubled regions in the world and their inhabitants, in Fellous's case, goes hand in hand with an unreserved disinterest

6. In this respect, too, she resembles the daughter of the immigrant protagonists in Annie Fitoussi's *La mémoire folle de Mouchi Rabbinou* (1985), who becomes a judge.

in the Jewish roots of her own family. These roots are not discernible in her reconstruction of the life of her relatives from the 1880s on through 1967, the year when Fellous arrived in Marseille. The "uprooting," the loss of this part of the heritage, predates the process of a migration whose many facets Fellous keeps evoking in her literary[7] as well as in her journalistic work, such as on her radio show *Carnet nomade* [Nomad Notebook] on channel France-Culture.

Effacements: Marlène Amar's *La femme sans tête*

The texts of this generation of Sephardic Jews of Maghrebi origins speak to the disenchantment with the French diaspora primarily by presenting the disillusionment of others, usually of the grandparents, parents, or older siblings, and their feelings of estrangement from the French nation, rather than elaborating on such experiences on the part of their young protagonists, who are often stand-ins for the authors themselves. Thus, it may be right to state that Marlène Amar's *La femme sans tête* (1993) [The Woman Without a Head] presents, metaphorically speaking, the decapitation of a Jewish woman from Algeria as the ultimate subordination of the immigrant to her new surroundings.[8] However, Amar's book is yet another example of a text that depicts not the protagonist's own drama of acculturation, but that of a relative, in this case an older sister. This difference in these texts is a substantive one: it presents the narrators as witnesses who were able to step back from the fate of those hurt by the strains of displacement, the dynamics of filial expectations, and the pressure of affiliation—to step back by writing about it.

The uncanny transformation that the older sister of the first-person narrator has undergone since her arrival from Algeria in *La femme sans tête* cannot be seen solely as a response to the pressure of becoming French. With the aid of cosmetic surgery, the sister changes her physical appearance to efface all corporeal traces of her North African origins: "Ma sœur, en se transformant, a fini par l'être pour de bon. Plus française que nature, même. Aujourd'hui, elle lit le Nouveau Testament et dit "israélite" en parlant d'un juif" (1993, 96) [My sister, in transforming herself, ended up being the real thing. More French than nature itself. Today, she reads the New Testament and says "Israelite"

7. In her *Midi à Babylone* (1994), for example, Fellous alludes to the fate of refugees from Albania arriving in Italy's port Bari in 1993.

8. This is the trajectory of the argument presented by Ireland 1998.

when speaking of a Jew]. Her transformation into the archetypical French woman is depicted in a mournful manner as a kind of metamorphosis, and as such it surely invites comparison with another archetypical figure: Franz Kafka's Gregor Samsa. Whichever of the countless interpretations of this canonical text of Jewish literature one would like to follow, one would be hard pressed to ignore the fact that Gregor Samsa's metamorphosis was a very direct response to filial submission to an emotionally grueling family dynamic. The overbearing pressure of having to relinquish essential notions of the self to parental expectations also provides the context in which "la femme sans tête" [the woman without a head] loses her physical as well as her psychological self. Her father commands total silence to avoid any ruptures in his home, which he has modeled in all details on the lifestyle of the French bourgeoisie:

> Le "tais-toi" de mon père s'adressait pourtant davantage à ma sœur, à ses débordements de mots, de rires, à tout ce qui, en elle, trahissait la terre d'où l'on venait. Elle a fini par l'entendre, ce commandement répété inlassablement, par s'y soumettre. Et aujourd'hui, même s'il n'y a plus d'air de famille, elle a fini aussi par nous ressembler. (1993, 109)
>
> [The "be quiet" of my father was, however, addressed more to my sister, to her excess of words, of laughter, to everything in her that betrayed the land from which we came. She finally heard it, this tirelessly repeated commandment, finally submitted to it. And today, even if there is no longer a family resemblance, she also finally looks like us in the end.]

Her mother, on the other hand, commands yet another form of cooperation: "Ma mère aspirait à l'éclat éternel, militait pour une féminité intemporelle. Et dans ce domaine, ma sœur était, sans aucun doute, sa meilleure disciple" (1993, 101) [My mother aspired to eternal brilliance, campaigned for a timeless femininity. And in this domain, my sister was, without a doubt, her best disciple]. The narrator can explain her sister's transformation into somebody else as a move within a dynamics in which the parents figure as agents promoting total assimilation, not without suffering more or less obviously from the costs they have to pay for obtaining their ideal:

> Je crois que le mal de dos de ma mère et les métamorphoses de ma sœur veulent dire la même chose: une rébellion de la chair contre la loi du silence imposée par l'exil. Comme si, en l'absence des mots, les corps se mettaient à parler. (1993, 93)

> [I believe my mother's back pain and my sister's metamorphoses mean the same thing: a rebellion in the flesh against the law of silence imposed by exile. As if, in the absence of words, the body begins to speak.]

Even if the narrative about the sister's metamorphosis does not result in a state comparable to the ugliness of Gregor Samsa's transformed self, but instead in a seemingly "nonethnic" body of beauty, it remains committed to Kafka's "Metamorphosis" precisely because it has such an anti-Kafkaesque twist. As a literary response to Kafka, Amar's *La femme sans tête* participates in the literature that speaks to the very physical aspect of anti-Semitism. Sander Gilman has shown in detail that inscribed in the history of anti-Semitism is a history of constructing a Jewish body as *the* anti-body, foreign both to nature and society. Gregor Samsa's metamorphosis, the pain of the narrator's mother in *La femme sans tête*, and her sister's self-mutilation in the name of French beauty: all can be read as forms of submission to the power of anti-Semitic constructs, as manifestations of a self-hatred that leaves these figures helpless and overwhelmed, ready to give in.

Recording the drama of exile as an act of the family drama, Amar's narrator (in many ways a stand-in for the author herself, who was born in 1949 in the Algerian Sahara) is the one who succeeds in articulating, via language, what her mother and sister display as physical symptoms. And in a manner similar to the son in Koska's *L'homme de paille*, the family reacts to this form of enunciation with silence, if not with indignation, as it threatens to breach the familial contract that binds all members to keep silent. Writing is a substitute for speaking, a form of clandestine articulation:

> Ce silence m'étonnait sans que je cherche à savoir d'où il venait. On ne s'interroge pas sur sa famille. Tout se passe comme si ce qui concernait les liens de chair et de sang "allait de soi." Parfois, il m'arrivait de penser qu'ils avaient dû, tout simplement, oublier que j'étais journaliste.
>
> Il m'a fallu entreprendre ce récit pour comprendre. Comprendre que dire était déjà de trop—alors écrire—dans cette famille qui avait choisi l'effacement comme la manière la plus sûre de se fondre dans la masse, de réussir à s'intégrer. La méthode caméléon. Un des leitmotive: "Motus et bouche cousue." (1993, 49)

> [This silence shocked me and I didn't try to understand where it came from. One doesn't ask oneself questions about one's family. Everything happens as if that which concerns the bonds of flesh and blood "comes from itself."

Sometimes, I came to think that they must simply have forgotten that I was a journalist.

I had to begin this story in order to understand. Understand that to speak was already too much—then to write—in this family that had chosen effacement as the most secure manner of planting itself in the masses, of succeeding at integrating itself. The chameleon method. One of the leitmotifs: "Words and mouth sewn shut."]

The narrator of Amar's second book, *Des gens infréquantables* (1996) [Bad Company], another young woman who became a journalist to break the parental silence, follows the path of Samuel, a cousin, from the Tunisian provinces all the way to France. In *La femme sans tête*, Amar had alluded to a new generation interested in everything their parents and grandparents had left behind, insisting on answers to their questions about a country of origin they had never seen: "Ils n'ont pas connu l'Algérie mais l'Algérie leur manque. Ils disent ne se sentir de nulle part, cherchent à savoir: 'Comment c'était là-bas?' " (1993, 97) [They have never known Algeria but they miss Algeria. They say they feel they don't come from anywhere, they try to understand: "What was it like there?"] Amar is writing on the very threshold of this generation, chronicling all the facets of its transitions between cultural, historical, and political systems, including the tensions between the arriving North African Jews (settling, for example, in the Parisian neighborhood "Le Sentier") and the Ashkenazim who did not always welcome them with open arms. She opens her second book with the description of an encounter that sets the stage for the entire book:

> Il sentait le savon, portait des vestes anglaises, légèrement étriquées, des pantalons trop courts. Je le croisais parfois dans la rue, avec son labrador. C'était un architecte d'une cinquantaine d'années, marié et père de deux enfants. Il avait un nom alsacien, d'origine ashkénaze. Il me jetait des regards brillants en m'entretenant de ses maîtresses qu'il prenait à la hussard dans les châteaux de vieux camarades ou sous des porches le soir, en promenant le chien. Il parlait fort, comblant les vides entre les mots d'un son continu et tremblé, comme le râle d'une bête amoureuse. Il n'aimait pas les Juifs d'Afrique du Nord. Il les appelait "la smala du Sentier." Un jour, il m'a dit: "Ils ne peuvent rien faire sans crier, s'agiter, gesticuler, sans faire de bruit. Ce sont des gens infréquentable." (1996, 17)

> [He smelled of soap, wore English jackets, a bit snug, pants that were too short. I passed him sometimes on the street with his labrador. He was an ar-

> chitect of about fifty, married and the father of two children. He had an Alsatian name of Ashkenazi origin. He threw me bright glances while telling me of his mistresses and how he would take her cavalierly in the chateaus of old friends or on the porch at night, while walking the dog. He spoke loudly, filling the spaces between his words with a continuous, trembling sound like the groan of an animal in love. He did not like Jews from North Africa. He called them "the Sentier's brood." One day, he said to me: "They can do nothing without shouting, bustling, gesticulating, without making noise. They are bad company."]

Amar may be in a position to pay attention to conflicts beyond the fault line of gentile society at large and the community of Jewish immigrants from the Maghreb because the social background of her own family put her into the upper echelons of the middle class. From this perspective, the issue of poverty, which not infrequently plays an important role in the works of her non-Jewish peers of immigrants to France, retreats into the background, while an awareness of finer shades of social interaction simultaneously opens up.

"Zulus from North Africa" in the French Provinces: Paule Darmon's *Baisse les yeux, Sarah*

In Paule Darmon's *Baisse les yeux, Sarah* (1980) [Lower Your Eyes, Sarah], the different routes Sephardi and Ashkenazi Judaism have taken over the course of the last century become a matter of contention between Sarah Levy, whose parents immigrated from the Maghreb, and the Ashkenazi family of her husband-to-be. Admitting that she never had to cry about a relative killed by the Nazis, never had to search for anyone lost in the war, and never had to suffer from apocalyptic visions of persecution, the young woman can summarize her life by stating that she is simply a young, happy Jewish woman of North African background, who only occasionally is plagued by the fact that her "naissance tardive" (1980, 163) [late birth] left her untouched by the suffering of her people.

This novel by Darmon (born 1945 in Casablanca) is an ironic look at a young, self-assertive Jewish woman of Maghrebi descent living in France in the sixties and seventies. The socially deconstructive efforts of the first-person narrator initially concern the status of her overpowering father, a lawyer from a Jewish-Algerian family. In his library the works of Sartre stand next to the Talmud, and his maxim, according to his daughter, is "Je suis juif, oui, et je vous emmerde" (1980, 23) [I am Jewish, yes, and I annoy you]. But the daughter's rebellion also finds a target in her mother, even though she is, as Sarah admits, one of the few Jewish Moroccan women living a relatively independent life. But Sarah can only see in her a woman who wasted her hard-earned education and her freedom by submitting totally to her husband, betraying the strong female tradition of a family that included a woman who had dared to defy a sultan and lost her life over it.[9]

Darmon's book pays attention to nuances of Maghrebi identity in which the aspects of gender and social background merge with the one of national belonging. The hybrid identity of the young protagonist consists not only in her growing up Jewish in an Islamic society (she was eighteen when her family left Casablanca for a town in the Midi), and not just in the fact that she is living as a North African in France, but also in a "mésalliance" [mismatch] looming in her family's past:

> les "aristocrates" venaient d'Algérie, alors que les "sauvages" étaient marocains.
>
> Mon père, juif français d'Algérie, avait donc commis une mésalliance, selon sa famille, en épousant une juive marocaine à laquelle il avait fait la charité de sa noble nationalité française. . . . La loi Crémieux . . . les autorisait à porter un regard horizontal sur le monde et les investissait d'un sentiment d'existence légale qui dégénéra en sentiment de supériorité vis-à-vis de leurs coreligionnaires moins heureux. (1980, 18)

> [the "aristocrats" came from Algeria, while the "savages" were Moroccan.
>
> My father, a French Jew from Algeria, had therefore committed a misalliance, according to his family, by marrying a Moroccan Jew upon whom he charitably bestowed his noble French nationality. . . . The Crémieux Law . . . allowed them to cast a horizontal look upon the world and invested them with a sense of legal existence that degenerated into a feeling of superiority over their less fortunate coreligionists.]

Darmon's narrator is fulfilling several tasks at once. Whereas the passage quoted above may address primarily a reader unaware of the Jewish hierarchies in the Maghreb and ignorant of the laws governing the citizenship of subjects in France's former territories and colonies, large parts of the book bear no such

9. For an interpretation of the issue of female sexuality in Darmon's novel, see Klein 1998, 70–72.

instructional intentions at all. Rather, they give voice to Sarah the *enfant terrible*, whose decision to "détester méthodiquement" (1980, 56) [hate methodically] her family produces a several-page-long list of all the things she hates about her clan. These include her grandmother's accent (which distorts the beautiful French language), her father's preferences for her brothers and his insistence that she should remain quiet, and the mezuzah attached to the door of a house in which the Jewish laws are observed on holidays and broken the following days. The life of acculturation is a hypocritical one in her eyes, led in a country of dubious reputation, "la France antisémite de ces milieux fermés de la grande bourgeoisie du Maroc ou des réactionnaires de la France de Pétain" (1980, 114) [the anti-Semitic France of those closed circles of the Moroccan upper bourgeoisie or the reactionaries of Pétain's France]. But these are not the associations of Sarah's father Charles, who left Morocco because of rampant corruption. His daughter's narrative pokes fun at his naïveté:

> La FFFFFrance (à prononcer avec extase), la FFFFFrance donc nous attendait.
>
> La justice, l'égalité, la liberté et la fraternité nous tendaient les bras.
>
> Effrayé par un Paris tentaculaire dont la réalité agressive métamorphosait son souvenir de Casablanca en petite ville, Charles Lévy . . . se rabattait avec courage sur la province française. . . . Restait à savoir dans quel trou, merveilleusement verdoyant et français, nous allions planter notre tente de nomade, dans quelle charmante petite bourgade, quelle ville historique, nous allions construire notre caravansérail. (1980, 112)

> [FFFFFrance (to be pronounced ecstatically), FFFFFrance awaited us.
>
> Justice, equality, liberty, and brotherhood greeted us with open arms.
>
> Terrified by a sprawling Paris, whose aggressive reality transformed his memory of Casablanca into that of a little city, Charles Lévy . . . decided courageously upon the French province. . . . It remained to be seen in which spot, marvelously green and French, we would pitch our nomad tent, in which charming little village, which historic town, we would erect our encampment.]

It is a desire to exaggerate the differences between home and exile by playing into the distorting stereotypes of the Maghrebi as exotic desert dwellers that drives the language of this passage.

Using a strategy similar to the observation that opened Amar's *Des gens infréquantables*, Darmon's *Baisse les yeux, Sarah* situates the immigrants from the Maghreb in a triangular constellation rather than in mere opposition to the French goyim. They appear as the savage Other both in the eyes of the French gentiles and the Ashkenazi Jews, who also treat them as invading newcomers without credentials, as colonial subjects:

> Comment avait-on pu imaginer une seconde que ces juifs du Maroc aient les mêmes coutumes que les juifs polonais? . . .
>
> *Ashkénaze*.
>
> C'était donc ça. Nous faisions partie du groupe sous-developpé des séphardim. . . . Nous étions exclus de la noblesse ashkénaze. Nous n'avions pas souffert le quart de ce qu'ils avaient eux souffert. Preuve irréfutable de notre barbarie, là-bas, au Maroc, les juifs ne parlent pas yiddish mais arabe, pis, judéo-arabe. Nous avions failli à la Culture hébraïque, aux grandes traditions, au sens de la famille. Certes, nous étions juifs, c'était déjà quelque chose. Mais juifs du Maroc. . . .
>
> Dans cette famille dégénérée de Zoulous d'Afrique du Nord, mon père, seul, aurait mérité d'être ashkénaze. (1980, 173–74)

> [How could they have imagined for a single second that these Moroccan Jews had the same customs as the Jews of Poland? . . .
>
> *Ashkenazi*.
>
> That was it then. We were part of the underdeveloped group of the Sephardic. . . . We were excluded from Ashkenazi nobility. We had not suffered a quarter of what they had suffered. Irrefutable proof of our barbarousness: there, in Morocco, the Jews do not speak Yiddish but Arabic, or worse yet, Judeo-Arabic. We had failed in Hebrew Culture, in the great traditions, in the meaning of family. Certainly, we were Jewish, that was something. But Jews from Morocco. . . .
>
> In this degenerated family of Zulus from North Africa, my father alone would have deserved to be Ashkenazi.]

With bitterness, sarcasm, but also disarming humor, Darmon dismisses the myth of "one Jewish culture" in France and dismantles the status Ashkenazi Jewry used to enjoy before the Sephardic immigrants managed to establish themselves as self-assertively as the other pillar of French Jewry. Declaring that it is the task of the authors of Maghrebi descent to reveal the tensions and conflicts within French Judaism, she follows these conflicts into the arena of conjugal life, as Sarah, surrendering her emancipated consciousness, goes on to marry an Ashkenazi Jew. She does not, however, succeed in finding happiness with him. Nobody escapes Darmon's authorial irony, not even her protagonist Sarah. The second-generation immigrant ultimately has not done much better than her mother, who as an adolescent certainly had not read de Beauvoir's memoirs, which Sarah keeps carrying around with her, trying to find the key for a life of female independence. What she finds instead is a lover.

Stories of Female Resistance

The relationship between the sexes as well as a woman's relationship to her body differs dramatically, the Sephardic women writers emphasize, with the cultural spaces women inhabit. Space, their works demonstrate, is indeed a gendered category, and, in the era predating the women's movement, the diasporic experience did not necessarily offer a more liberal attitude. Annie Goldmann in *Les filles de Mardochée* compares with her native Tunisia where "le rapport avec le corps était plus franc et plus violent" (1979, 122) [the relationship with the body was more frank and more violent]. Rubinstein's *Mémoire illettrée* reminisced in very frank terms about the heroine Kadem's introduction as a child into the realm of sexuality—an initiation into a sphere of pleasure that she later in life will not accept as a male domain. The texts by the Maghrebi-born women writers all testify to the claim of the anthropologist James Clifford that "diasporic experiences are always gendered" (1994, 313). Rubinstein and her younger female colleagues took it upon themselves to write the counterpart to Memmi's critique of colonialism from the perspective of the colonized woman. Gisèle Halimi, born in Tunisia in 1927, provided a highly visible model with her autobiographical works (*La cause des femmes* and *Le lait de l'oranger* [The Women's Cause; The Milk of the Orange Tree]) and her political activism promoting women's rights in France. While Annie Goldmann and Janine Gdalia in 1989 published their *Le judaïsme au féminin* [Judaism in the Feminine] attempting to align Jewish tradition with modern feminism, other women writers of Maghrebi descent traced in their fiction the price women have to pay for their passage as Jewish women into French society. "Voilà la diaspora: elle reçoit nos juives et nous renvoie des Françaises sans . . ." (Jacques 1987, 244) [This is the diaspora: it takes our Jewish women and sends back to us French women without . . .], an older Jewish woman who stayed in Egypt reprimands the young protagonist from Paris in Paula Jacques's novel *L'héritage de tante Carlotta* [Aunt Carlotta's Legacy]. Without having to finish her sentence, the readers understand that the old woman misses in the daughter of the émigré the proper respect for Jewish tradition (which, as the novel humorously reveals, is not easy to find in Cairo's diminished Jewish community either).

Paule Darmon in *Baisse les yeux, Sarah* pointed to the schizophrenic situation of the Jewish woman in the Maghreb who "en fille de l'Orient, la sexualité était pour elle une chose naturelle et heureuse, alors qu'en femme juive, son sexe était impur et sale" (1980, 27) [as a girl of the Orient, sexuality was for her something natural and happy, while as a Jewish woman, her sex was impure and dirty]. Women's autojudeographies speak to this inherent contradiction by reconstructing the tensions inherent in the female biographies of the older generations.[10] In Darmon's case, the personality of the young heroine appears to be the outcome of the mother's reaction of self-punishment to the dilemma of her situation. The daughter responds rebelliously to her mother's self-negation and she will continue to do so in dealing with the self-indulgence of her husband. Sarah conceptualizes her "refus de féminité" [rejection of femininity], perceived by her surroundings in misogynist terms as frigidity, in the language of anticolonization, ultimately referring back to the power struggle that had impacted so profoundly the fate of her family. Prepared to put up "une résistance acharnée et souterraine contre toute forme de colonisation et d'occupation autoritaires" [a fierce and secret resistance against all forms of authoritarian colonization and occupation], Sarah promises herself that she will never become "terrain conquis, le territoire occupé" (1980, 218) [conquered terrain, occupied territory]. Rubinstein's Kadem had uttered a very similar diatribe against female submission and the asymmetry of power relations governing the institution of marriage.

Whereas Janine Gdalia and Annie Goldmann in their Jewish feminist encyclopedia tried to situate the Jewish woman within the tradition of Judaism from the perspective of Western female emancipation, Chochana Boukhobza in her novel *Un été à Jérusalem* (1986) [A Summer in Jerusalem] traces how a young Jewish Parisian of Maghrebi origins tries to hold on to her female independence while experiencing a contemporary Israel caught up in male warfare. It is the story of Sarah, a seventeen-year-old girl who has persuaded her Tunisian parents to leave Belleville and to settle in Israel. Sarah herself, however, remains in France, as if promoting the family's aliyah ensured the

10. Thus, Pierre Horn is hardly right when he singles out Darmon's stance, stating that she "has employed an unusual frankness of tone and language, given her culture, ethnicity and sex, in presenting her heroine's revolt against resignation and role constraints" (Horn 1997, 154).

heroine's freedom in the *galut*, the French diaspora. Three years after her family's move to the Promised Land, she visits her parents and brothers in Israel. The encounter between the estranged members of the multiply displaced family is the center of the first-person narrative, which portrays the daughter as a "nomad," "une étrangère" (1986, 213) [a foreigner], who has more and more difficulties relating to her religious parents. A strong political dimension informs the text as both her brothers are fighting in the Chouf mountains against Lebanon, dismissing Sarah's abhorrence of warfare and desire for peace as typical of the naive Jew of the diaspora. Sarah's first-person narrative is concerned primarily with her identity as a Jewish woman returning to the Promised Land from the "exil goy" (1986, 166) [goy exile] and oscillates between moments of feminist self-assertiveness and moods of self-doubt and self-denigration. The "move from a literature of testimony to one of revolt," which the literary critic Odile Cazenave identified as a main feature of contemporary francophone women novelists from Africa, also characterizes Boukhobza's work (Cazenave 2000, 239).

The ominous warning of the prophet Jeremiah, according to which Jerusalem will become the whore of the nations, peculiarly begins to resonate with Sarah. Her fascination with Jerusalem is an ambiguous one; the modern, nonreligious woman experiences the city and its orthodox tradition as oppressive, as "hors des limites de ma logique" (Boukhobza 1986, 35) [beyond the limits of my logic]. Sarah's revolt and search for sexual liberation introduce her to a prostitute, whose original Arabic name connoted "mildness" before she changed the consonants of its Hebrew rendition to Mavrika, the "étincelante" (1986, 131) [glittering one]. In Sarah's imagination, Mavrika begins to personify Jerusalem's Other, and, moreover, the

> femme impénétrable que traquent depuis vingt siècles les cabalistes et les talmudistes. Drapée de noir, le visage dissimulé, elle s'introduit dans les fortins les plus défendus, grelotte devant les sépharim, s'oublie devant les disciples qui gémissent leurs prières, se donne sur les chemins de ronde aux soldats barbus. En hébreu, on l'appelle la Shehina. La Présence. (1986, 151)
>
> [impenetrable woman hounded for twenty centuries by the Kabbalists and the Talmudists. Draped in black, face hidden, she enters the most forbidden forts, trembles before the Sepharim, forgets herself before the disciples who murmur their prayers, gives herself to bearded soldiers on the highways. In Hebrew, they call her Shehina. The Presence.]

When Sarah learns, at the end of the book, about the death of her pacifist lover in Beirut, she seems to lose her mind and appears to identify herself with Mavrika. The image of the crazy prostitute, who publicly denounces the presence of God in a city whose sons all have been sent to die in the war, hovers over Sarah's pain.

Un été à Jérusalem revisits Jeremiah's prophecy and the sexual imagery of the (admittedly ambiguous) biblical warning that Jerusalem will become the whore of nations. Sarah's quest to define herself and her identities as a Jew, a daughter, and a lover have all been affected by her "exil hébraïque qui me transformait" (1986, 166) [Hebraic exile that transformed me]. Stripping away the misogynist connotations of the image of the whore—a move encouraged by the positive images of prominent prostitutes offered in the Bible—the book insists that it is the male politics of nationalism that have corrupted Jerusalem. In this battlefield, two women, Mavrika and her self-proclaimed alter ego Sarah, virtuously decry the tragic fate of Jerusalem's sons. Boukhobza merges the sexual and the political sphere against the backdrop of a highly evocative biblical imagery, no longer portraying a subversive heroine but instead a woman damaged, like Mavrika, by male sexual aggression.

The language of victimhood, of colonization, but also of resistance used in these texts connotes not by chance the Jewish experience of the twentieth-century. The narratives construed by these Jewish women writers explore the lot of female victims, but they are not narratives of victimization. Marlène Amar offers in the stance of her narrator a powerful counterexample to the headless woman who pays for her placement as a non-Jewish French woman first with her body and eventually with her soul and her life. In this and other more recent texts, the language of feminism at play in the novels of the 1980s has been replaced by a timbre that is less combative and less conceptual. Eliette Abécassis's most recent novel, *La répudiée* (2000) [The Repudiated Woman], directs the readers' attention to the female experience of Jewish space governed by male law without, however, using programmatic language. In this female bildungsroman set in Jerusalem, it becomes immediately apparent that the diaspora begins right outside of the Orthodox quarters of Israel's capital. Despite initial appearances, *La répudiée* does not break the pattern of the narrative geography of contemporary Jewish writing, which constantly compares locations by shifting settings from Belleville to the shtetl, from Champigny to the Maghreb, from Paris to the Warsaw ghetto, and from the Marais to Mea Shearim. This text, too, addresses the passage from one space to a very different one, and the crossing of cultural borders, even if Rachel, the young protagonist, never leaves the city limits of Jerusalem.

Rejected by her Orthodox husband because she has not borne him a child after ten years of marriage, Rachel leaves the Orthodox quarter for the first time in her life on a clandestine search for a gynecologist in the "quartier impie" [impious neighborhood]. She takes this short trip and accepts the risks associated with it not as a gesture of rebellion against Jewish law, but in order to find out whether it is indeed she who is the cause of the couple's childlessness. Rachel returns to the geographical core of Judaism as a different woman, because she now knows that she indeed is fertile, and because she has broken the law by showing herself naked to a man other than her husband.

Space, sacred and profane, is an essential dimension of Abécassis's work, which identifies the coordinates of the place allotted to women in the world of orthodoxy in a sphere beyond modern notions of the self. For Rachel, leaving this world behind can only be a temporary transition, one that will mark her for life.

Passageways Through the French Diaspora: The Itineraries of Claude Gutman

The thriving project of presenting counternarratives to the canonical French autobiography of the second half of the last century testifies to the confidence of young Jewish writers that there are stories to be told to which the nation ought to listen. Both in his semiautobiographical and his fictional works, Claude Gutman, who was born in 1946 in British Palestine and currently is the editor of the series *Fictions* of the Seuil publishing house, sheds light on French society from the point of view of the adolescent newcomer and religious outsider. The focus of his *Les réparations* (1981) [The Reparations] is the inner life of a child who has to grapple with a displacement whose historical reasons are foreign to him. His account is designed as a counternarrative to the autobiography of the members of established French society of deep historical roots: "J'ai acheté les *Mémoires d'une jeune fille rangée* à la librairie française. Pas mal. C'est les mémoires d'un jeune homme dérangé que je devrais écrire" (1981, 113) [I bought *The Memoirs of a Well-Behaved Girl* at the French bookstore. Not bad. It's the memoirs of a deranged young man that I should write]. The point of departure in Claude Gutman's semiautobiographical novel emphasizes the dividing impact of a single historical date on the relationship between the generations:

> Comment imaginer que mes parents s'étaient embarqués sur un *Exodus* en partance et que j'étais né, au bout du voyage, en terre autrefois biblique, et britannique par mandat? Je n'avais connu que la paix. J'avais cinq ans, noir de soleil, tout nu, tout rond, et je courais au bord de la mer, dégringolant les dunes pour tremper mes pieds nus dans la Méditerranée chaude, capturée dans les digues romaines de l'ancienne Césarée. (1981, 11)
>
> [How to imagine that my parents had boarded an *Exodus* about to set off and that I was born, at the end of the voyage, in a land once biblical and British by mandate? I had known nothing but peace. I was five, black from the sun, very naked, very round, and I ran along the seashore, racing down the dunes to dip my bare feet into the warm Mediterranean captured in the Roman dikes of the old Césarée.]

As a five-year-old in the early 1950s, Dany relocates with his father from a kibbutz to Paris, at a point in time when large numbers of Jews were settling in the newly founded state of Israel. A quick study, Dany soon realizes that the departure from Israel equals a departure from everything he knows, including his most familiar, intimate ideas: "Moi, j'avais perdu ma langue en atteignant Marseille. J'avais perdu mon prénom. J'étais devenu Claude. Je m'y suis familiarisé dans le train de Paris, dans le jour éclatant. Papa n'était plus *aba*" (1981, 15) [Me, I had lost my language upon reaching Marseille. I had lost my first name. I had become Claude. I familiarized myself with that in the train from Paris, in the bright daylight. Papa was no longer *aba*]. For Dany's father, the return to France is anything but difficult, since he has never thought of himself as a Jew but rather as a committed Communist of Eastern European background. His petition to emigrate to Canada unfortunately was turned down because he had written "atheist" rather than "Jew" on his visa application. Vexed by his son's superb performance in Hebrew language classes, his father is even more upset by the attempts of his wife's family to acquaint Dany—who in France goes by the name Claude—with the milieu of the *Amicale israélite*. The father's atheism, the Catholicism of society at large, and the Judaism of his Yiddish-speaking grandparents provide highly contradictory surroundings for Claude. His father addresses the situation by purchasing a crucifix for his son's room, preferring that the Christian church rather than the synagogue will make its impact on the child. Claude, on his part, reacts to a nun's effort to get him to pray by calling her a "whore."

A screening of Alain Resnais's *Nuit et brouillard* [Night and Fog] first introduces the young Claude to the deportation of the Jews during the Vichy regime. At this point, the tonality of the book changes dramatically from narration to analysis, delivered not from the position of the young narrator but by the adult author. Gutman comments on the legacy of the Shoah and its dislocating impact on his own generation:

> Pourquoi avoir vécu sans cimetière où ma mémoire ait put s'ancrer? Pourquoi rien qui m'ait enraciné à mon passé, aux miens? Rien qui m'ait permis d'inscrire ma vie à leur mort? Six millions d'êtres autrefois vivants, nourrissant de cendres et de poussières froides les charniers allemands, ne m'avaient pas légué la moindre parcelle de terre où je puisse pleurer. J'errais ainsi, tissant mon sous-sol de rêveries macabres. Enfant juif de l'après-guerre, j'ai grandi dans le souvenir d'impalpables moribonds. (1981, 76)
>
> [Why had I lived without a cemetery where my memory would have been able to anchor itself? Why nothing that would have rooted me in my past, with my people? Nothing that would have allowed me to join my life to their deaths? Six million beings once alive, feeding with ash and cold dust the German mass graves, had not left me the smallest piece of earth where I could cry. I wander thus, weaving my subterranean web of macabre reveries. A Jewish child from after the war, I grew up inside the memory of moribund impalpabilities.]

The passage speaks to different modes of displacement that have left the narrator without a proper place to mourn the dead, and therefore without a proper place to live. His is the experience of a social and ethnic outsider who, in addition, is displaced from his family: his mother stays behind in Israel, and his father moves in with a girlfriend while Claude is shipped off to boarding schools. His grandmother is the only person concerned with keeping the boy in touch with his Jewish roots, in a family that denies its ethnicity in public so that one of the relatives can marry a goy. Another relative has accepted an in-law who during the Occupation voluntarily filed a report with the authorities expressing his regret about his marriage to a Jewish woman. It comes as no surprise that the family is trying to compensate for such incidents with "covering memories" that take the place of the memory of past pain. In a few laconic words, the narrator points to the myth of the Resistance, which in his family, too, marks an effort to whitewash the actions of a non-Jewish in-law: "Comme tout le monde, il avait fait sa Résistance. Dans le métro, il avait tracé au rouge à lèvres une croix gammée dans le dos d'un officier" (1981, 87) [Like everyone else, he had made his Resistance. In the metro, he had drawn with lipstick a swastika on the back of an officer]. Claude lacks the necessary partners for the dialogue he wants to have about his heritage: those who have survived all turned into "Israelites," which leads him to believe that the real Jews were those who were killed.

Les larmes du crocodile [Crocodile Tears], published in 1982 as the sequel to *Les réparations*, continues the narrative from the perspective of the fifteen-year-old Claude by carrying on the leitmotiv of contemporary Jewish existence as a form of displacement that cannot look back to a space of origin. What Claude finds instead are the stories about the deportation of the Jews—stories told not by his taciturn father but by his grandmother:

> Tu te rends compte, des flics français! ç'aurait été les Allemands, on aurait encore compris. Mais des Français faire la grande rafle! Si tu avais entendu les hurlements dans la rue, le soir. Ils ont pris les enfants avec. Des ordures. Avec grand-père, on était cachés derrière les persiennes et on entendait tout. On croyait qu'ils allaient frapper à la porte. Tout était prêt. Mais non, ils n'ont pris que les étrangers. (1982, 58)
>
> [Believe it, the French cops! If it had been the Germans, we would have understood. But for the French to do the great roundup! If you had heard the shouting in the street at night. They took the children too. What filth. With grandfather, we were hidden behind the blinds and we heard everything. We thought that they would knock on the door. Everything was ready. But no, they took only the foreigners.]

The grandmother's memory recounts the roundup of the Jews as the clash between the indigenous and the foreign, between the French and the Jews—more precisely, the foreign Jews, who indeed had been targeted by the collaborators more fervently than had the French Jews. At the origin of the family's story of displacement is not a country of birth to which they can return in their reminiscences, but the act of deportation from a country in which they had sought refuge.

Upon his arrival in France, Claude had to give up his name to mark the shedding of his old identity. Participating in a social event of the *Amicale israélite* as an adolescent, he observes how, among the Jews, names are not fixed indicators of the self but rather tokens that change with the shifting locations of their bearers. They change either to shield their bearers from being recognized as Jews or to express a desire to break with the past and to mold the self to fit the new circumstances:

> Vers le milieu s'était égaré un Monsieur Pierre mais personne n'ignorait qu'il était Stein avant guerre. Après, ça lui a tout remué dans la tête et il est devenu Pierre en sortant du bureau de la Préfecture où ils changent les noms.

> A papa aussi la guerre avait tourné la tête, sans passer par le même bureau. Avant, il était Élie, après Robert tout seul, sans rien demander à personne. Moi, c'était la guerre dans ma tête mais ça ne changeait rien. (1982, 26)
>
> [Toward the spot a certain Monsieur Pierre had strayed, but everyone knew that he was Stein before the war. Afterward, everything was turned upside-down in his head and he became Pierre as he exited the office of the Prefecture where they change names. The war went to Papa's head too, though he didn't go to the same office. Before, he was Élie, afterward Robert alone, without asking anything of anyone. Me, there was war in my head but that changed nothing.]

Because proper names, in Claude's eyes, have lost their ability to delineate Jewish identity, his attention focuses on identity's corporeal aspect. His father tells him that the German occupiers initially had not recognized him as a Jew, and that only in the shower rooms, under German surveillance, was he afraid of being identified. Decades later, French police stop him in Saint-Quen because they believe him to be an Algerian. "A quoi se remarque un Juif?" (1982, 34) [What shows a Jew?] is the question that Claude poses about the relationship between space, body, and identity. It remains without an answer.

Another question that remains without a response is his diatribe against the constant references to the Nazi period, to the war and to the Resistance, which percolate in the Communist Youth group that Claude frequents: "Que j'en avais marre de vivre dans les souvenirs. Marre, marre et marre. Que les histoires de camps de concentration me filaient des cauchemars et qu'il serait temps d'arrêter" (1982, 127) [I was fed up with living in memories. Fed up, fed up, and fed up. If only the stories of the concentration camps would leave my nightmares and it be time to stop]. The steady return of the past deprives Claude of the space needed to define his own position with regard to a past that is omnipresent, both when it is distorted by society at large and when it is the constant point of reference for moralists. In this sense, Gutman's narrator is very much a child of his time. The author, in contrast, continues both in his fiction and in his books for young readers (such as *La maison vide*, *L'hôtel du retour*, and *Rue de Paris* [The Empty House, The Return Hotel, and Paris Street]) to tell the stories that the adolescent Claude is tired of hearing. It is in writing that Gutman seems to be able to settle this issue, and it is literature that may relate to the next generation, to the "passeurs de mémoire" (1989, 4) [carriers of memory] what it meant to have been displaced.

Gutman's novel *Les passages* (1997) [The Passages] offers the vita of a young man, Joseph Katz, who returned in 1946 from Palestine, where he had sought refuge, to France, where he concerns himself with the events that led to the deportation of his parents four years earlier. Already in *La maison vide*, Gutman had focused on the generational discrepancy between parents who were blindly—and tragically—loyal to France, and their children who in vain try to warn them of compatriots who are turning their backs on them. *Les passages* is the story of a returnee and his growing disillusionment with the country that killed his parents and with former friends and neighbors who hide their own problematic past by accusing those who, like Joseph Katz, fled. Joseph, too, is suspicious, and he cannot help hearing the ring of insincerity in the ready-made expressions of pity by the wealthy officials of the *Amicale*, who, in his eyes, hardly know what misery means.

Blended into the narrative of Joseph's attempt to reconcile himself with postwar France are flashbacks to the period of the Occupation, when Joseph was actively involved in rescuing young Jewish children. He had grown especially attached to one child and afterwards remained preoccupied by the question of whether little David had been lucky enough to survive the war. His record of active involvement in the lot of his people sets Joseph apart from some of the Jews he meets back home in France. He feels a growing discontentment with the ideological indoctrination practiced upon the children of persecuted and deported people in the orphanage where he works. He can accept neither the socialist streamlining of the curriculum nor the mystification of the victims as heroes of anti-Fascism. Quitting his job, he shares with the director his experience of working in a kibbutz orphanage where the murdered parents of the children were commemorated as the heroes of the Zionist cause. Demanding justice for both the victims and their offspring, Joseph insists that the victims were ordinary people, oblivious of the anti-Fascist or Zionist agendas, and that they have to be remembered as such, as

> simplement des gens ordinaires, conduits à la mort par des gens ordinaires, tués par des gens ordinaires. Hitler n'est pas le Diable de leurs cauchemars, les nazis étaient des êtres humains inhumains, mais la monstruosité n'est-elle pas humaine? Assez de ces salades qui transforment la vérité. (1997, 256)

> [simply ordinary people, brought to death by ordinary people, killed by ordinary people. Hitler is not the Devil of their nightmares, the Nazis were inhuman human beings, but isn't monstrosity human? Enough of these muddles that transform the truth.]

Gutman's Joseph Katz is a hero who, not unlike Kafka's Joseph K., resists enlistment into any ideological camp. Joseph will continue to fight for justice within a period of French history that had to struggle to see what was lying behind the cracks of the various myths the French nation had created about the past. He wages a fight against the displacement of the simple truths of the past, against another form of deportation that relocates the legacy of the victims into political and ideological spheres to serve certain dogmas and programs. As a portrayal of the immediate postwar era (in which the French did not always welcome back the Jewish survivors with expressions of remorse or enthusiasm), it complements in tone the novel *Quoi de neuf sur la guerre?* (1993) [What's New with the War?] by Robert Bober (born in Germany in 1931). Both books are texts of the 1990s, written with a distrust for political discourses that has been nursed by the collapse of the ideological master narratives.

The Pilgrimages of Anne Rabinovitch

The novels of Anne Rabinovitch (born 1945) offer an understanding of the notion of displacement that complicates further the idea of diasporic existence. The juxtaposition between the French diaspora and the fading memory of the home country that underlies many texts by Jewish Maghrebi writers is supplemented here by a multitude of national spaces and cultural locations. "Diaspora" here is understood both as a spatial concept and as one that unfolds in time, in history.

The female protagonists of Rabinovitch's slim novels view their return to the old centers of Judaism as a means of centering their own identity as contemporary Jewish artists or as global nomads of postmodernity. In her first novel, *L'hiver au cœur* [Winter in the Heart] (which appeared in 1983 and was later adapted into a film of international acclaim), the protagonist finds in Warsaw—which is also the title of a radio play authored by Rabinovitch's prominent father—the ability to reapproach the history of Judaism. As the daughter of the prominent former communist resistance fighter Wladimir Rabi, a prolific critic of France's Jewish establishment who died in 1981, Rabinovitch has to deal with a family legacy of Eastern European provenance. In *Comme si les hommes étaient partis en voyage* [As If They Had Left for a Trip], from 1995, a young filmmaker embarks on a trip to Vilna, the "Jerusalem of the North" and also the birthplace of Rabi. There, people take her for a reincarnation of "Une activiste lituanienne des années vingt, d'ascendance rabbinique, du bord de mer . . . Mais on sent que tu n'as pas subi de persécutions" (1995, 55) [A Lithuanian activist from the twenties, of rabbinical descent, beside the sea . . . But one senses that you have not endured persecutions].

The former Jewish ghettos, neglected Jewish cemeteries, and the sites of the former concentration camps are existential points of reference for Rabinovitch's protagonists. Experiencing the notion of diasporic existence painfully, as a life outside the centers of Jewish history and as a life at the margins of the gentile societies of Europe and the United States, she has her protagonists return to the concentration camps where her own ancestors were murdered. As a site of memory, a *lieu de mémoire*, the camp is a geographical as well as historical point of reference that reorients the trajectories of protagonists who are incessantly en route. Rabinovitch herself has lived in places as different as New York, Jerusalem, Warsaw, Paris, and California, and as a translator has worked on a range of Jewish-American writers. Like their author, her protagonists are women who are as familiar with Israel as they are with France, the United States, and Eastern Europe, and who are involved in the arts and in literature and who are surrounded by critics, filmmakers, and editors. What reverberates in their lives is George Steiner's notion of the text as the Jewish homeland (Steiner 1986) and Edmond Jabès's idea that the place inhabited by the Jew is the book, where the Jew "finds himself, in the book he questions himself, in the book he has his freedom, which has been forbidden him everywhere" (1991, 254).

The France of Rabinovitch's *Les étangs de Ville-d'Avray* (1987) [The Ponds of Ville-d'Avray] is a society where anti-Semitism runs rampant and the bloody terrorist attack in the rue des Rosiers of August 1982 is still in the foreground of the characters' minds. Eva Aronson, the protagonist of the novel, witnesses a conversation in a café in which Hitler and Le Pen are mentioned in a positive light:

> et puis, il y a les juifs, les Noirs, les Arabes, disait-il, élevant la voix. On n'en sort plus. On ne peut rien faire, on se fait tout de suite traiter d'antisémite, de raciste. Je vous le dis, la France est la poubelle du monde. Dans vingt ans, la race française n'existe plus. (1987, 91)
>
> [and then, there are the Jews, the Blacks, the Arabs, he said, raising his voice. We'll never get out of it. One can't do anything, one is immediately called an anti-Semite, a racist. I tell you this: France is the rubbish bin of the world. In twenty years, the French race will no longer exist.]

The French diaspora puts its Jew in a dilemma that Eva expresses in the following manner: "Me déraciner sans quitter Paris. N'être plus rattachée à rien" (1987, 15) [To uproot myself without leaving Paris. To no longer be attached to anything]. Corresponding to this wish is her desire to get involved with a man who, unlike her former lover Jérémie and many of her friends, had not met her father—an omnipresent character to whom all of her novels refer, albeit mostly in indirect ways. Yet Eva knows that there is no escape from the past, and her wanderings are just as much attempts at connecting intimately with all the various points of reference in her life and the lives of her people as they are attempts to cut herself off from them. An encounter with the "real," with the relics of the past, is the only remedy against the power of the constructs that tend to force aside history: "Une journée de juin éblouissante. Peu à peu les images du camp se superposent aux descriptions des livres. Le réel, plus fort que les cauchemars" (1987, 46) [A shining June day. Little by little the images of the camp superimpose themselves upon the descriptions in books. Reality, stronger than the nightmares].

In the passage introducing her visit to the camp at Auschwitz, the term "pilgrimage" ["pèlerinage"] stands in for the undertaking of visiting not the holy shrine destroyed with the temple but the site of the genocide that commands the respect of a sacred space. Ambiguously placed, the term refers as well to a pilgrimage of Catholics through a part of the town from which Eva commences her trip to Auschwitz. The camp's significance is both a communal and a personal one for Eva: on one of the displayed lists of the deportees she will find her family name. "Pilgrimage" evokes the notion of a long and burdensome journey that the pilgrim makes not so much as an individual but as part of a larger community. It is a journey whose path and stations often have been prearranged, as others have traveled the way before. Thus, the next move in the narrative does not really come as a surprise: a reflection upon Claude Lanzmann's film *Shoah* prefaces, so to speak, the protagonist's visit to the camp. Superimposing itself onto the real, the film becomes as much an image of the pilgrimage to Auschwitz as it has become a part of the pilgrimage itself: "*Shoah* comme un interminable voyage en car avec des arrêts toutes les deux heures" (1987, 46) [*Shoah* as an interminable bus trip with stops every two hours].

The account of Eva's visit to the camp (although strongly undernarrated, as is the novel in its entirety) points to all the elements that threaten to shape the visitor's perception of the place, including the presence of tourists as the secular pilgrims, listening to the explanations of their guides. Ready to give up and turn around, the narrator keeps being encouraged to go on by the friend who is accompanying her. They will return to the camp a second time, not by the trampled paths of the tourists, but by crossing a field and following the tracks of the old railway, with the swollen ankles of pilgrims:

> La fatigue, plus puissante que la mémoire.
>
> Dans un baraquement, je me suis assise à même la terre battue. La tête dans les mains. Autour de moi, les carcasses des lits à trois étages, les lavabos communs. Je ne supportais pas de m'en aller. Marek me regardait sans rien dire.
>
> Dehors, des fillettes cueillaient des fraises sauvages. J'ai voulu en goûter une. C'était acide.
>
> Nous avons marché jusqu'aux peupliers décharnés qui penchaient lamentablement. Les miradors se dressaient de loin en loin, intacts.
>
> Le ciel lumineux, la plaine à perte de vue. La journée finissait. Il était l'heure de retourner à la gare. Je refusais de passer la nuit à Auschwitz. (1987, 50)

> [Fatigue, more powerful than memory.
>
> In a barrack, I sat down on the beaten earth itself. Head in my hands. Around me, the carcasses of beds with three bunks, common bathrooms. I could not stand to leave. Marek looked at me without speaking.
>
> Outside, the girls gathered wild strawberries. I wanted to taste one. It was acidic.
>
> We walked up to the emaciated poplars which leaned pathetically. The watchtowers stood upright here and there, intact.
>
> The luminous sky, the plain as far as the eye could see. The day finished. It was time to return to the train station. I refused to spend the night at Auschwitz.]

The absence of any reference to Eva's emotional reactions to the environment is remarkable. Only her physical reactions are being narrated: the paralysis of her body speaks volumes. Neither does the narrator make any reference to her thoughts. The result is the image of a person who is at a loss for words in regard to the space she has decided to visit, which still manifests its menacing power, indicated by the watchtowers that continue to hover over the camp undamaged. Nature imagery—the acidity of the wild strawberries, the doleful movement of the poplars—provides an emotional timbre that otherwise would be strangely missing in the laconic description of the camp.

The usage of the term "pilgrimage" leads readers' expectations onto the wrong track. In hindsight, the journey to Auschwitz turns out to be an anti-pilgrimage because it negates any offer of consolation, let alone redemption, for which pilgrims are hoping and for which they have taken upon themselves the pain and effort of the journey to the sacred site. The camp, instead, is devoid of any transcendental meaning and neither does the pilgrimage offer the trajectory of redemption. Eva's decision to go to Auschwitz was an attempt to arrest her wanderings from one place to another, to return to the space that figures so centrally in the modern history of the Jewish people and in the history of her family. In this sense, Auschwitz represents the polar opposite, the antipode of the diaspora: a space that cannot be inhabited but that nonetheless represents, in its historical meaning, the epicenter of Jewish existence. The threat of paralysis elicited by the camp, which even affects memory ("La fatigue, plus puissante que la mémoire" [Fatigue, more powerful than memory]), is the counterimage to Eva's diasporic restlessness and her feeling of being haunted by the past. In *Comme si les hommes étaient partis en voyage*, the metaphor of the pilgrimage recurs to address the state of incessant displacement: "Pèlerinage avec elle-même, pour une rencontre sans heure ni lieu" (1995, 38) [Pilgrimage with herself, toward a meeting without a time or a place].

The vectors guiding the narratives of contemporary French-Jewish writing pull in different directions at once: they point toward former centers of Jewish life that fell prey to anti-Semitism and decolonization, toward a Holy Land whose promises are measured from the distance of the Diaspora and toward the sites of the Shoah. They orient the reader both toward sites of memory and the site of the Diaspora, measuring the distances between these points of reference. Emmanuel Moses's novel *Papernik* (1992) offers a diatribe of sorts against the French diaspora. The novel features an Israeli professor of French origin who, upon arriving in Paris for his sabbatical, immediately begins to regret his decision to spend a year in the country of his childhood. Having lived in Israel for the greater part of his life, he has become a secular Israeli who cares deeply about Israeli politics and who immediately tries to make friends in the Jewish community of Paris. His impressions about the French—the book takes place sometime in the 1980s—are anything but positive:

> Papernik avait eu beau attirer son attention sur la véritable nature du peuple français en général et parisien en particulier, sa xénophobie, son avarice, sa

> mesquinerie, sa lâcheté que l'occupation allemande, tel un réactif, avaient révélées au grand jour, et dont les Juifs, plus que tous, avaient fait les frais. (1992, 76)
>
> [Papernik tried in vain to draw his (friend's—author) attention to the true nature of the French people in general and the Parisian specifically: their xenophobia, their greed, their small-mindedness, their cowardice that German occupation had brought to daylight, like a chemical reagent, and for which the Jews, above all, had to pay.]

This middle-aged professor—a neurotic, self-conscious womanizer—bears much resemblance to the male protagonists featured in early novels by Saul Bellow and Philip Roth. He begins to feel even more estranged from his surroundings when he realizes that his wife and his children are apparently enjoying their stay in France. Moses clearly emphasizes the differences in age and, accordingly, attitude to life in the Diaspora between his characters. In this ability, he draws on his own background; the Casablanca-born author himself is the son of a famous literary critic of German extraction who had settled in the Jewish homeland. In his book *La danse de la poussière dans les rayons du soleil* (1999) [The Dance of the Dust in the Rays of the Sun], Moses crafted an autobiographical account of his family's complex story. He himself had left Israel in 1986 as a twenty-seven-year-old to return to France, where he had spent part of his childhood. Thus he looks at the cultural sensitivities of his protagonist with some sympathy, but primarily with the ironic skepticism of the child of immigrants who had decided finally to leave Israel and to live in the French diaspora.

Sylvie Weil's *Les vendanges de Rachi* (2000) [Rashi's Harvest] offers yet another perspective on the French diaspora. The narrator, the reader learns, had to come to live in the United States and gained interest in the life and works of Rashi, the medieval author of the famous commentaries to the Humash (the Pentateuch) and to the Talmud. When she tells her friends about her growing interest in the French rabbi (Rashi was born in Troyes, northern France), they respond with surprise to the national label she uses to refer to him—outside of France, Rashi is a Jew, rather than a "French Jew." The narrator's quest to study the life of Rashi has its point of departure in New York, the domicile of both the author and her narrator. In Brooklyn, she meets a descendent of the rabbi from the French region of Champagne. Weil's *Les vendanges de Rachi* is one of the few historical novels by a writer of the *générations d'après* that deals with an eminent figure of the Jewish tradition. It may not be mere coincidence that this book was written not in the French diaspora but in Brooklyn, which represents the other contemporary center of Jewish learning aside from Israel. Rashi appears in contemporary French Jewish literature a second time as the subject of a piece of fiction, Clément Weill Raynal's *Le tombeau de Rachi,* in 1997. This novel is a thriller that leads the reader from the calm of the French provinces to the underground world of Israeli intelligence operations, pursuing a very French theme, the nature of the *résistance* of French officials during German Occupation.

The narratives of all the authors presented in this chapter become maps that relate the experience of living as Jews in present-day France to these various points of the distant past and present. They orient readers to whom some if not all of these worlds may be foreign as well as those who may have traveled similar paths themselves. Yet, as much as these maps refer to historical places with precise coordinates, they are first and foremost documents of individuals' responses to difficult processes of cultural, national, and existential forms of displacement. However, the mourning for the lost worlds of Jewish life that characterized the narratives of their predecessors has given way to critical assessments of present-day France, which is no longer perceived as either an uninhabitable place or as a *locus amoenus* offering unlimited tolerance, freedom, and equality.

In her autobiographical piece "Mon algériance" (1997) [My Algeriance], the Algerian-born writer and critic Hélène Cixous reflects on how the family's experiences of persecution and emigration from Algeria to France have instilled in her the feeling of being merely a passer-through, a "passante." Cixous fashions an expression that aptly speaks to the ambivalence of her existence as a Jewish Algerian living in France when she writes, "Partir (pour) ne pas arriver d'Algérie, c'est aussi, incalculablement, une façon de ne pas avoir rompu avec l'Algérie" (1997a, 71–74) [To depart not to arrive from Algeria, that is also, incalculably, a form of not breaking with Algeria]. For Cixous, writing is a means of holding her arrival in France in suspense, a form of constant passing that remains conscious of one's roots without glorifying in hindsight the racism, violence, and misogyny that exist in her homeland. Writing is not at all a form of "nostalgérie." Thus, the trajectory of "homeward bound," which led earlier narratives to perceive of the Diaspora as quintessentially "nonhistorical" (Ezrahi 2000) sites, indeed has been redirected. The sites of the Diaspora are no longer seen as transitory spaces. This, however, does not contradict the feeling that many of the writers experience themselves as passing through these spaces that they are inhabiting for good. In his novel *Le chant des êtres*, Gil Ben Aych relates this ambivalence back to *ābar* [to cross over or beyond], the etymology of the word "Hebrew."

6 Postscripts

"As France becomes increasingly multicultural and multiethnic at the beginning of the twenty-first century, the history of French Jewry moves from the margins to the center," claimed the historian Paula E. Hyman in her study on Jews in modern France (1998, 218).

For this reason, a history of French literature at the beginning of this new century has to take into account the intriguing literary projections and aesthetic projects presented by writers of Jewish origin. Given the diverse backgrounds, styles, agendas, and voices of the writers encountered in this study, it would be misleading to talk about a "movement" or a "school" of contemporary Jewish writing in France. No such thing exists, and no such thing may ever come into being, given the individualism that governs the scene of writing and the attitudes of the writers toward Judaism. And yet, the readings offered here do suggest that over the past three decades, a large number of authors have emerged who do relate in their writing to their Jewishness in ways that cannot be found in previous eras of French letters. Theirs is a literature of difference that eagerly explores its ethnic heritage and assertively insists on its alterity, while not ignoring that—next to Judaism—its Frenchness presents yet another focus for its endeavors.

The beginnings of this literature fall within a period of transition from alluring societal programs of clear-cut design to indefinite personal agendas of unknown promise. The erosion in the 1970s of Marxist categories and of other sweeping historical systems allowed writers to discover new ways of conceptualizing the individual and his or her relationship to the Other. Simultaneously, the dominant notion of *Culture* became a multiplicity of forms of *le culturel*, and the predilection for the *universal* eventually became replaced with the appreciation of the *particular*. This powerful shift of intellectual paradigms was propelled by French theorists and philosophers, many of whom could trace their origins to Jewish or specifically Sephardic roots. There is no doubt that—as one critic once observed—this theoretical discussion is cut from the same cloth as the literature discussed in this book. It is also true, however, that the textures of the theories of postmodernism and poststructuralism have less in common with those of the literature surveyed here than one might expect. The authors born after the Shoah hardly ever venture into the deconstructive realms explored by, for example, Jacques Derrida. The nature of this difference needs clarification, and its reasons await explanation. It is striking that the radicalism of the philosophical inquiries finds its counterpart primarily in the works of the somewhat older writers, among them Hélène Cixous, Marcel Bénabou, and Georges Perec. The striking stylistic singularity of some of the works authored by Sephardic writers derives (with very few exceptions) from their indebtedness to the languages spoken at home and to the forms of oral and written tradition of the Jewish quarters of the Maghreb, rather than from an affinity with poststructuralist thought. Edmond Jabès's insistence that the difficulty of being a Jew coincides with the difficulty of writing may be to the point. However, the writers apparently have found ways of addressing this challenge that differ from the ones explored by the philosophers.

"Jewishness," to use the words of the anthropologist Daniel Boyarin, "disrupts the very categories of identity, because it is not national, not genealogical, not religious, but all of these, in dialectical tension with each other" (1994, 244). The very first texts of the first postwar generation of French Jews show that Jewishness also defied the societal contracts of postwar France. These early texts did so not by rejecting such contracts in their entirety, but by disrupting apparently seamless continuities and pointing directly to the tensions between the French ethnic and national tradition and the historical experience of its Jewish minority. They also flouted governing conventions of *écriture de soi*, thus articulating differences between the Jewish and the gentile experience of growing up in post-Vichy France. Yet neither Pierre Goldman nor Patrick Modiano—and the same could be said for their peers Katia Rubinstein, Guy Sitbon, or Marco Koskas—engaged in any effort to mediate these dialectical tensions. Instead of moderation, they were set on provocation; instead of adhering to the art of decorum, they went for satire, pastiche, and the macabre. Together with the dialectical tension of the genealogical, the national, and the religious, they exploded the dialectics of collaboration and resistance and left it to the fascinated French public to make sense of narratives that constituted the first act of an emerging literature that would subsequently take on a different tonality. Goldman, Modiano, and Rubinstein preceded the literary movement grounded in a "return to the roots," and—like an avant-garde—left behind their followers, who would in a much less ambiguous and ambivalent manner pursue ideologically less provocative and stylistically less risky paths.

Autojudeography, then, can also be understood as a new generation's challenge to a literary history only sparsely populated with Jewish writers who emphasized their Jewishness; in this sense of the term, it suggests that the young aspiring writers found themselves pretty much without precursors on whom they could have modeled their artistic personae, and without a tradition of French-Jewish letters on which they might build. The exceptions are few and far between, as the various debates on the topic have shown. Thus, the "auto" also alludes to the act of creating a literature from more or less nothing formed primarily along the contours of the self. That may also explain why so much of it is "auto"-presentation, autobiographically based writing that is last but not least preoccupied with the phenomenon of writing about the self. To see the reasons for this preoccupation only in the writers' situatedness as outsiders in a gentile society overestimates the sociological logic and understates the aesthetic dynamics of their writing. Facing the lack of a strong tradition of French-Jewish letters and responding to a dearth of intact Jewish traditions, this literature in stylistic respects differed not so much from the writing of non-Jewish peers as from previous expressions of Jewish writing in the French language.

In this respect, the position of the Jewish writer is reflected in Georges Perec's paradoxical sense of his estrangement as a Jew not from non-Jews, but from his own kin. To give autobiographical writing more and more the contours of Jewish writing was, if such a formula were permitted, a major aspiration in the instigation of *jeune littérature juive*. It can be argued that the proclivity toward autobiographical narratives exhibited in the early phase of contemporary Jewish writing did not derive simply from the relatively young age of most of the authors nor from an alleged deficit of experience that would supposedly reduce them to writing primarily about their own lives. On the contrary, these writers simply *had* to write primarily about themselves and their own experiences in order to fashion their own introduction to the covenant of Jewish letters.

Since the early beginnings, writers have emerged who, removed from the Vichy experience by two or even three generations, have pushed aside the occasionally formulaic modes of literary self-expression of the first post-Shoah generation to engage in less self-oriented genres, which they handle very playfully. Eliette Abécassis, to name but the most popular and successful example, provides in her mystery novels a literary *lieu de mémoire* for the testimony of the survivors, which many readers may judge as sensationalist and all-too-readable renditions of the horrors of the past. No longer does the provocative power of the text reside in an existential experience, and no longer is the provocation directed against those who preferred to keep the dossier of Vichy France closed. In other cases, like the work of Agnès Desarthe or Alain Gluckstein, the provocative impulse has vanished altogether and given way to narrative still lives of Jewish figures intimated against the backdrop of the mystical or narrative mazes of stories within stories within stories about life in prewar Poland. While his older colleague Cyrille Fleischman distills subtle melancholic vignettes from the vanishing milieu of Yiddish-speaking émigrés, Gluckstein rearranges the fragments in a colorful curiosity cabinet and installs as its curators an entire family consisting of narrators of vastly dissimilar ethnic, linguistic, and cultural backgrounds.

"J'écris pour naître à moi-même" (1990, 102) [I write to be born to myself]—this claim by Gilles Zenou points to the very core of autojudeography, which for the Sephardic writers becomes an endeavor rather different from the ones undertaken by their Ashkenazi peers. For those of them who grew up with families in which Judaism informed everyday life, the challenge obviously is not to reinscribe themselves into Judaism and its traditions, but first of all to inscribe themselves as Jewish writers of Maghrebi origins into the conventions and institutions governing French *belles lettres*. That is what for them the notion of autojudeo*graphy* primarily entails. Some writers choose to perfect a language that aspires to meet the celebrated literary standards of clarity, lucidity, and precision—paving stylistically a path to what Annie Goldmann describes as the lure of French literary culture, a lure that fascinated the young writer from the shore of North Africa:

> Être écrivain voulait dire être publié dans les grandes maisons d'édition de la rive gauche, apprécié par les critiques des grands journaux culturels français, être couronné, gloire suprême, par un prix littéraire français. (1995, 56)
>
> [To be a writer meant to be published by one of the great publishing houses from the Left Bank, to be esteemed by the critics of the great French cultural journals, to be crowned, ultimate glory, with a French literary prize.]

For a writer like Marlène Amar or Chochana Boukhobza, then, the challenge is to create within these conventions an idiom that can render justice to both the rhetorical traditions of the French letters and the cultural, ethnic, and linguistic experience of the Maghreb that they want to render. Others, like Katia Rubinstein, Marco Koskas, and Gil Ben Aych, capture instead the overdetermined situation of the Sephardic writer in a linguistic "mélange" and stylistic "patchwork" (Goldmann 1995, 58). This intermingling offers a genuine form of autojudeography that eschews these conventions while contradicting in both substance and form the claim made early in his career by Albert Memmi, the spiritual father of francophone Sephardic writing, according to which the diaspora can offer only estrangement to the Jews.

But regardless of their stylistic predilections, both groups of writers have presented texts that tend to display a much wider spectrum of contemporary Jewish life: the juxtaposition between gentile French society and Jewish minority that governs the relational amplitude of the Ashkenazi narrative is complicated in the texts of Sephardic writers by a strong awareness of the tensions between Ashkenazim and Sephardim.

The Ashkenazi narrative in contrast only very rarely speaks to encounters between the Sephardic and the Ashkenazi experiences. Only the writer Brigitte Peskine (born 1951 in Neuilly-sur-Seine) reciprocates this double perspective in some of her novels. Her family epic *Les eaux douces d'Europe* (1996) [The Sweet Waters of Europe] traces the descendants of the Jews expelled from Spain 600 years earlier through the ascent of Hitler. *Buena familia* (2000) [The Good Family] continues the narrative by focusing on the experience of an Istanbul-born descendant during the Nazi era who eventually found refuge in postwar France. Peskine's protagonist is a writer who tries to "faire revivre le monde judéo-sépharade" (2000, 243) [make the Judeo-Sephardic world come to life again] and grapples with the disdain that some of her peers from Constantinople bear toward what they perceive as the dominance of the Ashkenazim in post-Shoah Judaism in general and in the newly founded Jewish state in particular. The protagonist wants in the novel she is writing to break a taboo by portraying Auschwitz inmates not as saints but by looking at "des mères abusives et des pères autocrates, des sœurs sournoises, des frères hypocrites" (2000, 222) [the abusive mothers and autocratic fathers, the insidious sisters, the hypocritical brothers] who were among them. Peskine's narrative, however, is convincing only in the portrayal of the refugees' hardship under persecution and the family's dispersal—that is, in the description of a suffering experienced by both Ashkenazi and Sephardic Jews.

Aside from Peskine, it is interestingly enough only outsiders who attempt to look at both groups that constitute present-day France's Jewry. The Berlin-born writer Barbara Honigmann does this in her 1996 novel *Soharas Reise [Zohara's Journey]*, set in the Jewish community of her Strasbourg exile. Canadian-born (non-Jewish) expatriate Nancy Huston depicts in *L'empreinte de l'ange* (1998) [The Mark of an Angel] how the Fourth Republic dealt with North Africans. Most recently, the playwright Eric-Emmanuel Schmitt provides in his short tale *Monsieur Ibrahim et les fleurs du Coran* (2001) [Monsieur Ibrahim and the Flowers of the Koran] a fictional bridge between the worlds of Judaism and Islam. In the aftermath of September 11th and the escalation of the conflicts between Muslims and Jews in France—which has shifted the epicenter of anti-Semitic attacks from the political Right to Islamic fundamentalism—Schmitt's book has gained enormous popularity all over Europe by conveying a message of hopeful reconciliation between these two demographic constituencies of contemporary France.

While in the Sephardic texts the narrative fault lines meander along the border between Ashkenazim and Sephardim, the Ashkenazi texts find rifts within the main characters themselves. With the figure of the doppelgänger, the protagonist's alter ego, the authors create a multiperspectivism that the frequently undernarrated juxtaposition between gentiles and Jews usually does not provide. Henry Raczymow's *Un cri sans voix* almost leaves it up to the reader to determine whether Esther isn't merely a projection of the narrator. Some among Alain Gluckstein's "grand old men of Yiddish literature" have shed their Jewish background entirely to reemerge as gentile French writers, and one of Agnès Desarthe's heroines continues her life even after her death. In Eliette Abécassis's *L'or et la cendre*, the very identity of the (two?) main protagonists turn out to be mysteriously dubious: "Ils disent que Félix Werner est une création de mon esprit, un double idéal de moi" (1997, 373) [They say that Félix Werner is a creation of my mind, a doppelgänger of myself]. Patrick Modiano pursued in the historical figure Dora Bruder a kind of "elective affinity" indicated by the name "Bruder," whereas Goldman's picaro Rapoport can be seen as a convex mirror image of the memoir writer Goldman himself.

There are prominent models for this kind of fictional doubling up, ranging from the intriguing coexistence of the writer Romain Gary and his author persona Émile Ajar (not to mention the reincarnation of Gary's protagonist Moïché Cohn in the body of the "Hauptjudenfresser" ["Jew-Devourer-in-Chief"] Schatz) to the puzzling correlation between the self and the Viennese-born Gaspard Winckler in Georges Perec's *W, ou le souvenir d'enfance*. In the contemporary texts, however, such intriguing split configurations of Jewish non-German and non-Jewish German figures have more or less vanished. Here, the prominence of the protagonist's doubling should be regarded not simply as a rejuvenation of the literary type of the ever-changing *Zelig*. The phenomenon needs rather to be discussed as a response to the variety of challenges these authors face: a response to the philosophical and psychoanalytic dissolution of the concept of identity, to the need to deal with the confinements that tend to suffocate the literary discourse of identity, and last but not least to the desire to articulate in as many facets and refractions possible what it means to be Jewish in present times. Claude Gutman's image of the multiple reflections of his protagonist's countenance—"la glace qui reflétait l'autre glace qui renvoyait mon visage à l'infini, mon visage à l'infini, mon visage à l'infini" (1981, 88) [the window pane that reflected the other pane that returned the picture of my face infinitely, my face infinitely, my face infinitely]—speaks to the other, more unsettling side of this desire and to the fact that it may not always be easy to curb the connotative richness that the concept of the *"Juif de réflexion"* (Vidal-Naquet 1981, 12) is potentially capable of generating.

By and large, Anny Dayan-Rosenman's assertion that contemporary Jewish writers in France "restent étrangement silencieux sur le lieu et le temps de l'écriture" (1998, 341) [remain strangely silent about the place and time in which they are writing] cannot be confirmed by the readings offered in this study. On the contrary, rather than revisiting the biblical figures and sites at the origins of Judaism, rather than retracing the history that led French Jewry to the Vichy deportations, and rather than revisiting the memories of their kin's exodus from the Maghreb, these writers quite decisively turn their own and their readers' attention to the more recent era of Jewish life in France. In lieu of memories, they create fictional worlds in which the young respond to contemporary echoes of the past and to reverberations of the past felt in the present. Thus, their literature is a writing out of a void, against a void, and, initially, about a void (Wajcman). Not surprisingly then, the literary motif of the secret pervades large parts of this corpus: secrets of historical impact but also those of rather small importance, to allude to the title of Agnès Desarthe's novel. Detectives set out to solve racist hate crimes (Abécassis, Weill Raynal), tourists to solve mysteries (Jacques), scholars to put together the puzzles of literary history (Gluckstein). And over and over again, sons and daughters set out to turn the stones of their parents' pasts to discover traces of their pain and suffering (Anissimov, Fellous, Boukhobza) but also of other parts of their lives that they had not shared with their offspring (Amar, Spire, Koskas, Rozier).

Another powerful feature that pervades these texts is the tension between the genealogical principle of filiation and the individualistic principle of self-creation. Whereas filiation tends to become articulated primarily in the literary portrayal of a parent or grandparent (Ben Aych, Moses, Pachet, Fellous) or in the family tableau (Spire, Darmon, Golse), self-creation finds its expression in more autobiographical types of writing, most radically in the discussed forms of autojudeography. Myriam Anissimov's novels illustrate how difficult it is for an author to find a voice that can partake of both of these discourses at once. As an author belonging to the threshold generation, she finds herself too close to the horrors of persecution to structure her narratives around the notion of *juif de volonté*. From her family's history, she has derived a mission that she fulfills by dedicating her writing to the commemoration of their losses. The writer's desire not to dissolve entirely in this mission generates pictures of the writer-narrator that at times create a curious stereoscopic view of the pains suffered by the old and the emancipatory adventures enjoyed by the young generations.

In the narratives of Anne Rabinovitch, the father demands that his generation's ability to resurrect itself from catastrophe be honored; he casts a shadow so broad that the young protagonist's life and her accomplishments as a writer almost disappear from sight. In Antoine Spire's novel, the son seeks this paternal representative of the law, but he is left with a father who is the very incarnation of the *Israélite*. As such, the father is incapable of framing his offspring's coming-of-age narrative from the point of view of Jewish law and rite. It is in this image of the acculturated parent that certain Sephardi and Ashkenazi narratives converge. Authors from both groups create constellations of figures who engage in painful contests about the degree of acculturation that will allow them to remain who they were while permitting them to become who they want to be. The tension between the principle of filiation and the desire for auto-conception becomes the subject of acts of enunciation that Nicki Golse's or Marco Koskas's narrators conceive as acts of liberation either from a background of silence (the immigrant parents' *mutisme*) or from a background of paternal domination (the *Oriental patriarch*) that in the Western world appears quite literally out of place.

While history for Annie Goldmann provided the matrix for a process of generational development that gradually freed the subject from all sorts of boundaries, younger authors like Amar, Boukhobza, and Darmon have come to question and to fracture these early narratives of female liberation in the Western diaspora. The tenets of *écriture féminine* guided Goldmann's and to a certain extent also Rubinstein's narratives as they built on a female legacy of self-assertiveness. However, in the stories by the younger Sephardic women writers, these principles have retreated into the background and given way to reservations about the possibility of their emancipation. Such authors no longer just write from their "feminine libidinal economy" (Cixous 1975b, 42), but about an economy of desires that—to use Marlène Amar's metaphor—requires the Sephardic woman to change her face, her body as the bearers of her ethnic heritage to enter the libidinal zone of the French diaspora.

While as Jews the Sephardic authors write from a minority position that they share with their French-born Ashkenazi peers, they write as immigrants from a diasporic location that they share with non-Jewish francophone writers of different ethnic heritage and national background. Francophone African, Caribbean, or "Beur" literature has over the course of the last decades displayed narrative strategies that sometimes are similar to the ones of *jeune littérature sépharade*, which, however, is without a charter text of the kind Aimé Césaire offered in 1939 with his *Cahier d'un retour au pays natal*.

And yet, the fact that they share certain techniques must not give rise to the belief that the Jewish writers perceive this literature simply as an epiphenomenon that can be disregarded. Amar's *La femme sans tête* stands representatively in this regard: the narrative structure links the story of the young Jewish woman's transformation to Kafka's metamorphosis narrative. By clearly marking her heroine's Jewishness at all essential moments of the story, Amar pulls the Jewishness of Kafka's hero onto the surface of Kafka's text. Her novel remakes, one could argue, the tradition of Jewish writing. Thus, the very category of filiation refers not simply to biological ties and familiar bonds, but just as well to the "filiations imaginaries" (Robin 1995, 19) [imaginary filiations] that contemporary writers create in order to shape a legacy that they can accept. They stock this legacy with images of Jewish and non-Jewish provenance, French and non-French origin, and of literary and nonliterary characters—after all, the films of Woody Allen, Alain Resnais, and Jean Cayrol have influenced these younger generations just as much as the novels by Franz Kafka, Albert Cohen, or Saul Bellow. The tensions between the given principle of filiation and the yearning for self-conception approach resolution when the author models the image of the ancestors on his or her own image: the writer-narrator in Marcel Bénabou's *Jacob, Ménahem et Mimoun: Une Épopée familiale* (1995) [Jacob, Menahem, and Mimoun: A Family Epic] confesses that he presents his forebears thus so that "qu'en fin de compte ce seraient eux qui paraîtraient faits de moi, beaucoup plus que moi d'eux" (1995, 238) ["they would ultimately seem to proceed from me rather than I from them" (1998, 214)]. When this intriguing reversal of filiation is applied to the tension between literary affiliation with previous modes of writing and the conflicting desire to institute a new mode of writing, writers can find themselves in a paradox: they now can gaze into a mirror of illusory traditions that allows them to recognize first of all themselves.

Contemporary Jewish writers indeed enter in very complex negotiations with the canon of Jewish writing. Ruth R. Wisse, a custodian of the modern tradition of Jewish literature, professes that the "canonical impulse that brought the Bible into being" has in modern times given way to the "preeminence of the individual both in its form and content: it swears no prior allegiance to anything but itself" (2000, 348). And yet, authors as diverse as Ben Aych, Koskas, Rozier, or Raczymow all reappropriate narrative structures, genres, and themes that belong to the traditions of Jewish writing. They quote sources that speak to current concerns, they rejuvenate the tellers of tales told in the shtetl, the *mellah*, the *hara*, or the *ma'bara*, they borrow from the past modes that seem malleable enough to fit present needs, and ignore those parts of the tradition that would only forestall what they are trying to do.

Just as one can glean from the work of Amar how Jewish writing in present-day France negotiates the legacy of the modern Jewish writer par excellence Franz Kafka, one can appreciate in reading Gluckstein's novel how this same body of writing accepts the legacy of modern Yiddish fiction by bidding farewell to it. "As latecomers to modern literature," the literary historian Ken Frieden wrote of Yiddish writers, they "were obliged to rework prior traditions" and "parodied— appropriated, incorporated, and modified—diverse elements from European novels and stories" (1995, x). To rephrase Frieden's assertion, as a latecomer to Jewish literature, a writer like Gluckstein pays homage to the demise of this tradition precisely by parodying it.

When Bénabou's autobiographical narrator finishes his account of writing "pour le mellah de Mèknes, ce que d'autres avaient si magistralement réussi pour les ghettos et shtetl de l'Europe centrale et orientale" (1995, 81) ["for the Mellah in Mèknes what others had so masterfully done for the ghettos and shtetls of central and eastern Europe" (1998, 69)], he has to admit that he did not succeeded in fashioning the grand "familiale, judaïque et maghrébine epopee" (1995, 228) ["familial Judaic Morocccan epic" (1998, 205)] that he had planned since childhood. Bénabou's family epic and many of the texts by Marco Koskas, Gil Ben Aych, or Ami Bouganim offer instead self-conscious narratives with bits and pieces of family and colonial history, of Sephardic Judaism, and of the authors' careers as writers. Bénabou's narrator eventually comes to recognize his scattered narrative as a legitimate form of Jewish writing in the wake of the Kabbalist tradition: after all, once the opening of the Hebrew text of Genesis is replaced by one of its anagrams, the phrase "in the beginning" suddenly reads "with the remains."

The readers will judge which pieces of the rich beginnings of the literature surveyed here will endure and ultimately join the cause of Jewish literature.

Works Cited

Further Readings

Index

Works Cited

Abécassis, Eliette. 1996. *Qumran*. Paris: Ramsay.

———. 1997. *L'or et la cendre*. Paris: Ramsay.

———. 1998a. *Petite métaphysique du meurtre*. Paris: Presses universitaires de France.

———. 1998b. *The Qumran Mystery*, trans. Emily Read. London: Orion.

———. 2000. *La répudiée*. Paris: Albin Michel.

Abitol, Michel. 1983. *Les Juifs d'Afrique du Nord sous Vichy*. Paris: Maisonneuve & Larose.

———. 1994. "The Integration of North African Jews in France." In "Discourses on Jewish Identity in Twentieth-Century France." *Yale French Studies* 85: 248–61.

Adorno, Theodor W. 1977. "Commitment." In *Aesthetics and Politics*, ed. Ronald Taylor, 177–96. London: Verso.

———. 1984. *Aesthetic Theory*. London: Routledge and Kegan Paul.

Allouche, Jean-Luc. 1983. *Les jours innocents*. Paris: Lieu Commun.

Alter, Robert. 1994. "Jewish Dreams and Nightmares." In *What Is Jewish Literature?*, ed. Hana Wirth-Nesher, 53–69. Philadelphia: Jewish Publication Society.

Amar, Marlène. 1993. *La femme sans tête*. Paris: Gallimard.

———. 1996. *Des gens infréquentables*. Paris: Gallimard.

Anissimov, Myriam. 1973. *Comment va Rachel?* Paris: Denoël.

———. 1989. *La soie et les cendres*. Paris: Payot.

———. 1992. *Dans la plus stricte intimité*. Paris: Editions de l'Olivier.

———. 1995. "Écrivain yiddish de langue française." *Pardès* 21: 237–41.

———. 1996. *Primo Levi ou la tragédie d'un optimiste*. Paris: J.-C. Lattès.

———. 1999. *Sa Majesté la Mort*. Paris: Seuil.

Ascot, Roger. 1987. "Littérature juive: 'Je ne sais pas si elle existe, mais elle se porte bien.' " *Figaro Magazine* 390 (20 June): 48–50.

Astro, Alan. 1994. "Editor's Preface: Jewish Discretion in French Literature." In "Discourses on Jewish Identity in Twentieth-Century France." *Yale French Studies* 85: 1–17.

Auron, Yaïr. 1998. *Les Juifs d'extrême gauche en mai 1968: Une génération révolutionnaire marquée par la Shoah*. Paris: Albin Michel.

Avni, Ora. 1984. *Tics, tics, and tics: Figures, syllogismes, recit dans "Les chants de Maldoror."* Lexington, Ky.: French Forum.

———. 1994. "Patrick Modiano: A French Jew?" *Yale French Studies* 85: 227–47.

Axelrad, Catherine. 1988. *L'homme au car VW blanc de ma jeunesse*. Paris: Gallimard.

———. 1990. *La Varsovienne*. Paris: Gallimard.

———. 1993. *Vies et morts d'Esther*. Paris: Gallimard.

Bahloul, Joëlle. 1983. *Le culte de la table dressée: Rites et traditions de la table juive algérienne*. Paris: Métailié.

Barcellini, Serge, and Annette Wieviorka. 1995. *Passant, souviens-toi! Les lieux du souvenir de la Seconde Guerre mondiale en France*. Paris: Plon.

Bebe, Pauline. 2000. *Dictionnaire des femmes et du judaïsme*. Paris: Calmann-Levy.

Bénabou, Marcel. 1995. *Jacob, Ménahem et Mimoun: Une Épopée familiale*. Paris: Seuil.

———. 1998. *Jacob, Menahem, and Mimoun: A Family Epic*, trans. Steven Rendall. Lincoln: Univ. of Nebraska Press.

Ben Aych, Gil. 1981. *L'essuie-mains des pieds*. Paris: Presses d'aujourd hui.

———. 1983. *Le voyage de Mémé*. Paris: Pockette-Junior.

———. 1986. *Le livre d'Étoile*. Paris: Seuil.

———. 1988. *Le chant des êtres*. Paris: Gallimard.

———. 1997. *Les manuscrits de 1984: Critique de l'économie politique du signifiant*. Vol. 1 of *Au jour le jour: extraits*. Paris: L'Harmattan.

Bensimon, Doris. 1989. "Les Juifs d'Afrique du Nord entre la France et Israël." In *Les Juifs de France: Le Sionisme et l'etat d'Israël. Actes du Colloque Internationale 1987*, ed. Doris Bensimon and Benjamin Pinkas, 561–75. Paris: Langues'O.

Bensimon, Doris, and Sergio DellaPergola. 1984. *La population juive de la France: Socio-démographie et identité*. Paris: Centre national de la recherche scientifique.

Bensoussan, Albert. 1973. *La Bréhaigne*. Paris: Denoël.

Bernheim, Emmanuèle. 1993. *Sa femme*. Paris: Gallimard.

Bernheim, Gilles. 1997. *Un rabbin dans la cité*. Paris: Calmann-Levy.

Birnbaum, Pierre. 1995. *Destins Juifs: De la Révolution Française à Carpentras*. Paris: Calmann-Lévy.

———. 1999. *Jewish Destinies: Citizenship, State, and Community in Modern France*. New York: Hill and Wang.

Bitoun, Lazare. 1982. "Israélites hier, Juifs aujourd'hui." *Traces* 3: 79–88.

Blanchot, Maurice. 1980. *L'écriture du désastre*. Paris: Gallimard.

———. 1986. *The Writing of the Disaster*, trans. Ann Schmock. Lincoln: Univ. of Nebraska Press.

Bloom, Harold. 1985. "The Pragmatics of Contemporary Jewish Culture." In *Post-Analytic Philosophy*, ed. John Rajchman and Cornel West, 108–23. New York: Columbia Univ. Press.

Bober, Robert. 1993. *Quoi de neuf sur la guerre?* Paris: P.O.L.

Bouganim, Ami. 1981. *Récits du Mellah*. Paris: J.-C. Lattès.

———. 1983. *Le cri de l'arbre*. Tel Aviv: Stavit.

Boukhobza, Chochana. 1986. *Un été à Jérusalem*. Paris: Ballard.

———. 1987. *Le cri*. Paris: Ballard.

———. 1989. *Les herbes amères*. Paris: Ballard.

———. 1996. *Pour l'amour du père*. Paris: Seuil.

Boyarin, Daniel. 1994. *A Radical Jew: Paul and the Politics of Identity*. Berkeley: Univ. of California Press.

Boyarin, Jonathan. 1991. *Polish Jews in Paris: The Ethnography of Memory*. Bloomington: Indiana Univ. Press.

———. 1996. *Thinking in Jewish*. Chicago: Chicago Univ. Press.

Buber, Martin. 1936. "Die Sprache der Botschaft." In *Die Schrift und ihre Verdeutschung*, ed. Manfred Buber and Franz Rosenzweig, 55–75. Berlin: Schocken.

Cazenave, Odile. 2000. *Rebellious Women: The New Generation of Female African Novelists*. Boulder, Colo.: L. Rienner.

Chasseguet-Smirgel, Janine. 1988. *Pour une psychanalyse de l'art et de la créativité*. Paris: Payot.

Cheyette, Bryan. 1993. "The Culture of Apology: British-Jewish Literature." *Manna* 41.

———, ed. 1998. *Contemporary Jewish Writing in Britain and Ireland*. Lincoln: Univ. of Nebraska Press.

Cixous, Hélène. 1975a. *Un K incompréhensible: Pierre Goldman*. Paris: Bourgois.

———. 1975b. "Le rire de la Méduse." *L'Arc* 61: 39–54.

———. 1997a. "Mon algériance." *Les inrockuptibles*, August 20–September 3, 71–74.

———. 1997b. "My Algeriance, in other words, to depart not to arrive from Algeria," trans. Eric Prenowitz. *Tri-Quarterly* 100: 259–79.

Clendinnen, Inga. 1999. *Reading the Holocaust*. Cambridge: Cambridge Univ. Press.

Clifford, James. 1994. "Diasporas." *Cultural Anthropology* 9, no. 3: 302–38.

Coenen-Mennemeier, Brigitta. 1998. " 'Nous sommes tous des Juifs allemands': Mai 1968 und die literarische Behandlung der 'question juive.' " In *Jüdischer Republikanismus in Frankreich*, ed. Christoph Miething, 138–54. Tübingen: Niemeyer.

Cohen, Albert. 1954. *Le livre de ma mère*. Paris: Gallimard.

———. 1972. *O vous, frères humains*. Paris: Gallimard.

Cohen, Marcel. 1985. *Letras a un pintor*. Madrid: Amarab£.

Cohen-Azuelos, Jacqueline. 1999. *Fleur de Jasmin: Images et saveurs du Maroc*. Aix-en-Provence: Edisud.

Cohn-Bendit, Daniel. 1975. *Le Grand Bazar: Entretiens avec Michel Lévy, Jean-Marc Salmon, Maren Sell*. Paris: Belfond.

Czarny, Norbert. 1989. *Les valises*. Paris: Lieu Commun.

Darmon, Paule. 1980. *Baisse les yeux, Sarah*. Paris: B. Grasset.

David, Renée. 1993. "Le renouveau Juif laïque en France." *Les nouveuax cahiers* 114: 22–27.

David, Samuel Ben. 2000. "L'école juive en France: peu de moyens pour de grands rêves." *L'arche* 506: 86–87.

Dayan-Rosenman, Anny. 1998. "Mémoire, écriture, identitaire minoritaire." In *Les Juifs de France: De la Révolution Française à nos jours*, ed. Jean-Jacques Becker and Annette Wieviorka, 329–62. Paris: Liana Levi.

de Beauvoir, Simone. 1958. *Mémoires d'une jeune fille rangée*. Paris: Gallimard.

Debray, Régis. 1975. *Les rendez-vous manqués: Pour Pierre Goldman*. Paris: Seuil.

de Fontenay, Elisabeth. 1991. "Interventions." In *Le "quant-à-soi." Données et débats: Actes du XXXe colloque des intellectuels juifs de langue française*, 183–89. Paris: Denoël.

———. 1994. "On the *Quant-à-soi*." *Yale French Studies* 85: 217–24.

Delamarre, Alexandre J.-L. 1979. "Méditation sur la modernité." *Esprit* 29: 80–96.

Deleuze, Gilles, and Félix Guattari. 1975. *Kafka: Pour une littérature mineure*. Paris: Minuit.

———. 1986. *Kafka: Toward a Minor Literature*, trans. Dan Polan. Minneapolis: Univ. of Minnesota Press.

Desarthe, Agnès. 1992. *Les peurs de conception*. Paris: Ecole des loisirs.

———. 1996. *Un secret sans importance*. Paris: Editions de l'Olivier.

Dickstein, Juliette. 1997. "Born after Memory." Ph.D. diss., Harvard Univ.

Dollé, Jean Paul. 1997. *L'insoumis: Vies et légendes de Pierre Goldman*. Paris: Grasset.

Dugas, Guy. 1983. "Où en est la littérature sépharade d'expression française? Rapide bilan depuis 1980." *Revue Celfan-Celfan Review* 3, no. 1: 11–13.

———. 1990. *La littérature judéo-maghrébine d'expression française*. Paris: L'Harmattan.

"Editorial." 1979. *Combat pour la diaspora* 1: 6.

Elikan, Marc. 1995. "Le sentiment 'minoritaire' et identitaire dans la création romanesque de Myriam Anissimov." *Colloquium helveticum* 22: 41–53.

Ertel, Rachel. 1982. "Une littérature minoritaire." *Traces* 3: 88–91.

Even-Zohar, Itamar. 1978. "Israeli Hebrew Literature: A Model." *Papers in Historical Poetics*, 75–95.

Ezrahi, Sidra deKoven. 2000. *Booking Passage: Exile and Homecoming in the Modern Jewish Imagination*. Berkeley: Univ. of California Press.

Fellous, Colette. 1989. *Rosa Gallica*. Paris: Gallimard.

———. 1994. *Midi à Babylone*. Paris: Gallimard.

———. 2001. *Avenue de France*. Paris: Gallimard.

Fine, Ellen S. 1985. "New Kinds of Witnesses: French Post-Holocaust Writers." *Holocaust Studies Annual* 3: 121–36.

———. 1988. "The Absent Memory: The Act of Writing in Post-Holocaust French

Literature." In *Writing and the Holocaust*, ed. Berel Lang, 41–58. New York: Holmes and Meier.
Finkielkraut, Alain. 1980a. *Le Juif imaginaire*. Paris: Seuil.
———. 1980b. *The Imaginary Jew*, trans. Kevin O'Neill and David Suchoff. Lincoln: Univ. of Nebraska Press.
Fitoussi, Annie. 1985. *La mémoire folle de Mouchi Rabbinou: Le rabbin le plus pauvre du ghetto, le plus misérable de Tunis, plus fort que Mussolini, bien plus fort encore que la mort*. Paris: Mazarine.
Fleischer, Alain. 1999. *La femme qui avait deux bouches*. Paris: Seuil.
Fleischman, Cyrille. 1994. *Rendez-vous au métro Saint-Paul*. Paris: Le Dilettante.
———. 1995. "Modeste & subjectif." *Pardès* 21: 259–67.
Foucault, Michel. 1971. "Nietzsche, la généalogie, l'histoire." In *Hommage à Jean Hyppolite*, 145–73. Paris: Presses universitaires de France.
———. 1984. "Nietzsche, Genealogy, History." In *The Foucault Reader*, 76–101. New York: Penguin.
Francos, Ania. 1978. *Il était des femmes dans la Résistance . . .* Paris: Stock.
Fresco, Nadine. 1981. "La diaspora des cendres." *Nouvelle revue de psychanalyse* 24: 205–20.
Freud, Sigmund. 1917. "Mourning and Melancholia." *Standard Edition* 14: 243–58.
Frieden, Ken. 1995. *Classic Yiddish Fiction: Abramovitsh, Sholem Aleichem, and Peretz*. Albany: State Univ. of New York Press.
Friedlaender, Judith. 1990. *Vilna on the Seine: Jewish Intellectuals in France since 1968*. New Haven: Yale Univ. Press.
Friedländer, Saul. 1994. "Trauma, Memory and Transference." In *Holocaust Remembrance: The Shapes of Memory*, ed. Geoffrey L. Hartman, 251–63. Oxford, UK: Oxford Univ. Press.
Gandillot, Thierry. 1996. *L'héritage Windsmith*. Paris: R. Laffont.
Garnier, Dominique. 1980. *Nice, pour mémoire*. Paris: Seuil.
Gary, Romain. 1967. *La danse de Gengis Cohn*. Paris: Gallimard.
Gdalia, Janine. 1982. "Un âge d'or." *Traces* 3: 91–93.
Gdalia, Janine, and Annie Goldmann. 1989. *Le judaïsme au féminin*. Paris: Balland.
Genette Gérard. 1982. *Palimpsestes: La littérature au second degré*. Paris: Seuil.
Gilman, Sander L. 1991. *The Jew's Body*. New York: Routledge.
———. 1994 *Jews in Today's German Culture*. Bloomington: Indiana Univ. Press.
Glucksmann, André. 1984. "L'Occident est une diaspora." In *Aujourd'hui, être juif*, ed. Victor Malka, 167–75. Paris: Editions du Cerf.
Gluckstein, Alain. 1997. *Nos grands hommes*. Paris: Seuil.
Goldman, Pierre. 1975. *Souvenirs obscurs d'un Juif polonais né en France*. Paris: Seuil.
———. 1977a. *Dim Memories of a Polish Jew Born in France*, trans. Joan Pinkham. New York: Viking.

———. 1977b. *L'ordinaire mésaventure d'Archibald Rapoport*. Paris: Julliard.

Goldmann, Annie. 1979. *Les filles de Mardochée: Histoire d'une émancipation*. Paris: Denoël and Gonthier.

———. 1982. "Rencontres d'écrivains." In *Cultures juives méditerranéennes et orientales*, 315–30. Paris: Syros.

———. 1995. "Langue et création littéraire." *Pardès* 21: 55–59.

Golse, Nickie. 1980. *Dans le jardin de mon père*. Paris: B. Grasset.

Gorrara, Claire. 1998. *Women's Representations of the Occupation in Post-'68 France*. London: St. Martin's.

Guland, Olivier, and Michel Zerbib, eds. 2000. *Nous, Juifs de France*. Paris: Bayard.

Gutman, Claude. 1981. *Les réparations*. Paris: Mercure de France.

———. 1982. *Les larmes du crocodile*. Paris: Mercure de France.

———. 1988. *La folle rumeur de Smyrne*. Paris: Payot.

———. 1993. *La maison vide*. Paris: Gallimard.

———. 1997. *Les passages*. Paris: Seuil.

Gutman, Nelly. 1984. "Être juif en France en 1982." In *La France au pluriel?*, 90–99. Paris: L'Harmattan.

Halbronn, Jacques. 1996. "La problématique identitaire des Juifs français." In *Hier Juifs 'progressistes' aujourd'hui Juifs . . . ? Quelle identité juive laïque construire? Colloque organisé par les Amis de la Commission Centrale de l'Enfance, Sorbonne: 11 et 12 Février*, 49–79. N.p.: Les Amis.

Halimi, Gisèle. 1973. *La cause des femmes*. Paris: Gallimard.

———. 1988. *Le lait de l'oranger*. Paris: Gallimard.

Hall, Stuart. 1990. "Cultural Identity and Diaspora." In *Identity. Community, Culture, Difference*, ed. Jonathan Rutherford, 222–37. London: Lawrence and Wishart.

Halter, Marek. 1983. *La mémoire d'Abraham*. Paris: Laffont.

———. 1996. *Le Messie*. Paris: Laffont.

Hartman, Geoffrey H. 1994. "Introduction: Darkness Visible." In *Holocaust Remembrance: The Shapes of Memory*, ed. Geoffrey H. Hartman, 1–23. Oxford, UK: Blackwell.

Hass, Aaron. 1990. *In the Shadow of the Holocaust: The Second Generation*. Ithaca: Cornell Univ. Press.

Hazan-Aramar, Fortunée. 1987. *Saveurs de mon enfance: La cuisine juive du Maroc*. Paris: Laffont.

Hilsenrath, Edgar. 1966. *Night*. Garden City, N.Y.: Doubleday.

———. 1971. *The Nazi and the Barber*. New York: Doubleday.

Hirsch, Marianne. 1997. *Family Frames: Photography, Narrative, and Postmemory*. Cambridge, Mass.: Harvard Univ. Press.

Hoffmann, Stanley. 1995. Foreword to *Vichy France and the Jews*, ed. Michael R. Marrus and Robert O. Paxton, rev. ed. Stanford: Stanford Univ. Press.

Honigmann, Barbara. 1999. *Damals, Dann und Danach*. Munich: Hanser.

———. 2003. *Zohara's Journey*, trans. John Barrett. Boston: Godine.

Horn, Pierre. 1997. *Modern Jewish Writers of France*. Lampeter, Wales: Mellen.

Huston, Nancy. 1998. *L'Empreinte de l'ange*. Paris: Actes Sud.

Hyman, Paula. 1998. *The Jews of Modern France*. Berkeley: Univ. of California Press.

Ireland, Susan. 1998. "Writing the Body in Marlène Amar's 'La Femme sans tête.' " *French Review* 71, no. 3: 454–67.

Jabès, Edmond. 1985. *The Sin of the Book*, ed. Eric Gould. Lincoln: Univ. of Nebraska Press.

———. 1989. *Un Étranger avec, sous le bras, un livre de petit format*. Paris: Gallimard.

———. 1991. "This Is the Desert: Nothing Strikes Root Here." In *Routes of Wandering: Nomadism, Journeys, and Transitions in Contemporary Israeli Art*, ed. Sarit Shapira, 246–54. Jerusalem: Israel Museum.

———. 1993. *A Foreigner Carrying in the Crook of His Arm a Tiny Book*, trans. Rosemarie Waldrop. Wesleyan, Conn.: Wesleyan Univ. Press.

Jacques, Paula. 1987. *L'héritage de tante Carlotta*. Paris: Mercure de France.

Jamet, Dominique. 1975. "Patrick Modiano s'explique." *Lire* 1: 23–36.

JanMohammed, Abdul R., and David Lloyd, eds. 1990. *The Nature and Context of Minority Discourse*. Oxford: Oxford Univ. Press.

"Juifs, en France, aujourd'hui." 1968. *Esprit* 36: 370.

"Les Juifs en France." 1979. *Histoire* 3.

Kafka, Franz. 1935. *Der Prozess*. Berlin: Schocken.

Kahn, Annette. 1990. *Robert et Jeanne à Lyon sous l'Occupation*. Paris: Payot.

———. 1991a. *Personne ne voudra nous croire*. Paris: Payot.

———. 1991b. *Why My Father Died: A Daughter Confronts Her Family's Past at the Trial of Klaus Barbie*, trans. Anna Cancogni. New York: Summit Books.

Kanfer, Irène. 1974. "Une littérature juive: Pourquoi?" *Tribune juive* 300, 29 March–4 April, 12–17.

Kauffmann, Judith. 1984. "Modiano un 'Juif imaginaire'? Une relecture de *La Place de l'Etoile*." *Hebrew University Studies in Literature and the Arts* 12, no. 3: 130–45.

Klarsfeld, Arno. 1995. *Les dieux ne songent qu'à dormir*. Paris: Flammarion.

Klarsfeld, Serge, ed. 1978. *Le mémorial de la déportation des Juifs de France*. Paris: B. Klarsfeld Foundation.

———. 1983. *Vichy-Auschwitz 1942: Le rôle de Vichy dans la solution finale de la question juive en France, 1943–1944*. Paris: Fayard.

Klein, Judith. 1998. *Der feine Sand des Gedächtnisses. Jüdisch-maghrebinische Literatur der Gegenwart*. Hamburg: Europäische Verlagsanstalt.

Koskas, Marco. 1979. *Balace Bounel*. Paris: Ramsay.

———. 1982. "Rencentres d'écrivains." In *Cultures Juives méditerranéennes et orientales*, 315–30. Paris: Syros.

———. 1988. *L'homme de paille*. Paris: Calmann-Lévy.

———. 1994a. *Le roi des schnorrers*. Carnières: Lansman.

———. 1994b. *Yasser Arafat, ou Le Palestinien imaginaire*. Paris: J.-C. Lattès.

Koster, Serge. 1982. "Un roman juif en France?" *Traces* 3: 96–97.

———. 1991. *Trou de mémoire*. Paris: Critérion.

Kronfeld, Chana. 1997. "Beyond Deleuze and Guattari: Hebrew and Yiddish Modernism in the Age of Privileged Difference." In *Jews and Other Differences: The New Jewish Cultural Studies*, ed. Jonathan and Daniel Boyarin, 257–79. Minneapolis: Univ. of Minnesota Press.

Krygier, Rivon. 2000. "Non au retour du ghetto." In *Nous, Juifs de France*, ed. Olivier Guland and Michel Zerbib, 145–58. Paris: Bayard.

Langfus, Anna. 1965. "Qu'est-ce que la littérature juive?" *Les Nouveaux Cahiers* 2: 21–39.

Lasker, Michael M. 1994. *North African Jewry in the Twentieth Century: The Jews of Morocco, Tunisia, and Algeria*. New York: New York Univ. Press.

Lejeune, Philippe. 1975. *Le pacte autobiographique*. Paris: Seuil.

Lévy, Bernard-Henri. 1984. *Le diable en tête*. Paris: Grasset.

Lévy, Clara. 1998. *Écritures de l'identité: Les écrivains juifs après la Shoah*. Paris: Presses universitaires de France.

Lindenberg, Daniel. 1990. "Petit glossaire des questions juives d'aujourd'hui." *Esprit* 162: 81–87.

Lionnet, Françoise. 1995. *Postcolonial Representations: Women, Literature, Identity*. Ithaca: Cornell Univ. Press.

"La littérature juive." 1974. *Tribune juive* 300, 29 March–4 April, 12–17.

Lyotard, Jean Francois. 1984. *The Postmodern Condition. A Report on Knowledge*, trans. Geoff Bennington and Brian Massumi. Minneapolis: Univ. of Minnesota Press.

Malka, Salomon. 1980. "Le retour d'Alain Finkielkraut: La découverte du judaïsme sous les auspices du manque." *L'arche* 285: 51–52.

———. 1984. *Aujourd'hui, être juif*. Paris: Editions du Cerf.

Malka, Victor. 1972. "Patrick Modiano: Un homme sur du sable mouvant." *Les Nouvelles Littéraires* 30, October–5 November, 2.

Mandel, Arnold. 1965. "Qu'est-ce que la littérature juive?" *Les Nouveaux Cahiers* 2: 34–36.

———. 1980. "Le néo-diasporisme culturel." *L'arche* 282: 94–98.

Marienstras, Richard. 1965. "Qu'est-ce que la littérature juive?" *Les Nouveaux Cahiers* 2: 37–39.

———. 1975. *Être un peuple en diaspora*. Paris: Maspero.

Marks, Elaine. 1995. "Cendres juives: Jews Writing in French after Auschwitz." In *Auschwitz and After: Race, Culture, and the "Jewish Question,"* ed. Lawrence D. Kritzman, 35–46. New York: Routledge.

———. 1996. *Marrano as Metaphor: The Jewish Presence in French Writing*. New York: Routledge.

Memmi, Albert. 1953. *Le Statue de Sel*. Paris: Corrêa.

———. 1957. *Portrait du colonisé précédé du portrait du colonisateur*. Paris: Buchet/Chastel.

———. 1962. *Portrait d'un Juif*. Paris: Gallimard.

———. 1965. "Qu'est-ce que la littérature juive?" *Les nouveaux cahiers* 2: 32–34.

———. 1997. "Les fluctuations de l'identité culturelle." *Esprit* 21: 94–106.

Misrahi, Robert. 1963. *La condition réflexive de l'homme juif*. Paris: Julliard.

Modiano, Patrick. 1968. *La place de l'étoile*. Paris: Gallimard.

———. 1969. *La ronde de nuit*. Paris: Gallimard.

———. 1971. *Night Round*, trans. Patricia Wolf. New York: Knopf.

———. 1972. *Les boulevards de ceinture*. Paris: Gallimard.

———. 1974. *Ring Roads*, trans. Caroline Hillier. London: Gollancz.

———. 1997. *Dora Bruder*. Paris: Gallimard.

———. 1999. *Dora Bruder*, trans. Joanna Kilmartin. Berkeley: Univ. of California Press.

Morris, Alan. 1996. *Patrick Modiano*. Oxford: Berg.

Moses, Emmanuel. 1989. *Métiers*. Paris: Obsidiane.

———. 1992. *Papernik*. Paris: Grasset.

———. 1999. *La danse de la poussière dans les rayons du soleil*. Paris: Grasset.

Neher, André. 1969. *L'entretien infini*. Paris: Gallimard.

———. 1971. "Préface." In *Israël dans la conscience juive: Données et débats*. Paris: Presses universitaires de France.

Nevin, Thomas R. 1991. *Simone Weil: Portrait of a Self-Exiled Jew*. Chapel Hill: Univ. of North Carolina Press.

Nicoïdski, Clarisse. 1995. "Faux-papiers." *Pardès* 21: 275–84.

Nolden, Thomas. 1995. *Junge jüdische Literatur: Konzentrisches Schreiben in der Gegenwart*. Würzburg: Königshausen and Neumann.

Nora, Pierre. 1992. "La generation." In *Les lieux de mémoire. III. Les france. I. Conflits et partages*, ed. Pierre Nora, 931–71. Paris: Gallimard.

———. 1996. "Generation." In *Realms of Memory: Rethinking the French Past*, ed. Pierre Nora and trans. Arthur Goldhammer. New York: Columbia Univ. Press.

Orlando, Valérie. 1999. *Nomadic Voices of Exile: Feminine Identity in Francophone Literature of the Maghreb*. Athens, Ohio: Ohio Univ. Press.

Ouaknine, Robert. 1979. "Autojudéographie." In "Catalogue pour des Juifs de maintenant," ed. Luc Rosenzweig. *Recherches: Revue du Cerfi* 38: 123–49.

Ozick, Cynthia. 1983. *Art and Ardor*. New York: Knopf.

Pachet, Pierre. 1987. *Autobiographie de mon père*. Paris: Belin.

Partouche, Maurice. 1979. *Le sud profond*. Paris: Editions des autres.

———. 1982. "Rencontres d'écrivains." In *Cultures juives méditerranéennes et orientales*, 315–30. Paris: Syros.

Paxton, Robert O. 1972. *Vichy France: Old Guard and New Order, 1940–1944*. New York: Knopf.

Perec, Georges. 1969. *La disparition*. Paris: Denoël.

———. 1975. *W, ou le souvenir d'enfance*. Paris: Denoël.

———. 1978. *Je me souviens*. Paris: Hachette.

———. 1979. "Ellis Island: Description d'un projet." In "Catalogue pour des Juifs de maintenant," ed. Luc Rosenzweig. *Recherches: Revue du Cerfi* 38: 51–54.

———. 1988. *W, or The Memory of Childhood*, trans. David Bellos. Boston: Godine.

———. 1995a. *Ellis Island*. Paris: P.O.L.

———. 1995b. *Ellis Island*, trans. Harry Matthews. New York: New Press.

Perez, Hélène Gans. 1996. *Marrakech la Rouge: Les Juifs de la Médina*. Geneva: Editions Métropolis.

Peskine, Brigitte. 1996. *Les eaux douces de l'Europe*. Paris: Seuil.

———. 2000. *Buena familia*. Paris: Nil éditions.

Philippe, Béatrice. 1981. *Être juif dans la société française: Du Moyen Âge à nos jours*. Paris: Editions Montalba.

Rabi, Wladimir. 1979. "L'Establishment juif, structures et idélogie." In "Catalogue pour des Juifs de maintenant." *Recherches: Revue du Cerfi* 38: 9–27.

Rabinovitch, Anne. 1983. *L'hiver au coeur*. Paris: Barrault.

———. 1987. *Les étangs de Ville-d'Avray*. Arles: Actes Sud.

———. 1995. *Comme si les hommes étaient partis en voyage*. Paris: L'Harmattan.

Raczymow, Henri. 1979. *Contes d'exil et d'oubli*. Paris: Gallimard.

———. 1980. "Vous avez dit 'différent'?" *L'arche* 282: 91–93.

———. 1982a. "Aujourd'hui, le roman juif?" *Traces* 3: 71–78.

———. 1982b. *Rivières d'exil*. Paris: Gallimard.

———. 1985. *Un cri sans voix*. Paris: Gallimard.

———. 1986. "La mémoire trouée." *Pardès* 3: 177–82.

———. 1995a. "Avant-propos" to "Littérature et judéité dans les langues européennes," ed. Henri Raczymow. *Pardès* 21: 7–15.

———, ed. 1995b. "Littérature et Judéité dans les langues européennes." *Pardès* 21.

———. 1995c. *Writing the Book of Esther*, trans. Dori Katz. New York: Holmes & Meier.

———. 1995d. *Quartier libre*. Paris: Gallimard.

———. 2001. *L'homme qui tua René Bousquet*. Paris: Stock.

Rawicz, Piotr. 1965. "Qu'est-ce que la littérature juive?" *Les nouveaux cahiers* 2: 29–31.

Reich-Ranicki, Marcel. 1989. *Über Ruhestörer: Juden in der deutschen Literatur*. Stuttgart: Deutsche Verlags-Anstalt.

Robin, Régine. 1986. "L'identité juive ou le temps des incertitudes identitaires." *CinémAction* 37: 8–23.

———. 1989. *Le roman mémoriel: De l'histoire à l'écriture du hors-lieu*. Longueil, Quebec: Préambule.

———. 1995. "Kafka ou Maïmonide: Quelques filiations imaginaires chez les écrivains juifs." *Pardès* 21: 19–30.

Rosenzweig, Luc, ed. 1979. "Catalogue pour des Juifs de maintenant." *Recherches: Revue du Cerfi* 38.

———, ed. 1980. *La jeune France juive: Conversation avec des Juifs d'aujourd'hui*. Paris: Libres-Hallier.

———. 1994. "Interview with E. Weber." In *Jüdisches Denken in Frankreich*, ed. Elisabeth Weber, 183–203. Frankfurt: Suhrkamp.

Roskies, David G. 1995. *A Bridge of Longing: The Lost Art of Yiddish Storytelling*. Cambridge, Mass.: Harvard Univ. Press.

Roumani, Judith. 1984. "The Portable Homeland of North African Jewish Fiction: Ryvel and Koskas." *Prooftexts* 4, no. 3: 253–67.

Rousseau, Jean-Jacques. 1973. *Les confessions*. Lausanne: Bibliothèque romande.

Rousset, David. 1946. *L'univers concentrationnaire*. Paris: Éditions du Pavois.

Rousso, Henry. 1987. *Le syndrome de Vichy de 1944 à nos jours*. Paris: Seuil.

———. 1990. "Vichy-Syndrom und nationale Identität: Ein Interview mit H.R." *Frankreich Jahrbuch*, 105–17.

———. 1991. *The Vichy Syndrome: History and Memory in France since 1944*, trans. Arthur Goldhammer. Cambridge, Mass.: Harvard Univ. Press.

Rozier, Gilles. 1999. *Par-de là les monts obscurs*. Paris: Denoël.

———. 2001. *Moïse fiction*. Paris: Denoël.

Rubinstein, Katia. 1979. *Mémoire illettrée d'une fillette d'Afrique du Nord à l'époque coloniale*. Paris: Stock.

———. 1982. "Rencontres d'écrivains." In *Cultures juives méditerranéennes et orientales*, 322–28. Paris: Syros.

Ruszniewski-Dahan, Myriam. 1999. *Romanciers de la Shoah: Si l'écho de leur voix faiblit . . .* Paris: L'Harmattan.

Sartre, Jean-Paul. 1946. *Réflexions sur la question juive*. Paris: Morihien.

———. 1981. *Juifs and Israélites*. Paris: Gallimard.

———. 1983. *Jewish Identities in France: An Analysis of Contemporary French Jewry*, trans. Arthur Goldhammer. Chicago: Univ. of Chicago Press.

Schmitt, Eric-Emmanuel. 2000. *L'Evangile selon Pilate*. Paris: Albin Michel.

———. 2001. *Monsieur Ibrahim et les fleurs du Coran*. Paris: Albin Michel.

Schnapper, Dominique. 1983. *Jewish Identities in France: An Analysis of Contemporary French Jewry*, trans. Arthur Goldhammer. Chicago and London: Univ. of Chicago Press.

———. 1994. "*Israélites* and *Juifs*: New Jewish Identities in France." In *Jewish Identities in the New Europe*, ed. Jonathan Webber, 171–78. London: Littman.

Schulmann, Fernande. 1980. *Mémoires juives: L'enfance ailleurs*. Paris: Glancier-Guénaud.

Schwarz-Bart, André. 1959. *Le dernier des justes*. Paris: Seuil.

Shapiro, Susan. 1994. "Écriture judaïque: Where Are the Jews in Western Discourse?" In *Displacements: Cultural Identities in Question*, ed. Angelika Bammer, 182–201. Bloomington: Indiana Univ. Press.

Shurkin, Michael Robert. 2000. "Decolonization and the Renewal of French Judaism: Reflections on the Contemporary French Jewish Scene." *Jewish Social Studies* 6, no. 2: 156–76.

Silverman, Max. 1999. *Facing Postmodernity: Contemporary French Thought on Culture and Society*. London: Routledge.

Sitruk, Joseph. 2000. "Je ne veux pas perdre un seul Juif." In *Nous, Juifs de France*, ed. Olivier Guland and Michel Zerbib, 31–50. Paris: Bayard.

Spire, Antoine. 1988. *Le silence en héritage*. Paris: Laffont.

Steiner, George. 1986. "Our Homeland, the Text." *Salmagundi* 66, no. 5: 24–25.

Suleiman, Susan. 1999. "Rereading Rereading: Further Reflections on Sartre's 'Réflexions.' " In "Jean Paul Sartre's 'Anti-Semite and Jew.' " *October* 87: 129–39.

Tabori, George. 1994. "Die Kannibalen." In *Theaterstücke*. Frankfurt: Suhrkamp.

Tapia, Claude. 1986. *Les Juifs séphardes en France: Études psychosociologiques et historiques*. Paris: L'Harmattan.

Texier, Jean C. 1969. "Interview with Patrick Modiano." *La croix*, November, 9–10.

Trigano, Shmuel. 1979. *La nouvelle question juive: L'avenir d'un espoir*. Paris: Gallimard.

———. 1982. "De la nécessité de la lutte avec l'ange." *Traces* 3: 93–95.

———. 1984. "Critique de la modernité juive." In *Aujourd'hui, être juif*, ed. Victor Malka, 79–96. Paris: Editions du Cerf.

———. 1994. "The Notion of a 'Jewish Community' in France: A Special Case of Jewish Identity." In *Jewish Identities in the New Europe*, ed. Jonathan Webber, 179–88. London: Littman.

Valbert, Gérard. 1980. "N. Golse: 'Dans le jardin de mon père.' " *Magazine littéraire* 166: 55–56.

———. 1981. "Mémoire et identité dans *La place de l'étoile* et *Rue des boutiques obscures* de Patrick Modiano." *Yod* 7, no. 2: 87–91.

Vegh, Claudine. 1979. *Je ne lui ai pas dit au revoir: Des enfants des déportés parlent*. Paris: Gallimard.

Vidal-Naquet, Pierre. 1981. *Les Juifs, la mémoire et le présent*. Paris: Maspero.

———. 1991. *Les Juifs, la mémoire et le présent*. Vol. 2, *La découverte*. Paris: Maspero.

———. 1996. *The Jews: History, Memory, and the Present*, trans. and ed. David Ames Curtis. New York: Columbia Univ. Press.

Wajcman, Gérard. 1986. *L'interdit*. Paris: Denoël.

Wajsbrot, Cécile. 1995. "Être ou ne pas être." *Pardès* 21: 288–93.

———. 1996. *Mariane Klinger*. Cadeilhan, France: Zulma.

———. 1997. *La trahison*. Cadeilhan, France: Zulma.

Wardi, Charlotte. 1981. "Mémoire et identité dans 'La Place de l'Etoile' et 'Rue des Boutiques Obscures' de Patrick Modiano." In *Yod* 7:2: 87–91.

Wasserstein, Bernard. 1996. *Vanishing Diaspora: The Jews in Europe since 1945*. Cambridge, Mass.: Harvard Univ. Press.

Weil, Sylvie. 2000. *Les vendanges de Rachi*. Paris: Flammarion.

Weill Raynal, Clément. 1997. *Le tombeau de Rachi*. Paris: Le Cerf.

Wieviorka, Annette. 1979. *L'écureuil de Chine*. Paris: Presses d'aujourd' hui.

———. 2000. "Le Judaïsme laïc n'a pas d'avenir." In *Nous, Juifs de France*, ed. Olivier Guland and Michel Zerbib, 17–30. Paris: Bayard.

Wieviorka, Annette, and Itzhok Niborski. 1983. *Les livres du souvenir: Memoriaux juifs de Pologne*. Paris: Gallimard/Julliard.

Wilkomirski, Binjamin. 1995. *Bruchstücke: Aus einer Kindheit 1939–1948*. Frankfurt: Jüdischer Verlag.

Wisse, Ruth. 2000. *The Modern Jewish Canon: A Journey Through Language and Culture*. New York: Free Press.

Wolitz, Seth L. 1994. "Imagining the Jew in France: From 1945 to the Present." *Yale French Studies* 85: 119–34.

Yerushalmi, Yosef H. 1982. *Zakhor: Jewish History and Memory*. Seattle: Univ. of Washington Press.

Zenou, Gilles. 1987. *Mektoub*. Paris: Sillages, Blandin.

———. 1990. *La désaffection*. Paris: Blandin.

———. 2003. *Regards sur la condition juive*. Paris: Presses universitaires de France.

Zerdoun, Monique. 1990. *Rue de la Mémoire fêlée*. Paris: Albin Michel.

Further Readings

General

Astro, Alan, ed. 1996. "Jewish Studies in France." *Shofar* 14, no. 3.

Baumgarten, Jean, and Frank Alvarez-Pereyre, eds. 1990. *Les Études juives en France: Situation et perspectives*. Paris: Diffusion, Presses du CNRS.

Baumgarten, Jean, and David Bunis, eds. 1993. *Le yiddish: Langue, culture, société*. Paris: CNRS Editions.

Baumgarten, Jean, et al., eds. 1994. *Mille ans de cultures ashkénazes*. Paris: Levi.

Balhoul, Joelle. 1990. "Female Emancipation and Marriage Strategies: North African Jewish Women in France." *Jewish Folklore and Ethnology Review* 12, no. 1: 2–23.

Becker, Jean-Jacques, and Annette Wieviorka, eds. 1998. *Les Juifs de France: De la Révolution Française à nos jours*. Paris: Levi.

Benbassa, Esther. 1997. *Histoire des Juifs de France*. Paris: Seuil.

Benguigui, Georges, et al., eds. 1969. *Aspects of French Jewry*. London: Vallentine and Mitchell.

Bensimon-Donath, Doris. 1971. *L'intégration des Juifs nord-africains en France*. La Haye: Mouton.

Bensoussan, Georges. 1998. *Auschwitz en héritages? D'un bon usage de la mémoire*. Paris: Mille et une Nuits.

Birnbaum, Pierre. 1992. *Les fous de la République: Histoire politique des Juifs de l'État, de Gambetta Vichy*. Paris: Fayard.

Chouraqui, André. 1965. *Cent ans d'histoire: L'Alliance Israélite Universelle et la renaissance juive contemporaine (1860–1960)*. Paris: Presses universitaires de France.

———. 1985. *Histoire des Juifs en Afrique du Nord*. Paris: Rocher.

Cukier, Simon, et al., eds. 1987. *Juifs révolutionnaires: Une page d'histoire du Yiddichland en France*. Paris: Méssidor/Editions sociales.

Eder, Richard. 1980. "The Jewish Question in France." *New York Times Magazine*, 30 November.

Gilman, Sander L. 1992. *The Visibility of the Jew in the Diaspora: Body Imagery and Its Cultural Context*. Syracuse: Syracuse Univ. Press.

Girard, Patrick. 1983. *Les Juifs de France*. Paris: Huisman.

Hyman, Paula E. 1979. *From Dreyfus to Vichy: The Remaking of French Jewry, 1906–1939*. New York: Columbia Univ. Press.

Ikor, Roger. 1968. *Peut-on être juif aujourd'hui?* Paris: Grasset.

———. 1970. *Lettre ouverte aux Juifs*. Paris: Albin Michel.

Klein, Théo. 1994. "Quel avenir pour les Juifs de France?" *Plurielles* 3: 3–9.

Kritzman, Lawrence D. 1994. *Auschwitz and After: Race, Culture, and the "Jewish Question."* New York: Routledge.

Lévinas, Emmanuel. 1991. *Entre nous: Essais sur le penser-à-l'autre*. Paris: Grasset.

———. 1995. *Altérité et transcendence*. Saint-Clément-la-Rivière: Fata Morgana.

Lévy, Joseph, and Yolande Cohen. 1992. *Itinéraires séphardes: L'Odyssée des Juifs séphardes de l'Inquisition à nos jours*. Paris: Grancher.

Lévy, Justine. 1995. *Le rendez-vous*. Paris: Plon.

Lindenberg, Daniel, and Éric Conan. 1992. "Que faire de Vichy." *Esprit* 181: 5–16.

Lyotard, Jean-François. 1988. *Heidegger et "les Juifs."* Paris: Galilée.

———. 1990. "L'Europe, les Juifs et le livre." *Esprit* 162: 113–18.

Malka, Salomon. 1980. "Le retour d'Alain Finkielkraut: La découverte du judaïsme sous les auspices du manque." *L'arche* 285: 51–52.

Marienstras, Richard. 1986. "Histoire, mémoire, oubli." *Esprit* 120: 31–41.

Rosenman, Izio. 1993. "Les Juifs et l'Europe." *Plurielles* 1: 9–11.

Rousso, Henry. 1986. "Cet obscur objet du désir." In *La mémoire des français: Quarante ans de commémorations de la Seconde Guerre mondiale*, ed. Evelyne Damois and Jean-Pierre Rioux, 47–61. Paris: Editions du CNRS.

Schulmann, Fernande. 1979. "Je suis juive." *Esprit* 29: 60–64.

Simon, Patrick, and Claude Tapia. 1998. *Le Belleville des Juifs tunisiens*. Paris: Autrement.

Szafran, Maurice. 1990. *Les Juifs dans la politique française: De 1945 à nos jours*. Paris: Flammarion.

Thalmann, Rita. 1985. "Une lacune dans l'historiographie." In *Les Juifs dans la Résistance et la Libération: Histoire, témoignages, débates*, ed. Yves-Claude Aouate, 89–93. Paris: Scribe.

Weber, Elisabeth, ed. 1994. *Jüdisches Denken in Frankreich*. Frankfurt: Suhrkamp.

Wieviorka, Annette. 1992. *Déportation et génocide entre la mémoire et l'oubli*. Paris: Plon.

———. 1999. *Auschwitz expliqué à ma fille*. Paris: Seuil.

Criticism

Accad, Evelyne. 1987. "Chochana Boukhobza's *Un été à Jérusalem*." *World Literature Today* 61: 674.

Ascot, Roger. 1989. "Livres: Chochana, l'amour fou." *Figaro Magazine* 49, 23 September, 38.

Astro, Alan. 1991. "Bénabou bien abouti." *Pardès* 14: 252–59.

Casanova, Myriam. 1992. "Les rayons et les ombres de la mémoire juive." *Quinzaine littéraire* 609 (1–15 August): 13.

Charrière, Christian. 1988. "Le pardon à un stalinien repenti." *Figaro littéraire* 13764, 28 November, sec. I: 19.

Cheyette, Bryan, and Laura Marcus. "Introduction: Some Methodological Anxieties." In *Modernity, Culture, and the Jew*, ed. Bryan Cheyette and Laura Marcus, 1–23. Stanford: Stanford Univ. Press.

Cohen, Susan D. 1994. "Cultural Mixing, Exile, and Femininity in Paula Jacques' *Lumière de l'œil*." *French Review* 67, no. 5: 840–53.

Dana, Catherine. 1998. *Fictions pour mémoire: Camus, Perec, et l'écriture de la Shoah*. Paris: L'Harmattan.

Derrida, Jacques. 1997. *Adieu à Emmanuel Lévinas*. Paris: Galilée.

———. 2000. *Le schibboleth pour Paul Celan*. Noisy-le-Sec, France: La Marelle.

"Les écrivains français et le judaïsme 1880–1980." 1981. *Yod* 7, no. 1.

Eladan, Jacques. 1992. *Poètes juifs de langue française*. Paris: Blandin.

Elbaz, André. 1970. "Les romanciers juif français d'aujourd'hui." *Liberté* 12, no. 4: 32–105.

Frieden, Ken, ed. 1999. "Judaic Literature: Identity, Displacement, and Destruction." *Symposium* 52.

Jabès, Edmond. 1985. "There Is Such a Thing as Jewish Writing. . . ." In *The Sin of the Book: Edmond Jabès*, ed. Eric Gould, 26–31. Lincoln: Univ. of Nebraska Press.

"Judaéité et littérature." 1993–94. *Yod* 36/37.

Kéchichian, Patrick. 1989. "Les accents de vérité de Chochana Boukhobza." *Le monde* 13924, 3 November, 27.

Klein, Judith. 1991. "La belle étrangère et ses invités: Die französische Sprache und die Juden Nordafrikas. Zu einem wenig bekannten Gebiet der Frankophonie." *Lendemains* 16, no. 63: 69–76.

———. 1992. *Literatur und Genozid: Darstellungen der nationalsozialistischen Massenvernichtung in der französischen Literatur*. Vienna: Böhlau.

Koster, Serge. 1982. "Un roman juif en France?" *Traces* 3: 96–97.

Lazarus, Joyce Block. 1999. *Strangers and Sojourners: Jewish Identity in Contemporary Francophone Fiction*. New York: Lang.

Lévy, Bernard-Henri. 1987. "Y a-til une littérature juive?" *Figaro Magazine* 390 (20 June): 45–50.

Lionnet, Françoise. 1989. *Autobiographical Voices: Race, Gender, Self-Portaiture*. Ithaca: Cornell Univ. Press.

Mingelgrün, Albert. 2003. "Jeux de moi chez Patrick Modiano: De 'La Place de l'Étoile' à 'Dora Bruder.' " In *Zeitgenössische jüdische Autobiographie*, ed. Christoph Miething, 123–29. Tübingen: Niemeyer.

Miron, Dan. 2000. *The Image of the Shtetl and Other Studies of Modern Jewish Imagination*. Syracuse: Syracuse Univ. Press.

Motte, Warren. 1989. "Reading Jabès." *Romance Notes* 30, no. 2: 167–75.

———. 1997. "Playing It by the Book." *SubStance* 26, no. 1: 16–33.

Nolden, Thomas. 2002a. " 'Autojudéographie': 'Réjudaïsation' and Autobiographical Writing in France Since 1968." In *Zeitgenössische jüdische Autobiographie*, ed. Christoph Miething, 95–109. Tübingen: Niemeyer.

———. 2002b. "Qu'est-ce que la littérature juive? Jüdische Literatur nach 1968 in Deutschland und Frankreich." In *Deutsch-jüdische Literatur der neunziger Jahre: Die Generation nach der Shoah*, ed. Sander L. Gilman and Hartmut Steinecke, 189–203. Berlin: Schmidt.

———. 2003a. "Pierre Goldman and the Beginnings of *jeune littérature juive*." *French Forum* 28, no. 3: 57–76.

———. 2003b. "Strukturen autobiographischen Schreibens in der Literatur der jüdischen *générations d'après*." *Romanische Forschungen: Vierteljahresschrift für Romanische Sprachen und Kulturen* 4: 423–43.

Pudlowski, Gilles. 1982. "Le bon vieux temps du ghetto." *Nouvelles littéraires* (13 May): 54.

Rabi, Wladimir. 1971. "Littérature juive et écrivains juifs." *Les nouveaux cahiers* 24: 24–31.

Saavedra, Jean. 1990. "Le deuil de Norbert en jeune homme." *Quinzaine littéraire* 547 (16–31 January): 8.

Séguier, Marcel. 1985. *Le Juif de l'écriture*. Monaco: Rocher.

Spire, Antoine. 1994. "Les écrivains ashknénaze contemporains de France." In *Mille ans de cultures ashkénazes*, ed. Jean Baumgarten et al., 530–34. Paris: Lévi.

Steven, Jaron. 2002. "Autobiography and the Holocaust: An Examination of the Liminal Generation in France." *French Studies* 56, no. 2: 207–21.

Wahl, Jean-Jacques. 1987/88. "Chochana Boukhobza: 'Le cri.' " *Les nouveaux cahiers* 91: 65–66.

Wardi, Charlotte. 1973. *Le Juif dans le roman français. (1933–1948)*. Paris: Nizet.

———. 1986. *Le génocide dans la fiction romanesque, histoire et répresentation*. Paris: Presses universitaires de France.

Literary Texts

Abécassis, Eliette. 2003. *Clandestine*. Paris: Albin Michel.
———. 2004. *Le dérnier tribu*. Paris: Albin Michel.
Amran El Maleh, Edmond. 1980. *Parcours immobile*. Paris: Maspéro.
———. 1995. *Abner Aboumour*. Grenoble: La pensée sauvage.
Anissimov, Myriam. 2004. *Romain Gary: Le caméléon*. Paris: Denoël.
Assaraf, Albert. 1991. *L'hérétique: Elicha ben Abouya ou l'autre absolu*. Paris: Balland.
Bensoussan, Albert. 1973. *La Bréhaigne*. Paris: Denoël.
———. 1991. *Le Marrane, ou La confession d'un traître*. Paris: L'Harmattan.
———. 1993. *L'échelle séfarade*. Paris: L'Harmattan.
Boukhobza, Chochana. 1991. *Bel Canto*. Paris: Seuil.
Brami, Claude. 1990. *Parfums des étés perdus*. Paris: Gallimard.
Cixous, Hélène. 1995. *La fiancée juive: De la tentaion*. Paris: Des Femmes.
———. 1999. *Osnabrück*. Paris: Des Femmes.
———. 2000. *Le jour où je n'étais pas là*. Paris: Galilée.
———. 2001. *Portrait de Jacques Derrida en Jeune Saint Juif*. Paris: Galilée.
Clément, Catherine. 1999. *Marin et Hannah*. Paris: Calmann-Lévy.
———. 1992. *La señora*. Paris: Calmann-Lévy.
Dana, Jaqueline. 1981. *Le regard de Myriam*. Paris: Seuil.
Daniel, Jean. 1977. *Le refuge et la source*. Paris: Grasset et Fasquelle.
Debré, François. 1979. *Le livre des égarés*. Paris: Flammarion.
Doubrovsky, Serge. 1977. *Fils*. Paris: Galilée.
———. 1989. *Le livre brisé*. Paris: Grasset.
Fleischman, Cyrille. 1994. *Rendez-vous au métro Saint-Paul*. Paris: Le Dilettante.
———. 1995a. *Derniers rendez-vous au métro Saint-Paul*. Paris: Le Dilettante.
———. 1995b. *Nouveaux rendez-vous au métro Saint-Paul*. Paris: Le Dilettante.
Fleischman, Cyrille. 1999. *Un slow des années 50*. Paris: Le Castor Astral.
Forrester, Viviane. 1992. *Ce soir après la guerre*. Paris: C.-J. Lattès.
Frydman, Sarah. 1997. *La marche des vivants*. Paris: Albin Michel.
Garnier, Dominique. 1983. *La femme publique*. Paris: Seuil.
———. 1988. *J'attendrai la nuit et le jour*. Paris: Seuil.
Gille, Elisabeth. 1992. *Le mirador: Mémoires rêvés*. Paris: Presses de la Renaissance.
———. 1996. *Un paysage de cendres*. Paris: Seuil.
Giroud, Françoise. 1990. *Leçons particulières*. Paris: Fayard.
Gluckstein, Alain. *Bienvenu!* Paris: Seuil, 1993.
Goldberg, Jean-Michel. 1980. *Écorché juif*. Paris: Hachette.
Grumberg, Jean-Claude. 1979. *L'atelier*. Paris: Stock.
———. 1990. *Dreyfus*. Paris: Actes Sud.
———. 1999. *Zone libre*. Paris: Actes Sud.

Guedj, Max. 1986. *Mort de Cohen d'Alger*. Paris: L'Harmattan.
Gutman, Claude. 1991. *Les petits cailloux*. Paris: Julliard.
Haddad, Hubert. 1989. *Oholiba des songes*. Paris: Table Ronde.
Jacques, Paula. 1991. *Deborah et les anges dissipés*. Paris: Mercure de France.
Jay, Salim. [Irène Frain, pseud.]. 1982. *Le nabab*. Paris: J.-C. Lattes.
Kahn, Michèle. 1989. *Rue du roi doré*. Paris: Ramsay.
———. 2000a. *La pourpre et le jasmin*. Paris: Editions du Rocher.
———. 2000b. *Le Shnorrer de la rue des Rosiers*. Paris: Bibiophone-Daniel Radford.
Kattan, Naïm. 1981. *Le sable de l'île*. Paris: Gallimard.
Kayat, Claude. 1981. *Mohamed Cohen*. Paris: Seuil.
———. 1989. *Le rêve d'Esther*. Paris: Table ronde.
Kofman, Sarah. 1987. *Paroles suffoquées*. Paris: Galilée.
Konopnicki, Guy. 1989. *Au chic ouvrier*. Paris: Libres Hallier.
Koskas, Marco. 1981. *Destino*. Paris: B. Grasset.
Lentz, Serge. 1981. *Les années sandwiches*. Paris: Laffont.
Moati, Nine. 1983. *Les belles de Tunis*. Paris: Seuil.
———. 1989. *La passagère sans étoile*. Paris: Seuil.
Modiano, Patrick. 1977. *Livret de famille*. Paris: Gallimard.
———. 1981. *Une jeunesse*. Paris: Gallimard.
———. 1988. *Remise de peine*. Paris: Seuil.
———. 1989. *Vestiaire de l'enfance*. Paris: Gallimard.
Modiano, Patrick, and Louis Malle. 1974. *Lacombe Lucien*. Paris: Gallimard.
Moses, Emmanuel. 1989. *Un homme est parti*. Paris: Gallimard.
———. 2000. *Adieu Lewinter*. Paris: Denoël.
Nicoïdski, Clarisse. 1981. *Couvre-Feux*. Paris: Ramsay.
———. 1991. *Guerres civiles*. Paris: Payot.
Piat, Colette. 1991. *Adieu Moïse*. Paris: Belfond.
Rabinovitch, Anne. 1990. *Pour Budapest il est encore temps*. Arles: Actes Sud.
Silbert, Reine. 1980. *Il faut tojours quitter la Pologne*. Paris: Orbone.
Sitbon, Guy. 1980. *Gagou*. Paris: Grasset.
Spiraux, Alain. 1974. *Une fleur juive dans un jardin à la française*. Paris: Julliard.
———. 1976. *Hitler, ta maman t'appelle*. Paris: Belfond.
Valensi, Michel. 1983. *L'empreinte*. Tunis: Salambô.
Vigée, Claude. 1992. *Dans le silence de l'Aleph*. Paris: Albin Michel.
———. 1994–95. *Un panier de l'houblon*. Paris: J.-C. Lattès.
Wiesel, Elie. 1958. *Nuit*. Paris: Minuit.

Index

Abécassis, Eliette, 33, 106–9, 113, 155–58, 163, 199, 200, 217, 219–20; Works: *L'or et la cendre*, 108–9, 155–58, 219; *Petite métaphysique du meurtre*, 108; *Qumran*, 106–9, 155, 157; *La répudiée*, 199–200
Abitbol, Eliahou, 8
Abitol, Michel, 24, 26
Adorno, Theodor W., 85–86, 157
Ajar, Émile. *See* Gary, Romain
Aleichem, Sholem, 149–51; Works: "The Little Redheaded Jews," 149–51
Allen, Woody, 40, 222
Allouche, Jean-Luc, xiii, 5, 64, 164–68; Works: *Les jours innocents*, 164–68
Alter, Robert, 30, 69
Althusser, Louis, 8
Amalek, 104, 143
Amar, Marlène, xvi, 27, 77, 89–90, 174, 188–92, 199, 218, 221–23; Works: *La femme sans tête*, 188–90; *Des gens infréquentables*, 27, 89–90, 191–92, 194
Anissimov, Myriam, xv, 33, 39, 45, 52, 54, 64, 71–74, 77, 91, 93, 95–98, 113, 130, 143–45, 148, 163, 221; Works: *Comment va Rachel?*, 71–72, 91, 93; *Dans la plus stricte intimité*, 97, 143–45; *Sa Majesté la Mort*, 95–98, 144, 148
Arafat, Yassir, 33
Arafat, ou le Palestinien imaginaire (Koskas), 33
Aron, Raymond, 4
Artaud, Antonin, 127
Astro, Alan, xiii, 31, 66n. 7
Atlan, Liliane, 23
Auron, Yaïr, 64n. 6
Autobiographie de mon père (Pachet), 117
"Autojudéographie" (Ouaknine), 78–80
Avenue de France (Fellous), 111, 187
Avni, Ora, 56n. 3, 181
Avruch, Kenneth, 102
Axelrad, Catherine, 44–45, 148; Works: *L'homme au car VW blanc de ma jeunesse*, 44; *La Varsovienne*, 64n. 5, 45; *Vies et morts d'Esther*, 45, 148
Azoulay, Jacky, 23

bagages de sable, Les (Langfus), 15
Bahloul, Joëlle, 169n. 3
Baisse les yeux, Sarah (Darmon), 192–97
Barbie, Klaus, 15, 116–17, 131
Barcellini, Serge, 15
Barre, Raymond, 12
Barrès, Maurice, 57
Barthes, Roland, 105
Beauvoir, Simone de, 65, 181, 196, 200
Bebe, Pauline, 7
Begin, Menachem, 178
Bellow, Saul, 38, 40, 222
Ben, Myriam, 51
Bénabou, Marcel, xiv, 48, 51, 215, 223–24; Works: *Jacob, Ménahem et Mimoun: Une épopée familiale*, 48, 223
Ben Aych, Gil, xiii, xvi, 34, 168–73, 179, 213, 218, 221, 223–24; Works: *Le chant des êtres*, 34, 171–73, 213; *L'essuie-mains des pieds*, 169–70; "Ma langue," 169; *Le livre d'Étoile*, 170–71; *Le voyage de Mémé*, 170–71

Benjamin, Walter, 80, 108
Bensimon, Doris, 23, 24
Bensoussan, Albert, 39, 47, 52
Bensoussan, Georges, 15
Bernheim, Emmanuèle, 30
Bernheim, Gilles (Rabbi Bernheim), 7–8
Berranger, Olivier de, 13
Berri, Claude, 23, 59
Bettelheim, Bruno, 91
Bitoun, Lazare, 42–43, 63
Blanchot, Maurice, 33
Bloom, Harold, xiii, 103
Bober, Robert, 67n. 8, 206; Works: "Ellis Island: Description d'un projet" (Perec/Bober), 20, 67n. 8; *Quoi de neuf sur la guerre?*, 206
Boltanksi, Christian "Liberté," 23
Bouganim, Ami, xiii, 47, 167, 174–79, 224; Works: *Le cri de l'arbre*, 177–79; *Récits du Mellah*, 174–77
Boukhobza, Chochana, xv, xvi, 21, 77, 89–93, 119, 155, 159, 184–87, 197–99, 218, 221–22; Works: *Le cri*, 21; *Un été à Jérusalem*, 155, 197–99; *Les herbes amères*, 89–93; *Pour l'amour du père*, 159, 184–87
boulevards de ceinture, Les (Modiano), 120–22
Bousquet, René, 13, 61n. 4
Boyarin, Daniel, 215
Boyarin, Jonathan, 80
Braun, Eva, 57
Brenner, Frédéric, 23
Bruchstücke (Wilkomirski), 29
Buber, Martin, 23, 34
Buena familia (Peskine), 218
Burko-Falcman, Berthe, 52

Cahier d'un retour au pays natal (Césaire), 222
Camus, Albert, 55, 73, 166; Works: *La peste*, 73
Canetti, Elias, 130
"Catalogue pour des juifs de maintenant" (Rosenzweig), 4, 25, 40, 67n. 8, 79
cause des femmes, La (Halimi), 196
Cayrol, Jean, 14, 222; Works: *Nuit et brouillard*, 14, 201
Cazenave, Odile, 198
Celan, Paul, 86; Works: "Todesfuge," 86
Céline, Louis-Ferdinand, 57, 119
Césaire, Aimé, *Cahier d'un retour au pays natal*, 222
Chaban-Delmas, Jacques, 131
chagrin et la pitié, Le (Ophuls), 15
chant des êtres, Le (Ben Aych), 34, 171–73, 213
chants de Maldoror, Les (Lautréamont), 180–81
Chamisso, Adalbert von, 56
Chasseguet-Smirgel, Janine, 120n. 2
Cheyette, Bryan, 2n. 2
Chirac, Jacques, 13
Chmielnicki, Bohdan, 99
Cixous, Hélène, xiv, 61, 64, 212, 215; Works: "Mon algériance," 212
Clendinnen, Inga, 141
Clermont-Tonnerre, Comte de (Stanislas), 13
Clifford, James, 196
Cocteau, Jean, 153
Coenen-Mennemeier, Brigitta, 56n. 3
Cohen, Albert, 29, 40, 45–46, 178, 222; Works: *Le livre de ma mère*, 117; *O vous, frères humains*, 45–46
Cohen, Benny, 7
Cohen, Marcel, 51; Works: *Letras a un pintor*, 51
Cohen, Renaud, 23
Cohen-Azuelos, Jacqueline, 169n. 3
Cohn-Bendit, Daniel, 5, 18
Comment va Rachel? (Anissimov), 71–72
Comme si les hommes étaient partis en voyage (Rabinovitch), 206–7, 210
Confessions (Rousseau), 125
Contes d'exil et d'oubli (Raczymow), 65, 68, 69
Cours toujours (Desarthe), 153
cri, Le (Boukhobza), 21
cri de l'arbre, Le (Bouganim), 177–79
cri sans voix, Un (Raczymow), 135, 137–43, 219
Czarny, Norbert, 52, 113, 145–48, 163; Works: *Les valises*, 145–48

danse de Gengis Cohn, La (Gary), 59, 219
danse de la poussière dans les rayons du soleil, La (Moses), 211
Dans la plus stricte intimité (Anissimov), 97, 143–45

Dans le jardin de mon père (Golse), 132–35
Darmon, Paule, xiii, 77, 192–97, 221; Works: *Baisse les yeux, Sarah*, 192–97
Darquier de Pellepoix, Louis, 12
David, Renée, 8
Dayan-Rosenman, Anny, 220
Debray, Régis, 61, 64
de Gaulle, Charles, 5, 10, 11, 12, 15
Delamarre, Alexandre J.-L., 4
Delanoë, Nelcya, 77
Deleuze, Gilles, 34–35, 40, 41, 112
DellaPergola, Sergio, 24
dernier des justes, Le (Schwarz-Bart), 15, 52, 182–83
Derrida, Jacques, 45, 215
désaffection, La (Zenou) 166, 184
Desarthe, Agnès, 86, 151–54, 217, 219; Works: *Cours toujours*, 153; *Les peurs de conception*, 86; *Un secret sans importance*, 151–54
Desarthe, Dante, 23
"Deutéronome, 25, 17" (Moses), 103–5
Deutscher, Isaac, 36
diable en tête, Le (B. Lévy), 30
Dickstein, Juliette, 66n. 7
Didier, Christian, 61n. 4
dieux ne songent qu'à dormir, Les (A. Klarsfeld), 22
disparition, La (Perec), 80
Dollé, Jean Paul, 64n. 6
Dora Bruder (Modiano), 122–24, 219
Doubrovsky, Serge, 87
Drach, Michel, 23
Dreyfus, Alfred, 14, 36, 57
Drumont, Edouard, 5; Works: *La jeune France juive*, 5
Dugas, Guy, xiv, 46, 50, 76, 158n. 11, 169
Dugowson, Martine, 23

eaux douces de l'Europe, Les (Peskine), 218
Eco, Umberto, 108
écureuil de Chine, L' (Wieviorka), 18
Eichmann, Adolf, 14
Elikan, Marc, 72n. 10
"Ellis Island: Description d'un projet" (Perec/Bober), 20, 67n. 8
empreinte de l'ange, L' (Huston) 219
enfance ailleurs: Mémoires juives, L' (Schulmann), 4
Epstein, Helen, 91
Ertel, Rachel, xiv, 40–41
essuie-mains des pieds, L' (Ben Aych), 169–70
étangs de Ville-d'Avray, Les (Rabinovitch), 207–10
été à Jérusalem, Un (Boukhobza), 155, 197–99
étranger avec, sous le bras, un livre de petit format, Un (Jabes), 39
Être un people en diaspora (Marienstras), 8
évangile selon Pilate, L' (Schmitt), 103n. 4
Even-Zohar, Itamar, 32
Ezrahi, Sidra deKoven, 213

Fackenheim, Emil, 108
Faurisson, Robert, 12
Fellous, Colette, 109–13, 118, 187–88, 220–21; Works: *Avenue de France*, 111, 187; *Midi à Babylone*, 111, 188n. 7; *Rosa Gallica*, 109–12, 118, 148
femme sans tête, La (Amar), 188–90, 222
filles de Mardochée: Histoire d'une émancipation, Les (Goldmann), 47, 65, 74–75, 116, 196
Fine, Ellen, 66n. 7, 68n. 9, 142n. 10
Finkiel, Emmanuel, 23
Finkielkraut, Alain, xii, 5, 19–22, 31, 54, 72, 164, 183; Works: *Le Juif imaginaire*, xii, 5, 19–20
Fitoussi, Annie, 187–88; Works: *La mémoire folle de Mouchi Rabbinou*, 187n. 6
Fleischer, Alain, 118–19
Fleischman, Cyrille, 52, 98, 217
folle rumeur de Smyrne, La (Gutman), 103
Fondane, Benjamin, 52
Fontenay, Elisbath de, 11n. 5 114
Foucault, Michel, 126
Francos, Ania, 136; Works: *Il était des femmes dans la Résistance . . .*, 136
Frank, Anne, 86
Fresco, Nadine, 91n. 1
Freud, Sigmund, 52, 57, 116, 132
Frieden, Ken, 102, 223
Friedlaender, Judith, 60
Friedländer, Saul, 52, 141

Gandillot, Thierry, 157–58; Works: *L'héritage Windsmith*, 157–58

Garnier, Dominique, 71–74; Works: *Nice, pour mémoire*, 71–74
Gary, Romain, 33, 59, 219; Works: *La danse de Gengis Cohn*, 59, 219
Gdalia, Janine, 41, 76n. 11, 196; Works: *Le judaïsme au féminin*, 196
Genet, Jean, 127
Genette, Gérard, 103, 151
gens infréquentables, Des (Amar), 27, 89–90, 191–92, 194
Gide, André, 44, 166; Works: *L'immoraliste*, 166
Gilbert-Lecomte, Roger, 123
Gilman, Sander, 2n. 1, 190
Giscard d'Estaing, Valéry, 10, 12, 17
Glucksmann, André, 19
Gluckstein, Alain, xiii, 98–102, 183, 217, 219–20, 223; Works: *Nos grands hommes*, 98–102, 183
Goldman, Pierre, xiii, xv, 5, 59–64, 74, 77, 81–85, 113, 116, 124–28, 136–37, 163, 215–16, 219; Works: *L'ordinaire mésaventure d'Archibald Rapoport*, 59, 83–85, 116, 124–28, 136, 219, *Souvenirs obscurs d'un Juif polonais né en France*, 59–64, 82–83, 124, 137
Goldmann, Annie, xv, 47–48, 65, 74–77, 116, 196, 217, 221–22; Works: *Les filles de Mardochée: Histoire d'une émancipation*, 47, 65, 74–75, 116, 196; *Le judaïsme au féminin*, 196
Goldmann, Lucien, 75
Golse, Nickie, 119, 132–35, 163, 221; Works: *Dans le jardin de mon père*, 132–35
Gorrara, Claire, 74
Grumberg, Jean-Claude, 23
Guattari, Félix, 34–35, 40, 41, 112
Gutman, Claude, 21, 33, 103, 135, 200–206, 220; Works: *La folle rumeur de Smyrne*, 103; *Les larmes du crocodile*, 203–4; *La maison vide*, 33, 135, 204–5; *Les passages*, 204–6; *Les réparations*, 21, 200–203; *Rue de Paris*, 204

Hajdenberg, Henri, 10
Halbronn, Jacques, 17n. 6, 27
Halévy, Daniel, 57
Halimi, Gisèle, 196; Works: *La cause des femmes*, 196; *Le lait d'oranger*, 196
Hall, Stuart, 165
Halter, Marek, xi, 52; Works: *La mémoire d'Abraham*, 52; *Le Messie*, 52
Hartlaub, Felix, 123
Hartman, Geoffrey H., 32, 67, 68
Hass, Aaron, 138n. 6
Hazan-Aramar, Fortunée, 169n. 3
Heine, Heinrich, 57, 86
Heraclitus, 173
herbes amères, Les (Boukhobza), 89–93
héritage de tante Carlotta, L' (Jacques), 167, 196
héritage Windsmith, L' (Gandillot), 157–58
Hilsenrath, Edgar, 59; Works: *The Nazi and the Barber*, 59; *Night*, 59
Hirsch, Marianne, 68
Hitler, Adolf, 33, 205, 207
hiver au cœur, L' (Rabinovitch), 206
homme au car VW blanc de ma jeunesse, L' (Axelrad), 44
homme de paille, L' (Koskas), 158–62, 184, 186, 190
Honigmann, Barbara, 2, 162; Works: "Selbstporträt einer Jüdin," 162; *Soharas Reise*, 219
Horn, Pierre, 197n. 10
hôtel du retour, L' (Gutman), 204
Huston, Nancy, 219; Works: *L'empreinte de l'ange*, 219
Huysmans, Joris-Karl, 127
Hyman, Paula E., 25, 214

Il était des femmes dans la Résistance . . . (Francos), 136
immoraliste, L' (Gide), 166
interdit, L' (Wajcman), 32, 85–89
Ireland, Susan, 188n. 8

Jab, Edmond, 33, 39, 207, 215; Works: *Un étranger avec, sous le bras, un livre de petit format*, 39
Jacob, Ménahem et Mimoun: Une épopée familiale (Bénabou), 48, 223–24
Jacques, Paula, 47, 167, 196, 220; Works: *L'héritage de tante Carlotta*, 167, 196
JanMohammed, Abdul R., 41n. 2
Jay, Salim, 183
Je me souviens (Perec), 61
Je ne lui ai pas dit au revoir (Vegh), 4, 91

jeune France juive, La (Drumont), 5
jeune France juive, La (Rosenzweig), 5, 63, 115
Joanovici, Joseph, 57
Joffo, Joseph, 59
Jospin, Lionel, 13
jours innocents, Les (Allouche), 164–68
judaïsme au féminin, Le (Goldmann/Gdalia), 196
Juif imaginaire, Le (Finkielkraut), xii, 5, 19–20

Kafka, Franz, xii, 34, 40, 46, 49, 57, 61, 82, 129, 189–90, 206, 222–23; Works: "Metamorphosis," 129, 189–90, 222; *Der Prozess*, xii, 61n. 4, 62, 82, 206
Kahn, Annette, 116–17; Works: *Personne ne voudra nous croire*, 117; *Robert et Jeanne à Lyon sous l'Occupation*, 116n. 1; *Why My Father Died: A Daughter Confronts Her Family's Past at the Trial of Klaus Barbie*, 116–17
Kanfer, Irène, 39–40
Kannibalen, Die (Tabori), 59
Kauffmann, Judith, 56n. 3
Klarsfeld, Arno, 22; Works: *Les dieux ne songent qu'à dormir*, 22
Klarsfeld, Beate, 15, 22
Klarsfeld, Serge, 10n. 4, 15–16, 22, 25, 87; Works: *Le mémorial de la déportation des Juifs de France*, 16, 22, 87
Klein, Judith, xiv, 166n. 1
Kolbe, Maximilian, 156
Koskas, Marco, xiii, xvi, 33, 47–48, 65, 119, 163, 173–74, 179, 184, 186, 190, 215, 218, 221, 223–24; Works: *Arafat, ou le Palestinien imaginaire*, 33; *L'homme de paille*, 158–62, 190; *Le roi des schnorrers*, 33; *Palais Bounel*, 65, 159
Koster, Serge, 29, 32, 42–43; Works: *Trou de mémoire*, 32
Kronfeld, Chana, 41n. 2
Krygier, Rivon, 7

Lacan, Jacques, 52
la Fayette, Madame de (Marie-Madelaine Picohe de La Verge), 44
lait d'oranger, Le (Halimi), 196
Lampe, Friedo, 123
Langfus, Anna, 15, 36, 103; Works: *Les bagages de sable*, 15
Lanzmann, Claude, 15, 208; Works: *Shoah*, 15, 208
Lanzmann, Jacques, 59
larmes du crocodile, Les (Gutman), 203–4
Lasker, Michael M., 26
Lautréamont, Comte de, 179–81; Works: *Les chants de Maldoror*, 180–81
Lejeune, Philippe, 96
Le Pen, Jean-Marie, 10, 207
Letras a un pintor (M. Cohen), 51
Levi, Primo, 33
Lévinas, Emmanuel, 8, 22, 29
Lévy, Benny, 8
Lévy, Bernard-Henri, 10, 30; Works: *Le diable en tête*, 30
Lévy, Clara, xii, 31, 39, 164
Lévy, Justine, 30
Lévy, Raphaël (pseud. Ryvel), 51, 166, 173
Lindenberg, Daniel, 1
Lionnet, Françoise, xvi, 50, 179
"Little Redheaded Jews, The" (Aleichem), 149–51
livre de ma mère, Le (Cohen), 117
livre d'Étoile, Le (Ben Aych), 170
livres du souvenir, Les (Wieviorka), 18
Lloyd, David, 41n. 2
Lunel, Armand, 52
Lyotard, Jean-Francois, 16

Maimonides, Moses, 7
maison vide, La (Gutman), 33, 204–5
Malamud, Bernard, 38, 40
"Ma langue" (Ben Aych), 169
Mandel, Arnold, 5, 36, 39, 51, 166
Mann, Thomas, 95n. 2
Mariane Klinger (Wajsbrot) 95n. 2
Marienstras, Richard, 8–9, 35, 37–38, 40; Works: *Être un peuple en diaspora*, 8
Marks, Elaine, xii, 29
Marrakech la Rouge: Les Juifs de la Médina (Perez), 170
Marx, Karl, xii, 17, 57, 76
Marx Brothers, 40
Mattéoli, Jean, 16, 19
Maurois, André, 57
Mektoub (Zenou), 165–66

Memmi, Albert, xiii, 9, 37, 39, 51, 77, 181–82, 196, 218; Works: *Portrait du colonisé précédé du portrait du colonisateur*, 37, 181–82; *Portrait d'un Juif*, 37, 77; *La statue de sel*, 181–82
mémoire d'Abraham, La (Halter), 52
mémoire folle de Mouchi Rabbinou: Le rabbin le plus pauvre du ghetto, le plus misérable de Tunis, plus fort que Mussolini, bien plus fort encore que la mort, La (Fitoussi), 187n. 6
Mémoire illettrée d'une fillette d'Afrique du Nord à l'époque coloniale (Rubinstein), 179–83, 196–97
Mémoires d'une jeune fille rangée (de Beauvoir), 181, 200
mémorial de la déportation des Juifs de France, Le (Klarsfeld), 16, 22, 87
Mendès France, Pierre, 10
Messie, Le (Halter), 52
"Metamorphosis" (Kafka), 129, 189–90, 222
Métiers (Moses), 105
Midi à Babylone (Fellous), 111, 188n. 7
Misrahi, Robert, 21
Mitrani, Michel, 23
Mitterand, François, 13, 15
Mizrahi, Moshe, 23
Modiano, Patrick, xv, 33, 39, 44–45, 55–60, 64, 77, 116, 119–24, 127, 163, 215, 219; Works: *Les boulevards de ceinture*, 120–22; *Dora Bruder*, 122–24, 219; *La place de l'étoile*, 55–60, 120, 122
Moïse fiction (Rozier), 103
"Mon algériance" (Cixous), 212
Monsieur Ibrahim et les fleurs du Coran (Schmitt), 219
Moscovici, Serge, 166n. 1
Moses, Emmanuel, 103–5, 155, 210–11, 221; Works: *La danse de la poussière dans les rayons du soleil*, 211; "Deutéronome, 25, 17," 103–5; *Métiers*, 105; *Papernik*, 155, 210–11

Nazi and the Barber, The (Hilsenrath), 59
Neher, André, 19
Niborski, Itzhok, 18
Nice, pour mémoire (Garnier), 71–74
Nicoïdski, Clarisse, 53
Night (Hilsenrath), 59
Nolden, Thomas, 2n. 1
Nolte, Ernst, 108
Nora, Pierre, 68, 158
Nos grands hommes (Gluckstein), 98–102, 183
Nouvelle question juive (Trigano), 4
Nuit et brouillard (Cayrol and Resnais), 14, 201

Ophuls, Marcel, 15; Works: *Le chagrin et la pitié*, 15
ordinaire mésaventure d'Archibald Rapoport, L' (Goldman), 59, 83–85, 116, 124–28, 136, 219
or et la cendre, L' (Abécassis), 108–9, 155–58, 219
Orlando, Valérie, 168–69
Ouaknine, Robert, 32, 78–80, 113, 116
O vous, frères humains (A. Cohen), 45–46
Ozick, Cynthia, 34–35

Pachet, Pierre, 117, 221; Works: *Autobiographie de mon père*, 117
Palais Bounel (Koskas), 65, 159, 173–74
Papernik (Moses), 155, 210–11
Papon, Maurice, 22
Par-delà les monts obscures (Rozier), 148–51
Partouche, Maurice, 18, 47
passages, Les (Gutman), 204–6
Paxton, Robert O., 11
Pellepoix, Darquier de, 5
Perec, Georges, xiv, 20, 31, 58, 61, 66–68, 80–81, 87, 119, 173, 215–16, 219; Works: *La disparition*, 80; "Ellis Island: Description d'un projet," 20, 67; *Je me souviens*, 61; *La vie, mode d'emploi*, 173; *W, ou le souvenir d'enfance*, 66, 81, 219
Perez, Hélène Gans, 169–70; Works: *Marrakech la Rouge: Les Juifs de la Médina*, 169–70
Personne ne voudra nous croire (Kahn), 117
Peskine, Brigitte, 218–19; Works: *Buena familia*, 218; *Les eaux douces de l'Europe*, 218
peste, La (Camus), 73
Pétain, Henri Philippe, 13, 194
"petit bureau d'à coté, Le" (Fleischman), 98
Petite métaphysique du meurtre (Abécassis), 108
peurs de conception, Les (Desarthe), 86

Phénoménologie de la condition juive en France et en Allemagne, au XXe siècle (Zenou), 167
place de l'étoile, La (Modiano), 55–59, 60, 120, 122
Pompidou, Georges, 12
Portrait du colonisé précédé du portrait du colonisateur (Memmi), 37, 181
Portrait d'un Juif (Memmi), 37, 77
Pour l'amour du père (Boukhobza), 159, 184–87
Proust, Marcel, 46, 49, 57, 61
Prozess, Der (Kafka), xii, 61n. 4, 62, 82, 206

Quartier libre (Raczymow), 139n. 7
Qumran (Abécassis), 106–9, 155, 157
Quoi de neuf sur la guerre? (Bober), 206

Rabi (Rabinovitch), Wladimir, 25, 106, 118
Rabinovitch, Anne, 25, 118, 206–10, 221; Works: *Comme si les hommes étaient partis en voyage*, 206–7, 210; *Les étangs de Ville-d'Avray*, 207–10; *L'hiver au cœur*, 206
Raczymow, Henri, xiii, xiv, xv, 5n. 3, 33, 44, 51–52, 61n. 4, 65–70, 77, 98, 135–43, 219, 223; Works: *Contes d'exil et d'oubli*, 65, 68–69; *Un cri sans voix*, 135, 137–43, 219; *Quartier libre*, 139n. 7; *Rivières d'exil*, 136–37
Rashi (Solomon ben Isaac), 33, 211–12
Rawicz, Piotr, 36
Récits du Mellah (Bouganim), 174–77
Reich-Ranicki, Marcel, 2
réparations, Les (Gutman), 21, 200–203
répudiée, La (Abécassis), 199–200
Resnais, Alain, 14, 201, 222; Works: *Nuit et brouillard*, 14, 201
Rivières d'exil (Raczymow), 136–37
Robert et Jeanne à Lyon sous l'Occupation (Kahn), 116n. 1
Robin, Régine, xiv, 69
roi des schnorrers, Le (Koskas), 33
ronde de nuit, La (Modiano), 120
Rosa Gallica (Fellous), 109–12, 118, 148
Rosenzweig, Franz, 23
Rosenzweig, Luc, xv, 4–5, 19, 22, 25, 63, 67n. 8, 79, 115, 119; Works: "Catalogue pour des juifs de maintenant," 4, 25, 40, 67n. 8, 79; *La jeune France juive*, 63, 115
Roskies, David G., 69–70, 98
Rossif, Frédéric, 14
Roth, Philip, 40, 155
Rousseau, Jean-Jacques, 125
Rousset, David, 112
Rousso, Henry, 11, 121
Rozier, Gilles, xiii, 33, 103, 119, 148–51, 221, 223; Works: *Moïse fiction*, 103; *Par-delà les monts obscures*, 148–51
Rubenstein, Richard, 108
Rubinstein, Katia, xiii, 47–50, 65, 77, 179–83, 196–97, 215–16, 218, 222; Works: *Mémoire illettrée d'une fillette d'Afrique du Nord à l'époque coloniale*, 65, 179–83, 196–97
Rue de la mémoire fêlée (Zerdoun), 174
Rue de Paris (Gutman), 204
Ryvel (Raphaël Lévy), 51, 166, 173

Sachs, Maurice, 57, 123
Sade, Marquis de (Donatien Alphonse François), 127
Sa Majesté la Mort (Anissimov), 95–98, 144, 148
Sarraute, Nathalie, 29
Sartre, Jean-Paul, 8, 14, 19, 38, 57, 114, 153, 162, 192
Schmitt, Eric-Emmanuel, 33, 103; Works: *L'évangile selon Pilate*, 103n. 4; *Monsieur Ibrahim et les fleurs du Coran*, 219
Schnapper, Dominique, 4, 6, 31, 105
Schulmann, Fernande, 4; Works: *L'enfance ailleurs: Mémoires juives*, 4
Schwarz-Bart, André, xi, 14, 52, 182–83; Works: *Le dernier des justes*, 15, 52, 182–83
secret sans importance, Un (Desarthe), 151–54
"Selbstportät einer Jüdin" (Honigmann), 162
Shoah (Lanzmann), 15, 208
Shurkin, Michael Robert, 21n. 7
silence d'héritage, Le (Spire), 128–32, 134
Silvera, Charlotte, 23
Silverman, Max, 53
Sitbon, Guy, 215
Sitruk, Joseph, 3, 7
Soharas Reise (Honigmann), 219
"Song of Songs," 152

Souvenirs obscurs d'un Juif polonais né en France (Goldman), 59–64, 82–83, 124
Spire, André, 119, 128–32, 134, 163, 221; Works: *Le silence d'héritage*, 128–32, 134
Spire, Antoine, 52
statue de sel, La (Memmi), 181–82
Stein, Edith, 156
Steiner, George, 207
Stroheim, Erich von, 57
Styron, William, 130
Suissa, Steve, 23

Tabori, George, 59; Works: *Die Kannibalen*, 59
Tapia, Claude, 9
temps du ghetto, Le (Rossif), 14
Texier, Jean C., 127
Thaelmann, Ernst, 56
"Todesfuge," (Celan), 86
tombeau de Rachi, Le (Weill Raynal), 113, 212
Touvier, Paul, 12, 15
trahison, La (Wajsbrot), 92–95
Trigano, Shmuel, 4, 12, 21, 23–24, 43–44, 49; Works: *Nouvelle question juive*, 4
Trou de mémoire (Koster), 32
Tsevi, Shabbetai, 33

valises, Les (Czarny), 145–48
Varsovienne, La (Axelrad), 64n. 5, 45
Vegh, Claudine, 4, 91; Works: *Je ne lui ai pas dit au revoir*, 4, 91
vendanges de Rachi, Les (Weil), 103, 211–12
Vidal-Naquet, Pierre, 13, 16, 81
vie, mode d'emploi, La (Perec), 173
Vies et morts d'Esther (Axelrad), 45, 148
Vigée, Claude, 39
Voltaire (François-Marie Arouet de), 49
von Chamisso, Adalbert, 56
voyage de Mémé, Le (Ben Aych), 170–71

Wagner, Richard, 56
Wajcman, Gérard, xiii, 32, 85–89, 220; Works: *L'interdit*, 32, 85–89, 220
Wajsbrot, Cécile, 52, 53, 54, 92–95, 113; Works: *Mariane Klinger*, 95n. 2; *La trahison*, 92–95
Wardi, Charlotte, 55
Weil, Simone, 13, 129, 132
Weil, Sylvie, 33, 103, 211–12; Works: *Les vendanges de Rachi*, 103, 211–12
Weill Raynal, Clément, 33, 113, 212, 220; Works: *Le tombeau de Rachi*, 113, 212
Wessel, Horst, 56
Why My Father Died: A Daughter Confronts Her Family's Past at the Trial of Klaus Barbie (Kahn), 116–17
Wiesel, Elie, 10, 39, 117
Wieviorka, Annette, 3, 15, 18, 19; Works: *L'écureuil de Chine*, 18; *Les livres du souvenir*, 18
Wilkomirski, Binjamin, 30; Works: *Bruchstücke*, 29
Wisse, Ruth R., 30, 223
Wolitz, Seth L., 14, 23
W, ou le souvenir d'enfance (Perec), 66, 81, 219

Yerushalmi, Yosef Hayim, 16

Zauberman, Yolande, 23
Zenou, Gilles, xvi, 165–67, 184, 217; Works: *La désaffection*, 166, 184; *Mektoub*, 165–66; *Phénoménologie de la condition juive en France et en Allemagne, au XXe siècle*, 167
Zerdoun, Monique, 174; Works: *Rue de la mémoire fêlée*, 174
Zilbermann, Jean-Jacques, 23